ABOUT ISLAND PRESS

Island Press is the only nonprofit organization in the United States whose principal purpose is the publication of books on environmental issues and natural resource management. We provide solutions-oriented information to professionals, public officials, business and community leaders, and concerned citizens who are shaping responses to environmental problems.

In 1994, Island Press celebrates its tenth anniversary as the leading provider of timely and practical books that take a multidisciplinary approach to critical environmental concerns. Our growing list of titles reflects our commitment to bringing the best of an expanding body of literature to the environmental community throughout North America and the world.

Support for Island Press is provided by The Geraldine R. Dodge Foundation, The Energy Foundation, The Ford Foundation, The George Gund Foundation, William and Flora Hewlett Foundation, The James Irvine Foundation, The John D. and Catherine T. MacArthur Foundation, The Andrew W. Mellon Foundation, The Joyce Mertz-Gilmore Foundation, The New-Land Foundation, The Pew Charitable Trusts, The Rockefeller Brothers Fund, The Tides Foundation, Turner Foundation, Inc., The Rockefeller Philanthropic Collaborative, Inc., and individual donors.

ABOUT THE WILDERNESS SOCIETY

The Wilderness Society is the only national conservation organization that is devoted primarily to the protection and management of public lands. Founded in 1935 by two foresters, Bob Marshall and Aldo Leopold, the society uses a combination of advocacy, analysis, and public education in its campaigns to improve the management of America's national parks, forests, wildlife refuges, and Bureau of Land Management lands. The Wilderness Society is headquartered in Washington, D.C., and currently has over three hundred thousand members nationwide.

THESE
AMERICAN
LANDS

THESE
AMERICAN
LANDS

Parks, Wilderness, and the Public Lands

DYAN ZASLOWSKY AND T. H. WATKINS

The Wilderness Society

ISLAND PRESS

Washington, D.C. ■ Covelo, California

Preceding pages: Mount Sanford at sunrise, Wrangell-St. Elias National Park and Preserve, Alaska (photo by T. H. Watkins).

Library of Congress Cataloging-in-Publication Data

Zaslowsky, Dyan.
    These American lands : parks, wilderness, and the public lands /
Dyan Zaslowsky and T.H. Watkins, the Wilderness Society. —Rev. and
expanded ed.
        p. cm.
    Includes bibliographical references and index.
    ISBN 1-55963-239-9. — ISBN 1-55963-240-2 (pbk.)
    1. National parks and reserves—United States—History.
2. Wilderness areas—United States—history.   3. Public lands—
United States—History.   I. Watkins, T. H. (Tom H.), 1936–
II. Wilderness Society.   III. Title.
E160.Z37 1994   94-16293
973—dc20   CIP

Printed on recycled, acid-free paper ♾ ♻
Manufactured in the United States of America
10 9 8 7 6 5 4 3 2 1

Dedicated to the memory of
WALLACE STEGNER
1909-1993

CONTENTS

CONTENTS

FOREWORD TO THE REVISED EDITION

The substantial and impressive document you hold in your hands was launched, I'm happy to report, as the result of a long-standing complaint of mine that there was no single source to which interested Americans (conservationists included) could turn that would tell them everything it was important to know about the most magnificent natural inheritance enjoyed by any nation on earth: the 634 million acres (nearly a million square miles) of America's public lands. One could find individual books about the national parks, or the national forests, or Alaska, or wildlife refuges, and even a couple that dealt with the lands of the Bureau of Land Management. Few such books, however, combined the past and present in a coherent narrative, fewer still discussed with sufficient detail and authority the manifold problems afflicting the nation's public lands, and none presented a blueprint for the future management and expansion of this splendid legacy. I suggested that The Wilderness Society produce a modest series of reports—I dubbed them the "white papers"—that would satisfy the needs outlined above and do so in a manner palatable to the general reader.

The result was instead *These American Lands*, and no man's complaint ever had a happier ending. It was all there in one comprehensive package: the history, problems, and prospects of America's national parks, national forests, Bureau of Land Management lands, wildlife refuges, designated wildernesses, Alaska lands, wild and scenic rivers, and national trails. Each chapter outlined in a lively fashion the history of the unit of public lands under discussion, clarified the resource use and policy conflicts that were currently besetting it, then followed with a prescription from The Wilderness Society for the future protection and management of these lands and resources. Finally, an appendix offered—for the first time in a single place—all relevant statistical information regarding these lands (including the only existing comprehensive list of names, location, and acreage of the entire current National Wilderness Preservation System), together with a handy chronological history of all major public land legislation.

There was no other book quite like *These American Lands* anywhere when it was first published in the fall of 1986, and it soon proved itself one of the most reliable and often used tools available to the conservation community, Congress, policymakers, land managers, and, indeed, any citizen in search of a true and solid understanding of our national patrimony of lands. There still is no book quite like that original edition, but much environmental water has passed under the conservationist bridge since 1986. We believe that the time is right for a new edition, one that not only brings the history up-to-date with discussions about new legislation, new wilderness designations, new conflicts, new conservation campaigns, and much else, but also begins to frame its discussion of what still needs to be done in a context that includes more sophisticated concepts in the protection and preservation of land and wildlife.

From the conservationist point of view, of course, perhaps the most important development since 1986 has been a revolutionary change in the atmosphere here in Washington, D. C. The Reagan administration that once gave the conservation community so much grief is no more, and the Bush administration that followed it, hardly better, did not survive its first term. A new, more environmentally-committed administration under President Bill Clinton has come to power, and both the new President's appointments and many of his actions in his first year in office suggest that while some decisions may still fall short of the environmental ideal in many areas of concern, a new age of responsibility and stewardship clearly has begun.

It is up to the conservation community to meet these fresh circumstances with a new commitment of its own. I am not necessarily talking about the kinds of initiatives that have punctuated the long history recounted so tellingly in the pages of this book—the fights against dams and for birds, against clearcutting and for wilderness designation, against road-building and for park protection, against overgrazing and for Mining Law reform. All of this and more has been necessary, indeed inescapable, and much of it will remain necessary even in this new time, when environmentalism now seems to blossom in the Executive Branch. We will always have battles that will have to be fought, as the Sierra Club's Daniel B. Luten once said, "So long as Americans con-tinue to value both the useful and the beautiful qualities of the land-scape, so long as they cherish both fields and wilderness, so long as they are beset by both nostalgia and wanderlust. . . ." But the conservation struggle has too long been a matter of barricades and battles, each fought singly and exhaustingly. Each battle over the Forest Service's RARE II process or the preservation of wild rivers or the designation of wilderness or any other conservation cause has cost time and energy, and with every day spent much of the very resource we were trying to protect inevitably has vanished. The continuing saraband of struggle and compromise nearly obliterated the last of the ancient forests of the Pacific Northwest, precipitated the alarming loss of wetlands everywhere in the country, reduced the nation's reserves of true wilderness, impaired the natural qualities of national parks, accelerated the extinction of species, destroyed the financial base and quality of life in human communities, and weakened the fabric of biodiversity.

And so it has tended to go: while the principals get lost in dust clouds of conflict over policies, proposals, and programs, the overall abundance and quality of natural habitat is steadily diminished.

It is time to change the character of the struggle. Conservationists can no longer afford to dissipate our strengths in a piecemeal attempt to overcome an assault here, repel an invader there, until our resources are so thinly spread that we lose the fort itself. What is needed is a true coherence of vision—the kind of certainty of purpose that the long brave campaign for the creation of a National Wilderness Preservation System once provided.

The one item in our philosophical arsenal that can meet the need for such purpose is something I will have to call ecosystem protection, for want of a better and more precise term. The phrase is a little troubling mainly because its cousin, "ecosystem management," already is going the rounds of the land-management agencies and is being just about as freely misinterpreted as "patriotism" or "justice." Like these other noble terms, the phrase attempts to define an ideal—and, as The Wilderness Society's Karin Sheldon has written, "therefore is vulnerable to the human tendency to distort such sentiments when convenient. Some federal land managers, consequently, have taken to using 'ecosystem management' to explain (and therefore justify) the misguided things they do or allow to be done to the land. Authorizing a clearcut that wrecks a streambank that silts up a river that destroys a salmon fishery is management, all right, but it has precious little to do with preserving the health of anyone's ecosystem."

Indeed. We must focus on the core of what should be meant by ecosystem protection. However little human beings still know about ecosystem mechanics or even what precisely *defines* an ecosystem, what we must remember is that ecosystem protection is a concept that is deeply rooted in Aldo Leopold's land ethic. "All ethics so far evolved," he wrote, "rest upon a single premise: that the individual is a member of a community of interdependent parts. . . . The land ethic simply enlarges the boundaries of the community to include soils, waters, plants, and animals, or collectively, the land." The key word here is "community" and it is becoming more and more clear that while traditional wilderness designation—drawing lines around pristine areas of wild country to be kept "untrammeled by man"—may still be the most immediately effective means of protecting many individual areas, it can no longer be the only tool we use if we are going to preserve the land as community. Nor, given its capacity for damage, can we operate as if the human element in the natural community is without force or function.

It is the whole system of life that must be protected, because if we do not do so, the salvation of any given part of that system will be futile. For example, however glorious a victory the passage of the California Desert Protection Act will be, if the burgeoning civilization that surrounds and uses the ecosystem of the entire protected and unprotected desert does not learn to understand how interdependent and fragile this great wholeness is, wilderness designation and national park status will not prevent its eventual, inexorable disintegration.

So in the pages that follow, especially in those devoted to The Wilderness Society's hopes for the land, you will, every now and then, see discussions that not only outline specific continuing conflicts and preservation goals, but emphasize the means by which a coherence of vision and management can be achieved. That is only as it should be. In its own way, the ideal of ecosystem protection may prove to be as revolutionary a notion as the original vision of a National Wilderness Preservation System was when it was first conceived more than forty years ago. For the term essentially is conceptual: it is a way of seeing as well as of doing. If we human beings learn to see the intricacies that bind one part of a natural system to another and then to us, we will no longer argue about the importance of wilderness preservation, or over the question of saving endangered species, or how human communities must base their economic futures not on short-term exploitation but on long-term, sustainable development. If we learn, finally, that what we need to "manage" is not the land so much as ourselves *in* the land, we will have turned the history of American land use on its head.

Gaylord Nelson
Counselor
The Wilderness Society
Washington, D. C.
April 1994

A NOTE FROM THE AUTHORS

This revision of *These American Lands* was possible only with the expert assistance of many present and former staff members of The Wilderness Society. We want to thank, especially, Bennett Beach and Burnita Bell of the Public Affairs Department; William C. Reffalt, former director of Refuge Programs, and Pamela Eaton, present director of Refuge Programs; Michael Francis, director of Forest Programs; Nancy Green, director of BLM Programs; Allen Smith, director of the Alaska Regional Office; James Webb, director of the Florida Regional Office; Patricia Byrnes, managing editor of *Wilderness* magazine; and, especially, computer specialist Patricia Holmes, who guided this revision through the typesetting process. We also owe a debt of gratitude to the good work of many other conservation organizations whose reports and other material have provided the fundament on which much of this book was built. Any errors of fact or interpretation that may remain after the diligence of all these individuals and organizations are the sole and exclusive property of the authors.

With regard to the appendix material, the reader should note that all wilderness areas, national parks, wild and scenic rivers, and other land classifications made after this book was first published have been gathered in a separate section, "Appendix B." Similarly, the "Selected Bibliography" of the first edition is now followed by "Additional Readings," a selection of particularly useful and important books and articles published since *These American Lands* was issued.

THE VIEW
FROM HOME

From my house and neighborhood I can see the difference between private and public land. In this mountain suburb the privately owned lots are two acres or more, and the houses built on them are large. The yards are decorated with swings and redwood decks. There are hot tubs, and dog runs slant down the sunny slope. Some residents have fenced out others. I can see that more and more people are installing satellite dishes to pick up cable-television programs, and one of our neighbors has planted an orange windsock on his roof to guide his helicopter onto a landing pad. A llama farm occupies the valley below. Our property expresses ourselves; we do what we like with the land we own.

The houses are oriented to achieve the best views, which lie beyond the llama farm, to the south and west. A forest of pine, fir, and spruce drapes one million acres of rugged country, and depending on the season, the higher elevations are streaked with the pale green, gold, or silver of aspen. All the trees play out at twelve thousand feet. The Continental Divide, outstretched like an eagle's wing, soars another 2,400 feet above the treeline. At night the forest is as black and concentrated as pitch, making the sky light by comparison. This is all national forestland, all belonging to that portion of the continent that will never be subdivided and subjected to impulse. Such is our understanding as, with a hypocritical sense of relief, we welcome the knowledge that limitations have been imposed on the spread of the sort of temporal pleasures that confuse even our own yards. The exercise of free choice on private property has resulted in a patchwork of development, raising our living standards possibly, yet leaving us unsatisfied. Where we live, the value of our property is mostly determined by the permanence of the big, raw reach of public land. We have bought proximity to a national forest, and with it a view that astonishes us every morning. But it is hard to forget that the land, the source of our astonishment, is commonly owned. The land beyond the llama farm is our shared patrimony and, as long as major distinctions are enforced, our greatest material bequest.

One-third of the nation's land is publicly owned, and managed by various bureaus of the federal government for the perpetuation of America's natural resources. The public land systems compensate for the chief shortcoming of free enterprise—which is its inability to respond to any but its own pressing demands, all of them originating, understandably, in the need to maximize profits as quickly as possible. "On the evidence of several generations of exploitative freedom no one could guarantee the future its share of the American earth except the American government," wrote Wallace Stegner in *Beyond the Hundredth Meridian.* Despite the accumulating evidence of land abused through economic incentives, the federal government did not assume the role of conservator easily, or in one bold leap forward. Congress dispensed federal assistance only as a last resort— approaching, then avoiding, matters that questioned the ultimate wisdom of unchecked private initiative.

Consider the 1872 debate surrounding the reservation of Yellowstone, the first national park. "I have grave doubts about the propriety of passing this bill," said Senator Cornelius Cole of California in 1872. "The geysers will remain, no matter where the ownership of the land may be, and I do not know why settlers should be excluded from a tract of land forty miles square. . . . I can't see how the natural curiosities can be interfered with if settlers are allowed to appropriate them." The park was finally set aside after assurances from the politically savvy geographer Ferdinand V. Hayden that the Yellowstone region was as worthless as it was magnificent, and hence of no use to future settlers. From that time to this, nature preservation has always been submitted to an economic calculus for which it is poorly suited. Ironically, the national parks were quickly accepted as the embodiment of democracy. They were, in fact, "a predictable response to despoliation and avarice," noted Joseph L. Sax, a law professor and public-land theorist. National parks, according to Sax's *Mountains Without Handrails*,

> harmonized with a principle that was at the very crest of its influence in American land policy. The Yellowstone era was also the time of the Homestead and Desert Land Acts, when every American family was to have its share of the public domain free of monopolization by the rich. The application of that principle to the great scenic wonders could not be realized by granting a sequoia grove or Grand Canyon to each citizen. But it was possible to preserve the spectacular sites for the average citizen by holding them as public places to be enjoyed by all.

The same principle logically extends to the public land systems that followed the establishment of national parks.

Apart from the politically understandable desire to avoid restraining the Great White Hope of free enterprise, there was another, more deeply seated reason why a broad consensus in favor of nature conservation and appreciation took longer than necessary to take root. To the earliest European arrivals, land that had not been subdued to man's ends was wilderness, and the word had only terrifying connotations. Pioneer concepts of wilderness had been shaped by the Bible, and, according to those who have counted, the Old and New Testaments contain some three hundred disparaging references to it. The ancestral memory of Europe's frontier during the Dark and Middle Ages bound the meaning of wilderness even more closely to brutish existence. "Successive waves of frontiersmen had to contend with wilderness as uncontrolled and terrifying as that which primitive man confronted," wrote Roderick Nash, a historian of the American wilderness movement, in *Wilderness and the American Mind*.

> Safety and comfort, even necessities like food and shelter, depended on overcoming the wild environment. For the first Americans, as for

3

medieval Europeans, the forest's darkness hid savage men, wild beasts and still stranger creatures of the imagination. In addition civilized man faced the danger of succumbing to the wilderness of his surroundings and reverting to savagery himself. The pioneer, in short, lived too close to wilderness for appreciation.

Americans had to become more citified before they could abide wildness in their world.

Possibly too much has been blamed on the Judeo-Christian teachings calling for the subjugation of the earth. Often cited in this argument is Genesis 1:28, in which man is given dominion over nature and is divinely blessed. But environmental degradation occurred long before many civilizations had any contact with biblical writings. China, for instance, was deforested years before the first Christian missionaries arrived. Besides, the early teachers in almost all religions instructed their adherents on how to take care of the land. Hebrews were commanded to let fields lie fallow every seventh year so that soil nutrients would be restored. "Woe unto them that join house to house, that lay field to field, till there is no place where one may be alone in the midst of the earth," Isaiah admonished. Noticing the disparity between the preaching and the practice, the scientist René Dubos said that "the professed ideals of a culture, like those of its politicians, are rarely translated into actual practice, but this is at least as true of Orientals as of Western peoples." According to Dubos, deforestation, combined with ignorance of the long-range effects of intensive agriculture, is the main reason for the deterioration of land, rather than a conscious effort to destroy it.

While no single culture holds the patent for land abuse, the newly formed United States was gifted with more wild land than any other modern nation in the world. The land was wasted at an appalling rate, accelerated further still by such improved axes, saws, and firearms as the colonists could acquire. Nineteenth-century artists and authors recorded numerous instances of profligacy. James Fenimore Cooper's Leatherstocking novels, glorifying the noble savage, warned of excess. Richard Jones, a fool in Cooper's *The Pioneers*, scoffs when he is told not to burn too much wood. "Why, you might as well predict that the fish will die for want of water in the lake!" he retorts. Actually, by the 1820s, wood shortages were severe in many New England

4

towns, and poorer families froze to death in winter. In Vermont alone, so much of the forest cover had been cut or burned that the land was good only for grazing sheep, which made the situation worse.

A reckless attitude toward natural resources had quickly become a national trait, just as Europeans were beginning to curse their own habit of waste. For them it was too late; hardly any open land remained. In America, the critics were rising. Among them was an odd man named Henry David Thoreau, observed in his native Concord, Massachusetts, standing in downpours for hours, or staring at mallards on a pond long after his neighbors deemed there was any purpose in it. He won national acclaim for *Walden, or, Life in the Woods*, published in 1854. *Walden* recorded Thoreau's experiment of living in the woods alone, in a cabin he built himself. "If a man walks in the woods for love of them half of each day, he is in danger of being regarded as a loafer, but if he spends his whole day as a speculator shearing off those woods and making the earth bald before her time, he is esteemed as an industrious and enterprising citizen," he wrote. In an essay for *The Atlantic Monthly* four years later, Thoreau wrote, "The pine is no more lumber than man is, and to be made into boards and houses is no more its true and highest use than the truest use of a man is to be cut down and made into manure. There is a higher law affecting our relation to pines as well as to men." To Thoreau, who died in 1862 at the age of forty-five, the perfect man in the perfect place would permit civilization into no more than half his life, letting nature rule the other half.

And that portion was hardly enough for bearded, peripatetic John Muir, who had come from Scotland when still a boy. Temporarily blinded in an accident while working in a wheel factory, Muir vowed that once he regained his eyesight he would live only in wild places. Light returned, and Muir set out, wandering for years, studying the earth, botanizing, and dodging the draft that had been instituted during the Civil War. Before his explorations led him into the remotest pockets of the North American continent, including Alaska, Muir greatly admired Thoreau, and Thoreau's own mentor, Ralph Waldo Emerson. But Muir was as fervently committed to making changes as these men were to talking and writing about them. Eventually Muir dismissed Thoreau as "the captain of a huckleberry party."

Muir's accounts of his travels and opinions on man's role in nature were published in the widely read *Century Magazine* and elsewhere. "The world, we are told, was made for man, a presumption that is totally unsupported by facts," Muir wrote, repudiating his Calvinist upbringing. "Nature's object in making animals and plants might possibly be first of all the happiness of each of them, not the creation of all for the happiness of one. Why ought man to value himself as more than an infinitely small composing unit of the great unit of creation, and what creature of all the Lord has taken the pains to make it less essential to the grand completeness of the unit?"

And Muir acted: he vigorously championed the nascent national park movement, and the addition of Yosemite was his almost exclusive contribution to the system. Muir knew the valley better than any man, having debunked the prevailing theories of its geological origins. Before most people could accept the idea, Muir knew that the only hope for nature's preservation lay with the U.S. government. Decisive protection was needed desperately in all the national parks, although Frederick Law Olmsted, the principal planner of New York's Central Park, had beaten Muir to that conclusion before there even were national parks. Muir also believed forests needed to be nationalized, and he applied himself to that end. Being famous in his own right made the famous seek him out. He became nature's most eloquent spokesman, a man who knew the language of both trees and Americans, and initiated a vital communication between them. In one of those delightful instances of historical convergence, President Theodore Roosevelt invited Muir to meet him in Yosemite and to tell him more about government's duties in preservation. During their time together, Roosevelt asked only that they "keep away from civilization." Then, for three nights, "two major figures in American history enacted in microcosm the culture's persistent dream: creative truancy in the wild heart of the New World," wrote Frederick Turner in *Rediscovering America*, his biography of Muir.

Although the federal role in land preservation did not evolve exactly as Muir had advised, there is no doubt that many of his opinions influenced Roosevelt, the first chief executive to put conservation on the national agenda. Even with Roosevelt's great strides, however, public land management has, since the beginning of the century, withstood the various thrusts and parries of the political system. Until the last twenty years or so, public lands lacked a unifying theme: units of land for the many aspects of preservation were added piecemeal; false hopes lingered. Some administrations have been more mistrustful than others of the purpose of the public lands and of those directed to fulfill it, believing, as Senator Cole did in 1872, that the private sector can do everything right, given a chance. Any slippage from the slowly emerged ideal can have serious long-range consequences. A friend of mine from the former Soviet Union once asserted that American preservation policies still made too many concessions to private enterprise to do any good. Wilderness areas for public recreation? Air-conditioned hotels in national parks? What message was being sent to the people? he asked. Such lenience would lead to failure, he predicted, resulting in weakened nature and soft people. This friend, who was in private a harsh critic of his own regime in most matters, praised the strict Soviet approach to preservation. "Nature must be left completely alone somewhere," he insisted. It certainly was in the days of the Soviet Union: Armed guards were posted around nature reserves, and access to most of them was restricted to scientists.

These are unacceptable measures in the United States, where effective perpetuation of all publicly held resources must begin with the recognition that public land is not an anomaly in American life, but an integral part of it. Side-by-side systems of private and public land can function symbiotically. Maintaining a large base of land in its natural, healthy condition makes it possible for us to prosper. Meanwhile, the material indications that the nation is very well off also suggest that the United States can afford to protect its landed estate. As Israel's prime minister, David Ben-Gurion, remarked when he flew over the West in the early 1960s, "Who but America can afford to keep such deserts?" Nature, wrote Professor Sax, "is also a successful model of many things that human communities seek: continuity, stability, and sustenance, adaptation, sustained productivity, diversity and evolutionary change. . . . Natural systems renew themselves without any exhaustion of resources . . . they thrive on tolerance of diversity and [they] resist the arrogance of the conquerors. . . ." Natural systems are good ones to emulate, but at this point in our cultural evolution, government must show us how, by emphasizing always that health, beauty, and permanence are the only

7

important goods, and by educating us to the fact that productivity, measured longitudinally, is the by-product, and not the overriding commitment. Wrote Wallace Stegner:

> If that government contained quarreling and jealous bureaus, that was too bad. If it sheltered grafters . . . too bad. If it was too far from the resources in question to make every decision right, too bad.
>
> Too bad. But the alternative was worse. The alternative was creeping deserts, flooded river valleys, dusty miles of unused and unusable land, feeble or partial or monopolistic utilization of the available land and water. The alternative was great power and great wealth to a few and for a brief time rather than competence and independence for the communities of small freeholders on which [the] political economy unchangeably rested.

As this book will relate, America's history is rife with such grim alternatives. America's future, with regard to its parks, forests, wildlife, rivers, and nonrenewable resources, can tell another story.

Dyan Zaslowsky
Evergreen, Colorado
November 1985,
March 1994

Marymere Falls, Olympic National Park, Washington (T. H. Watkins).

1

THE PLEASURING GROUNDS

The National Park System

By moonbeam and the bagged yellow light of two hundred glowing *farolitos*, fifty foreign guests steered their way down a tight passage into the Cliff Palace Ruin at Mesa Verde National Park in southern Colorado. Out on the far edge of candlelight, in the back of an Anasazi chamber, a Ute Indian sat cross-legged and played the oboe. "I have wanted to come here for a thousand years," murmured a man from Kupang, Indonesia, cradling himself against a slick-rock pillow. In the gently orchestrated darkness of this late summer's night in 1984, he and the others must have felt the truth in the fact that the world would be poorer without such places as Mesa Verde—without, on a grand scale, the whole national park system of the United States.

Along with free public education and private philanthropy, the creation of natural national parks ranks among the few thoroughly American contributions to world culture. And the success of the United States' venture has encouraged the establishment of more than 1,200 national parks in over one hundred countries. The hundreds of units in our own national park system, encompassing more than 89 million acres, are the portion of federally retained lands that Americans encounter soonest, understand best, and cherish most. Touching affirmation of this is evident in letters written to National Park Service officials by battle-worn soldiers during several wars. A soldier wrote one such letter from Europe during World War II:

Yosemite National Park, 1900 (Seaver Center for Western History Research, Natural History Museum of Los Angeles County).

11

I had no conception of how much the national parks could mean in wartime until I came here. If you could hear the men talk of our parks and forests, you know how great a part they play in the American scene. When the talk turns to "before the war," it is invariably . . . the hours spent with rod and reel on lake and stream, the camping trips, the quiet nights in the pine woods . . . and it is those things that these men are fighting for, as well as for their homes, sweethearts, wives and families.

The fifty-one full-fledged parks cover about 80 million acres. Many of these—Yosemite, Yellowstone, Olympic, for example—are considered the "crown jewels" of the system by virtue of their extraordinary natural beauty and wildness, but the system has grown well beyond its original and revolutionary purpose of preserving spectacular landscapes for the pleasure of the public. In the past century it has sprouted numerous monuments, preserves, lakeshores, rivers, seashores, historic sites, memorials, military parks, battlefield parks, historical parks, recreation areas, parkways, and other additions— all preceded by the word "national" in official usages, and all intended to inspire or edify the public. The diversity of the group commemorates not only the continent's natural gifts, but the course of its human events as well. This combination has at times strained the National Park Service's ability to cover all bases. The jurisdiction of the Park Service, with its billion-dollar annual budget and more than eight thousand full-time employees, ranges from the 8.3-million-acre Wrangell–St. Elias National Park and Preserve in Alaska to the one-third-acre Ford's Theatre National Historic Site in the District of Columbia. The agency must perpetuate the backwoods solitude of Wyoming's Grand Tetons, and accommodate an audience of 9,500 on the rolling lawn of the Wolf Trap Farm Park for the Performing Arts in Virginia.

Such diverse responsibilities have aroused the complaint that the mission of the National Park Service has been muddied. Rather than concentrate on administering a few things very well, some critics charge, the Service diffuses its energies and talents among too many duties of a contradictory nature. If so, it is symptomatic of a paradox that has haunted the agency ever since 1916 and the Organic Act that created it. The Service's mission in regard to the national parks, that act stated, was "to conserve the scenery and the natural and historic objects and wildlife therein and to provide for the enjoyment of the same in such manner and by such means as will leave them unimpaired for the enjoyment of future generations." But at no point did the act define precisely how this delicate balance between preservation and public pleasure was to be accomplished or maintained— and there still are no precise guidelines to solve one of the Park Service's most persistent modern dilemmas, as succinctly outlined by Ronald A. Foresta in *America's National Parks and Their Keepers*: "If use destroys, how can a management policy both accommodate use and preserve the natural area? A mandate which is inherently contradictory must, by logical extension, become a management dilemma—a problem for which there is no solution that does not violate a restraint."

Ironically, contradictions in American society itself once provided the national park system with its greatest support. As Joseph L. Sax wrote in *Mountains Without Handrails: Reflections on the National Parks*:

> The happy convergence of many disparate interests permitted Congress and the public to sustain contradictory, but compatible beliefs that permitted a park system to flourish: On one side the repugnance of the seemingly boundless materialism that infused American life, a spiritual attachment to untrammeled nature, and a self-congratulatory attitude toward the preservation of nature's bounty; and on the other a commitment to economic progress wherever it could be exacted, nationalistic pride, and the practical uses of nature as a commodity supportive of tourism and commercial recreation.

TOWARD A "NATION'S PARK"

It was a long journey from the happy condition described by Sax to the frustrations of today. It began in 1832, but not, as one might expect, because that was the year that Congress withdrew the region of Hot Springs, Arkansas, from appropriation by the various land laws and declared it the first natural federal preserve. Hot Springs was valued not for its scenic grandeur or even its claim as a natural

13

wonder, but for its perceived medicinal value; this was the great age of hydrotherapy, and Congress believed that all Americans should have access to the curative waters that bubbled up in that part of the Ozarks (Hot Springs, in fact, did not formally enter the modern national park system until 1921). The real beginning that year took place a thousand miles to the northwest, at the confluence of the Missouri and Yellowstone rivers, where a young artist stood amazed at the beauty of the country all around him. His name was George Catlin. His specialty was painting Indians, and to find them he had gone aboard the first steamboat to ascend the Missouri as far as the mouth of the Yellowstone. He surveyed the untamed landscape along the river and wrote in his journal that that place, or some other place in the West, ought to be set aside as a "nation's park, containing man and beast, in all the freshness of their nature's beauty." Catlin added that "I would ask no other monument to my memory, nor any enrollment of my name among the famous dead, than the reputation of having been the founder of such an institution."

As an artist who used nature as the backdrop of his paintings, Catlin was more sensitive to natural beauty than were many of his countrymen. Yet he may also have been reacting to the sense of cultural inferiority that penetrated the young, entrepreneurial nation. National park historian Alfred Runte maintains that the park movement sprang originally from America's desire to appear as refined as the older nations of Europe. But the United States, barely emerged from the cleared forests, had no cathedrals, no Roman ruins, and no intricate gardens that bespoke human triumph and national greatness. Writing in his *Sketch Book* in 1819, Washington Irving shared a common view when he said he preferred to "wander over the scenes of renowned achievement—to tread, as it were, in the footsteps of antiquity—to loiter about the ruined castle—to meditate on the falling tower—to escape, in short, from commonplace reality of the present, and lose myself among the shadowy grandeurs of the past." At about the same time, James Fenimore Cooper acknowledged that Europe contained the "sublimer views," unless the United States resorted to "the Rocky mountains and the ranges of California and Mexico"— which at that time were as foreign to the United States as was Europe. Aggravating this sense of cultural anxiety was the fact that Americans had generally left their most scenic areas in a shambles. Niagara Falls had been recognized as the nation's greatest natural spectacle, but by the 1830s its cliffs were combed by rogues and unscrupulous operators, who laid claim to the best overlooks and then charged tourists exorbitantly for the view. Fly-by-night enterprise cluttered the area, turning the place into a cheap circus. The setting had become so tawdry that when Alexis de Tocqueville visited the Falls in 1831, he urged an American friend to "hasten" to see the place before all its grandeur was lost. Delay, Tocqueville warned, would mean that "your Niagara will have been spoiled for you. Already the forest round about is being cleared. I don't give the Americans ten years to establish a saw or flour mill at the base of the cataract."

The fact that some Americans were beginning to see the disgrace for themselves and realize (as Catlin did) that symbols of national greatness lay in another direction was not sufficient to make Congress try to protect "scenery," not even in 1864, when it turned the Yosemite Valley over to the state of California for operation as a park. This casual gesture, made by a Congress preoccupied with the Civil War, hardly preserved the valley. Since the state did not mind commercial enterprise—but, indeed, encouraged it—the valley was soon victimized by the same kind of exploitation (including grazing and logging this time) that had made such a mess of Niagara Falls.

Yosemite was sublime even in disgrace, but little known outside its own state. In Wyoming Territory, however, a few hundred miles southwest of the spot where Catlin had discerned his vision of a "nation's park," lay the Yellowstone country, the subject of widespread if sometimes incredulous fascination almost from the beginning of the nation's expansion into the trans-Mississippi West. It lay untouched by anything but wonder, and had for a long time.

First word of the Yellowstone region was brought to civilization in 1807, when John Colter returned from a solo trip. Colter had been a member of the Lewis and Clark expedition, but, in 1805, enticed by the possibilities of fur trapping, he asked to take his leave. He was released, and Lewis's journal makes this note: "The example of this man shows us how easily men may be weaned from the habits of civilized life to the ruder but scarcely less fascinating manners of the woods. Just at the moment when he is approaching the frontiers,

15

he is tempted by a hunting scheme to give up those delightful prospects and goes back without the least reluctance to the solitude of the woods."

The solitude of the woods led Colter to Yellowstone Lake, the land of geysers and of falls higher than those of Niagara. He returned to St. Louis with rich pelts and richer tales of boiling springs and towers of water that rose one hundred feet. Apparently he "saw too much for his reputation as a man of veracity," wrote the historian Hiram Martin Chittenden. No one believed him. The place he described was jeeringly known as "Colter's Hell." It did not help matters that Jim Bridger, a mountain man, was apparently the next English-speaking person to return from the area with breathless descriptions. Bridger was well-known as a man who played fast and loose with the truth. He confirmed Colter's sighting of geysers and hot springs, but he embellished these realities with glittering reports of petrified birds that sang petrified songs, of mountains made entirely of glass that had the property of telescopes and so transparent that a person could walk right into them if he wasn't watchful. And so the region of the Yellowstone remained little more than a fantasy land for most of the busiest years of the westward movement. Between 1804 and 1870 there were 110 scientific explorations west of the Mississippi River, but only one of them was assigned to the Yellowstone region, and that was not until 1859. In that year, Captain W. F. Raynolds was ordered to report his findings around Yellowstone, so that the stories of nature's opulence could be either confirmed or denied. At one point Captain Raynolds stood where he could see the entire region of the park. But he got no closer. News that the Civil War had erupted reached him, along with orders that sent him back to the States. In his wistful report, Captain Raynolds noted that duty compelled him to content himself with "listening to marvelous tales of burning plains and immense lakes without verifying these wonders."

Finally, in 1870, an exploration party of nineteen men from the Montana Territory organized a trip that would once and for all set the record straight. Cornelius Hedges, the member of the party who usually receives credit for coming up with the national park idea, noted that "a more confirmed set of skeptics never went out into the wilderness than those who composed our party, and never was a party more completely surprised and captivated with the wonders of nature." Even Old Faithful cooperated. When the party came within several hundred feet of the geyser, a massive flume of water shot 150 feet into the air. The popular story is that while Hedges, Nathaniel P. Langford, and other expedition members sat around their campfire at the junction of the Gibbon and Firehold rivers one night, they discussed Yellowstone's possibilities. Once their reports were published, Yellowstone would, of course, be exploited to the fullest. Hedges, with Langford supporting him, rejected this scenario and decided that the Yellowstone country should be set aside as a national park, preserved in its natural state. Whether or not such a conversation took place is debatable. Historians now believe an employee of the Northern Pacific Railroad by the name of A. B. Nettleson first passed this suggestion on to his superiors in Washington, D.C. Moreover, even if Hedges did bring up the subject of a national park, he did not originate the idea, because a few years earlier he had heard a Jesuit missionary make the same suggestion while giving a talk on Yellowstone in Helena, Montana. And as early as 1865, Montana Territorial Governor Thomas E. Meagher had voiced a similar proposal. Whoever originated the notion, it was clearly an idea whose time was near. In 1871, Ferdinand Vandiveer Hayden took his Geological and Geographical Survey of the Territories into Yellowstone with artist Thomas Moran and photographer William Henry Jackson. Moran's paintings and Jackson's photographs were added to the support material of a growing number of park promoters. By now, these included no less than Jay Cooke of the Northern Pacific Railroad, who backed the idea on the quite proper assumption that anything that promoted the wonders of the West could do wonders for his railroad.

The promotional flurry paid off on March 1, 1872, when Congress created Yellowstone National Park as "a public park or pleasuring ground for the benefit and enjoyment of the people." With the easy establishment of Yellowstone, Congress inaugurated the dubious tradition of creating a park without appropriating money for its protection. The government operated under the delusion that the park would pay its own way once visitors started streaming in. The delusion was a fortunate one insofar as it led to the establishment of the park; once it was created, however, there was no money to operate it. For the first five years Superintendent Nathaniel Langford donated his time and services. For the next twenty-two years no superintendent had the legal authority to detain or discipline the countless vandals and poachers who infiltrated the park once its fame spread. A superintendent could do no more than evict an offender from the park; the closest seat of justice lay 250 mountainous miles away, in the town of Evanston. Moreover, Yellowstone's enabling act contained no provision for the protection of wildlife, leaving game vulnerable to slaughter. The buffalo in the park constituted one of the few wild herds left in the country, but poaching reduced their number from 541 to twenty-two before Congress finally appropriated funds to buy domesticated specimens to breed with the remaining wild ones.

Tourists, rare as they were at first, added to the headaches. Visitors painted their names on any surface they could reach, and threw boots and small trees into the geysers and hot springs. Anyone who visited the park in its earliest years deserved some credit, however, because getting there was no weekend excursion. Congress had sternly rejected the railroads' frequent bid to lay track right through the park, and it was many years before even a branch line served it. Consequently the best route to Yellowstone was the northern one, from Bismarck in Dakota Territory. But first the traveler would have to take a steamboat up the Missouri River 400 miles to the Yellowstone River, up that another 360 miles to the mouth of the Bighorn, then another 60 miles up the Bighorn to Clark's Fork. At this point a coach would take travelers the last 72 miles to the park's border. The distance from Bismarck was 1,050 miles, and the round trip took from three to four weeks. This was not only the shortest route—in terms of mileage—it was the cheapest, although the $100 it cost was a princely sum at the time.

And the hardships were just beginning. Lodging was unreliable—unbuilt, in fact, for several years after its predicted completion. Food could be downright poisonous. From the outset, Congress had intended preservation to go hand in hand with use, and in 1882 it made the first concession agreement with a pair of businessmen from Dakota Territory. In exchange for the free use of 4,400 acres of prime scenic land, Carroll T. Hobart and Henry F. Douglas would feed and shelter park visitors via their Yellowstone Improvement Company. Unfortunately, the company's "improvements" included a planned luxury hotel, the killing and consumption of wild game ostensibly under park protection, and the stripping of timber for construction of the Mammoth Hot Springs Hotel. The agreement was canceled, and in its aftermath Congress decided that certain standards had to be established and enforced. For example, no longer could forests be logged arbitrarily, nor could construction take place within one-quarter of a mile of the park's most important wonders. Still, the word "improvement" continued to be used in reference to levels of accommodation, ranging from tents on platforms and a zealous effort to produce hot meals to more palatial appointments. The term was vague enough to inspire one European-trained landscape artist to devise a plan that would have placed an observatory, a rowing club, a forest institute, a swimming pool, a racetrack, and health spas throughout the park. He also recommended setting aside "thousands of acres for private villas."

Congress may not have been at all sure of what it meant by "improvement," but it made great strides in defining it after a commission visited Yellowstone in 1885 and made some important suggestions. The park, commission members agreed, should be "spared the vandalism of improvement" as much as possible. Yellowstone's "great and only charms are in the display of wonderful forms of nature, the ever-varying beauty of the rugged landscape, and the sublimity of the scenery. Art cannot embellish them," the report stated. Nevertheless, anarchy continued in Yellowstone, while Congress continued to refuse to empower or adequately fund a park supervisory staff. Desperate for assistance, the Secretary of the Interior had only one avenue open to him. He could, at his discretion, ask the Secretary of War to station troops in the park, which is exactly what Lieutenant General Philip Sheridan had suggested years earlier. And so, late on the evening of August 17, 1886, Troop M of the United States Cavalry rode into Yellowstone and relieved the civilian superintendent of his duties. The cavalry's presence was assumed to be temporary. It remained there, however, for thirty-two years, and by all accounts did an excellent job. Army supervision was later established in Yosemite, Sequoia, and General Grant parks as well, and in the performance

19

of their duties the military park rangers even earned the praise of John Muir. "In pleasing contrast to the noisy, ever-changing management or mismanagement of blustering, blundering, plundering, moneymaking vote sellers . . . the soldiers do their duty so quietly that the traveler is scarcely aware of their presence," Muir wrote. "Blessings on Uncle Sam's soldiers. They have done their job well, and every pine tree is waving its arms for joy."

A SYSTEM WITHOUT SYSTEM

In the eighteen years following the establishment of Yellowstone, only one other national park was created, and that temporarily: Mackinac Island National Park in Michigan, established in 1875, and twenty years later turned over to Michigan to be conserved as that state saw fit. The next flurry of park creation came in 1890, when Yosemite, Sequoia, and General Grant (later incorporated into Sequoia) national parks were established within days of one another.

On the flanks of the Sierras surrounding the Yosemite Valley, sheep had stripped the grass down to the soil, which, once exposed, quickly eroded away. John Muir—"Muir of the Mountains," as he was known even then—called the sheep "hoofed locusts," and campaigned hard for the creation of a federal reserve in the high country above the valley. The resulting national park, called Yosemite, was a peculiar place for the first fifteen years of its existence. It was shaped like an enormous doughnut, the hole being the state-owned and woefully abused valley in its center, with fenced ranges, houses, hotels, stores, and saloons; the last advertised such corrosive beverages as "corpse revivers" and "Samsons with the hair on." In 1905, again largely through the efforts of Muir and his Sierra Club, the state returned the valley to the federal government and it was added to the national park.

Sequoia and General Grant were known primarily as "tree parks," and were reserved to stop the vandalism of the world's largest tree— *Sequoiadendron giganteum*. Acres of the great trees had been logged for the sheer wonder of them. They were hard to cut down and their wood was too brittle to be of much use, but they were up to four thousand years old and the novelty of their age and size attracted attention. A tree would be felled just so a section of it could be

20

displayed in sideshows back East and in Europe. (At least one such enterprise went bankrupt because the public refused to believe a tree that large could be real, and crowds stayed away.) Some of the most impressive groves remained in private hands after the parks were created, and it took a funding drive initiated by the National Geographic Society to purchase the best of these and add them to the federal reserve.

Slowly, in such piecemeal fashion, and with varying degrees of opposition and confusion, the system grew: Mount Rainier, 1899 (but only after the Northern Pacific won a right-of-way as the price of its support); Crater Lake, 1902 (the vision of a single individual, Judge William Gladstone Steel, who then had to fund the park's care himself and serve as its superintendent without pay); Mesa Verde, 1906; Petrified Forest, 1906 (generally attributed to the efforts of John Muir); Grand Canyon, 1908; Zion, 1909; Olympic, 1909; Glacier, 1910; Rocky Mountain, 1915; Hawaii Volcanoes, 1916. Growth of the system had been accelerated (however inadvertently) in 1906, when Congress responded to the gross vandalism and theft of Anasazi relics among ancient Indian cliff dwellings in the Southwest by passing the Antiquities Act, which authorized the preservation as national monuments of sites containing scientific, historic, or scenic treasures and gave the President the power to designate them without first seeking congressional approval. By 1916, twenty national monuments had been declared by Presidents Roosevelt, Taft, and Wilson. The ability to create national monuments by executive order strengthened the national park movement enormously because it circumvented long debates and the possible rejection, for political reasons, of important sites. About one-quarter of today's national parks started out as national monuments.

By 1916, then, one might charitably say that a national park system was in place—but if so, it was a system without system. It was, first of all, headless; nowhere in official Washington could "an inquirer find an office of the national parks or a single desk devoted solely to their management," remembered J. Horace McFarland, president of the American Civic Association and one of the best friends the national parks ever had. "If the national parks were to meet the demands of the motor age," he recalled, "if they were ever to have enough money, enough publicity and enough protection, they had to be administered by a bureau of their own. They could not go on as the responsibility of a few clerks freighted with a superabundance of other matters classed as more important." In 1912, McFarland and other park supporters persuaded President Taft to send a special message to Congress. "I earnestly recommend," the President said, "the establishment of a Bureau of National Parks." But opposition from the Department of Agriculture's powerful Forest Service lobby, which was convinced that the parks should be folded into the national forest system, managed to forestall action over the next four years.

Nothing demonstrated the need for a protective agency for the parks more than the conflict over Hetch Hetchy, a valley in the northwest corner of Yosemite National Park whose beauty John Muir considered second only to that of Yosemite Valley itself. San Franciscans had wanted to build a dam on the Tuolumne River since before 1900, largely for the generation of municipally owned hydroelectric power. But since the dam would have flooded the Hetch Hetchy Valley, the city petitioned Congress in 1901 to grant the necessary permission. Congress gave its assent, but Interior Secretary Ethan Allen Hitchcock refused to authorize the reservoir, as did his successor, James Garfield. To President Theodore Roosevelt, Muir wrote that the Hetch Hetchy dam promoters demonstrated "the proud sort of confidence that comes of good sound irrefragable ignorance," and for eight years preservationists successfully fought the project. But in 1913 Franklin K. Lane, former city attorney of San Francisco and a firm believer in the city's dam, became Secretary of the Interior and began promoting it himself. In the final vote on enabling legislation that year, Congress backed Lane and the dam proponents, and within a few years the Hetch Hetchy Valley had disappeared beneath the waters behind the O'Shaughnessy Dam.

"I'll be relieved when it's settled," Muir had said earlier that year, "for it's killing me." After the dam's approval, friends noticed that he was sick quite often; a little more than a year after his greatest defeat, he died of pneumonia at the age of seventy-six.

STEPHEN MATHER: PRESSURE AND PROMOTION

With the loss of Hetch Hetchy, efforts to create a park service heated up again. The first step in this resurgence was taken in 1914 when

Interior Secretary Lane himself, ironically enough, hired an old class-mate of his named Stephen Tyng Mather to be his assistant in charge of the parks. Mather, a forty-seven-year-old millionaire who had spent twenty-two years in the borax business, had made the mistake of writing Lane to complain about the horrid food and lodging in Yo-semite Valley. Lane, not completely insensitive to the meaning of parks, wrote back: "Dear Steve, If you don't like the way the parks are being run, come on down to Washington and run them yourself." Mather decided to try, if just for a year.

Mather, who traced his lineage back to Cotton Mather, turned out to be precisely what the ailing parks needed. He was dynamic and tireless and, it seemed, could sell anything. He had promoted his 20-Mule Team Borax into the American household, and he gave the national parks the same frenzied devotion, determined to make the parks something Americans simply could not live without. In the year he was allowing for the job, Mather planned to sweep the superfluous and tacky concessions from the parks, prevent further commercial intrusions, add worthy units to the system but keep out what he called the "dead cats" that were too often the pork-barrel pets of congress-men, and, above all, increase both the friends and the funds of the parks. To help achieve these high-minded goals, he selected as his assistant Horace Albright, an idealistic and very able young lawyer who was working elsewhere within the Interior Department.

It took him thirteen years, not one, but Mather accomplished much of what he set out to do. The first order of business was to get a National Park Service bill through Congress, and he immediately began drumming up support for the idea. To the argument that the Forest Service was the proper custodian of natural wonders, he re-plied, with some justification, that in the care of the Forest Service natural beauty would always be measured against utilitarian values and beauty would come out the loser. Trees on national forest land, he said, were viewed as a crop. They required cultivation and har-vesting, like cotton or corn, and preservation was a slim prospect under such conditions. To counter congressional apathy, he organized a media blitz of respectable dimensions. First, he financed, out of his own pocket, extravagant park tours and invited along congressmen and carefully chosen men of influence, such as George Horace Lor-imer of *The Saturday Evening Post* and Gilbert Grosvenor of *National*

Geographic. Next, again out of his own pocket, he hired journalist Robert Sterling Yard (a former editor of *Century Magazine*) to write and place magazine articles, generate news stories, and produce descriptive booklets concerning the glories of the parks. Finally, he persuaded such railroads as the Southern Pacific and the Santa Fe to finance the publication of an elegant book, the *National Parks Portfolio*, which was then distributed free of charge to 250,000 people by the General Federation of Women's Clubs. This frenzied effort came to fruition in 1916, when Congress passed and President Woodrow Wilson signed the act creating the National Park Service with its noble (and later difficult) adjuration "to conserve the scenery and the natural and historic objects and the wildlife therein, and to provide for the enjoyment of the same in such manner and by such means as will leave them unimpaired for the enjoyment of future generations."

The imprimatur of Congress had little behind it in the way of practical aid. "The Service was a small agency with a limited charge," Ronald A. Foresta notes in *America's National Parks and Their Keepers.* "It ran a mere fifteen parks. Its field staff numbered a few hundred and its Washington staff, consisting of Mather, Albright, a draftsman, a few clerks, messengers, and secretaries, could be housed in a couple of offices." This situation slowed Mather down hardly at all. Before illness forced his retirement in 1929 (he died in 1930), he doubled the size of the park domain from 7,500 to 15,846 square miles by adding seven new parks and thirteen new monuments to the system, carved increasingly larger appropriations out of Congress, and built the agency into an institution comparable in public estimation—if never in size—to the Forest Service.

For the most part, he did it with the same methods that he had used in creating the Park Service: pressure and promotion. Until Mather's affection for tourist development—particularly the building of roads—estranged the two men permanently, Yard continued to publish scores of magazine articles, hundreds of news features, and thousands of copies of booklets, maps, and pamphlets, and together they gave lectures in churches, clubs, and schools all over the country, accompanied by Mather's amateurish but enthusiastic home movies of his own edifying park experiences.

Mather often infused the National Park Service with his own money

24

in other ways, the propriety of which might be called into question in these more modern times. He bought the old Tioga Road into Yosemite and financed part of its improvement, for example. He also purchased the ranger headquarters at Glacier National Park for $8,000 and donated it to the service. (In this instance the property was a privately owned parcel within the park, which had been foreclosed upon when Mather bought it. The only condition was that the owner had the option to buy back the property within a year of its sale. And the owner would have done so, had he not fallen down and died on the steps of the courthouse where he was going to file for possession.) In yet another burst of goodwill and generosity, Mather lent $200,000 to a park concessioner to make necessary additions and improvements to a hotel. He also lobbied businessmen for financial support, and among his earliest allies were, as noted, railroad executives.

Promoting the parks fit in well with the railroads' own "See America First" campaign, which depended on good train transportation before the proliferation of the automobile. "Every passenger that goes to the national parks, wherever they may be, represents practically a net earning," said Louis W. Hill, head of the Great Northern Railroad. Mather particularly encouraged sizable railroad investment in the form of luxury hotels. The Great Northern underwrote Glacier, the Northern Pacific built hotels in Yellowstone, and the Union Pacific took care of Bryce, Zion, and the north rim of the Grand Canyon. Since the railroads expected to earn their greatest profits on passenger service to and from the parks, hotel prices were kept at reasonable levels. Mather assured the companies that sponsored the hotels that they would be allowed a controlled monopoly of the parks they served. Uncontrolled free enterprise had merely cluttered and degraded the parks before his tenure, and Mather believed monopoly was the answer, so long as profits and the manner in which they were made were closely scrutinized by the Park Service. In return for the guaranteed monopoly, licensed concessioners financed capital improvements to serve their captive audience.

Mather was no primitivist when it came to park accommodations. Having toured Switzerland, he believed that comfortable lodgings and good food enhanced the travelers' admiration of the landscape. In America's parks he ordered a range of services from the luxurious to the spartan. Scenery, Mather maintained, "is a hollow enjoyment to a tourist who sets out in the morning after an indigestible breakfast and fitful sleep on an impossible bed." He was a man of decent tastes, however, and was very firm about how far commercialism should be allowed to venture. One day he visited Coney Island in New York with park landscape architect Gilbert Stanley Underwood for "an object lesson." The two men spent the day wandering through the crowds, stuffing themselves with hot dogs and raw onions, and washing it all down with orange pop. At one point Mather turned to Underwood and said, "This is exactly what we don't want in the national parks. Lots of people seem to like it and if they do, they ought to have it, but not in the national parks. Our job in the National Park Service is to keep the national parks as close to what God made them and as far as we can from a horror like this."

Perhaps the most famous story about Mather's insistence upon refinement in the parks took place at Glacier one August. On his arrival he noticed that a sawmill used to build the Great Northern Railroad's hotel at the Many Glacier site had not been dismantled as he had repeatedly ordered. Furious with this disobedience, he assembled a group of visitors to watch as he lit the fuse to thirteen charges of dynamite and blasted the sawmill to flinders. When asked by amazed onlookers why he had done this, Mather replied that he was merely celebrating his daughter's nineteenth birthday.

The most far-reaching decision Mather made during his directorship was to allow automobiles into the parks. Shortly after he took charge, he gave support to Western automobile enthusiasts who were demanding a park-to-park road system. To Mather, the plan was one more way to promote the parks and increase their visitations—easily translated into more money and prestige. At the dedication of Rocky Mountain National Park, over which Mather presided in 1916, three hundred cars and their drivers attended, forming "the greatest automobile demonstration ever seen in Colorado." Even without adequate roads, automobiles in great numbers were soon rumbling through most of the parks—only some ten thousand vehicles a year at first, but by 1919 the number had soared to 98,000. People were happy to shed that "horrid fiend, the railroad timetable," as the Lincoln Highway Association called it, and those who arrived by car outnumbered by four to one those who arrived by train. Few people realized then that the automobile would also be the parks' great undoing. One who did was James Bryce, the percipient British ambassador to the United States, who, after a visit to Yosemite in 1913, said, "If Adam had known what harm the serpent was going to work he would have tried to prevent him from finding lodgement in Eden; and if you were to realize what the result of the automobile will be in that wonderful, incomparable valley, you will keep it out." No one was listening, least of all Steve Mather.

"IN ABSOLUTELY UNIMPAIRED FORM"

Looking for park friends wherever he could find them, Mather realized that his greatest need was to get support east of the Mississippi River. All national parks lay to the west, and it was easy for Eastern congressmen to argue that they were not "national parks" at all, and should therefore be the responsibility of the states in which they were located. For the sake of the parks in the West, then, Mather and Albright embarked on a park-hunting expedition in the East. The big problem here was that nearly all the land had passed into private or state hands, and most of what remained was under the administration of the Forest Service. Nevertheless, a search committee scoured the Eastern and Southern regions in the early 1920s and finally came up with two worthy possibilities in the Appalachian Mountains: the Shenandoah Valley in Virginia, and the Great Smoky Mountains in Tennessee and North Carolina.

While the Great Smokies were fairly remote by the standards of their part of the country, the Shenandoah was a place where you could feel the "nearness of mankind," the first park to broaden the basic dictum that "a national park is where you find it" to "a national park is where the people are." In 1925 Congress stated its intent to establish these two parks in the East, provided that the states involved could raise the money to purchase the necessary private lands. It was a messy, drawn-out business. The Shenandoah, which covers about 195,000 acres along the crest of the Blue Ridge Mountains, was authorized by Congress in 1926 but was not fully established until 1935, by which time the state of Virginia had bought some seven hundred private land holdings in the area. The money for the purchases came from donations large and small. Schoolchildren gave their allowances to the cause. "I ain't so crazy 'bout leavin' these hills," said historian Freeman Tilden, an eighty-three-year-old lifetime resident, "but I never believed in bein' agin the government . . . besides, I always said these hills would be the heart of the world." Authorization to dedication of Great Smoky Mountains National Park took almost fourteen years, even though its half-million acres of private land were acquired with the help of John D. Rockefeller, Jr., through the Laura Spelman Rockefeller Memorial. Rockefeller offered $5 million in honor of his mother, and his donation was matched by smaller contributions from the states of North Carolina and Tennessee.

In addition to finding new parks and expanding old ones so that such things as elk and deer habitats would be protected (and the elk and deer along with them), Mather was frequently confronted with the threat of inappropriate uses. During World War I the parks, supposedly off-limit to most grazing, were open to stockmen who maintained that it was an act of patriotism to increase the nation's food supply. Several of the national parks had private landowners in their midst, which complicated management of the parks. On some private lands, logging continued, as did hunting and other activities outlawed in the parks. The number of private properties in Glacier, Mount Rainier, and Rocky Mountain National Park increased the fire hazards in those places, since private owners could not be required to take the same precautions the federal government took. To this day, private inholdings, which account for about 600,000 acres in the park system, create a major headache for park officials striving for uniform management over a large area.

In the wake of the Hetch Hetchy debacle, which he inherited and could do nothing to stop, Mather had a number of other in-park development projects he could and did fend off. Recurrent among these were plans to dam Yellowstone and other lakes as part of irrigation projects designed to help Idaho farmers. One plan given initial approval would have submerged ten thousand acres of prime meadows and forests. Secretary Lane, who tended to favor reclamation over preservation, gave his tentative permission for the park to be used in this fashion. This bestirred Mather to tender a letter of resignation. "Every plan to exploit Yellowstone has failed to receive the consideration of Congress," he wrote. "Mighty railroad projects have gone down to everlasting defeat. Must all the victories of the past now become hollow memories by the granting of reservoir rights that will desecrate its biggest and most beautiful lakes and form the precedent for commercial exploitation of all scenic reservoirs?"

Lane did not accept Mather's resignation, and he himself resigned before giving the final go-ahead on the project. Interestingly, before Lane stepped down he issued an important policy statement—perhaps dictated by Mather—that has remained one of the guiding lights of park management.

The statement declared, first, that national parks "must be maintained in absolutely unimpaired form for the use of future generations as well as those of our own time"; second, that "they are set aside for the use, observation, health and pleasure of the people"; and third, that "the national interest must dictate all decisions affecting parks."

This final assertion, unfortunately, allowed consideration of hundreds of projects that might otherwise have been considered detrimental and contradictory to the park ethic from the outset. Dams in Yellowstone, for instance, looked like a sure thing when Albert Fall, a devotee of schemes promoting oil, mineral, and even livestock exploitation of public resources, was appointed Secretary of the Interior in 1921. When Mather pleaded with him to disavow the dam project, Fall was noncommittal. "Every generation since Adam and Eve has lived better than the generation before," said Fall. "I don't know how they'll do it—maybe they'll use energy of the sun or the sea waves—but those boys will live better than we do. I stand for opening up every resource." Yet for some unknown reason he never did sanction the Yellowstone dams before the Teapot Dome scandal drove him from office, and for that he remains a kind of strange bedfellow in the preservationists' camp.

THE BATTLE OF JACKSON HOLE

After Mather's departure in 1929, the directorship fell to his colleague and protégé, Horace Albright, who brought to the position the same enthusiasm Mather had shown, and accomplished a great deal during his own four-year term. At the beginning he stated that his job was "to consolidate our gains, finish up the rounding out of the park system, go rather heavily into the historical park field, and get such legislation as is necessary to guarantee the future of the system on a sound permanent basis, where the power and the personality of the Director may no longer have to be controlling factors in operating the Service." American history was Albright's pet interest, and he made it an important part of Park Service administration, beginning in 1930, when Congress appropriated funds for the reconstruction of George Washington's birthplace on the Wakefield Plantation in Virginia. Under Albright, the Park Service also advanced its unique program of "interpretation" of sites, through which a park ranger might not merely guide visitors, but make them *feel* the essence of a particular park.

Albright's goals prepared the way for a major reorganization of the Park Service in 1933. After a brief conversation during an automobile ride with Albright, it is said, President Franklin Roosevelt transferred jurisdiction of all memorials, military cemeteries, battlefields, and numerous other sites to the National Park Service. From then on, the guardians of Yosemite looked after the Statue of Liberty and Antietam as well. One residual effect of reorganization was to exacerbate relations with the Forest Service, which had never been very good, by transferring the administration of Mount Olympus and Bandolier national monuments from the Forest Service to the Park Service. (Relations grew even worse when New Deal economist Rexford G. Tugwell suggested moving forests out of the Department of Agriculture and into the Department of the Interior; Harold L. Ickes, Interior Secretary, liked this idea and pursued it, unsuccessfully, for the next thirteen years.)

In 1931, at Albright's instigation, Senator George Nye had introduced a bill that would rid the national parks of some of the destructive practices that had plagued them from the beginning. Mineral prospecting in Mesa Verde and Grand Canyon was prohibited; summer home permits were rescinded at Glacier; all provisions that had previously authorized the Secretary of the Interior to grant railroad rights-of-way through parks were finally and fully revoked. Another precedent-setting expansion of Park Service authority under Albright had to do with roadbuilding. Before 1931, Park Service funds were to be used for in-park road construction and maintenance only. After that year, the Park Service was authorized to spend part of its appropriation on "approach roads" outside the parks. The new practice was supported by the states, which felt that the burden of building roads into the parks from major highways was excessive.

The question of roads had catapulted Albright into the middle of one of the fiercest and longest Park Service controversies ever. The conflict concerned Grand Teton National Park, created shortly after he became Park Service director. Albright had loved Jackson Hole, the valley out of which the Tetons rose some seven thousand feet, as much as any scene in America. However, the park he had been given did not include the valley, but only the east side of the mountains. It was a "stingy, skimpy, niggardly little park" in some estimations, and Albright itched to expand it. Jackson Hole was filled with dude ranches, gas stations, hot dog stands, and a few working ranches where cattle were intensively grazed, and Jackson Lake had been dammed for irrigation. Albright thought that perhaps the people of Wyoming would be happy to trade the valley for a good road system through the area—which was precisely what the powerful coalition of dude ranchers did not want, since their business depended on the attraction of unroaded wilderness to guests. For their part, the working ranchers feared restrictions and cutbacks on their grazing habits.

Amid a flurry of abuse, the Park Service withdrew its suggestion. Albright kept his hopes for Jackson Hole to himself, for he had already set a plan in motion. In 1924, while accompanying John D. Rockefeller, Jr., on a tour of the Tetons, Albright had maneuvered Rockefeller into a place where the whole valley spread out before him, and with this vista in sight, he began to talk about how wonderful it would be if the place could be restored to its natural condition. Rockefeller agreed. He told Albright he would buy the valley from its private owners and turn it over to the Park Service. But the work had to be done slowly and surreptitiously, lest prices increase with the knowledge of a Rockefeller on the loose.

Throughout the years of his tenure as Park Service director, and for years after Albright left the service at the end of 1933 to head the American Civic Association, Rockefeller's dummy corporation, the Snake River Land & Cattle Company, managed to buy up most of the private land in Jackson Hole—spending more than a million dollars in the end.

But Rockefeller couldn't give it away. Congress, bowing to pressure from delegations from most of the Rocky Mountain and some other Western states, made it clear that it had no intention of adding Jackson Hole to Grand Teton National Park, and under those circumstances the Interior Department could not accept the gift of land. Finally, in 1942, after fifteen years of paying taxes on land he had entertained no notion of owning for so long, Rockefeller gave Interior Secretary Harold Ickes an ultimatum: Take the land now or Rockefeller's people would start selling it off. Ickes turned to President Roosevelt and persuaded him to declare Jackson Hole a national monument, incorporating the Rockefeller holdings within it. Roosevelt did so on March 5, 1943.

The ensuing uproar was predictable, though fruitless. Wyoming's congressman Frank Barrett compared Roosevelt's action to those of Adolf Hitler and immediately introduced a bill rescinding Jackson Hole's national monument status. It failed to move during that session, the session that followed, and in fact through all of the several congressional sessions in which he presented it until he left Congress. By 1950, public sentiment even in the region of Jackson Hole had shifted, and that year the monument was incorporated into Grand Teton National Park—just as Albright and Rockefeller had intended.

A LEGACY IN TRANSITION

One residual effect of the Jackson Hole controversy was a certain presidential hesitancy about invoking the Antiquities Act as a means of reserving land for park purposes; not until the 1970s would any large-scale national monuments be created again. In the meantime, the National Park Service had plenty with which to occupy itself.

The legacy of promotion and expansion established by Mather and Albright held strong even during the Depression, when the new Park Service director, Arno Cammerer, was forced to cut his budget to $5 million—half that of previous years. Physically, the system was markedly improved through the efforts of the Civilian Conservation Corps, which did an enormous amount of fix-up work in both the national forests and the national parks. By some estimates the 118 camps operating in the parks did the work of fifty years in only ten. The CCC built roads, trails, and campgrounds. It cleared trees and planted them. The CCC boys performed hard, clean work under a program considered one of Roosevelt's greatest New Deal successes.

But the CCC work also tended to widen the gap between strict preservationists like Robert Sterling Yard, first president of the militant National Parks Association and later cofounder of the equally militant Wilderness Society, and development-minded officials like Cammerer. CCC roadbuilding was offensive to many preservationists, but not to national park officials, who stood by their ambitions to have roads constructed to and through as many parks as possible. Disappointment with the Park Service's emphasis was part of the sentiment that led to the formation of The Wilderness Society in 1935 (see chapter 5). Ironically, four of the eight founders of The Society were either employed by or had close ties to the Forest Service, once the nemesis of preservation, and the new conservation organization threw much of its support to the Agriculture Department's agency, while aiming most of its barbs at the Park Service, no longer considered by like-minded conservationists the true savior of primitive America.

In spite of criticism from conservation groups, the Park Service continued to steer an expansionist course. Beginning with Lake Mead in 1935, when the reservoir began filling up behind the newly built Hoover Dam, the Park Service was assigned responsibility for the administration of such man-made recreation areas. Under Cammerer, the Park Service also became more interested in adding seashores to its domain. In 1937, Cape Hatteras National Seashore, in North Carolina, was the first to be authorized, with the slow and costly job of private land acquisition left up to the state. In 1938, Interior Secretary Ickes stated the case eloquently for seashore reservations:

When we look up and down the ocean fronts of America, we find that everywhere they are passing behind the fences of private ownership. The people can no longer get to the ocean. When we have reached the point that a nation of 125 million people cannot set foot upon the thousands of miles of beaches that border the Atlantic and Pacific Oceans, except by permission of those who monopolize the ocean front, then I say it is the prerogative and the duty of the Federal and State Governments to step in and acquire, not a swimming beach here and there, but solid blocks of ocean front hundreds of miles in length. Call this ocean front a national park, or a national seashore, or a state park or anything you please—I say that the people have a right to a fair share of it.

Cammerer retired in 1940, his health broken by six years of work without a day off in the first five. When Newton Drury assumed the directorship, the parks were in better shape than they had ever been, but now they faced a new set of challenges. World War II placed severe demands on the parks, and Drury, the most preservation-minded of the early directors (he was a close friend of Robert Sterling Yard, for one thing), staved off assaults from stockmen and other commercial interests. The pressures of war did force him to relent on some mining intrusions in the parks: copper was extracted from the Grand Canyon, manganese came out of Shenandoah, and Yosemite was opened to yield a meager fifty-five tons of tungsten. But nothing was as serious as the threat to Olympic National Park's Sitka spruce. It was because of the spruce that timber interests had fought the designation of the park in the 1930s, but the onset of war imbued their sentiments with patriotism. The Sitka spruce were essential for building airplanes, they said. The War Production Board agreed, and recommended that the Sitka spruce be cut and used for defense. In so dark a time, the use seemed legitimate and unavoidable. Drury resisted, however, and Secretary Ickes supported him, with the statement that "the virgin forests in the national parks should not be cut unless the trees are absolutely essential to the prosecution of the war, with no alternative, and only as a last resort. Critical necessity rather than convenience should be the governing reason for sacrifice of an important part of our federal estate." Lending a helping hand, the Park Service then found healthy stands of spruce in Canada and Alaska, shortly after which aluminum replaced wood in most aircraft construction anyway.

34

THE PITFALLS OF PEACE

Efforts to exploit national park commodities did not lessen after the war. If anything, they increased, for the demands of peacetime growth were more pervasive and lasting than the focused exigencies of war. In 1950, while Director Drury was thumbing through the *Federal Register*, he noticed that the Bureau of Reclamation was planning to build two dams in Dinosaur National Monument as part of its comprehensive Colorado River Basin Storage project. Drury assumed there had to have been a mistake. After all, he had never even been consulted about the dam proposals. But it was not a mistake. Drury protested. Interior Secretary Oscar Chapman believed in the project and gave it his endorsement. According to the historian John Ise, "The traditional, bureaucratic thing would have been for Drury to agree that dams in Dinosaur were absolutely necessary and good and holy." Drury did not do the bureaucratic thing, and Chapman pressured him to resign.

On his way out of the Park Service, Drury spoke from his heart:

> No resources should be consumed or features destroyed through lumbering, grazing, mining, hunting, water control developments or other industrial uses. This is a cardinal point, which park agencies and executives have learned they must adhere to as closely as possible. Nearly always there is arrayed against it the multiple-use philosophy of public resource management which holds that scenic and recreational resources may be used for numerous other reasons without sacrificing the scenic and recreational values; that grazing will reduce the fire hazard; that damming of lakes and streams for irrigation and power will make them more useful for recreation, will do little harm, and will bring economic benefits. This is an attractive argument to the utilitarians but it misses the point. . . . If we are going to succeed in preserving the greatness of the national parks, they must be held inviolate. They represent the last stand of primitive America. If we are going to whittle away at them we should recognize at the very beginning that all such whittlings are cumulative and that the end result will be mediocrity. Greatness will be gone.

Public opinion persuaded Congress to kill the Dinosaur dams in 1956. Publicity against the project was powerfully mounted by a coalition of conservation groups, chief among them The Wilderness Society, the Sierra Club, and the Izaak Walton League, a combination unprecedented in conservation history and one with enough visible and vocal public support to make any future attempts to violate park sanctity increasingly difficult to engineer. It was this coalition, more than any other factor, that managed to block immense dams at Bridge Canyon and Marble Canyon that would have inundated major portions of Grand Canyon National Monument and even parts of Grand Canyon National Park in the 1960s, and it was this coalition that formed the core of the modern environmental movement.

Meanwhile, when the parks were not in danger of injury from megadams and other resource development, they were in danger of being loved to death. After the war, the public returned to the parks by the millions—30 million a year by 1950. But roads and services had remained at 1940 levels. Buildings, trails, and campgrounds were dilapidated, and more of everything seemed to be needed. In 1956, Conrad Wirth, Drury's replacement, presented a "wish list" for the parks to Congress—and for the first time in the history of its dealings with the parks, Congress approved a major financial commitment: an $800 million to $1 billion appropriation for a program of improvement and expansion. Wirth dubbed the project "Mission 66" in honor of the year it was scheduled to be completed—not coincidentally, also the fiftieth anniversary year of the creation of the Park Service—by which time the parks would be equipped to handle as many as 80 million visitors a year. Or so the projections said.

However ambitious, Mission 66 simply could not keep up with the numbers; in just four years, visitation had jumped to 72 million a year and the projected figure of 80 million visits was reached and passed long before the anniversary year of 1966. Fifteen new recreation areas were designated in this period, and in 1961, 27,000 acres of the Cape Cod shore were added to the park system, closely followed by significant additions at Point Reyes in California and Padre Island in the Gulf of Mexico, just off the coast of Texas. All of this did little to relieve the population pressure. As early as 1958 the problem was so obvious that Congress had established an Outdoor Recreation Resources Review Commission (ORRRC) to look into the situation nationwide. In 1962 it issued its report, which declared that there was nothing less than "a crisis in outdoor recreation." Secretary of the Interior Stewart Udall responded by creating the Bureau of Outdoor Recreation, designed to advise and administer the development of recreation facilities on public lands under the Interior Department's aegis—and answerable directly to his office.

Park Service Director Wirth resented both the Review Commission and the bureau that followed it, both of which were out of the control of his department. His cooperation with both was minimal, and Udall became so disenchanted with him that he forced Wirth's resignation in 1964. As Udall explained it in a letter to Horace Albright, who retained his strong interest in and influence on park policy all his life, "We have sometimes been critical, even strongly critical, of the stiff-necked attitude of the National Park Service. When it stands like Horatius at the bridge, patience runs low." Wirth was replaced by George Hartzog, a former Park Service official who had returned to private law practice before being rehired as director by Udall. Hartzog, like Mather before him, was an idiosyncratic type who did not often stand on protocol; among other legends that grew up around his tenure was the reported time when he grew so frustrated at the swollen mass of rules, regulations, and guidelines that had grown up around Park Service management over the years that he cleared off of the bookshelves of his office all but three volumes: one covering administrative policies for natural areas, one for historic areas, and one for recreational areas. More than a yearning for simplicity, however, commended him to Udall. Hartzog was a devoted supporter of what Udall called the "New Conservation," one of whose principal tenets was that the Park Service could no longer function in isolation from the needs of the larger society, that it was far more than just a caretaker of natural beauty, and that recreation as one of its administrative functions could not be viewed as something merely incidental in American life. Rather, it was an utter necessity to the spiritual and emotional well-being of each and every citizen. That said, the Park Service must move to provide recreational opportunities over a broad spectrum of the nation—including its cities.

While Udall and Hartzog fine-tuned park policy, Congress moved to build up the system itself—or at least make such an expansion possible. Except for those minor additions noted earlier, not much along these lines had been done within recent memory. Of the 23.8 million acres of national park natural areas in existence in 1964, 22.9 million had been reserved before World War II. Realizing that park acquisition might remain at a standstill—while visitations could only continue to soar—Congress broke with its long-standing tradition of not appropriating funds for land acquisition and, in 1964, passed an act creating the Land and Water Conservation Fund (LWCF) to ensure that money always would be available for such purchases; funding would come from the sale of excess federal property, from park entrance and permit fees, from a tax on motorboat fuel, and, after 1968, from receipts for oil and gas leases on the outer continental shelf. (These last receipts now amount to about 90 percent of the total of $900 million in annual income to the fund.) Since 1964 the LWCF has served as the source for nearly all parkland purchases—including those necessary for the creation of Redwood National Park in 1968, the largest addition to the system since the Great Smoky Mountains in the 1930s. The fund has been so successful that James Watt, while head of the Bureau of Outdoor Recreation during the Nixon administration, called it "one of the most effective conservation programs in America."

THE URBAN EXPLOSION

Among the most enduring legacies of Udall's New Conservation was to bring life to the concept of urban parks. There had been urban parks, of a sort, in the system for years—Rock Creek Park and the smaller parks in the District of Columbia were paramount among these—and with some park planners there had always been a mild conviction that there should be more. But it was the 1962 report of the ORRRC that brought the idea out of the realm of speculation and into the light of urgency. "Over a quarter-billion acres are public designated outdoor recreation areas," the report noted, "however, either the location of the land, or restrictive management policies, or both, greatly reduce the effectiveness of the land for recreation use by the bulk of the population." This land, then, the report continued, was "of little use to most Americans looking for a place in the sun for their families on a weekend, when the demand is overwhelming. The problem is not one of total acres but of effective acres."

The most effective acres, clearly, would be in or near major metropolitan centers. "The new conservation," President Lyndon B. Johnson said, "is built on a new promise—to bring parks closer to the people." Udall and his park director, George Hartzog, put their minds and hearts behind this goal, but it was easier said in a speech than done in the field. Any significant move in the direction of urban park development would encounter a whole new system of problems outside the Park Service's experience, problems tied inextricably to those afflicting every aspect of life in urban America—including poverty, crime, racial turmoil, and congestion. Moreover, as Ronald A. Foresta points out,

> the agency had no proven criteria for urban park selection. It did not have a good idea of which parks would be good ones from the standpoints of management ease or political support. It did not even know which ones would be able to meet their stated objectives. One thing was certain, however; the urban parks would require large staffs, large development outlays, and large budgets, perhaps large enough to starve the other parks in the system. These questions and facts meant that a major urban commitment would be a very large gamble at unknown odds.

Still, the commitment was made, albeit haltingly and on a generally piecemeal basis. By the time Hartzog left office in 1972, only a few major additions had been made to the system that qualified—by proximity if sometimes little else—as urban parks, among them Delaware Water Gap National Recreation Area, Fire Island National Seashore, and Indiana Dunes National Lakeshore. But under subsequent directors, and with an increasingly active role from Congress, the urban park system expanded dramatically through the seventies, with the addition of Golden Gate National Recreation Area, around San Francisco; Gateway, in the environs of New York City; Cuyahoga Valley, between Cleveland and Akron; Chattahoochie River, near Atlanta; Santa Monica Mountains, near Los Angeles; and Jean Lafitte National Historical Park and Recreation Area, scattered in and around New Orleans.

39

THE WATT INTERLUDE

If the 1970s saw a major shift in emphasis away from the traditionalist view of the national parks as a collection of scenic jewels, and the Park Service as little more than their custodian, it was a situation largely confined to the lower forty-eight states. In Alaska, it was quite a different matter. As will be discussed in chapter 6, controversy surrounding the construction of the Trans-Alaskan Pipeline had accelerated concern over the future of the Alaska lands, including the preservation and expansion of the state's own park and monument system. That concern ultimately would be expressed in passage of the Alaska National Interest Lands Conservation Act (ANILCA) in 1980—but even before then, President Jimmy Carter had evoked memories of earlier presidential actions when he moved in 1978 to create, by executive fiat, millions of acres of national monuments in Alaska as an interim measure to protect them while their ultimate fate was decided by Congress. This was park-making on a grand scale, and very much within the traditions of the past, a fact given even greater reality when ANILCA firmly embedded more than 43 million acres in the national park and monument system.

Passage of ANILCA was a watershed in another, less benign fashion. It stood squarely at the end of the only administration of President Carter, the most conservation-minded President since Franklin Roosevelt, and at the beginning of the first administration of Ronald Reagan, whom most environmentalists would characterize as the *least* conservation-minded President since Dwight D. Eisenhower. At issue, almost immediately, was future policy regarding the national park system, a question put into focus by Reagan's first Interior Secretary, James Watt, early in 1981. Less than ten years before, Watt had praised the virtues of the Land and Water Conservation Fund, but now he no longer believed it should be used for park expansion; in fact, he did not think the parks needed expansion at all. They needed fixing, and LWCF money should be used for that and that alone. The crown jewels, he asserted, were in a "shameful condition." In truth, some of the parks *were* looking as bedraggled as they had before the Mission 66 project had refurbished them. Visitations had increased to more than 300 million a year, with the heaviest use concentrated in such Eastern parks as Shenandoah, which in 1980 received 7.5

40

million visitors, while Yellowstone and Yosemite each received about two million. In some of the parks, roads and sewage systems needed repair, and Watt declared many park buildings "hazards." He said that it would cost $1.6 billion to make the necessary capital improvements, and acquiring new lands would be irresponsible if the old ones were not repaired first. Watt's estimate was too high by more than half a billion dollars, according to a later estimate by the Park Service, and in any case Congress refused to permit LWCF money to be used in any way other than for acquisition.

The conservation community tended to look upon Watt's assertions skeptically, contending that his lament over the sorry condition of the national parks was nothing more than an act to camouflage his ingrained antagonism toward park expansion. During the first four years of the Reagan administration, the Interior Department consistently proposed spending millions of dollars less in LWCF acquisition money than Congress just as consistently appropriated—and even with more money than it had requested, the Interior Department, after Watt declared a "moratorium" on parkland acquisitions, spent very little of it. In the end, the Park Service launched a massive rehabilitation effort with separate funding. Before the budget crunch of 1985 brought it nearly to a halt, the agency managed to spend $800 million or so of what was billed as a "billion-dollar program."

THE THREATS WITHIN

The Reagan administration's reluctance to expand the system significantly—or even to buy out private inholdings in order to "expand" parks from within—exacerbated a problem that had been steadily growing even as the parks grew in the seventies: the ironic fact that many of the original parks were in some ways becoming quite as "urban" as the urban parks. In an interview in 1980, Park Service Director Russell Dickenson conceded the problem: "Any time that you take a park like Yosemite or Grand Canyon that handles up to 25,000 cars a day, you have an impacted situation. You have an urban situation." One park planner voiced the still-heretical opinion that the superintendents of many parks ought not to be chosen from the rank and file of the Service but from the administrative offices of cities with a population of about 150,000.

As early as 1968, Edward Abbey, the iconoclastic author of *Desert Solitaire*, had spoken for many who felt that the Park Service had only itself to blame and that the trouble stemmed primarily from the agency's affection for roads and elaborate visitor centers. "'Parks are for People' is the public relations slogan," he wrote. "Which decoded means that parks are for people-in-automobiles. Behind the slogan is the assumption that the majority of Americans, exactly like the managers of the tourist industry, expect and demand to see the national parks from the comfort, security, and convenience of their automobiles." James Watt's own improvement program—"Mission Fixit," some conservationists called it—included many road projects that could be accused of merely substantiating Abbey's indictment in the 1980s. But it was not merely elaborately engineered roads that threatened to change the face of the national parks. There was, for instance, the question of concessioners. Ever since Mather's time, concessioners had operated as supervised monopolies in the parks. Some—perhaps most—of the early concessioners took their responsibilities to the integrity of the parks themselves seriously. The Curry Company in Yosemite, for example, was a family-owned business that served the park well for three generations. But by the 1960s, the situation had begun to change, particularly in the major parks, where small family operations were bought out by major corporations. Amfac, a sugar conglomerate, became the concessioner for most of Grand Canyon National Park; Trans World Corporation took over the concessions in Bryce Canyon, Zion, and part of Grand Canyon; The General Host Company took over operations in Yellowstone (and ran things so badly that it had to be bought out by the Park Service in 1979 at a cost of nearly $20 million); and the Music Corporation of America—MCA—acquired the Curry Company itself in 1973.

The National Parks Concessions Policy Act of 1965 attempted to exercise some degree of control, but its provisions were honored more often by being ignored or misinterpreted than by being enforced. Moreover, the act's financial provisions gave back to the federal government an appallingly small share of concessioner profits; the Curry Company, for instance, only had to pay three-quarters of one percent of its gross revenue to the government for the privilege of doing business in Yosemite. It was the Yosemite experience, in fact, that perhaps most precisely demonstrated the concessions problem (as well as other internal difficulties). From the moment that MCA assumed control of visitor facilities in the seven-mile-long, one-mile-wide Yosemite Valley, it began to approach management in a manner one might have expected from what was, after all, an entertainment company. New brochures now proclaimed the park to be "Nature's eloquent answer to convention city." Modern motel rooms, saloons, beauty parlors, swimming pools, and tennis courts were put in place. There was a bank, a dog kennel, assorted boutiques. "This Isn't No Man's Land. Or Primitive Wilderness," one brochure boasted. "This is Civilization." Indeed—but it had little to do with the purpose of the national parks. Those who objected to such development and the resulting traffic and air pollution found a focus for their anger when MCA's own film company decided to "enhance" some Yosemite rocks with paint for a short-lived television series. Outrage was widespread and vehement. MCA backed off, and the Park Service itself began to put together a General Management Plan for the future administration of the park. Its first draft, published in 1978, drew 63,000 written comments from the public, and when it was issued in final form in 1980, the plan met with much approval from the conservation community—particularly when it announced as its principal goals the removal of such resort-like facilities as tennis courts and golf courses, as well as 59 percent of day-parking facilities, 68 percent of employee housing, and 17 percent of overnight visitor accommodations.

Neither the Reagan nor the Bush administrations pushed for reform, however, and the Park Service, whose officials are not ordinarily the most revolutionary of bureaucrats, continued to let development abide in the increasingly cluttered valley. By the beginning of the 1990s, only one golf course had been removed, parking spaces had increased, most employees still lived in the valley, and the number of overnight facilities had actually been allowed to increase—from 1,528 beds to 1,549. In the meantime, MCA and all its subsidiaries, including the Curry Company was sold to Matsushita, a Japanese corporation, which showed no more inclination to institute reforms on its own than had its American predecessor. In frustration over the National Park Service's continuing vacillation with regard to the implementation of the master plan, a number of conservation groups, led by The Wilderness Society, established in September 1990 the Yosemite Restoration Trust, an organization dedicated to the protection of the park's natural values.

Ultimately, early in 1991, MCA-Matsushita sold the Curry Company to the National Parks Foundation, which declared its intention to turn over the company's assets to the National Park Service. "This deal gets ownership of the buildings into Park Service hands and allows real competition for the 1993 contract," George T. Frampton, Jr., then president of The Wilderness Society, said. "But it does not yet guarantee that the General Management Plan will be implemented. The important question remains: Will the agreement lead to more resource protection and less commercialization? On this point, the jury is still out." The jury was still out in December 1992, when the National Park Service awarded the concessions contract to Delaware North Companies, Inc., a New York corporation with absolutely no experience in national park operations. Conservationist efforts to persuade the National Park Service to reconsider the decision proved fruitless.

THREATS WITHIN AND WITHOUT

In part as a consequence of the situation in Yosemite National Park, bills to reform the Concessions Policy Act of 1965 had been introduced in the 1980s, and another was put forth in 1991, only to get lost in a legislative mire; it was still unacted upon when in January, 1993, Bill Clinton was inaugurated President of the United States—the first president in our history who had run on a strong and unmistakable environmental platform. Shortly afterward, Bruce Babbitt, former governor of Arizona and an outspoken environmentalist himself, was appointed Secretary of the Interior. Shortly after that, The Wilderness Society's George T. Frampton, Jr., was appointed Assistant Secretary of the Interior for Fish, Wildlife, and Parks. And shortly after that, Roger G. Kennedy, director of the Smithsonian's National Museum of American History and a longtime vocal environmentalist, was appointed Director of the National Park Service.

Measured by his appointments alone, then, Clinton seemed likely to vindicate the high hopes the conservation community had placed in his election—and among those hopes was reform of concessions policy in the national parks. It remained, however, only a hope by the end of Clinton's first year in office, legislation barely moving in Congress. In the meantime, the new administration had inherited a gaggle of threats to go along with all the problems of inappropriate concessions management —including constantly inadequate funding for scientific research, public education and interpretation, staffing, and proper housing for Park Service employees. Many problems stemmed from simple population pressure. Americans continued to love their national parks throughout the 1980s in increasing numbers. By the end of the decade, park visitation had reached an estimated 275 million a year—roughly ten times what it had been in 1950—and showed no signs of abating (which helped to explain the appeal of concessions contracts in the parks). With all the people came traffic congestion, as well as overcrowded campgrounds, over-hiked trails, degraded meadows and other sensitive natural areas, garbage and litter problems, and rising crime rates that in some parks forced park workers to perform more like urban cops than wilderness rangers.

And if such internal problems were not enough, there were all the threats that came from outside the parks, some of them of monumental proportions. The Park Service was equipped to deal with very few of them. In *Mountains Without Handrails* (1981), Joseph L. Sax remarked that the Park Service had succumbed to an "enclave mentality," meaning that the Service had lost the ability to influence, and even the desire to try to influence, what happened beyond the boundaries of the parks. There were a number of reasons for this attitude. For one thing, the nature of its mission emphasized the differences between parks and the rest of the country. For another, the first parks themselves were sheltered, situated deep within unexploited regions of public domain, hundreds of miles from society's most debilitating characteristics, and all the lands around them remained more or less innocent of resource extraction, commercial development, and urban growth. People came to visit, perhaps, sometimes in great numbers, but when the season was over the crowds left, usually giving flora and fauna time to recover.

In recent times, however, the relative safety of isolation has been all but obliterated for most of the parks, not least because of the growing intrusion of non-parklike activities on "inholdings," private lands that remain in many parks. "Inholdings are the worm in the apple," National Park Service Director George Hartzog complained in 1967. "They might not take up much of the total park area, but they tend to cluster around the prime scenic attractions. . . . On private lands within parks you will find lumberyards, pig farms, gravel pits, logging operations, and sheep and cattle ranches, plus power plants and mine shafts, auto junk-yards, garbage dumps, private plane landing strips, and proliferating residential subdivisions." After passage of the Land and Water Conservation Act in 1964, which provided funding for the acquisition of park inholdings, the government had the means to act. The fund authorized the expenditure of as much as $900 million a year (to be taken out of proceeds from offshore oil leases and other revenue sources) for such purposes, and by the end of 1980, $2.85 billion had in fact been allocated. But in 1981, the Reagan administration declared a "moratorium" on any further park purchases and did not request any money from the fund (except for one small allocation in 1984). Even when President George Bush's administration approved the release of funds, the amount of money allocated remained far below what was needed. And to the disappointment of the conservation community, the Clinton administration, driven less by antagonism to park expansion than by budgetary worries, so far has been reluctant to appropriate as much money as necessary to resolve the most troublesome problems once and for all. Thousands of inholdings, with all their nagging difficulties, remain firmly fixed in the national park apple.

By the end of the 1970s, civilization in all its forms had advanced to the gates from outside as well. Fearing the consequences, Congressman Phillip Burton—a parks advocate who had engineered the passage of the Omnibus Parks Act of 1978, legislation that added to the system such urban units as the Santa Monica Mountains and Golden Gate national recreation areas in California and Gateway National Recreation Area in New York—was moved to request a comprehensive study of park problems from the National Park Service. The report, issued in 1980, was entitled *State of the Parks* and identified no fewer than 4,345 individual threats to the system's integrity, more than half of which originated out-side the parks themselves. "No area is immune," the report stated. "Although some impacts are subtle and not immediately obvious, long-term consequences can be disastrous." Outside threats included air pollution from sulphur dioxide and hydrocarbon emissions and water pollution from toxic-waste disposal, oil spills, dredging materials, and sewage effluents; resource extraction, especially oil

46

drilling, strip-mining, hard-rock mining, and timber clearcutting on national forest and Bureau of Land Management lands adjacent to parks; and commercial, residential, and road developments near the parks. "There is no question," the report's executive summary stated, "but that these threats will continue to degrade and destroy irreplaceable park resources until such time as mitigation measures are implemented. In many cases, this degradation or loss of resources is irreversible. It represents a sacrifice by a public that, for the most part, is unaware that such a price is being paid."

The National Park System, Congressman Burton lamented, "one of the talismans of the United States as a civilized community, is in trouble. Desperate trouble. Trouble so desperate that if we do not take steps *right now* to make needed changes we will be standing on the edge of a situation that will make the idea of the national parks a grim and bitter jest." The Congressman could be forgiven his hyperbole, for many of the parks were indeed in desperate trouble. There were some positive actions in the years that followed the report. A proposed residential development at the edge of Black Canyon of the Gunnison National Monument in Colorado was thwarted, as was an attempt by the Department of Energy to establish a nuclear waste dump near the boundaries of Canyonlands National Park in Utah. After the *State of the Parks* report was issued, a National Park System Protection and Resources Management Act was introduced in the House of Representatives; it would have enabled park adminstrators to keep track of the condition of the parks' natural and cultural resources and would have given the National Park Service much more control over the kinds of actions taken by other federal agencies on land outside park boundaries. The bill passed the House twice, only to be blocked in the Senate. For the most part, the 1980s were marked by the continuing growth of problems that the federal government did virtually nothing to alleviate. Indeed, an Interior Department memorandum of 1986 went so far as to order employees to stop using the term "threats" when discussing park problems and use "adverse actions" instead.

Nevertheless, threats they were and threats they remained—and in most cases, still remain. Clearcutting in the seven national forests surrounding Yellowstone has badly damaged habitat necessary to support the park's wandering population of grizzly bears, which do not recognize manmade boundaries, while attempts to tap into the complex system of geothermal sources outside the park continue to put Old Faithful itself—the most popular single attraction in the park—in jeopardy. A major wildlife migration corridor linking Glacier National Park and the Bob Marshall Wilderness in Flathead National Forest has been threatened by proposed oil drilling permits, while Canadian officials in nearby Waterton National Park entertain development proposals that would further endanger the migration needs of grizzlies and other species that inhabit Glacier. Denali National Park in Alaska has been threatened on the one hand by state officials attempting to capture ownership of the riverbeds in the park and on the other hand by the attempt of those same officials to open up roads in the park by citing an ancient, little-known, and often misinterpreted federal law regarding rights of way (S2477; see also chapters 3 and 7). Everywhere, air pollution becomes an increasingly insidious threat—in the "golden circle" of seven Southwestern parks that includes Grand Canyon itself, summer visitors often have trouble seeing what they have come to see because southerly winds have carried tremendous loads of pollutants into the region from sources in California, Arizona, New Mexico, and even Mexico, while in numerous parks scattered from Sequoia in California to Acadia in Maine, ozone levels regularly reach and exceed levels considered dangerous to humans and acid rain eats at trees and destroys the ability of lakes to support life.

The fate of no single park, however, illustrates the problem of outside threats more dramatically than that of Everglades National Park in Florida—which at the insistence of Interior Secretary Harold L. Ickes was described as a "wilderness" park in the legislation that established it in 1934, but which is today so beleaguered by activities taking place outside its boundaries that the description is given a certain grim irony. At the heart of the problem is water, for the Everglades is a supremely complex natural system that depends absolutely on the persistent flow of a fifty-mile-wide sheet of water from Lake Okeechobee just north of the park to Florida Bay on the south. But two generations of human engineering—presided over by the U. S. Army Corps of Engineers and the South Florida Water Management District—shunted much of the water away from the park in order to drain lands for agriculture and urban development and to supply water to sugar plantations, industries, and homes that developed on those "reclaimed" lands. According to a January 1991 Wilderness Society study, agriculture was the biggest consumer of the region's water, but urban users paid more than one hundred times as much as farmers for each gallon supplied from the regional management system. What is more, Lake Okeechobee itself was seriously polluted by phosphates and other contaminants from upstream dairies and in excess waters pumped back into the lake from sugar fields. As part of a plan to slow eutrophication of the lake, sugar growers were ordered to pump most of their used water southward, increasing pollution burdens on both Loxahatchee National Wildlife Refuge and Everglades National Park.

Engineering the Everglades has been disastrous for the natural system of the park, which no longer supports the abundance of wildlife that once gave the 'Glades its essential character. Alligators, the definitive resident species, were nearly exterminated by a combination of over-hunting and habitat loss; by the end of the 1960s, one scientist estimated, the park's original population of about one million had been reduced by at least 80 percent. Emergency measures taken in the 1970s managed to help the population recover somewhat, but it remains far below its historic levels. The Florida Panther, an endangered species, has suffered even more grievous harm; loss of habitat, mercury poisoning, and deaths from automobiles have reduced the population so profoundly that only about thirty of the great cats remain in the wild portions of Everglades and Big Cypress National Preserve just north of the park. Wading-bird populations—including the wood stork, considered an indicator species by park biologists—have been reduced by as much as 95 percent over the past fifty years. In 1934, biologists counted 245,000 wading-bird nests in the park; less than-sixty years later the count had dropped to 9,500. "This place isn't exceptional anymore," wildlife biologist John Ogden told reporter Norman Boucher in the summer of 1991. "I've been here 25 years, and the change in that time has been just overwhelming. The pace of degradation since the 1960s has drastically increased to the point where this entire ecosystem is in the process of collapse."

By then, conservationists, the state government, the Congress, and even the Bush administration were involved in measures they hoped would at least begin to rectify the damage of decades. In 1983, then-

49

Governor Bob Graham announced a Save the Everglades Program and in March 1984 numerous conservation organizations joined in an Everglades Coalition to support the governor's initiative. In 1988, Congress authorized a 146,000-acre addition to Big Cypress National Preserve and in October of that year the U. S. Justice Department filed a lawsuit against the South Florida Water Management District and the State Department of Environmental Regulation, charging them with failure to meet state water-quality standards for water discharged to the Everglades. In 1989, Congress passed the Everglades National Park Protection Act, which authorized the purchase of 107,000 acres on the eastern boundary of the park to establish a "buffer" between urban environs and the park. The U. S. Army Corps of Engineers, meanwhile, was ordered to begin reversing some of the most pernicious effects of its historic engineering efforts. Upstream from Lake Okeechobee, the Kissimmee River had been thoroughly "channelized," draining adjacent wetlands; a program was now launched to restore much of the river's original course and natural habitat. In the Shark River Slough, the park's central water course, the Corps would penetrate dikes that restricted flow to the park and add gates to permit a more accurate replication of the slough's natural water regime.

In 1991, newly elected Governor Lawton Chiles dropped the state's opposition to the claims in the water quality suit. The federal government and state agencies worked out a plan for the treatment of phosphates and other agricultural waste through on-farm management tactics and thousands of acres of filtering marshes to be established on converted agricultural land. The sugar companies filed a blizzard of lawsuits to prevent the terms of the state-federal settlement from being executed. For two years there have been various and intricate efforts to settle the conflict instituted by Interior Secretary Babbitt, engaging the industry, environmentalists, state and federal agencies, and the Florida legislature. Tentative agreements have raised expectations and antagonisms and thus far have resulted only in disappointment and delay. But as *The New York Times* editorialized, "Mr. Babbitt's heart is clearly in the right place. . . . As the Secretary knows better than anyone, there is no end to preserving the Everglades."

"Just so," says The Wilderness Society's Florida director, Jim Webb. "Having taken dominion of the Everglades, our society is now forever

50

challenged to preserve and restore their natural values and simultaneously provide for burgeoning human activity. Given the region's
gene-rous endowment of rainfall, it remains possible to do that, but only
if we address fundamental errors that we have made in the design and
execution of our purposes." He salutes the efforts of the U. S. Army
Corps of Engineers and a federal inter-agency task force to restore the
natural integrity of the park, for he believes that the water system must
be rebuilt to provide for a large human population as part of a regional
ecosystem, not just an imposition on it. "Since we've accepted direct
and permanent responsibility for the health of the ecosystem, the right
design for the park, and for the millions who live nearby, is one that
will help future generations deal with problems that we cannot now
identify—a design that conserves water rather than wastes it, one that
provides first for the natural system and then fairly allocates an abundant surplus. The wrong design, like the one this generation has inherited, will make it harder. And if the problems of the Everglades get
much harder, the failure of the Everglades is certain."

AN AGENDA FOR THE NATIONAL PARKS

The story of the past, present, and potential future of Everglades National Park stands as a cautionary tale illustrating the complex and, it
sometimes seems, nearly insurmountable problems that now afflict "the
best idea we ever had." If there is "no end" to preserving the Everglades from the encroachment of civilization, as *The New York Times*
wrote, there also is no end to the task of saving the rest of the parks
from various levels of threat, whether from within, as with Yosemite, or
from without, as with the 'Glades. We must begin the process of making a genuine, long-term commitment to a shift in emphasis in park
administration. The Organic Act of 1916 stipulated that the parks were
to be preserved "unimpaired, for the enjoyment of future generations."
By the year 2010, visitation to the parks is expected to reach an
astonishing half-billion people a year, and if we do not take action,
those "future generations" may have little to enjoy that has not been
significantly, perhaps permanently, impaired. William Penn Mott, who
served well, if briefly, as director of the National Park Service, said
shortly after taking office in 1985, that "we must err on the side of

preservation." That is as good a rallying cry as any to serve as the theme for the future administration of the parks.

As the preceding narrative suggests, there are a number of specific reforms that could be instituted in the short run. The Wilderness Society has prepared a list of the most important:

The funding for the base operations for each park should be increased to levels proper management demands. There is a tendency to view national park funding as a "luxury" that we can cut back on in difficult financial times. That is simply wrong. Our national parks are nothing less than essential to the public; they pay a major return on investment in the form of education, clean air and water, the conservation of biological diversity, international tourist dollars, improved mental and physical health, and many other ways. Yet we spend only a pittance on them. Less than two percent of the federal budget is devoted to environmental protection, and just a fraction of that goes to the national parks. If for example, Congress were to dedicate just a half-penny of the federal gasoline tax to the parks, their budgets would increase by 50 percent. And according to a 1991 survey undertaken by Citibank, 67 percent of Americans want "more money to go into preserving and maintaining the national parks."

A greater percentage of park funding should be invested in basic scientific research. An August 1992 report by the National Research Council of the National Academy of Sciences declared that the National Park Service "must give the science program immediate and aggressive attention. Pressures on these national treasures are increasing rapidly. It is shortsighted to fail to organize and support a science program to protect the parks for future generations. And it is a waste of a unique resource if the parks are not used, with proper safeguards, to help address the scientific challenges faced throughout the biosphere." To do so, parks need more money, and Congress should appropriate the funds as a separate line item.

Concessioners should be required to pay higher fees to the Park

Service for the privilege of operating in the parks. Reports by the Interior Department's Inspector General have found that concessioners, most of whom still enjoy monopolies, pay meager amounts. Moreover, they often are the primary beneficiaries of utility improvements, road construction, and other infrastructure work underwritten by the Park Service. The Clinton administration should vigorously support and Congress should pass legislation similar to bills introduced in 1993—by Dale Bumpers in the Senate and Mike Synar in the House—to reform the Concessions Policy Act of 1965 to ensure that the government gets fair measure, that bids for park concessions be vigorously competitive, and that the concessioners be regulated more stringently with regard to operations that may impact the natural integrity of the parks.

Appropriations from the Land and Water Conservation Fund must be increased. Each year, $900 million goes into this fund, mostly from offshore oil and gas royalties. The money is supposed to be invested primarily in the acquisition of land for the national parks and other federal and state public-land systems. Over the past decade, an annual average of only about $250 million has gone for its intended purposes. In 1993, Senator Bennett Johnston of Louisiana introduced legislation that, among other things, would have guaranteed that the Interior Department would receive $600 million a year for five consecutive years, much of which could be earmarked for national park acquisitions. The passage of such legislation should be one of the main priorities of the National Park Service and the Clinton administration.

The National Park System should be expanded. The most recent significant national park designations were those for Great Basin National Park in Nevada in 1986, Samoa National Park in American Samoa in 1988, and Dry Tortugas National Park in Florida in 1992. A number of other areas are deserving of park status, both for their value as unique ecosystems and for the natural grandeur they encompass. Major candidate areas would include Grasslands National Park in Wyoming, Tallgrass Prairie National Park in Kansas and Oklahoma, and Siskiyou National Park in Oregon and California.

In the long run, even such necessary measures will not be enough to guarantee the permanent protection of the National Park System. We can only hope to provide long-term protection if we begin to manage parks not as isolated units—as if this were still the middle of the nineteenth century—but as integral parts of coherent systems of public and private lands, many of them enormous in scope and complexity. This is hardly a revolutionary notion. Many parks, together with the lands around them, have been designated as units of the International Biosphere Reserve System, an informal but eminently useful attempt to identify those regions of the globe most crucial to its overall ecological health. They stand as institutional representations of John Muir's remark that "When we try to pick out something by itself, we find it hitched to everything else in the universe."

So it should be, but is not, for the national parks. The principal reason that Everglades is in such peril, for example, is because the public and private land around it has been administered almost as if the park and its own needs did not exist. Its rescue, if it can be achieved, will only come if that tradition is reversed permanently. Yellowstone National Park, for another example, lies at the heart of the Greater Yellowstone Ecosystem, a 13-million-acre complex of lands that includes seven national forests, two national wildlife refuges, and even some Bureau of Land Management land—not to mention state and private land and many human communities. Together, they make up one of the most important land systems on the continent, yet for decades the various federal public-land agencies—especially the U. S. Forest Service—have continued to manage their lands with virtually no consideration for what effect they might be having on the land and wildlife resources of the national park that is their most important neighbor. The closest thing to regular cooperation among the federal entities is the Interagency Grizzly Bear Committee, and even this noble attempt to establish management guidelines to ensure a healthy population of the ecosystem's most important predator has been riven by contention and inconsistency.

In 1983, conservationists joined to establish the Greater Yellowstone Coalition, an organization designed to monitor the management of all the public lands of the region and encourage cooperation among the agencies involved. The coalition has built itself into what any regional

54

conservation organization could envy—a force respected not just in the Yellowstone region but in the warrens of the nation's capital as well. But even this organization so far has not been able to persuade the managers of the ecosystem to work together for the common good. More is needed. "At the very least," Yellowstone ecologist Tim W. Clark told reporter Charles E. Little in the Winter 1987 issue of *Wilderness* magazine, "we're going to need some federal legislation to state that this piece of geography is unique in a national and global sense and to say, 'We expect you guys out there—Forest Service, National Park Service, and so forth—to come up with specific management principles that recognize this uniqueness and to apply them through rigorous management programs, plus monitoring and evaluation.' That is the kind of broad umbrella-type policy that is needed."

Similar vision must be applied to every other area in which national parks are the core of public-land regions big and complex enough to be described as ecosystems—Lassen, Yosemite, Sequoia, and Kings Canyon national parks in the Sierra Nevada, for example; or the "Golden Circle" of national parks, chief among them Grand Canyon, that ornament the Colorado Plateau; or Great Smoky Mountains National Park, the jewel that lies surrounded by national forests in four states; or the two great parks of the northern border, Glacier in Montana and North Cascades in Washington, both of which are bracketed by national forests.

There should be, finally, no place for anarchy in the preservation of the best idea we ever had.

2

A HEART OF WOOD

The National Forest System

When Bill Kreutzer went to work on the White River Plateau Timber Reserve in Colorado, he soon grew accustomed to being ambushed and beaten, even shot at. The year was 1905 and Kreutzer was a forest ranger, one of the first in a tiny new agency called the U.S. Forest Service. His story, matter-of-factly told in the reports and other documents of what is now White River National Forest, was typical. Day or night, on horseback or on foot, he patrolled the Delaware-sized forest reserve alone, watching for fires and putting them out when he could, keeping an eye out for illegally cut timber, making sure the number of grazing cattle and sheep did not exceed the number allowed on government land, and sometimes risking his life in defense of an idea—though he would not have been likely to couch it in such a high-toned manner.

For Kreutzer and a handful of other sturdy young foresters were representative of something utterly new in American history: the first serious challenge by the government of the United States to those who, for at least two generations, had been using and abusing federal lands almost entirely without hindrance. President Theodore Roosevelt had bluntly stated the case against such traditional practices shortly after taking the oath of office a second time. "In the past we have admitted the right of the individual to injure the future of the Republic for his present profit. The time," Roosevelt declared, "has come for a change."

The national forest system is the embodiment of that change. Now

---

Felling a redwood in California in the 1860s (Bancroft Library, University of California at Berkeley).

191 million acres in size, it comprises about 18 percent of the remaining commercial forestland in the country, with 153 individual national forests and eighteen grassland units in forty states. The national forests cloak the slopes of nearly every major mountain range in the nation in a chevron pattern of tree and shadow: Alaska's Chugach and Tongass; the Far West's Cascades, Coast Range, Sierra Nevadas, and Siskiyous; the arid West's Rockies; the central region's Black Hills, Ozarks, and Ouachitas; the Northeast's White Mountains and Green Mountains; the South's Appalachians. Among their rocky pinnacles, rivers are born of rain and snowmelt, metamorphosing at lower elevations into white flumes of crashing power or placid skeins of muddy water that are, in either form, the lifeblood of hundreds of small towns and large cites. In the Intermontane West, where rainfall is scarce, 85 percent of all water originates on 25 percent of the land—land that is located, not accidentally, within the boundaries of national forests.

Water and earth, along with trees and grass, are only the most visible resources of national forests. Additionally, they contain deposits of nonreplenishables such as gold, silver, chromium, molybdenum, nickel, tungsten, copper, and zinc, along with reserves of oil and natural gas. Drive through any national forest, and at its perimeter you will see a faintly rhomboidal sign in brown and ivory, proclaiming that here is the "Land of Many Uses," these being outdoor recreation, range, timber, watershed, and wildlife and fish habitat. Since 1964, wilderness preservation has also received official sanction. "Many uses" means that there are many users. There are loggers who come to cut timber, and recreationists who crave rugged beauty and solitude, in numbers surpassing those who visit national parks. Fourteen thousand ranchers graze 7 million sheep and cattle on the forest ranges, while more than 70,000 individuals or groups have been granted special-use permits for their television transmission stations, ski slopes, reservoirs, lodges, camps, and even public schools where land in adjacent towns is in short supply.

This multiple-use orientation is the most distinct characteristic of the national forest system. It is also the watchword of the United States Forest Service, the bureau in the Department of Agriculture that manages and protects forestlands on behalf of the public interest.

In a letter signed by Agriculture Secretary James Wilson on February 1, 1905, and disseminated for all to read, the Forest Service's guiding principle was first elegantly proclaimed: "Where conflicting interests must be reconciled the question will always be decided from the standpoint of the greatest good of the greatest number in the long run." William Greeley, who served as chief forester in the 1920s, explained in his autobiography that the phrase "multiple use" expressed "our zeal for the utmost public service from a section of land. We had the thrill of building Utopia and were a bit starry-eyed over it."

Perhaps too starry-eyed. Today, multiple use does not mean that every activity must be allowed on every acre in the national forests. It means instead that there must be a sense of balance throughout the entire system. The point at which this balance has been achieved, however, can be arguable. Thousands of times a year, Forest Service officials have the chance to upset or stabilize the national forests' equilibrium. Whether to permit clear-cutting on one thousand acres of Gunnison National Forest in Colorado, whether to build logging roads through de facto wilderness in Flathead National Forest in Montana, whether to chemically treat an infestation of spruce budworm, whether to approve a new ski slope, whether to add trails, whether to close campsites, whether to proceed with all of these things or none of them right now entails the making of numerous decisions that affect balance. And each is a decision that cuts to the heart of America's resource choices. This is the way Teddy Roosevelt might have seen it. "As a people," he said, "we have the right and duty, second to none other but the right and duty of obeying the moral law, of requiring and doing justice, to protect ourselves and our children against the wasteful development of our natural resources, whether that waste is caused by the actual destruction of such resources or by making them impossible of development hereafter."

Roosevelt spoke, of course, from his knowledge of what had gone before.

THE ANCESTRAL FOREST

To those who set eyes upon it first, the American forest—the largest and most varied in the world outside of the tropics—seemed utterly indomitable. Pilgrims considered the scene before them with dread. The bravest among the early arrivals ventured out, according to Pilgrim chronicler William Bradford in the 1620s, "for a view of a more goodly country to feed their hopes; for which way soever they turned their eyes (save upward to the heavens) they could have little solace or content in respect of any outward objects." The forest washed inland over the continent far beyond a Pilgrim's ability to imagine it, clear to the Mississippi River he did not know existed, and was bounded on its outer edge by a pale hem of shore the length of which he could only guess. Yet the sense of human defeat was momentary. It gave way to the conviction that the industriousness of the people was as boundless as the forest. And neither, it seemed, would ever give out.

"Unlike Europe, the wooded continent was prediction, not chronicles, it was dreams, not traditions," wrote Richard Lillard in *The Great Forest*. "It implied new chapters in the history of commerce and agriculture and politics and statesmanship." Forests were cleared for settlements and fields and pastures. Wood was fashioned into houses and fences and fuel at so rapid a pace that the effects of deforestation were felt in the most populous regions within fifty years of settlement. In 1681, William Penn attempted to prevent widespread clear-cutting when he established the colony of "Penn's Woods." He decreed that for every four acres of trees cut, one acre was to be left standing. Nevertheless, an astute Pennsylvanian observed in 1753 that "our Runs dry up apace, several which formerly wou'd turn a fulling Mill, are now scarce sufficient for the Use of a Farm, the Reason of which is this, when the Country was cover'd with Woods & the Swamps with Brush, the Rain that fell was detain'd by These Interruptions." Yet such commentary was rare in that age, the more common view being one expressed by Isaac Weld, Jr., a tourist from England, who remarked that the man who could cut down the most trees was "looked upon as the most industrious citizen, and one that is making the greatest improvements in the country." By unanimous consent, the forest was only as good as what was made of it.

A capable settler learned to read his patch of forest like a treasure map, for the kind of trees that grew in a place told him what crops might thrive in their stead, explained Rutherford Platt in *The Great*

American Forest. In Virginia, for example, land bearing the largest oaks was known to be good for yielding fine tobacco; in Georgia, hickory land was cleared for corn; everywhere, soft maple and birch were not worth the trouble of clearing, since these breeds grew in places considered too cold and wet for proper cultivation. And certain trees themselves could be a useful treasure. Oak and hickory were hard to split and so made the sturdiest wagon parts. Oak, along with maple and walnut, was turned into furniture that lasted generations. Supple ash made the best bows and arrows, while birch, maple, and cherry burned very hot, and the small, tight fires kindled from them were ideal for cooking. Chestnut, with its long, ropy grain, could be split the length of an eight-foot log, and so lent itself to the ubiquitous split-rail fence. Favoring one tree over another did not mean that only the desired specimen was cut. Sometimes it was easier to clear the whole stand as though trees were weeds, and leave it barren for future use.

Life in the broadleaf interior of the East was different from life amid the evergreens farther north and west, and the standard equipage of each made this plain. In the deciduous forest a settler was associated with "the ax, the cornpatch, the split rail fence, a dog, a cow, a woman in the cabin and children," wrote Rutherford Platt. "In the conifer forest the symbols were the canoe, snowshoes, fur-bearing animal traps, the spoor of bear and moose, a trading post and lonely campsite." The trees of the conifer forest offered shelter and fuel, but no special services like those of the deciduous forest. In both forests profligacy flourished, perhaps unavoidably, according to the forest historian Samuel Trask Dana. He wrote in *Forest and Range Policy*:

> Labor and capital, being scarce and therefore expensive, were used as sparingly and intensively as possible. In modern terminology, they were "conserved." Natural resources, being abundant and therefore cheap, were used as liberally and extensively as possible. In other words, they were exploited. There was nothing "ruthless" or reprehensible about this procedure. It was merely the application of sound common sense to the economic problem of making the most effective use of the productive factors at the disposal of the colonists.

61

THE GREAT ASSAULT

Colonial expedience became a national industry in the years of growth that followed the War of Revolution, and in a continuing climate of abundance, the forests fell as the industry moved. First through New England, then into the Adirondacks and Catskills of New York and Pennsylvania, south into the Appalachians, through the Blue Ridge Mountains and the Great Smoky Mountains, clear to the edge of Florida. Up into the old Northwest, where Michigan lost its original forest in a single lifetime, where the old forests of Wisconsin were cut, rough-sawn into billions of board feet of unfinished lumber, packed together into rafts the size of football fields, and floated down the rivers to market. By the turn of the century the industry had jumped the continent to the West Coast, first to California, where the coast redwoods and the sugar pine of the Sierras fell to the saw and the donkey engine; then to Oregon and Washington, where spruce and Douglas fir disappeared into the holds of coastwise lumber schooners; then back into the interior of the continent, to the Rocky Mountains, through Colorado, Wyoming, Montana, and Idaho, where another industry consumed wood to timber its mines and to build its boom cities.

In its scope, in the amount of wood taken, and in the swiftness of its passage, there was nothing in human history to compare with the decades of this astonishing assault on the natural world. And there was precious little done to stop it. By some accounts, Congress passed more than one thousand land laws in the century following the Revolution, but only five of these up to 1873 dealt specifically with forests, or with the keeping of them in that condition. All five, the first of which was passed in 1799, affirmed the government's right to reserve timber on the public domain for shipbuilding and its intent to prosecute those caught taking wood for unauthorized use. "Trespass" became the polite word for what amounted to stealing timber from naval timber reserves, although it applied quite well to the pilfering of any sort of timber from the public domain at large. Not that the laws had much effect. The American attitude then toward government reserves was about the same as it had been toward those reserves established under King George III. Great Britain's "broad arrow" reserves of colonial white pine for the Royal Navy's masts had been branded a form of tyranny, period. There had even been a "Pine Tree Riot" in 1772, during which more than twenty rebellious Down-Easters crossed out, with switches and clubs on the British sheriff's bare back, "the account against them of all logs cut, drawn and forfeited," making the sheriff "wish he had never heard of pine trees fit for masting the royal navy."

Throughout most of the century following the Revolution, such attitudes fostered a tradition of laissez-faire, the conscious policy not to defend seriously against trespass or to prosecute those suspected of depredations. This represented a major reversal of President Thomas Jefferson's assertion that lands to which the government held title would be protected from exploitation. From the moment Jefferson left government office, his dictate was ignored. "In its place was tacitly substituted the rule that the public domain is a vast commons on which all may freely go and take," wrote Thomas LeDuc in 1964. "By continuous refusal of adequate appropriations for police protection, Congress expressed its clear intent that federal power should not be used to protect public property." The timber barons understood this fully, and it was with clear consciences that they not only took the trees they wanted where law did not prevent them, but ignored and subverted those laws that did finally evolve—as we shall see in chapter 4.

A few government officials did make the mistake of trying to enforce the law in spite of laissez-faire tradition. Carl Schurz, Secretary of the Interior from 1877 to 1881, took timber depredation very seriously. He had been born and raised in Germany, where the science of forestry was commonly practiced and plundering had long since fallen out of favor. He fired land agents who had gained their positions through patronage or who had developed a knack for looking in the other direction when corruption approached. Schurz replaced them with tougher, independent men. He also lobbied for the novel idea of selling timber-cutting privileges while retaining the land to prevent its mistreatment. These efforts got him nowhere, for Congress grew uneasy about his burst of enforcement and in 1880 responded by passing a law that actually excused timber violators on public lands from civil or criminal prosecution, if they paid $1.25 an acre for the land they had unlawfully cleared. Critics of the measure, who were mostly in the East and the Lake States, where gutting the landscape had such destructive consequences, sarcastically called it "the bill to license thieves on the public domain," or "the bill to condone crime and invite trespass and encourage theft."

Frustrated in his efforts to restore sanity to public land matters, Schurz resigned. Almost immediately his successor backed off from Schurz's reforms. He even apologized to Congress, stating that "extenuating circumstances surrounding the acts of trespass" would always be dug up to avoid further prosecution of wrongdoers. But the appointment of William Andrew Jackson Sparks, a former congressman, to the post of General Land Office commissioner in 1885 brought yet another crusader for land reform. For frauds involving various land laws, particularly the Timber and Stone Act of 1878, Sparks suspended all entries in the regions where the flimflam had been uncovered: in Dakota, Idaho, Utah, Washington, Colorado, and Wyoming—in other words, in the greater part of the public domain. Sparks's campaign to end "widespread, persistent public land robbery committed under the guise of various forms of public land entry" impressed Congress as little as had the Schurz crackdown, and he did not remain on the job for long. Soon after he was dismissed, Interior Secretary Lucius Q. C. Lamar revoked his program, even though Sparks had reported, before leaving his position in 1887, that more than 41 million acres of fraudulently claimed land had been restored to the public domain for honest disposition.

Unfortunately, reformers within the government, like Schurz and Sparks, were so rare as to be easily identified—and gotten rid of. For the most part, during that period of the nineteenth century, which the social historian Vernon L. Parrington called "the Great Barbecue," the timber industry did its cooking unencumbered by federal sanctions or concern.

THE PRESCIENCE OF GEORGE PERKINS MARSH

Even as the timber industry went about its business, however, a body of sentiment for the protection of the forests was slowly coalescing. Some of it, remarkably, developed out of studies commissioned by the government itself. In 1876, Congress had established a Division of Forestry in the Agriculture Department, and had placed Franklin

B. Hough, a physician and amateur forester, at its head. Hough, who had served as superintendent of the 1870 U.S. Census, won his appointment by conducting his own study of American forests, using census data, and submitting independent reports to Congress. His studies revealed that timber-cutting had dropped off entirely in some areas but was accelerating dramatically in others. The emerging pattern revealed forests in various stages of depletion. Congress gave Hough $2,000 to conduct further investigations into "the annual amount of consumption, importation, and exportation of timber and other forest products, the probable future supply for future wants," and "the means best adapted to their preservation and renewal." Almost all of this, however, was confined to private lands; try as he might, Hough could not convince Congress that his studies ought to be applied to the lands of the public domain as well. In 1880 another government study, this one conducted by Harvard botanist Charles Sargent, predicted that if the present rate of timber-cutting continued, the remaining American forests would be gone in ten years. Sargent's forecast may have been too pessimistic, but few who studied the situation could believe that the forests would hold out much more than thirty years. In the course of a Victorian lifetime, an area the size of Europe already had been deforested in the United States.

In the face of such investigations, agitation for federal protection of forests was growing among the ranks of amateur foresters who had joined to form the American Forestry Association in 1875. Many of them had been profoundly affected by one of the most prescient books in the nation's history: George Perkins Marsh's *Man and Nature*, first published in 1864. A renowned polymath, Marsh had much besides this book to occupy him. He was, at the beginning of his public life, an impoverished Vermont statesman who had served as the state's railroad commissioner and fish commissioner. As an architectural authority, Marsh had designed the Vermont capitol building and determined the final proportions of the Washington Monument. After the deaths of his wife and young son and a second marriage to a woman who was bedridden the rest of her life, Marsh immersed himself in Scandinavian history, compiled Icelandic folklore, and popularized the travels of the Vikings. His reputation as a historian and linguist caught Abraham Lincoln's attention, and Marsh was appointed minister plenipotentiary to the Kingdom of Italy in 1861. He served in this capacity until his death in 1882, making his term one of the longest in American diplomacy. The undemanding duties of the post gave him the leisure to research and write his most famous work.

Man and Nature, entitled *Man, the Disturber of Nature's Harmonies* until the publisher objected on the grounds that it simply could not be so (Marsh retitled the 1874 edition *The Earth as Modified by Human Action*), surveyed the decline of ancient civilizations through the decline of the lands they occupied. For example, Marsh said, the Fertile Crescent, which had spawned some of mankind's brighter cultural achievements, had been turned into "an assemblage of bald mountains, barren, treeless hills and Swampy and malarious plains"; the abused land of ancient Greece and Rome revealed "a desolation almost as complete as the moon," and parts of China were hardly better. All of this, he made clear, was the direct consequence of deforestation, and he did not neglect his own native land: "Man has too long forgotten that the earth was given to him for usufruct alone, not for consumption, still less for profligate waste," he wrote. In the United States "we are, even now, breaking up the floor and wainscoting and doors and window frames of our dwelling, for fuel to warm our bodies and seethe our pottage, and the world cannot afford to wait till the slow and sure progress of exact science has taught it a better economy."

RUIN AND REDEMPTION

In Michigan, for instance, science and economy were progressing in a different direction. This was just one of the states where the lumber industry was running full-tilt in the last half of the nineteenth century. By the 1870s more than one hundred sawmills were operating in the Saginaw–Bay City area alone—six days a week, twelve hours a day. In 1882, the peak year, these mills turned out more than one billion board feet of lumber. By 1897, Michigan sawmills had produced more than 160 billion board feet of white pine, leaving only 6 billion board feet in the entire state. To reach this point had taken less than fifty years.

In more pedestrian terms, 160 billion board feet of timber can be translated into about 10 million six-room houses, or enough planks to build a pine floor over Michigan and Rhode Island together. Much of it actually did go into the construction of houses and barns between the Lake States and the Rockies. But public demand alone did not push Michigan, or any other state, to the brink of deforestation. Technology had developed beyond the ability of the resource to regenerate. Mills that had once peaked at 10 million board feet a year were, by the end of the nineteenth century, cutting 40, 50, even 200 million feet a year. In his memoirs the Civil War historian Bruce Catton, who grew up on the far side of Michigan's timber boom, described the recurring circumstances: "One of the baffling factors of the age of improved technology now made its appearance. The cost of production became lower but only on the condition that the producer was able to put more and more money into it . . . big operators had to invest a lot of money and they could not get it back unless they operated at capacity."

Fire was another big consumer of wood, much of it the result of wasteful timber practices. Until the later days of the era, timbermen could afford to take only the best trees, stripping logs of their crowns and branches before hauling them out. The residue was left on the forest floor beneath the remaining "undesirable" trees. After years of accumulation and drying, such detritus made living tinderboxes out of many forests—imminent fires waiting for the strike of lightning, the spark from a passing locomotive, the flames from a runaway cookfire. The results were often horrific. So it was with the Peshtigo Fire of Wisconsin in 1871, when 1,280,000 acres were burned and more than 1,500 people were killed; so it was in Michigan in 1881, when fire killed a million acres of trees and 138 people; so it was in Minnesota in 1894, when the Hinckley Fire destroyed 160,000 acres of forest, twelve towns, and 418 people. After fire, quite often came flood—an inadvertent demonstration of watershed ecology. Hillsides with little left but black snags and soot could not hold the water during seasons of rain. Rivers swelled with runoff and debris and carried it all into downstream towns with devastating effects.

As the forests went, so did the economy they had directly supported. Catton described the sound of ruin he heard as a boy:

When the buzz saws and the edgers and the jolting game saws and the clattering conveyers at last fell idle for good, the boss would pull the whistle cord, tie it down, and let the steam go up to join the clouds. One long haunting blast—the same that had been rousing the townspeople and calling men to work for a generation or more— would go echoing across the plains, slowly losing its pitch and its volume as the pressure died, falling at last to a dispirited moan and at last fading out altogether . . . and that mill was out of action forever, and possibly the town along with it, and people would begin to wonder what they were going to do next.

It was too late to help Michigan, but when Congress passed the General Revision Act of 1891, relief from the perils of unchecked deforestation was on the way. Not that Congress intended any such thing, for the act brought succor in a form most of the legislators had never seriously contemplated, and certainly would not have condoned if they had. The only thing they had meant to do on March 3, 1891, was rescind some of the most ill-suited and flagrantly abused of the land laws. Instead, owing to vigorous arm-twisting by Interior Secretary John W. Noble, a conference committee attached a rider to the bill (later called the Forest Reserve Act) that altered the course of public land history. The rider authorized the President to "set apart and reserve . . . any part of the public lands wholly or in part covered with timber or undergrowth whether of commercial value or not, as public reservations." Noble had been convinced of this measure's urgency by Bernard Fernow, who had succeeded Hough at the Division of Forestry.

Fernow and others had tried for about two years to convince Congress of the need for federally protected forests, but had not even been able to get a serious hearing. Yet once Noble's rider slipped through, a "long chain of peculiar circumstances" kept most congressmen from noticing its presence, according to the historian John Ise. The only notable criticism was voiced by Arkansas Senator Thomas C. McRae, who denounced the rider as "an extraordinary and dangerous" power to give a President. The bill with its provocative rider nevertheless passed, "not through the initiative of Congress," Ise wrote, "but rather because Congress had no good opportunity to act on the provision." Exercising his new authority, President Benjamin Harrison proclaimed the Yellowstone Timberland Reserve next to the park, and the White River Plateau reserve in Colorado. He soon added four more, encompassing 13 million acres.

At first it seemed as though no one had noticed, and those few who did cautiously praised Harrison's proclamations on the grounds they would prevent carelessly set fires and floods. No one was exactly sure what else the reserves might be for. Naturalist John Muir convinced himself that they were another form of national park, and rejoiced at the advancement of preservation. Others were not so sure. People in Meeker, Colorado, a town near the White River reserve, did not share Muir's joy, feeling that any such thing would stifle their economic development. The *Meeker Herald* suggested that local communities join hands "in a solid phalanx against the dude design for an outdoor museum and menagerie." The uncertainty irritated President Grover Cleveland. He added another 20 million acres of reserves, but refused to set aside any more until Congress defined their purpose. Congress obliged on June 4, 1897 (again in an amendment to a larger bill), by passing the Forest Organic Act.

The act stated that reserves were established "to improve and protect the forest within the boundaries for the purpose of securing favorable conditions of water flow, and to furnish a continuous supply of timber for the use and necessities of citizens of the United States." The act also specified what kind of timber could be removed from the forests—and required each tree to be "marked and designated" before it was cut and sold. Administration of the forest reserves was handed over to the General Land Office in the Department of the Interior. Perhaps the most far-reaching provision in the act was its authorization of the Interior Secretary to "regulate the occupancy and use" of the forests without providing a clue as to what was meant by this term. Charles Wilkinson, a professor of natural resource law, has labeled the Organic Act "a blank check" because of this. Gifford Pinchot, who assumed control of the Division of Forestry in 1898, called it "the milk in the coconut."

THE FIRST CHIEF FORESTER

Pinchot, a hatchet-faced Yale graduate belonging to a well-to-do family of French extraction, began to figure prominently in forestry matters shortly after completing his silvicultural studies in France.

The neat rows of commercial timber there, with the ground swept as clean of clutter as a living room floor, and with roads and paths intersecting at regular intervals, was a vision he wanted to transplant into the unruly forests of America. It was time, he felt, to introduce the European tradition of growing trees like a crop to the United States. On his return from Europe in 1891 at age twenty-six, Pinchot opened a forestry consulting office. Demand for his services was predictably light, but he did find a few opportunities to demonstrate the practicability of the European system. At the 1893 World's Fair in Chicago, Pinchot exhibited his impressive results from managing the seven-thousand-acre forest on the Biltmore estate of multimillionaire George Vanderbilt.

In 1896, Pinchot tagged along with the National Academy of Science's Forestry Commission on a tour of Western forests. The commission's recommendations led to the passage of the Organic Act the following year, and to the addition of another 21 million acres of reserves. Fernow, who did not believe that forestry could be practiced on a grand scale under the American political system, was replaced in 1898 by Pinchot, who with all his heart believed precisely this. But with no control over the federal forests, still in Interior, Pinchot and his small staff in Agriculture's Division of Forestry could do little more than provide individuals and lumber companies with silvicultural advice regarding their own private forests. He called his first year at the division a "halcyon and vociferous time," but it was not enough. He wanted those Western forest reserves, and, not a man to keep his opinions to himself, he lashed out at the General Land Office, for its "executive incompetence and political toad-eating." When Land Office Commissioner Binger Hermann asserted that his office was "fully competent to deal with forestry," Pinchot retorted that not only was the land office "incompetent to deal with it, but it understood so little about forestry even to know that it was incompetent."

"Obviously to bring Uncle Sam's forests and foresters together was nothing more than common sense," Pinchot stated in his autobiography, *Breaking New Ground.* "Brought together they were going to be, if I had any luck, and when they were I proposed to be the forester in charge." Luck had little to do with it; determination and a firmly developed friendship with Theodore Roosevelt did. After struggling for seven years, Pinchot finally achieved his heart's desire. With the prodding of Roosevelt after he assumed the presidency, Congress eventually transferred all the reserves over to the Department of Agriculture for safekeeping in 1905. Soon afterward, the reserves were renamed national forests and the Division of Forestry became the Forest Service, reflecting the more active role the agency would assume. Immediately, Pinchot set his program into motion, clarifying it first in a letter of instruction that bore Agriculture Secretary James Wilson's signature, but was pure Pinchot. "It must be clearly borne in mind that all land is to be devoted to its most productive use for the permanent good of the whole people and not for the temporary benefit of the individuals or companies," the instructions began. "All the resources of the Forest Reserves are for *use* and this use must be brought about in a thoroughly prompt and businesslike manner, under such restrictions only as will insure the permanence of these resources. . . ." Pinchot had learned in Europe that the success of any forestry effort depended on community support. Therefore, in his agency he promised that "local questions will be decided on local grounds," with first consideration being given to the dominant industry.

INVENTING CONSERVATION

To promote the gospel of wise use, Pinchot replaced the timber agents of the General Land Office, most of them political appointees, with men of his own, civil service people all. According to one of Pinchot's first employees, the newcomers formed "a corps of inspectors Pinchot knew he could trust; men who knew the West and how to get around; men who would go, look, see and not take anybody's word for nothing; men who couldn't be bribed or bluffed." Pinchot was considered a "tough hombre" to work for, but those who were selected from the hundreds of applicants considered their time well spent. Most, in fact, felt there was no better way to spend it. The Forest Service's esprit de corps was unmatched by any other government bureau. Its men were respected for their courage and efficiency. It operated as though it were oblivious to the existence of political expediency.

Those who worked in the Washington office were regularly invited

71

to Pinchot's mansion for gingerbread and baked apples, served with long discussions of forestry. To these soirees Pinchot also invited illustrious guests to mingle with his staff. In the backcountry, things were different. "It was a world of strings of packhorses or men who walked alone—a world of hoof and foot and the rest done by hand," Norman Maclean wrote in *A River Runs Through It*. Rangers never went without a .45 revolver, with which they could "hit a postage stamp stuck to an aspen tree at fifty feet," and, after 1907, a forty-two-page book entitled *The Use of the National Forests*, which fit into a shirt pocket. The *Use* book was Pinchot's way of preaching to his men when there was no one around to tell them what to do. "The man who skins the land and moves on does the country more harm than good," was one of the book's pronouncements. "He may enrich himself and a few others for a very brief time, but he kills the land." Despite the Forest Service's righteous attitude and the unshakable conviction that foresters knew what was best, the agency made peace with those it regulated. Before too long, men like F. E. Weyerhaeuser, the son of the lumber company's founder, were talking in a way that signified Pinchot's effectiveness. At one timber convention Weyerhaeuser asserted that "practical forestry ought to be of more interest and importance to lumbermen than to any other class of men."

Even though Pinchot's doctrine of utility was an inspiring and highly commendable departure from the profligacy that had gone before, it had some shortcomings from the outset. It bound the forest to materialism. If something could not be produced to sell on the open market, it was not considered valuable. Pinchot dismissed recreation as "quite incidental" to the ultimate purpose of the forest (although today it is second in priority only to logging). He had no appreciation for plain and simple scenic preservation. So unattuned was Pinchot to the national park idea that he became a champion of the Hetch Hetchy project in Yosemite National Park, and every park bill that came up before Congress was disputed by the Forest Service. Finally, Pinchot and Muir, who had gotten along very well while traveling with the 1896 Forestry Commission, broke off their friendship because of vastly different expectations of the natural world. In his autobiography, Pinchot tells the story of the time he was hiking

72

with Muir in the Grand Canyon when they came across a tarantula. Pinchot was ready to shoot it, but Muir stopped him. "He wouldn't let me kill it," Pinchot wrote. "He said it had as much right there as we did." Pinchot was amazed.

While the word "conservation" is most often associated these days with the advocates of John Muir's worldview, it was Pinchot's word at the start. He coined it, not long after discovering what it meant. The meaning of conservation came to Pinchot on a gloomy day in February 1907, while he was riding through Rock Creek Park in Washington, D.C. It suddenly struck him that the "wise use" of all natural resources was "the key to the safety and prosperity of the American people, and all the people of the world, for all time to come." Together with a fellow forester, Pinchot derived the word "conservation" from the forest conservancies of British-ruled India. Later, while riding with Roosevelt, Pinchot described his philosophy and told Roosevelt what he called it. Roosevelt "understood, accepted, and adopted it without the smallest hesitation," wrote Pinchot. "It was directly in line with everything he had been thinking and doing." The concept of conservation had been at the heart of Roosevelt's administration all along. And now there was a word to keep it there, forever.

THE BIG STEAL

Even before the 43 million acres of forest reserves were transferred from Interior to Agriculture, Pinchot worried about the fate of the remaining unreserved forestlands on the public domain, most of them scattered through the Rocky Mountain region. Without federal protection, they would be open to the same ravages evident to a large degree elsewhere. Timber in the Rocky Mountain West grew in rough terrain, and its species of Engelmann spruce and ponderosa and lodgepole pine were considered commercially inferior to the Douglas fir and Sitka spruce of the Northwest. As a result, except in mining regions, the Rockies had not been raided as thoroughly as other parts of the country. Pinchot did not believe this could last, and he convinced Roosevelt that surveys had to be made before the inevitable assault. During 1903 and 1904—even before creation of the Forest Service—Pinchot had fifteen men fresh out of forestry schools making

73

field investigations to determine the proper boundaries of future reserves.

He had other reasons as well. Under the terms of the "lieu-lands" clause of the 1897 Organic Act, owners of property enclosed within a forest reserve could exchange that property for land anywhere outside the confines of the reserve. However much lumber companies detested forest reserves, few were reluctant to take advantage of this clause, trading land they had already harvested for virgin territory elsewhere. Millions of acres of previously untouched forest had gone into private hands in this manner; the Weyerhaeuser company alone acquired more than 900,000 acres of new land in exchange for its cut-over property.

Understandably, Pinchot detested the lieu-lands clause, and his surveyors were instructed to draw reserve boundaries in such a way as to exclude large private landholdings wherever possible. His men complied readily, even with a certain arrogance. "The boundary men were a corps d'elite," asserted Coert duBois in his memoirs (published in *Forest History*). "We strutted around and lorded it over the working plan boys and would scarce deign to spit at a tree planter." During his first summer, duBois was assigned to Colorado: "The area that each examiner was to cover was painted with Pommeroy's yellow drawing ink on General Land Office state maps on a scale of half an inch to the township," duBois wrote in his memoirs. "When [supervisor] Allen handed me the map indicating my first season's job I thought he had spilled the bottle of Pommeroy's ink all over southwest Colorado. It covered all the mountain country in the nine counties in the southeast corner of the state and slopped all over both sides of the Continental Divide." In two summers the boundary men walked and mapped about 150 million acres of potential reserve lands. When completed, the boundary men's work was to be put to a use as controversial as any in the annals of conservation.

Angered by Roosevelt's reserve-making tendencies, Western congressmen succeeded in having this executive power repealed in a rider to the 1907 agriculture funding bill. The bill with this stipulation passed, and although Roosevelt could easily have pocket-vetoed it as the closing act of his administration, Pinchot had a more dramatic exit in mind for the President. With Roosevelt's "enthusiastic consent," Pinchot and his staff drew up all the reserve proclamations for which the boundary men had already done the legwork. "We set every available man at work drawing proclamations for the national forests in six states," wrote Pinchot. "We knew precisely what we wanted . . . our office worked straight through, some of them working thirty-six and forty-eight hours on end to finish the job." When the work was done, Roosevelt signed into existence another twenty-one new national forests totaling 16 million acres. Then, and only then, did he sign the agricultural bill denying every President after him the privilege of doing what he had just done. During the course of his presidency, Roosevelt had set aside about 80 million acres of national forests.

The West, as predicted, exploded when it learned what Roosevelt and Pinchot had done. Pinchot, according to Washington's governor at the time, "has done more to retard the growth and development of the Northwest than any other man." The editor of the *Seattle Post-Intelligencer* avowed that "the recent abuses of power have grown to the point that there will be bitter revolt against the entire policy of forest reserves and an appeal to Congress to repeal all laws on the subject." Roosevelt perhaps described the situation best when he said, gleefully, that "the opponents of the Forest Service turned handsprings in their wrath, and dire were the threats against the executive, but the threats could not be carried out, and were really a tribute to the efficiency of our action."

Out of his respect for Roosevelt, William Howard Taft retained Pinchot in 1909 as his "administration's conscience" but drastically curtailed his rabble-rousing. Taft, who did not share Roosevelt's preoccupation with conservation, though he felt strongly about it, thought Pinchot was "a good deal of a radical and a good deal of a crank." After Pinchot publicly insinuated that Interior Secretary Richard Ballinger had committed improprieties regarding the leasing of Alaskan coal lands and triggered a Senate investigation into the matter, Taft, in 1910, fired his chief forester for insubordination. Such cross fire between departments, particularly when it was a lower official sniping at a higher one, could not be tolerated. Pinchot eventually returned to Pennsylvania, entered politics, became governor, considered running for President, and remained a potent force in conservation and forestry until his death in 1948. "I have since been a governor, every now and then," he was heard to say on more than one occasion. "But I am a forester all the time—have been, and shall be, all my working life."

RESCUE IN THE EAST

Pinchot's unceremonious departure from the Forest Service did not injure the agency at all. It continued to gain strength in its enforcement policies and earned the respect even of those who detested governmental interference. Henry Solon Graves, dean of the Yale Forestry School, replaced Pinchot, becoming one of the few chief foresters who did not work his way up through the ranks as a career man. One thing that troubled Graves and his successors was the fact that the Forest Service returned so little income to the U.S. Treasury from the sale of timber. Not more than 5 percent of the nation's supply came from the national forests in any year, and all timber sales were restricted to those needed for forest custodial reasons. But Graves hoped the Forest Service could one day be self-sufficient. To challenging legislators he explained why it was not already. Forests had values other than those associated with sawn timber, Graves said. If the Forest Service stopped all noncustodial timber operations and ignored the importance of watershed protection "the forests could easily be made to show a net profit." He quickly added, however, that forests were never to be looked at as a source of short-term income. They were a long-term investment. Also, the Forest Service understanding with private timber operators was that government land would not compete with private land. Chief Forester Greeley, who followed Graves, asserted that the agency would never be allowed to "sacrifice the intrinsic value" of public property by a "bargain-day policy" of dumping timber on the market (a policy that did not survive into modern times, as we shall see).

Conflicts with Stephen Mather's new National Park Service also occupied forestry officials. With almost every new national park that came along, some national forestland was transferred from Agriculture's "multiple use" department—the Forest Service—to Interior's "preservation" department—the Park Service. Possibly as a way to stanch the outflow of its lands, the Forest Service began to promote the national forests' recreational opportunities. In 1929 the agency began to designate parts of national forests as primitive, which meant they were left alone as much as possible (see chapter 5).

From the standpoint of environmental protection, which is to say watershed and timber protection, the National Forest System in the West was so successful that Eastern states began to agitate for similar help. This was harder to accomplish, since there was little public domain left east of the Mississippi; most had passed into private hands almost a century before. In 1901, Agriculture Secretary Wilson recommended the establishment of a forest reserve in the Southern Appalachians, but there was no federal money for the necessary purchases, and efforts to attract it failed. Support for the idea was growing in the East, however, where the cycle of fire, floods, and erosion had been particularly severe. "During March 1907, heavy rains brought flood waters down the Monongahela River," wrote C. R. McKim in his history of the area. "The trees and other healthy vegetation were no longer there to regulate the rainwater's flow. It devastated all the agricultural land in the basin of the Monongahela River, causing some $100 million in damages—a gigantic sum for those times—then descended in all its fury upon the helpless city of Pittsburgh, causing there additional damages of $8 million, drowning people and ruining homes."

This disaster was enough to make the West Virginia legislature ask Congress to purchase the despoiled lands for reforestation. In 1911 the passage of the Weeks Act authorized these purchases, as well as those of similar cut-over lands in other Eastern states. This act, named for Massachusetts congressman John W. Weeks, appropriated $9 million to buy 5 million acres in the Southern Appalachians and another million acres in the White Mountains of New Hampshire. It provided for the acquisition of "forested, cut-over or denuded lands within the watersheds of navigable streams. . . ." The emphasis on stream protection was necessary, for it appeared to be the only way Congress could constitutionally buy land, using its power to regulate interstate commerce by maintaining navigable streams. The "production of timber" was added to navigable stream protection in 1924 when the Clarke-McNary Act was passed. Clarke-McNary also introduced the notion of "cooperation to inspire voluntary action" and offered incentives to private landowners to improve the condition of their forests and manage their land more soundly. Finally, the act required that states put up funds matching those of the federal government for fire protection.

The Pisgah National Forest in North Carolina was the first established in the East, in 1916, near the Biltmore estate where Pinchot had done his forestry apprenticeship. Acquisition of forestlands gained momentum during the 1920s, and again during the 1930s, when twenty-six new forests were established. The Great Depression was a boom time for Eastern national forests, because people were desperate to sell their land, and nobody but the federal government was in a position to buy it. Most of the land purchased for Eastern forests cost less than five dollars an acre. "Nearly all were lands that had been abused, poorly protected or ignored, whose owners were happy to unload on the federal government," one commentator of the era noted. Federal investment in reforestation, fire protection, and timber-stand improvement, mostly through the Civilian Conservation Corps, returned the lands to their original heavily forested condition. A comparatively mild climate and abundant rainfall allowed the reforestation work to take hold sooner than most people expected.

Reforestation everywhere was given a boost by the passage of the Knutsen-Vanderberg Act in 1930, which required that money received from the sale of federal timber be set aside for reseeding and planting, in addition to what Congress could be convinced to appropriate every year. By Chief Forester Greeley's count, the high tide of denuded forestlands in the nation had been 81 million acres; much of this had now been given new life.

POINTS OF CONTENTION

The comfortable, almost symbiotic relationship between the Forest Service and the timber industry that had developed during the first three decades of the system got a rude jolt in 1933. That was the year of the Service's Copeland Report, which urged the federal government to buy a good deal more forestland for the national forest system and exert tighter controls over logging on private lands. "The period of voluntary private forestry is over," declared Robert Marshall, one of the young Turks in the agency, who also advocated, in

78

a book called *The People's Forests*, the outright nationalization of all forests. It was just such pronouncements that soon made loggers cast the agency in an ominous shade of red and sparked a letter-writing campaign between timber executives and agency officials regarding "the tremendous impetus given socialism." Fear of creeping socialism finally forced the Copeland recommendations out of the realm of consideration, and the report disappeared into the maw of the bureaucracy.

Pinchot, watching from the wings, had said he was pleased that a bit of a wedge had been driven into the logger-forester relationship. Things between the regulators and the regulated had gotten too cozy even for his taste; in 1928, for example, Chief Forester Greeley had quit the Service to manage the West Coast Lumbermen's Association, thus setting in motion what later critics came to call the Service's "revolving door" tradition of employee exchanges between the government agency and private industry. But when President Franklin D. Roosevelt appointed Ferdinand A. Silcox, a forester who had spent most of his time working in labor relations, to the position of chief forester, Pinchot was relieved. He said that once again his Forest Service might become "the aggressive agent and advocate of the public good, and not the humble little brother of the lumbermen."

In this second Roosevelt the Forest Service acquired another fond admirer; it seemed to run in the family. As a child, Franklin Roosevelt had developed a deep affection for trees on his Hyde Park estate. There, he raised them as a cash crop and as a way to reclaim the land. By 1944 Roosevelt, who listed his occupation as "tree grower" when he went to vote, had supervised the planting of half a million trees on his land. He transferred his "gospel of conservation" to many of his New Deal programs—at least those having to do with making land and water available for planned and regulated human use. (Parks and wilderness and refuges, on the other hand, were not quite so high on his list of priorities.) While Roosevelt was campaigning for the presidency, someone remarked that he seemed to dwell on the importance of land, trees, and water as the solution for perhaps too many of America's most pressing concerns. "I fear that I must plead guilty to that charge," he replied.

Under Roosevelt it was not always easy to tell a Forest Service friend from a Forest Service foe, because in Harold Ickes, Secretary of the Interior, they were one and the same. Not long after taking office, Ickes conceived the notion of turning the Department of the Interior into what he called a "true" Department of Conservation. It probably was New Deal "brain truster" Rexford G. Tugwell who first proposed this to Ickes, along with suggesting that the Forest Service would be a natural part of such an agency. In any case, Ickes soon made the idea his own. The possibility of transfer had arisen before. In 1886, Fernow had thought that the division of forestry belonged in the Interior Department, since that was where all the other federal land responsibilities were housed. During the Graves administration, the states had tried several times to have national forests turned over to them, and during Greeley's tenure Interior Secretary Albert Fall had tried to recover the forests Pinchot had taken. Fall might even have succeeded, had he not been interrupted by the Teapot Dome scandal and suddenly found his hands quite full.

Ickes, who called himself "as hard-boiled and enthusiastic a conservationist as there is in the country," was a more serious challenger than Fall. "I'm going to get the Forest Service," he announced, and for nearly ten years he tried. Roosevelt encouraged him, but never went so far as to use his personal influence on Congress; there were too many other things he wanted done and he feared overextending himself. Moreover, Ickes was opposed vigorously by Agriculture Secretary Henry A. Wallace, who looked upon the Ickes attempts at a raid with no enthusiasm whatever. Neither did Pinchot, who reminded everyone within earshot of the sorry record of the Interior Department before Ickes's arrival there and implied that it could well revert to old habits once Ickes was gone. "Ickes is sincere and honest," Pinchot said, "but he cannot live forever." In the end, although he did get the U.S. Biological Survey and the Bureau of Fisheries in the Reorganization Act of 1939 (see chapter 4), Ickes never did get his Conservation Department—or the forests.

Following World War II, a serious attempt was made not merely to transfer the national forests but to dismantle them. This scheme, beginning in 1946, was forged by a handful of powerful Western ranchers who had always been rebellious against federal intervention, and against paying the grazing fees instituted in 1906. What triggered this particular attack was the Forest Service decree that livestock on national forest ranges would have to be cut back to give the land time to recover from the overgrazing permitted during the war. Stockmen had never developed the camaraderie with the Forest Service that loggers enjoyed. And rangers were accused of not liking stockmen any more than stockmen liked them, a point made clear in Norman Maclean's story "USFS 1919: The Ranger, the Cook and a Hole in the Sky" in *A River Runs Through It*: "Bill Bell was the toughest [guy] in the Bitterroot Valley, and we thought he was the best ranger in the Forest Service. We were strengthened in this belief by the rumor that Bill had killed a sheepherder. We were a little disappointed that he had been acquitted of the charges, but nobody held it against him, for we all knew that being acquitted of killing a sheepherder in Montana isn't the same as being innocent."

And so stockmen gathered in Salt Lake City in the summer of 1946 and began to think about how they might acquire 80 million acres of national forest range—and, while they were at it, the 142 million acres of Taylor Act grazing lands as well (more on this in chapter 3). The states in which the lands were located, they decided, would serve as a conduit, taking possession of the ranges until a select group of ranchers could buy them, at nine cents an acre, and keep them for their exclusive use. Western politicians, traditionally under powerful obligation to the livestock industry, went along cheerfully. Then the historian and social critic Bernard DeVoto got wind of the idea and spread it before the nation in the pages of *Harper's*. He called it "one of the biggest landgrabs in history," and accused the stock business of wanting "to shovel most of the West into its rivers." According to DeVoto, overgrazing had done more damage to the West than anything else. He kept the heat on the ranchers until there was no hope of success. They retaliated by calling for congressional field hearings into Forest Service grazing policies. Congressman Frank A. Barrett, a Wyoming rancher, served as chairman as the hearings traveled to Western cities. For their lack of decorum the whole series was dubbed "Barrett's Wild West Show," as audiences packed with angry ranchers "yelled, stamped and applauded" every time a charge was leveled against the Forest Service.

It was all very much in keeping with the sentiments expressed by

81

one J. Elmer Brock, a Wyoming stockman who repudiated DeVoto's outrage with some of his own. "The users of grazing lands must conform to the whims of numerous federal bureaus," he wrote in a guest column in the *Denver Post*. These bureaus were "all predacious and most of them tinged with pink or even deeper hue." Federal ownership and management of land, Brock asserted, was nothing other than a "form of communism." Charges of socialism failed to arouse the public's sympathy for ranchers; their plan to acquire the national forest ranges in the name of free enterprise failed completely. The forests would stay put in the Department of Agriculture, and, for the time being, continue under government protection.

ROADS-FOR-TIMBER-FOR-ROADS-FOR . . .

At the start, the U.S. Forest Service was understood to be a caretaker agency, for the most part. Trees were cut largely for custodial reasons rather than for commercial ones, and the annual harvest from national forests remained below 2 percent of the national total annually until World War II. From the beginning, in fact, lumber industry executives constantly had sought assurances that national forest timber would not compete with that taken from their own forests. Almost 75 percent of the woodlands in the country belonged to private landowners or the lumber industry. Since these lands had originally been selected for their superior productivity and accessibility, it was generally agreed that with the application of wise forestry, private and commercial forests could meet the needs of the nation almost indefinitely. Much of the Forest Service's early work, after all, had concentrated on teaching the right management techniques to the private forestry sector. (The agency still does this through its State and Private Forestry Division, dwarfed though it is by other Forest Service programs.) The national forests were to be saved for the Future, a shadowy time that might one day arrive, like the Apocalypse, beyond dispute. When the right time came, the national forests would be there, in prime condition to render their share of timber.

By Forest Service and timber industry reckoning, the right time coincided with the end of World War II. The pace of logging had gained momentum during the war, but it was not to be temporary. Soldiers became civilians with pent-up purchasing power and a keen desire for houses. War-torn Europe needed to be rebuilt, and a great deal of American lumber was exported for that purpose. Faced with depletion on its own lands, the timber industry began looking toward the national forests to furnish what its own forests could not. Under this pressure, cutting in the national forests accelerated until, as Forest Service historian Harold K. Steen put it, "timber management had ceased to be largely custodial, and good logging practices were no longer to be advocated on private lands alone."

In 1952, Assistant Chief Forester Christopher Granger wrote an article in *American Forest* announcing that national forest harvests would continue to increase significantly. The increase was due not only to heavier industrial demand for the wood, but also to "the initiative of the Forest Service men going out and getting business." Granger, among others, expressed delight in the prospect of expanded logging in the national forests because it looked as though the agency might be able to realize one of its most elusive dreams: the operation of the entire forest system "in the black," as though it were a business and not a long-term investment. The major obstacle to this goal was the lack of roads into merchantable stands. For years the Forest Service had complained about both the number and the condition of its roads, but Congress had not appropriated enough money to improve the situation, according to agency officials. With the press of timber demands, funds could no longer be denied, particularly in light of the argument that greater harvests would help the national forests pay their own way, as well as cover the cost of road construction. It was not long before a roads-for-timber-for-roads mentality began to take root, producing ever-greater amounts of both. Between 1950 and 1969 the amount of timber cut from the national forests jumped from 5.6 billion to 12.8 billion board feet. The roadbuilding budget soared, and the hiring of civil engineers became a priority. Today more than 350,000 miles of roads run through the national forests, making it the most extensive road system in the world, and civil engineers, the next largest professional group after foresters, number about 3,500 (among them Chief Forester Max Peterson). The accelerated cutting did not improve the Service's bottom line at first (and, as we shall see, in some areas it never did), largely because of the increased roading costs; the Service began to attribute more benefits to logging

83

roads than might ordinarily pass inspection—such as the somewhat tortuous claim that logging itself was a multiple-use tool, since it made roads possible, and roads, after the trees had been hauled out over them, served many other uses.

One of these uses, the Service admitted, was recreation, although a bias against this activity had reemerged by now, almost as if foresters once again viewed it through Pinchot's eyes as "quite incidental." It wasn't. From a fairly constant prewar level of 10 million visitors a year, recreation visits in the national forests leaped to 190 million a year in just three decades. As early as the 1950s, recreationists were beginning to compete seriously with the timber industry for choice lands—lands that the Service and the industry wanted to log and recreationists wanted to enjoy. The two desires were not compatible. To those who ventured into the national forests for something other than a flatbed of timber, "it seemed that the agency was adopting the very methods it had held up for so many years as examples of bad land management," wrote Steen. It did not look as though the Forest Service was protecting the forest from "rampaging, greedy lumbermen," as the public had been told all these years. And a crisis of confidence was in the making.

HOW MULTIPLE IS MULTIPLE USE?

In his 1955 annual report, Chief Forester Richard E. McArdle had written that the "needs for water, timber, and forage, for recreation, wilderness areas, and for hunting and fishing, mount constantly. This places our multiple-use principle of management under severe strain and tests our skill in both resource management and human relations." Caught between the demands of the timber industry and the nature-seeking public, the Forest Service decided it was time to go back to basics, to a reaffirmation of multiple use, and to a clearer statement of precisely what the term meant. The Forest Service turned to Congress in the late 1950s to codify the words it had tried to live by for half a century under its own administrative edict. It would not seem that legislative adoption of something as democratic-sounding and as historically significant as multiple use could generate controversy. But it did. Comments within the agency ranged from "It's about time" to a puzzled "We've been practicing this all along." Outside of the

Forest Service, some people were even more wary of a multiple-use law. The National Lumber Manufacturers Association opposed multiple use because its leaders felt it diluted the intent of the 1897 Organic Act specifying the need for national forests for watershed protection and for a continuous supply of timber. One spokesman for the lumbermen's association told Chief Forester McArdle that multiple use held no advantage for the lumbermen; they already had what they needed. "By making all uses equal in priority the forest manager will probably act on the basis of public pressure," industry spokesman Ralph Hodges explained. "This doesn't give protection to the lumber industry."

The Sierra Club (the only conservation organization to do so) also opposed what finally emerged in 1959 as the Multiple Use–Sustained Yield Bill (sustained yield being the historic operating principle that timber harvesting must ensure a continuous supply of timber into the future; simply put, you must not cut more than you can grow). As far as the Sierra Club was concerned, the foresters were not trained to choose between such uses as lumber and scenery. Rather than place all uses on an equal footing with timber, the club's leaders worried, the bill would instead sanction existing agency attitudes toward logging. "The Forest Service is not as well equipped administratively as it needs to be to deal with the problems of conflict in land use which it must face in the years to come," warned an article in the Sierra Club *Bulletin*. The club did not drop its opposition until sponsors of the bill agreed to a clause stipulating that wilderness preservation qualified as a legitimate use under the umbrella of recreation, and in that form the bill was passed and signed into law by President Dwight D. Eisenhower on June 12, 1960.

For the first time in national forest history, five major uses, listed alphabetically to avoid the appearance of favoritism, were accorded equal billing in one law: outdoor recreation, range, timber, watershed, and wildlife and fish habitat. As some had feared, however, the law did not slow the growth of logging, nor was there any substantial shift in favor of the other prescribed uses. According to a growing number of conservationists, multiple-use planning had not achieved the "preeminent stature" they had hoped for. Many claim it still has not. Barry Flamm, a forester then in the employ of the Wilderness Society, testified in 1985 in regard to the Reagan administration's proposed 1986 budget and outlined the problem: "The basic laws guiding the management of the National Forests are founded on the principle of multiple-use conservation," he said. He then pointed out that the proposed 1986 Forest Service budget simply undercut the whole idea of multiple use: "The resource development and exploitation line items (e.g., timber sales, minerals, grazing) total approximately $600 million. In contrast, the resource stewardship programs (e.g., soil and water, wildlife and fish, recreation and trails, and land acquisition) are allocated one-fourth this amount—$170 million."

A CLEAR-CUT CONTROVERSY

The Forest Service defended itself vigorously against the critics of its multiple-use policies from the beginning—but not always successfully, or sometimes even logically. In 1971, for example, Chief Forester Edward Cliff asserted that thanks to the Forest Service's interpretation of the multiple-use principle, "the national forests are producing more goods and services for the use and enjoyment of the American people, and in greater variety than ever before." This was not the sort of defense to engender confidence in the agency among those who were its severest critics, particularly when in plain view was the Forest Service's increasing reliance on clear-cutting as a way to fulfill such multiple uses as proposed by Chief Forester Cliff. Clear-cutting, in which all trees were removed from large expanses of forest in a single operation, was, after all, the single most dramatic and visible manifestation of logging's impact. To most people who happened upon a clear-cut site, the stumpy land looked no different from the way it might have looked in the generation of the scoundrel loggers who cut and ran.

Once shunned by the Forest Service, clear-cutting had become normal procedure. By 1969, 61 percent of the harvest from the Western national forests was clear-cut, while about 50 percent of the Eastern national forest harvest was obtained this way. Before clear-cutting became so common, foresters had practiced various types of selective cutting, being careful to leave enough trees in a patch to regenerate the stand, with or without artificial reseeding. The Forest Service maintained that clear-cutting was cheaper and faster and for insect-infested stands, it claimed that this was sometimes the only way to contain the damage. Mostly, however, foresters expressed a sharp interest in raising trees of commercial value, and believed that many of these species would not regenerate in the shade provided by trees left standing after selective cutting. Douglas fir, for example, needed broad, open light as a seedling, and clear-cutting was the only way to ensure its return. Clear-cutting prepared the ground for even-aged stands and so maximized the yield of more desirable species.

But clear-cutting on a grand scale also had significant ecological consequences. It accelerated the rate of erosion and water runoff, which sapped nutrients from the soil, and allowed too much sediment in too short a time to enter streams, destroying natural stream vegetation and organisms. (Excessive sedimentation buried newly laid fish eggs or smothered hatchlings.) In addition, stream temperatures were raised by three or four degrees while flowing through unshaded clear-cut areas, and the higher water temperatures were lethal to salmon and trout. Finally, the municipal water treatment plants downstream of a clear-cut area had a more difficult time removing abnormal amounts of siltation from the water supply, and required additional investments from local governments to expand their silt-removal capacity. Dredging of community reservoirs also would have been needed more frequently if sedimentation were not controlled at the entry point. Nor could the fact that a clear-cut area is an ugly area be dismissed, since many towns near national forests relied on natural beauty for tourism.

The case against clear-cutting was perhaps made most tellingly in regard to Bitterroot National Forest in Montana and the Monongahela National Forest in West Virginia during the 1960s and 1970s. Residents of the towns closest to the afflicted forests were the first to protest. A logger from Darby, Montana, charged that "the Forest Service is knocking down and burying and burning the next 150 years of future in our area. They're destroying our forest and our livelihood." G. M. Brandborg, who had worked as forest supervisor on the Bitterroot between 1935 and 1955, told a reporter fourteen years later that "forestry practices today are entirely different from those applied when I was associated with the Forest Service." To Brandborg, it seemed modern foresters had "lost feeling for the good earth."

The verdict of a task force appointed by the Forest Service itself to consider clear-cutting on the Bitterroot was not much better. In 1969 the committee criticized the agency for its "preoccupation with timber management objectives." A second damning report, this one in 1970, came from a committee chaired by Arnold Bolle, dean of the University of Montana's forestry school. "Multiple-use management in fact does not exist as the governing principle of the Bitterroot National Forest," the Bolle report concluded. The rate and method of cutting could be defended only "on a purely technical basis." On environmental and long-term economic grounds, however, the technology was insupportable.

Similar disagreements with the Forest Service were meanwhile developing about the Monongahela National Forest in West Virginia. In 1964 the Forest Service switched from an all-age management program of the hardwood forest to an even-aged management program, which required extensive clear-cutting in a forest largely supported by recreational users. Local residents and the state legislature protested because clear-cutting would undermine the region's considerable tourism business, which depended almost entirely on good hunting and fishing and the rolling beauty found in the national forest. The West Virginia division of the Izaak Walton League filed a suit against the Forest Service on the grounds that the agency was ignoring the 1897 instruction to "mark and designate" individual trees before cutting them. A 1975 court of appeals decision upheld the league's argument, and the Forest Service finally declared a system-wide moratorium on clear-cutting.

In the meantime, Senator Frank Church of Idaho, chairman of the Senate Subcommittee on Public Lands, conducted hearings on the subject both in the field and in Washington, D.C., in which his committee heard damning testimony on every hand and sifted through piles of corroborating evidence. In the end, the committee issued a series of suggested guidelines to the Forest Service in regard to clear-cutting abuses; perhaps the most significant of these was a stipulation that no clear-cutting should be undertaken unless it could be proved that the area in question could be restored to full growth within five years—an almost impossible goal in many areas (which the committee probably knew full well), thus effectively taking them out of production.

88

FORESTS AND THE FUTURE

Throughout this long process of questioning Forest Service practices, a movement grew in support of congressional legislation to spell out management policies in a far more precise manner than that reflected in the Organic Act of 1897. Even the timber industry, frustrated by a confusion of policy, backed such an idea, and conservationists rallied behind it as a means of bringing up for public consideration the environmental soundness of all standard forestry practices. Congress responded in 1976 with the National Forest Management Act (NFMA), the single most far-reaching piece of legislation for the national forests since their inception more than eighty years before.

The NFMA did not ban clear-cutting outright, but by adopting the so-called Church guidelines it did limit its applications severely. Furthermore, the NFMA stated that the sale of timber from each forest had to be limited to a quantity equal to or less than that which the forest could replace on a sustained-yield basis, provided all multiple-use objectives were met. The Forest Service also was instructed to maintain species diversity and not just maximize the growth of trees that were commercially sought. Finally, all uses of the forest were to be laid out in detailed fifty-year plans, which were to be completed in 1985, one plan to a forest, and subject to public review.

Probably the act's most significant provision was to mandate the public's role in reviewing and formulating forest plans. Nothing so formal as a comprehensive plan had ever existed before, but if one had, public contributions to its preparation would certainly not have been sought by the Forest Service, an agency understandably jealous of its long tradition of autonomy. Before World War II, ordinary Americans never questioned the wisdom of the Forest Service on such matters as timber-cutting and environmental protection. In two of the very few lawsuits ever filed against the Service in regard to management practices in its first fifty years, the courts emphasized in their decisions that it was the agency's responsibility to "fill in the details"; it had grown accustomed to functioning with no one looking over its shoulder. With the passage of the NFMA, this changed. Scrutiny, rather than blind trust, would characterize the relationship of the public—and Congress—to the Forest Service from now on.

Forestry analyst and professor of natural law Charles Wilkinson, for one, considered this a good thing. "Within just fifteen years," he wrote in a 1984 law review article, "we have seen, if not a near-revolution, at the very least a deep and fundamental change in Forest Service law and policy." The nation's "oldest and proudest conservation agency" no longer stood outside the law. Whether the agency would adjust to the new realities was another question, he said. Law and tradition remained new to each other, and "the relationship is not remotely a comfortable one."

THE BRIGHT RED BOTTOM LINE

The relationship did not grow notably more comfortable in the years that followed Wilkinson's assessment. The 1980s, in particular, witnessed levels of increasingly angry contention between the conservation community and the Forest Service—both in the field and in Washington, D. C. —a steady disputation that rivaled the most bitter conflicts over clear-cutting in the 1960s and the 1970s. And much of it stemmed from what environmentalists believed was the agency's slipshod implementation of the law as expressed in the NFMA.

Consider, for example, money. Section 6(k) of the NFMA stipulated that management plans for each of the national forests "shall identify lands within the management area which are not suited for timber production, considering physical, economic and other pertinent factors to the extent feasible . . . and shall assure that, except for salvage sales or sales necessitated to protect other multiple-use values, no timber harvesting shall occur on such lands for a period of ten years." In the mid-1970s and early 1980s, resource economists at the Natural Resources Defense Council and The Wilderness Society began to take a look at the "economic" reference in Section 6(k) in the light of what they were beginning to learn about "below-cost sales" on the national forests. There was nothing new about this except the amounts involved. The selling of some timber off the national forests at prices below the cost of administration had been a traditional part of Forest Service policy for years. It operated on the assumption that the National Forest System was never meant to turn a profit. It was an investment in the nation's dis-tant resource future. But before World War II, when the Forest Service was generally more particular about where and how it allowed timber to be cut, below-cost sales were kept to a minimum. They occurred and were tolerated—but never encouraged.

By the 1980s, when between 10 and 12 billion board-feet of timber (as much as one-fourth of all the timber used in the country) were being taken off the national forests every year, below-cost timber sales had become far more routine—and routinely more and more expensive for the taxpayer. A Wilderness Society study issued in 1983 calculated that in 1982 timber sales in 97 out of 155 forest units (many of which did not even have timber programs) had cost the Forest Service more to prepare and manage than they garnered in receipts. Seven out of nine regions in the lower 48 states lost money; both Alaskan forests lost money. The total lost? $219,508,000. In 1984, the General Accounting Office did its own report, analyzing sales in the Rocky Mountain and Intermountain regions for 1981 and 1982; more than 88 percent of the sales, it concluded, had lost money. By the end of 1985, Wilderness Society economists were estimating that during the previous ten years, the federal government's cost of growing and selling timber in numerous forests exceeded receipts—after accounting for inflation—by a total of $2.1 *billion*.

From the point of view of conservationists, of course, it was not entirely a question of money, however horrendous the figures. Most had no particular argument with the Forest Service's non-profit traditions. But they did argue that most of the timber operations being promoted by the Forest Service were slovenly and destructive—especially the road-building program, far and away the most expensive of all timber-related costs. In Alaska's Tongass National Forest, where timber sales were returning less than two cents for every dollar spent, every mile of logging road cost $250,000 to construct. By the middle of the 1980s there was enough road mileage in the national forests to reach to the moon and back, then halfway back again, and such roads, many constructed on the steepest of slopes and built to standards that enabled logging trucks to rip through the woods at near-highway speeds, fragmented wildlife habitat, accelerated erosion patterns (thus helping to silt up riverbeds and destroy spawning grounds for salmon and steelhead populations), and contributed noise and air pollution to the general ambiance of the forest. Altogether, the Forest Service's below-cost program was a case of double jeopardy, critics complained. It was not only making the degradation of the land inevitable, it was forcing taxpayers to foot the bill for the corruption of a resource that belonged to all of them.

For years, the Forest Service responded to such charges simply by denying that it was losing money. The critics had misunderstood the figures or did not comprehend the agency's accounting system, it said. R. Max Peterson, then Chief of the Forest Service, explained the problem to an interviewer in 1986: "Let me make it very clear. I'm not saying that every timber sale necessarily benefits other resources. . . . In fact, in any given case it might be better for some other resource that a particular sale not be made. But I'm saying that . . . the benefits to the other resources from these timber sales need to be considered. What's more, the long-term implications need to be considered. You need to amortize some of the costs, instead of considering them in the same year. . . . So it's been an inappropriate interpretation of what we call cash-flow that's led to a lot of the confusion. I don't know of any economist who would be a part of that kind of analysis."

The Chief's comments did not get a good review from The Wilderness Society's chief economist, Peter Emerson, who was particularly unhappy with Peterson's implication that properly trained economists would not use the kind of cash-flow methods of analysis commonly used by critics of the plan—and that their conclusions were consequently out of whack. "Economists have used cash-flow analysis—the annual comparison of timber receipts and expenditures—as one means to identify what has become known as the below-cost timber sales program," he responded. "You can do it over longer spans of time with other kinds of analyses—even factoring in reasonably projected long-term trends—but in the end you can't escape the fundamental problem. It exists, and to say that it doesn't simply because one particular method doesn't meet whatever standards the Chief may have in mind is just sophistry. The Forest Service is planning to log millions of acres where timber values are so low that the land should be *abandoned* for timber growing purposes."

The argument moved back and forth between these two points for several more years, while taxpayer losses rose, road construction and logging continued to degrade the forests, and public outrage over the "pay as you destroy" program reached the editorial pages of newspapers all over the country. Finally, Dale Robertson, who had succeeded

Peterson as Chief, admitted in 1990 that, indeed, there had been below-cost timber sales on some of the forests (though his estimate of losses fell far short of anything put forth by conservationists) and that the Forest Service was now institutionally dedicated to phasing out at least the most egregious of them.

THE BOUNDARIES OF LOSS

Chief Robertson's admission was a quiet victory for conservation analysis, but the environmental community was in no position to rest on its laurels. A new controversy had blossomed by then, one that spoke even more precisely to the conflict between use and preservation than below-cost timber sales—and it centered on the most profitable forests in the system. That, indeed, was the problem. The western red cedar, Sitka spruce, and Douglas fir of the Pacific Northwest were the most economically valuable trees in the country, and at the same time the very heart of rare and complex forest communities hundreds of years old that could still be found in the wide band of twelve national forests that stretched from north-central Washington to northwestern California. The timber industry and Forest Service timber-sale planners called such forests "decadent," celebrated the extraordinarily valuable straight-grained lumber their trees produced, and wanted to increase the cut. Environmentalists called such old-growth "ancient forests," which, once gone, would to all intents and purposes be gone forever and with them all the ecological, aesthetic, and spiritual qualities that justified their preservation. And, environmentalists insisted, the forests were going—and going fast.

The Forest Service and the Bureau of Land Management (which administered some heavily-timbered old railroad grant lands that had been returned to the government in southwest Oregon) calculated that there were approximately 19 million acres of old-growth forests in the region at the time of the first logging operations in the middle of the nineteenth century. All parties agreed that by the 1980s only a fraction of that original abundance remained—but there was considerable disagreement as to the *size* of the fraction. By 1987, the draft management plans for the twelve national forests involved had been released by the Forest Service. The plans included, among other things, estimates of the amount of old growth that remained in each of the forest units. These estimates were highly suspect, even though Forest Service scientists in 1986 had developed a set of definitions that everyone, including environmentalists, had agreed was both accurate and useful in determining just what qualified as old growth. Most of the draft plans, as it happened, studiously ignored the agency's standards in calculating remaining stands of old growth, apparently operating on the principle that a stand of old growth was what convenience said it was. In *End of the Ancient Forests*, an analysis issued by The Wilderness Society in June 1988, it was noted that the plans "employ a wide range of definitions in arriving at their inventories of old growth. Most of these definitions fall far short of scientific accuracy. Some plans do not even *distinguish* between old growth and mature forests; others employ definitions so simplistic as to be almost meaningless."

In an attempt to discover the gap between Forest Service estimates and a more likely reality, forest ecologist Peter Morrison calculated existing old growth on six of the national forests under question, using the definitions established in 1986 by Forest Service scientists, then compared his findings with those of the agency's planners. The discrepancies were alarming. In the Mt. Baker-Snoqualmie forest complex, the planners said they had discovered 667,000 acres of old growth; Morrison and his colleagues found only 297,000 acres; in Siskiyou National Forest, the planners said, there were 443,000 acres; Morrison said there were only 141,000; in Willamette National Forest, the Forest Service announced the presence of a whopping 868,350 acres; Morrison said there were only 399,000. And so it went. All told, the difference between Forest Service estimates and those of Morrison on the six forest units amounted to more than 1.6 million acres. Later environmental studies—including a series of highly detailed computer-generated GIS (Geographic Information Systems) maps produced by The Wilderness Society's office in Seattle—supported Morrison's conclusions, and it was soon apparent that no more than 2.4 million acres of the original 19 million acres of old growth forest remained in the Pacific Northwest, far less than half that which the Forest Service had claimed.

Such numbers amounted to more than just a terrible error in arithmetic on the part of the Forest Service. They were a prediction of doom, environmentalists feared, for Forest Service planners apparently had convinced themselves that there was plenty of old growth left and

94

that they could proceed apace with the massive increase in planned harvest levels over the next fifty years without doing significant damage to the last remnants of old growth. To block them, more than twenty-five national and local conservation groups joined in an Ancient Forest Alliance and began putting substantial pressure on both Congress and the Executive Department, especially through the courts. One of the most visible points of contention was the previously unpublicized northern spotted owl, a species dependent upon old growth for healthy populations. In spite of rapidly disappearing habitat and steadily declining numbers, the U. S. Fish and Wildlife Service steadfastly had refused to list the owl as an endangered species under the provisions of the Endangered Species Act of 1973 (for more on the act, see chapter 4), but a lawsuit filed by the Sierra Club Legal Defense Fund on behalf of the Alliance asked the courts to force the agency to reconsider its decision, and in November 1988 the U. S. District Court in Seattle ordered the agency to do precisely that. Meanwhile, later suits filed by or on behalf of the Alliance won temporary injunctions on 1.1 billion board feet of planned timber sales of old-growth forest.

By then, in the words of *The Washington Post*, the debate had "evolved from a parochial conflict between conservationists and timber companies into one of the principal environmental battles of the 101st Congress." Conservationists were not the only ones exerting pressure: the timber industry, unions, local timber-dependent communities, and their political allies, all predicting a calamitous loss of jobs as the result of a reduction in logging, put in place their own, equally vigorous campaign, including proposed legislation that would have retained high levels of harvests, rescinded the injunctions against the destruction of spotted owl habitat, and prohibited the courts from issuing temporary restraining orders or preliminary injunctions against timber sales on any grounds. In the fall of 1989, a compromise agreement reached in Congress lifted the court injunctions granted earlier, but directed the Forest Service to minimize cutting and fragmentation, utilize its own stringent (though previously ignored) scientific definitions in calculating the existence of old growth, and increase the amount of protected owl habitat by 25 percent. The agreement also prohibited timber sales in any forest land administratively designated as spotted owl habitat.

The compromise, described by leaders of the Ancient Forest Alliance

95

as "more pragmatic than pleasing," in fact pleased almost no one at all, and soon was rendered all but moot. In June 1990, the Fish and Wildlife Service, in answer to the court's directive, declared that the northern spotted owl was, if not "endangered," at least "threatened," which meant that the Forest Service and the Bureau of Reclamation (on its Oregon railroad lands) had to develop interim plans to protect owl habitat. An Interagency Scientific Committee was formed to come up with a strategy, which was promptly challenged in the courts as inadequate by the Ancient Forest Alliance; The suit was upheld and a moratorium on further timber sales was ordered. In 1992, the Bush administration responded by exercising a little-used provision of the Endangered Species Act that authorized the creation of a special committee—dubbed "the God squad" —to adjudicate disputes regarding the law. To no one's surprise, the committee upheld the ban on timber sales on only 13 of the 44 areas under contention. The Ancient Forest Alliance promptly challenged this conclusion by taking the issue to court once again—and once again, the courts upheld a moratorium on timber sales. The impasse continued, while the Alliance increased its support for congressional legislation that would establish a permanently protected Ancient Forest Reserve System. By the spring of 1993, the often fractious campaign to save the last of these forests was well into its eighth year—and after nearly a decade of conflict, litigation, analysis, and activism, the fate of the forests remained trapped in an ecological, economic, and political quagmire. No wonder, then, that the spring seemed to promise so much hope, most of it bubbling out of a conference held by President Bill Clinton in Portland, Oregon, in April. Environmentalists of all stripes, timber industry representatives, working men and women, politicians, and other folk were all invited to a highly visible, nationally-televised discussion over what was at stake. At the conclusion of the conference, the President directed the Forest Service and the Bureau of Land Management to develop a management plan for the 19.4 million acres of national forests and 2.7 million acres of BLM land in the region that would be "scientifically sound, ecologically credible, and legally responsible."

In the late summer of 1993 the Forest Service and the BLM dutifully issued a draft environmental statement that described several alternative management strategies for the forests. Among the alternatives was one called "Option 9." Following the lead of the two agencies, the

Clinton administration offered this option as its "preferred alternative," invited public comment, as the law required, and made plans to issue a final draft in January 1994. The response to Option 9 on the part of the environmental community was immediate and negative. In spite of a superficially impressive attempt to establish new kinds of administrative areas in which old growth would either be protected outright or managed sensitively, the conservationist critique stated, the balance of the option favored timber production over preservation—so much so that at least 1.6 million acres of ecologically significant old-growth forests would remain available to logging. This would have amounted to no less than one-fourth of all the most vital old-growth forests that remained unprotected in wilderness areas and national parks—and the option would have rendered the remaining groves of protected forests so fragmented in so many areas as to remove the very foundation of their survival as coherent ecosystems. Finally, as the government scientists who had evaluated the option had themselves estimated, it would eventually lead to the extinction of no less than 403 out of the 1,079 species dependent upon old-growth habitat, including many local populations of salmon, steelhead, and other fish species.

The Clinton administration, appalled and unaccountably surprised by the vehemence of the opposition, asked for, and received, an extension on the deadline for a final plan until March 1994. Some changes were indeed made in the final proposal, but not enough, conservationists believed, to seriously diminish the harm the "Clinton Plan," as it became known, would accomplish. They accelerated their campaign for an Ancient Forest Protection Act and considered another series of court challenges that promised to keep the fight over the preservation of these old forests a major priority in the environmental movement for years.

AN AGENDA FOR THE NATIONAL FORESTS

For all its individual complexities, the continuing struggle over the fate of the old growth forests of the Pacific Northwest still serves as a useful simile for the problems that beset most of the national forests in the system. The dominance of timber production as the primary use in these "multiple use" forests is a problem throughout the system, as is the disappearance of old growth, with its abundance of diversity. There is

97

old growth, after all, even in the forests of the east—isolated groves in the national forest units that surround Great Smoky Mountains National Park in the Southern Appalachians, for example, or patches that remain in White Mountain National Forest in New England—and most of it, too, is threatened with extinction. East and West, there are too many logging roads being built, too many streambeds being degraded, too many fish populations being threatened, too much clearcutting going on, too much overall destruction being pursued in order to maintain one industry to the detriment of recreation, wilderness values, the taxpayer's pocketbook, and, above all, the preservation of biodiversity. In many forests of the West, logging is joined by drilling for oil and gas, grazing, and hardrock mining to compound the problem, but in most of the forests it is timber production that still has the most devastating impact.

The decisions to be made about the future of what remains of the once-great American forest will test, finally and with stark clarity, just how committed our political system really is to the notion that we owe an enormous obligation to the community of life that it so abundantly represents. The forest and the idea of the forest, to borrow from Joseph Wood Krutch, has largely shaped us as a nation, has given us a sense of adventure, of possibility, of the mysterious about to be made known. It has colored our imaginations, become a part of our cultural heritage. A little of Natty Bumppo resides in all of us, and Daniel Boone still walks at the back of our minds. Along the way, it also has sustained us as an engine of life—giving us much of the air we breathe, the water we drink, the genetic diversity on which our own future depends. Such is the way of forests.

As these pages have demonstrated, we have given little enough back in the way of care. Indeed, for generations we ripped at our forests in a frenzy of ignorance until, appalled by what we had accomplished, we fumbled toward a concept we chose to call "wise use." We fumble still, and it is time now to clarify in no uncertain terms the means whereby we fully can achieve a working combination of utility and ethics in the management of our national forests. In both the short term and the long run, there are a number of programs that should be initiated as soon as possible. The recommendations that follow share a single principle: For too long, the great weight of policy governing the management of these lands has been placed on the extractive end of the scales. That dominance must end. While the forests can and should continue to serve the immediate commodity needs of American citizens, this should not be allowed to compromise the priceless assets that are nearly unique to the national forests—as natural storehouses of pristine wilderness, biological diversity, and spiritual enrichment—qualities that are no less real and in the long run infinitely more important than our transient economic demands for timber and paper, oil and gold.

Take immediate steps to protect the ancient forests of the Pacific Northwest. Whether by revision of the "Clinton Plan" for the old-growth forests or by congressional passage of an Ancient Forest Protection Act, the last remaining groves of these complex systems of life must be preserved. While the economic impact on local communities through the loss of timber jobs will be real, it will not even begin to approach the tens of thousands of jobs that the industry and, at times, the Forest Service itself have claimed. Over the longest term, the most likely number of lost jobs will not exceed 9,000, a figure that begins to take on some perspective when it is compared with the 26,000 jobs that are known to have been lost over the past decade or so because of mill modernization and the flight of many timber companies to private-land "tree-farming" in southern states, where costs are lower, trees regrow faster, and environmentalists are fewer—none of which has had anything to do with environmental actions in the Pacific Northwest.

Still, neither the government nor the environmental community can or should ignore the very real impacts of change. One thing the government can do immediately is to reduce raw-log exports, which from 1980 to 1989 grew from 2.6 billion board-feet a year to 3.7 billion board-feet. Reducing the volume of log exports would help alleviate the loss of timber because of environmental constraints. Furthermore, the government should encourage an increase in the production of manufactured wood products in the region—an option not fully utilized. Both of these goals could be accomplished if Congress:

> Closed loopholes that permit substitution of federal timber by private companies that export their own logs, make the ban on export of raw logs from federal lands permanent, and extend the ban to timber species not currently covered;

Authorized and encouraged the states to impose an export tax on raw logs at least equal to the premium paid for export logs;

Established an Education and Economic Development Trust Fund for the use of states that enact an export tax on raw logs. Trust fund assets would be generated through the export tax and real-located to states based on their deposits into the fund. Fifty percent of the reallocation would be used to fund local education needs according to the state's plan for education and 50 percent would be used to fund economic diversification, job training, industry modernization, and secondary manufacturing development; and

Provided an investment tax credit and allowed accelerated depreciation for capital investments in new facilities to produce export grades of lumber, or secondary wood products such as laminated beams, doors, furniture, and the like.

The Forest Service should reduce the timber sales levels on the national forests. In fiscal year 1993, The Forest Service prepared timber sales for 4.55 billion board feet. This figure, like the figures that preceded it in other years, showed a steady decline in timber levels, but the goals are still much too high. Research undertaken by The Wilderness Society, among other groups, indicates that a truly sustainable level of logging—taking into account the elimination of below-cost timber sales and management policies designed to enhance the biological productivity of the forests instead of their commercial productivity—would be considerably less than two billion board feet a year. That is the level at which all future timber-sales planning should be based. The Forest Service's own ecosystem management policy commits it to "using an ecological approach in the future management of the national forests." This cannot be accomplished so long as allowable logging levels remain above two billion board feet. "The most important resource in the national forests," Michael Francis, director of forest programs for The Wilderness Society, has told Congress, "but rather the one resource that makes them all possible: biological diversity. The diversity of life is the basis of sustainable forestry and ecosystem management. . . . The goal of

100

national forest management and budgeting should be to maintain the structure and function of natural forest ecosystems."

The Forest Service should expand and accelerate its phase-out program for below-cost timber sales. As one important means of achieving the lower timber cut every year, the agency should be directed, through an Executive Order, to phase out below-cost timber sales by eliminating the most costly sales first and curtailing *all* such sales within five years. Afterward, each commercial timber sale must assure a positive net return to the U. S. Treasury. In the future the Service's planning process must avoid below-cost sales and its accounting systems must monitor sale costs accurately for more improved reports to Congress.

The Forest Service should establish a moratorium on construction of new forest roads. Forest Service logging roads cost the taxpayers of this country anywhere from $120 million to $150 million every year just for their construction—not to mention the costs of mitigating the erosion, sedimentation, and habitat destruction roading causes. With a road system already in place that, taken together, is long enough to encircle the earth fourteen times, the time has come for the agency to admit that enough is enough; it should stop major road construction now and should not request additional money from Congress for further road building.

Reforestation programs must be administered to ensure that they meet the biological requirements of the NFMA. The National Forest Management Act of 1976 prohibits logging on national forests except where reforestation is assured within five years. This directive has been whittled away in regulation and practice. Reforestation "assurance" now apparently requires only the assertion that the appropriate technology to accomplish reforestation exists somewhere in the world—whether or not it is ever likely to be actually applied to any piece of ground under consideration for logging. The broad application of this kind of standard has led the Forest Service routinely to ignore reforestation constraints when determining areas it deems "suitable" for logging. The Forest Service should direct its planners to behave as if "assured" reforestation within five years means exactly what it says—an honest assurance based on solid, practical probabilities, not gaseous, theoretical possibilities. No timber sale anywhere on the national forests should be declared appropriate unless and until there is a real certainty that it can be—and will be—adequately reforested.

Finally, the national forests should be preserved and managed so as to flourish as the heart of coherent systems of land devoted principally to the survival of biological diversity. If, as will be discussed in greater detail in chapter 5, our traditional means of preserving wild country—as national parks, refuges, and wilderness areas—are no longer entirely adequate to ensure that true diversity of plants and animals can be maintained, we will have to turn to the lands of the present National Forest System as the most important single units in the designation of large, ecosystem-wide enclaves. National forests include most of the 261 major terrestrial ecosystem types that have been identified within the continental United States, including Alaska. A majority of all wild species of plants and animals in the country almost certainly occur somewhere within the 191 million-acre National Forest System, and national forests are the primary—sometimes the only—havens for increasingly rare species that once spread freely across the land. They provide habitat for at least 150 species that the U. S. Fish and Wildlife Service has designated as endangered or threatened. They also include as many as 1,300 species considered likely candidates for such designation. In short, without the forests, all hope of preserving the diversity and ecological integrity of any system of large enclaves of protected land would be fruitless; this "use," of all the "multiple uses" to which the forests might be heir, must take precedence over all others.

The obligation we owe to the forests, to use a device much-loved in political rhetoric, should be viewed not so much as a task, but as a gift. Indeed, given the abundance of life, wildness, scenery, and natural resources represented in the forests, we have a legacy whose richness alone should be enough to move us. What other nation on earth even has the *opportunity* to wisely manage such abundance? We must exercise the wit and courage to embrace that opportunity. Both certainly will be needed. "Make no little plans," architect Daniel Burnham is said to have remarked once. "They have no magic to stir men's souls."

Even in outline, the recommendations we make here for the future management of the national forests comprise no little plan. It is a program whose application could help to tranform the future of the nation's entire system of public lands and could inspire us for the first time in our history to make an intelligent, functioning, applied land ethic a living reality.

What better place to start than in the forests—the very home of the nation's memory?

3

THE LEFTOVER
LEGACY

The National Resource Lands of the BLM

Gertrude Stein, the sometime poet and playwright, was not ordinarily given to trenchant observations regarding the relationship of geography to history, but on one occasion she did give voice to such a thought: "In the United States," she wrote, "there is more space where nobody is than where anybody is. That is what makes America what it is." Poets seem to have liked this idea; Charles Olson, in Part One of *Call Me Ishmael*, his study of Herman Melville, says: "I take SPACE to be the central fact to man born in America. I spell it large because it comes large here." Space, in the form of land, was indeed a major factor in shaping the character and institutions of America. It offered, among other things, a freedom of movement and opportunity denied to most other peoples, and in that freedom there was room for quite a lot of dreaming—three billion acres or so in the beginning.

Most of it is gone now. The lands under discussion in this chapter—some 236 million acres of them in the coterminous United States and Alaska—are all that remain of that original inheritance, after withdrawals for parks and forests, national grasslands and wildlife refuges, monuments, reservoir sites, and defense installations, after land grants to states, colleges, canal companies, veterans of domestic wars, and railroads, after creation of the Indian reservation system, after sale and disposal through hundreds of land laws over the past two centuries. They are sometimes idly dismissed as the "leftover lands," the "lands no one knows," or—a little harshly—the "lands nobody wanted." More

Placer mining on the San Juan River, Utah (Collections in the Museum of New Mexico).

propitiously, they have officially been designated the National Resource Lands and placed under the administration of the Bureau of Land Management.

It is a complex and demanding inheritance the BLM monitors, "rich in a spectrum of resources," as one conservationist has described it, "from the wilderness that illuminates the spirit to the coal that lights a city." More than 174 million acres outside Alaska are contained in the eleven Western states—more than 48 million in Nevada alone (69 percent of the state's total acreage)—but odd lots crop up in a number of Eastern states: 589 acres in Wisconsin, 12 in Illinois, 3,962 in Louisiana, for example.

With so much land under its stewardship, the duties of the BLM are multitudinous. It is the chief administrator of public grazing lands, on which some 21,000 ranchers graze 7 million cattle, sheep, and goats. It controls the leasing program for oil, gas, coal, oil shale, and geothermal sites and the administration of claims for gold, silver, iron, copper, lead, molybdenum, and uranium mining on its own lands as well as those on another 370 million acres of national forests and other federal land units. It manages 7.9 million acres of commercial forest, from which it produces about 1.3 million board feet of timber each year, most of it from a 2.1-million-acre parcel in western Oregon once given to the Oregon and California Railroad and later taken back. Its domain includes 35 million acres of wetlands, 85,935 miles of fishable streams, and thousands of archaeological sites, petroglyphs, pictographs, and fossil remains—all reminders that the American continent was not always governed as it is now, and that civilization as we think we know it has lasted but a moment in the long stretch of human history and geologic time. Finally, by its own reckoning, the BLM administers some 25 million acres of land that are potential additions to the National Wilderness Preservation System.

An extraordinary legacy, these "leftover lands"—and perhaps the least understood and most underappreciated of all the nation's public lands. But then they always have been. In 1861, Daniel Webster gazed westward and perceived little but trash: "What do we want of that vast and worthless area, that region of savages and wild beasts, of wind, of dust, of cactus and prairie dogs? To what use could we ever hope to put those great deserts and those endless mountain ranges, impenetrable and covered to their base in eternal snow?" We know a little better now, but it has been a long journey to understanding the West, "a transition from fable to fact," as Wallace Stegner has described it. Its course follows the outline of the history of the unappropriated, unreserved public domain—which is what, at the beginning, the national resource lands were called.

WHERE DID THEY COME FROM? WHERE DID THEY GO?

The idea of a national public domain owes its existence to the state of Maryland. In 1778 this tiny, landless state led a protest against states whose claims to western lands put them at an advantage. There was nothing modest about these claims. Under the royal charter that the colonies went to war to revoke, Virginia, for example, had been granted ownership to all the territory west to the Mississippi River and north into the Upper Peninsula of what would become Michigan, and still claimed this territory after the war. Massachusetts claimed enormous sections that now run through Michigan and Wisconsin. Maryland, not as blessed as such other states, threatened that it would not sign the Articles of Confederation until the landed states surrendered their claims to the newly formed central government. All lands, according to Maryland's statesmen, had been fought for by the "common blood and treasure" of the thirteen states, and therefore should be commonly owned.

On October 10, 1780, the Continental Congress agreed, and formally made the donation of these claims to the government a condition of equal membership in the federal union. Congress also resolved that "the unappropriated lands that may be ceded or relinquished to the United States, by any particular states . . . shall be disposed of for the common benefit of the United States, and be settled and formed into distinct Republican States, which shall become members of the Federal Union, and shall have the same rights of sovereignty, freedom and independence as other states."

In 1802 these transfers were completed and the infant government had become the landlord for more than 233 million acres. The following year the nation doubled its size when President Thomas Jefferson agreed to pay France $27 million for its Louisiana Territory,

107

and over the next fifty-one years diplomacy, war, and purchase spread the sovereignty of the federal government to more than 1.4 billion acres.

The Northwest Ordinance of 1785 had spelled out the method by which such lands were to be surveyed and prepared for sale by auction to citizens moving westward. All lands were to be uniquely identified by the metes and bounds designated in what is called the rectilinear survey. They would be divided up into townships six miles to a side. These, in turn, would be subdivided into thirty-six numbered sections of one square mile each (640 acres). Whole townships as well as individual sections would be offered for sale—at a minimum bid of one dollar an acre—at public auctions to be held in each of the original thirteen states. Congress reserved to the federal government sections 8, 11, 26, and 29 in each township, and section 16 was to be set aside for the support of public schools. Later, in 1812, the General Land Office was established in the Treasury Department to handle all land sales.

From the beginning, there was a basic conflict between the philosophy held by such as Thomas Jefferson, who believed that land should be put into the hands of yeoman farmers ("the most precious part of the state," Jefferson called them), even if it came down to giving it away, and that held by Alexander Hamilton and his allies, who believed that land sales would remain the only sure source of income for the federal government and should therefore bring in the highest possible price. While this debate sputtered, the speculators and the squatters (who often were one and the same) moved in on the land itself. Corruption, bloated land booms, and consequent bankruptcies made a travesty of the orderly land sales program envisioned by the Ordinance of 1785. Land speculation, one Kentucky newspaper complained, was "the most portentous evil that ever existed in America," one that "threatened the dissolution of the union." For their part, pioneers subverted the stipulations of the ordinance by simply ignoring them. As Jefferson himself had predicted, the landless poor "would settle the lands in spite of everybody." They simply squatted on the land and would not be moved; by 1828, for example, two-thirds of the residents of Illinois lived on land that still belonged to the federal government.

As a result of all this, land sales never accounted for more than 10 percent of the government's operating revenue. Gradually, Congress accepted the inevitable and no longer looked upon the land as a great bank account. With the Preemption Act of 1841, it legitimized the squatter's impulse by allowing him to go out into the unsurveyed domain and stake a claim to a piece of it, at $1.25 an acre. The government also started giving land away to promote settlement and progress through a succession of gifts to wagon-road companies (3 million acres), land-grant colleges (77 million acres), swamp-reclamation projects (65 million acres), and railroads (94 million acres). But it was the Homestead Act of 1862 that demonstrated the final capitulation of the Hamiltonians.

Under the provisions of the Homestead Act, any citizen twenty-one years old or the head of a household could lay claim to 160 acres of government land; he could live on it for six months, then buy it for $1.25 an acre, or live on it for five continuous years and cultivate it, after which he would receive title for nothing more than the small filing fee. Here was the Jeffersonian impulse given full expression; between 1862 and 1882, 552,112 homestead entries were filed, and the term "land-office business" took on substance. In *The Northern Tier*, a contemporary account of Midwestern life, one E. Jeff Jenkins described a typical scene when the General Land Office opened its doors in Concordia, Kansas, on January 16, 1871:

> The door opened—a shout—a rush—a scramble over each other—a confused shouting of the number of the range and township, as a half-dozen or more simultaneously presented their papers to the officers, who, in the tumult, could as well have told which animal was first taken into the ark, as to have designated which one of the settlers was prior in time with the presentation of his papers. . . . The following day was a repetition of the previous one and the rush continued for months. . . .

For all its noble intentions, the Homestead Act was based on experience learned in the humid and subhumid lands of the eastern third of the continent. The farther west the settlers scrambled to stake their claims, the greater the distance from reality. Beyond the 100th

Meridian, which bisects the country from a point a little east of Minot, North Dakota, to a point a little west of Laredo, Texas, aridity became the unifying geographic factor. Rainfall beyond this point averaged less than twenty inches a year. What had been true in one circumstance remained true in another; before the Civil War, the South's expansion of its cotton economy was checked in west Texas by what Daniel Webster called "the ordinance of nature, the will of God." Now, in the last quarter of the nineteenth century, what had stymied the South was killing the Western settler. "The possibilities of trouble, which increased in geometrical ratio beyond the 100th meridian, had a tendency to materialize in clusters," wrote Wallace Stegner in *Beyond the Hundredth Meridian.* Even if spring looked promising with green grass and blossoming wildflowers, later "the brassy sky of drouth might open to let across the fields winds like the breath of a blowtorch, or clouds of grasshoppers, or crawling armies of chinch bugs. Pests always seem to thrive best in drouth years. And if drouth and insect plagues did not appear there was always a chance of cyclones, cloudbursts, hail. It took a man to break and hold a homestead of 160 acres even in the subhumid zone. It took a superman to do it on the arid plains."

A lot of them tried, as Stegner notes, and a lot of them failed. Of those 552,112 claims filed in the first twenty years of the Homestead Act, only 35 percent ever "proved up" to full ownership. "The government," Senator William E. Borah noted cynically, "bets 160 acres against the filing fee that the settler can't live on the land for five years without starving to death."

Still, much of the land was gone—80 million acres of it by 1900—and not all of it to the benefit of the small family farmer it was meant to sustain. Fraud, usually through the medium of dummy entries, enabled already outsized ranching and farming operations to grow even larger with the gift of government land. The pattern continued with each of the land laws that followed, desperate efforts to reconcile the hope of land for the landless with the hard realities of the geography in which it was meant to flourish—chiefly the Timber Culture Act of 1873, which granted an additional 160 acres to homesteaders who promised to plant forty acres of the grant in trees, and the Desert Land Act of 1877, which made 640-acre tracts available at $1.25 an

110

acre, providing the claimant could prove that he had "brought water" to his claim in an effort to irrigate it. Both of these offered sterling opportunities for anyone with gumption enough to evade the strict observance of law, and the General Land Office, understaffed and underpaid throughout its existence, could do little to monitor the situation. Millions of acres of public land were joined to private monopolies.

THE ONE-ARMED REVOLUTIONARY

Even while giving it away in ever-increasing chunks, the government was investigating what it had in the public domain. In the years immediately following the Civil War, it had launched four major surveys of its Western lands: Ferdinand V. Hayden's Survey of Nebraska Territory, Clarence King's Survey of the 40th Parallel, Lieutenant George M. Wheeler's Survey of the Territory West of the 100th Meridian, and John Wesley Powell's Survey of the Plateau Province of the Colorado River. All of these expeditions enriched and enlarged the nation's knowledge of its patrimony (and Hayden's survey, as noted in chapter 1, led directly to the creation of Yellowstone National Park), but only Powell's gave birth to an idea—an idea that could have changed the history of the West.

The one-armed major (he gained the rank and lost his right arm during the Civil War) had achieved a measure of fame on an exploring expedition in 1869, when he and his men made the first recorded journey down the Colorado River through the Grand Canyon; his report of that journey, *Exploration of the Colorado River of the West and Its Tributaries*, published in 1875, came as close as any government document ever has to best-sellerdom. His next major publication, *Report on the Lands of the Arid Region of the United States, with a More Detailed Account of the Lands of Utah*, issued in 1879, was less well received—particularly by those who had a stake in the status quo as far as the administration of the public domain was concerned. For Powell was talking common sense and rational planning in a program designed to restructure the whole system; in other words, revolution.

First, he contradicted the claims of the boomers that the land west of the 100th Meridian was a garden waiting only for the plow and a

111

little water to make it blossom (and there were those who claimed that rain would *follow* the plow, according to the dictates of some never-explained physical law). Wrong, Powell said: Only part of the land was arable under any circumstances, and only part of that could be irrigated with the finite resource of water that was available. There were limits to this growth. Second, he pointed out that an irrigated farm of 160 acres was far too much for an ordinary family to handle; he recommended that the single-family farm be reduced to eighty acres. Conversely, the nature of pasturage in the West—which required anywhere from thirty to sixty acres to support each animal—meant that the 160 acres available under the Homestead Act or even the 640 acres available under the Desert Land Act were not enough to maintain a family ranch; pasturage land, he said, should be carved into tracts of 2,560 acres each. Third, he laid bare the fact that in this land of little rain, he who controlled the available water controlled the land around it—a condition that had already made land monopoly endemic in the West. He recommended that the system of rectilinear surveys be scrapped and that all eighty-acre family farm units and all 2,560-acre pasturage units be drawn so as to give each equal rights to available water.

There was more: he strongly recommended that all pasturage lands be held in common by Western communities, unfenced so as to make the most efficient use of the forage and to further ensure common access to water. Finally, since it was demonstrably impossible for individual families to finance irrigation projects for each family farm, he proposed that the federal government encourage the formation of cooperative irrigation districts whose common financing could build the necessary distribution systems.

An accommodating soul, the major included in his report sample legislation designed to meet these goals. These prototype bills, like the rest of the report, were quietly applauded by a few brave members of Congress, loudly condemned by a few others, and studiously ignored by most. Congress was not yet ready to accept limitations to growth, or even commonsense planning—especially planning that included proposals that smacked suspiciously of socialism. In the meantime, the National Academy of Sciences (on whose deliberations Powell exerted some considerable influence) recommended to Congress that the four Western surveys be consolidated into one, that the century-old rectilinear survey system be revised, and that a public land commission be established to examine all existing land laws with an eye toward revising or eliminating them. At the request of Interior Secretary Carl Schurz, Powell drafted legislation on all three recommendations. These were introduced in Congress and two of the proposals got passed; the surveys were put under the aegis of a new agency, the U.S. Geological Survey (Clarence King was named its first director), and a Public Lands Commission was created, with the major as a member. (In addition to all of this, Powell slipped through legislation creating a Bureau of American Ethnology, which he would direct until his death, in 1902.)

The Public Lands Commission issued its report in 1880. It included the first codification of the nearly three thousand land laws and regulations that had been applied to the public domain since 1785, as well as a number of arguments reminiscent of Powell's thinking, among them the statement that the West's most important characteristic was its heterogeneity: "One region is exclusively valuable for mining, another solely for timber, a third for nothing but pasturage, and a fourth serves no useful purpose whatever. . . . Hence it has come to pass that the homestead and preemption laws are not suited for securing the settlement of more than an insignificant portion of the country." It, too, recommended that the traditional survey be scrapped and the lands classified instead according to their mineral, grazing, timber, and irrigation resources.

The report was ignored. In 1881, Powell replaced King as director of the U.S. Geological Survey and began the project of mapping the entire country, quadrant by quadrant (the task is still unfinished). In 1888 he joined in an unlikely alliance with Senator William D. "Big Bill" Stewart of Nevada, one of the leading boomers of the West, to engineer a joint resolution in Congress that ordered the Geological Survey to examine the public domain and identify all irrigable lands and potential reservoir sites. Stewart, of course, wanted to stimulate growth, and was furious when a rider was attached to the resolution that would remove all lands "susceptible to irrigation" from settlement under the various land laws; he got this amended to include a provision allowing the President to reopen such lands at his discretion, though only under the stipulations of the Homestead Act.

Powell methodically began work on the irrigation survey. Too me-

113

thodically, by Stewart's lights. Months passed, then a year, then two years, and still there was no report from Powell. In the meantime the land was closed to settlement. Stewart lost patience. In 1890 he got Powell's budget trimmed from $720,000 to $162,500 and persuaded his colleagues to cancel the withdrawal of the lands under study. Two years later the budget was cut another $90,000 and sixteen staff positions were eliminated, and two years after that, Powell gave up; he resigned as director of the U.S. Geological Survey.

Ironically, in that same year of 1894, Congress passed the first of two pieces of legislation that reflected, at least in part, Powell's arguments in his *Arid Region* report of 1879: the Carey Act, which authorized the transfer of as much as one million acres of the public domain to individual states, providing those states then turned around and sold it cheaply to irrigation companies, who, in their turn, would sell it to individual farmers, with attached water rights, in order to finance irrigation works. The second piece of legislation was the Reclamation (or Newlands) Act of 1902, which created the Reclamation Service (later renamed the Bureau of Reclamation), whose function it would be to build federal dams and irrigation works in the West. The major almost certainly would have approved one stipulation of this act: water derived from federal irrigation works would be made available only to farm units of 160 acres (or 320 acres, in the case of a man and wife) and only to those who would live on and work the land. The major would not have approved of the fact that at no time in the next eighty years, during which period more than $11 billion in taxpayers' money went to dam most of the major rivers in the West, would the 160-acre limitation be enforced with any consistency at all—and in 1982 would be removed entirely by another act of Congress.

USING IT UP

While the vision of John Wesley Powell was being formulated (then casually dismissed), the exploitation of the public domain proceeded at an alarming rate—sometimes with consequences Powell could have foretold. Except for those reservations involved in the beginning of the national park and national forest systems (see chapters 1 and 2), the land was vulnerable, governed by laws too easily sub-

114

verted and in any case, as we have seen, inadequate to the task of protection.

Among the first of those to venture into the farthest reaches of this domain were the miners, and it is instructive to remember that every single major mining strike in the history of the West was made on public land—gold in California in 1849, gold in Colorado in 1859, silver in Nevada in 1859, gold in Montana in 1862, silver in Idaho in 1864. In these and half a hundred other early mining developments, the treasure was claimed and extracted from land owned by the federal government. It was not until 1872 that Congress got around to imposing federal law on the extraction of federal treasure from federal land—and this General Mining Law, as it was called, was less than draconian. Under its provisions, a mining patent could be obtained by making a "valid" mineral discovery, paying for a boundary survey, applying to a land office for the land included in such a survey, paying $2.50 an acre for placer (surface) mining and five dollars an acre for lode (underground) mining, and investing one hundred dollars a year in improvements for five consecutive years. That was it—that was the government's share of the estimated $20 billion in gold, silver, and other minerals taken from the public lands during the busiest decades of mining in the nineteenth-century West. The law is still with us, still active, and still being applied in national forests and the "leftover lands" of the Bureau of Land Management.

Broadly speaking, the extraction of gold, silver, and copper had minimal impact on the whole sweep of the public domain. Not as much can be said of the other major Western industry of the nineteenth century. The grazing of cattle and sheep had a profound effect on the land from the beginning. When Powell suggested that livestock homesteads of 2,560 acres be established, congressmen from the East and Midwest were shocked by the amount of land he was suggesting was necessary to a grazier. Yet not even his amount was sufficient, and in practice stockmen were in possession of far greater areas. One Mormon cattle enterprise ruled 2 million acres, or about 3,500 square miles of open range. While this was larger than most, it was not uncommon to find other stock operations of similarly impressive proportions.

The American stock industry grew out of Texas after the Civil War,

115

when the demand for beef in the North and East encouraged the raising of larger and larger herds. The animals were driven straight north to railheads like Abilene, Kansas, for shipment to Chicago, or even farther north to fatten on the sweet grass of the High Plains. Within ten years after the Civil War the herds had spread over the grasslands of Kansas, Nebraska, the Dakotas, Colorado, Wyoming, Montana, and Utah, consuming the fine, free grass of the public domain before being shipped to market. Operating expenses on the range were irresistibly low. It might cost four dollars to buy a single calf. To feed the calf cost nothing, since it fed itself on the range. In a year the animal would bring forty dollars in the northern markets. The business began to attract investors from the East and from as far away as Canada, England, and Scotland.

In less than fifteen years the northern range was stocked to capacity. Running out of water and grass, ranchers began squabbling among themselves, resorting to gang wars on occasion in the competitive struggle. There was unity, however, in their shared contempt for the homesteader, a benighted soul who often fenced the open range in patches of 160 acres (making sure to enclose the water, if there was any), depriving the cattle of free movement. "Now there is so much land taken up and fenced in that the trail for most of the way is little better than a crooked land," grumbled one trail hand in 1874, the year barbed wire was invented and made its appearance on the plains. "These fellows from Ohio, Indiana and other northern and eastern states—the 'bone and sinew of the country,' as politicians call them—have made farms, enclosed pastures and fenced water holes until you can't rest; and I say, Damn such bone and sinew! They are the ruin of the country, and have everlastingly, eternally now and forever, destroyed the best grazing-land in the world."

In retaliation—and quite illegally in many cases—ranchers began fencing in vast areas to keep homesteaders out. The scene was set for the enactment of what the biologist Garrett Hardin would call "the tragedy of the commons": limited resources, when subjected to unlimited use, reduced the welfare of all.

As Theodore Roosevelt learned during his brief tenure as a Dakota rancher, "overstocking [the range] may cause little or no harm for two or three years, but sooner or later there comes a winter which

116

means ruin to the ranches that have too many cattle on them. It is merely a question of time as to when a winter will come that will understock the ranges by the summary process of killing off about half of all the cattle throughout the Northwest."

In 1886 the northern range was stocked well beyond its carrying capacity. Drought that spring and summer reduced the available forage, leaving hundreds of thousands (no one knows precisely how many) of cattle undernourished. Winter came early and stayed long. Snow drifted so deep throughout the West that cattle and people were buried alive in it. Temperatures stayed well below zero for weeks, and the wind whipped the plains. Cattle piled up like driftwood in all the fenced-in corners of the range. When the snowdrifts melted away, the damage was tallied. About three-fourths of all the herds in the West had been killed off. Roosevelt, who came back to survey the catastrophe, recalled riding through the Dakota country for three days without seeing a live animal. It was, he said, "a perfect smashup."

A smashup for the land, too; millions of acres had been stripped as clean as a billiard table by the combination of drought and too many cattle, and it would be decades before recovery. Some areas never did recover, and the consequent erosion left true wastelands where once the grass had grown belly-high to a horse.

A DAWNING REALITY

Reform of the sweeping nature called for in Powell's *Arid Region* report was beyond the capabilities of a Congress and a federal bureaucracy resistant to change under the best of circumstances, but by the turn of the century it was clear that the nation's stewardship of the public domain was a travesty. Something had to be done, and something was—reluctantly and cautiously, at first, but with increasing scope in the first decade of the twentieth century.

In 1891 the General Revision Act repealed the Preemption Act of 1841, the Timber Culture Act of 1873, and the auction sale of land; it also reduced the land obtainable under the Desert Land Act from 640 acres to 320—and, as noted in chapter 2, the act's "Forest Reserve" clause empowered the President to make withdrawals of any forest areas the Secretary of the Interior deemed necessary for

117

watershed protection and timber preservation. In 1897 these forest reserves were placed under the control of the General Land Office, and when that agency proved too amenable to corruption, an act of 1901 moved the reserves from the Department of the Interior to the Department of Agriculture.

In 1902, Theodore Roosevelt's first Secretary of the Interior, Ethan Allen Hitchcock, launched an investigation of land frauds that ultimately returned more than one million acres to the public domain. In 1904, Congress passed the Kincaid Homestead Act, which allowed entries of 640 acres in the Sand Hills region of Nebraska; it proved so successful that a demand rose for its extension to the rest of the public domain. In 1905 an executive order put a moratorium on entries under the provisions of the Timber and Stone Act of 1878; this law, which allowed the negotiated sale of public lands unfit for cultivation, had been as cheerfully abused by timber companies as the Homestead and Desert Land acts had been by livestock companies.

Coal lands got special attention during the Roosevelt years. In 1873 an act modeled after the General Mining Law of 1872 allowed claims to be filed on 160 acres of coal-bearing lands, at a sale price of ten dollars an acre; the law stipulated that no more than four such claims could be owned by a single individual or corporation. Nearly 30 million acres had been disposed of by the turn of the century, and most of this, through dummy entries and prearranged agreements with the original purchasers, had ended up in the hands of a few companies. To prevent the spread of this kind of monopoly, in 1906 Roosevelt withdrew 66 million acres of coal lands, including a million in Alaska, where hundreds of mining claims were pending. It was the controversy over these claims during the administration of William Howard Taft that led to the dismissal of Chief Forester Gifford Pinchot in 1910 (as described in chapters 2 and 6).

The reformist movement began sputtering out during the Taft and Wilson administrations. An Enlarged Homestead Act of 1909 did increase the size of a homestead claim to 320 acres, but only on those lands not suitable for irrigation. The Pickett Act of 1910 authorized the President to make withdrawals for "any public purpose," but the lands so withdrawn were still open to mining for metalliferous minerals under the General Mining Law. The Stock-Raising Homestead Act of 1916, inspired by the imminence of World War I and the projected need for additional beef, did include stipulations that range improvements were mandatory, but the 640 acres obtainable simply made it easier for already huge ranching operations to grow bigger. The mandated improvements were largely ignored by those who began expanding their operations during the war and the boom years of the twenties, until the same kinds of mistakes that had brought the cattle industry down in the 1880s were being repeated—and would have even more spectacular consequences.

THE TEAPOT DOME–ELK HILLS AFFAIR

Perhaps no single incident from the history of the public domain more accurately demonstrated its vulnerability to the excesses of greed and ignorance than the Teapot Dome–Elk Hills imbroglio of the 1920s. The public resource on the public lands here was oil, and for once the federal government developed an intelligent law for its extraction. The Mineral Leasing Act of 1920 allowed oil companies access to petroleum reserves on the public domain, national forests, and wildlife refuges by a leasing system. The leases were awarded through a competitive bidding process, and the government would receive a royalty on all oil extracted. (By folding coal lands into this same law, Congress also rationalized the extraction of this resource; natural gas, phosphate, and sodium were also covered in the legislation.) Later, the states in which the extraction took place would get a cut of the royalties.

Still off limits, however, were the petroleum reserves that had been withdrawn for the exclusive use of the navy. President Taft had established reserves for defense purposes in the Elk Hills and Buena Vista Hills of California. Similar reserves at the Teapot Dome formation in Wyoming and on the North Slope of Alaska were later added, all of which were closely guarded by Secretary of the Navy Josephus Daniels. His successor, Edwin Denby, was more lax. In 1920, Denby secretly agreed to transfer responsibilities for the naval reserves over to Interior Secretary Albert B. Fall, who had requested them. Just as secretly, President Warren G. Harding approved the transfer in 1921. Trouble began shortly thereafter, for Fall, a Kentucky gentleman transplanted to New Mexico, had plans for these

119

reserves. In April 1922 he leased all of the Teapot Dome reserve to Harry F. Sinclair of Sinclair Oil, without the inconvenience of competitive bidding. A little over two weeks later, Fall turned over the Elk Hills Reserve to Edward L. Doheny of the Pan American Petroleum and Transport Company—also without the benefit of competitive bids. As well, he waived Doheny's royalty payment to the government, allowing Doheny to build storage tanks and other facilities for the navy at Pearl Harbor and San Pedro instead.

Fall's agreements with Sinclair and Doheny were never meant to become public knowledge, but word of them leaked out within weeks. An aroused resident of Wyoming wrote to Senator John B. Kendrick about the rumor concerning Teapot Dome. Kendrick in turn asked for an explanation from Secretary Fall. Finding no satisfaction there, Kendrick called for a Senate inquiry. Fall stonewalled the investigators, saying that the reserves had been transferred to his department for reasons of national security. He also explained to Senate questioners that he had used his discretionary powers to convey the privileged leases so that the country might have some of its oil reserves developed as quickly as possible.

The investigation could not proceed beyond that point; there was no evidence of wrongdoing, although Senator Thomas J. Walsh of Montana, who chaired the committee inquiry, remained suspicious of Fall's motives. In 1923, for reasons that Fall claimed had nothing to do with the stalled investigation, the Secretary resigned. He joined Sinclair's company as a negotiator for an oil-drilling contract on Russia's Sakhalin Island, taking himself to the ends of the earth to dodge Walsh's suspicions. The press sympathized with Fall, who had heroically weathered several personal tragedies. Walsh was denounced for hounding an innocent man as ruthlessly as Javert had pursued Jean Valjean in Victor Hugo's *Les Miserables*. Even Doheny's admission during the Senate inquiry that he expected to make $100 million from his preferential lease with Fall did not seem to offend the press.

So things might have remained, had it not been for the discovery of a sudden rise in Fall's buying power. He had never been rich. He had, in fact, pronounced himself "dead broke" in 1920. But in 1921 he paid ten years of back taxes on his Three Rivers Ranch in New

Mexico, and bought land adjacent to his ranch for $91,500. Home from Russia, Fall declined to testify before the Senate committee about the source of his extra income, on the grounds that he was ill. Finally he admitted that he had borrowed $100,000 from *Washington Post* owner Edward B. McLean. McLean admitted that Fall had asked him for such a loan and that he had gladly given it, but that Fall had later returned his check uncashed, saying that he had gotten the money he needed from someone else. Fall was back on the front pages, which prompted Edward Doheny to come forward and tell how he had lent Fall $100,000 in an unsecured loan ("a personal loan to a lifelong friend," Doheny called it), this at about the same time Fall handed Doheny the Elk Hills oil reserve. Doheny insisted he saw nothing peculiar in this. In the meantime, it seemed that Fall had also accepted at least $172,000 from Sinclair in exchange for the oil in the Teapot Dome reserve. Sinclair refused to answer questions from Senate investigators and was cited and later indicted for contempt. Doheny, angered by months of questioning at the hands of perfidious Democratic congressmen (during a Republican administration at that), finally turned on them all and provided the names of all those legislators who had been willing to sell him their votes. By the time Doheny was through, his account of influence-peddling implicated many of America's finest in Congress, on both sides of the aisle. Harding died of food poisoning in office before these scandals were exposed, but his administration went down in history as the nation's most corrupt. In October 1929, more than eight years after Fall's leasing arrangement had been made, he was convicted of accepting bribes and sentenced to jail. Fall earned the ignominious distinction of being the first and (until the Watergate debacle) only Cabinet member to go to prison.

Even before Fall's imprisonment, federal courts rescinded the Doheny and Sinclair leases and returned Teapot Dome and Elk Hills to the navy. Shortly after taking office in 1929, President Herbert Hoover announced that henceforth no federal oil lands would be leased unless Congress expressly requested it. The ban remained in force until 1932, by which time vast deposits of oil had been struck in east Texas and Oklahoma—all of it on private property. For the moment, the pressure to exploit the public reserves had cooled.

CLOSING THE DOOR

Hoover's swift move to bar the oil reserves from exploitation was not an indication of his administration's deep regard for the public domain. What the Hoover administration, particularly Interior Secretary Lyman Wilbur, wanted to do, in fact, was get rid of it altogether. It was time, Wilbur told those attending the annual conference of governors in 1929, for the states to start taking care of their own internal affairs—including the public lands within their borders. He proposed to turn these lands over to the states.

Not all the lands, however; not the national parks or the national forests. And the federal government would retain rights to all subsurface minerals. The states looked askance at this gift and decided they did not want it. "The West doesn't care much about getting the lid without the bucket," observed an editorial in the *Billings* (Montana) *Gazette*. Governor George H. Dern of Utah agreed. "The states already own," he said, "in their school land grants, millions of acres of this same kind of land, which they can neither sell nor lease, and which is yielding no income. Why should they want more of this precious heritage of desert?"

Wilbur's plan died.

What may have been lurking in the back of Governor Dern's mind was the simple fact that his state and the rest of the Western states were not eager to assume responsibility for what was clearly a disaster in the making. Ever since the cattle boom of the prewar and war years, followed by the lush times of the 1920s, the Western range had been crowded with more and more animals, just as in the years preceding the "Big Die-Up" of 1886–87. Unlike grazing in the national forests, which was regulated to some degree (too much so, according to Western ranchers), that on the public domain remained almost entirely unregulated; the land was open to anyone who cared to put an animal there. It was brutally overgrazed, and by the early years of the Depression, wind erosion combined with drought to produce dust storms the size of half a state, blackening the skies from New Mexico to the Dakotas, sucking detritus into the upper atmosphere, where it drifted to bring twilight at noon to cities as far east as New York.

This was too much, even for a Western congressman. Even for

Representative Edward I. Taylor of Colorado, heretofore a vigorous foe of federal ownership of Western land. Shortly after President Franklin D. Roosevelt took office in 1933, Taylor introduced legislation designed to establish strict regulation of grazing on the public domain—the federal domain. As he later explained,

> I fought for the conservation of the public domain under federal leadership because the citizens were unable to cope with the situation under existing trends and circumstances. The job was too big and interwoven for even the states to handle with satisfactory coordination. On the Western Slope of Colorado and in nearby states I saw waste, competition, overuse, and abuse of valuable range lands and watersheds eating into the very heart of the Western economy. Farmers and ranchers everywhere in the range country were suffering. The basic economy of entire communities was threatened. There was terrific strife and bloodshed between the cattle and sheep men over the use of the range. Valuable irrigation projects stood in danger of ultimate deterioration. Erosion, yes, even human erosion, had taken root. The livestock industry, through circumstances beyond its control, was headed for self-strangulation.

The Taylor Grazing Act became law on June 28, 1934. Although it postdated the creation of the national forest system by almost fifty years, the act was billed as "the Magna Carta of conservation," for its conscientiousness and for its immediate scope. More than 80 million acres, later increased to 142 million, were closed to entry under any of the land laws, and New Deal economist Rexford Tugwell declared that "the day on which the President signed the Taylor Act, which virtually closed the public domain to further settlement, laid in its grave a land policy which had long since been dead and which walked abroad only as a troublesome ghost within the living world." Tugwell's glib analysis was a little premature.

THE STOCKMEN TAKE CARE OF THEIR OWN

The Taylor Act created grazing districts, within which qualified (which is to say well-established and influential) local ranchers would be issued grazing permits every year for an allotted number of animals.

123

The Interior Secretary was authorized to set grazing fees, of which 25 percent was earmarked for range management and improvement. The act also established a Division of Grazing (later the Grazing Service), which would coordinate the program. Interior Secretary Harold L. Ickes selected Farrington R. Carpenter, a Colorado lawyer and rancher, to head the new agency. The Taylor Act was offered as a prime example of democracy in action, because it established "advisory committees" made up of local stockmen to cooperate with district managers. This, however, was the act's chief weakness, for the power these committees exercised was nearly absolute. District managers rarely went out of their way to antagonize men who were, after all, their neighbors, and even Service Director Carpenter sided so often with those he was supposed to be regulating that Interior Secretary Ickes reprimanded him on numerous occasions. Ickes was also upset with Carpenter's staffing—nine people had been hired to supervise the 80 million acres initially covered by the Taylor Grazing Act. "You have not developed sufficient personnel even to protect the government's interest, let alone develop adequate range conservation programs," Ickes scolded.

Even with all their power, stockmen were still unsatisfied. Possibly nothing angered them more than the fact that grazing fees had been instituted for something they had always taken at will. The first grazing fee set in 1936 was five cents per cow per month, a fraction of what private grazing lands cost to lease, but still, it rankled. Patrick A. McCarran of Nevada, who first won his Senate seat in 1934, heard his constituents' complaints and became an effective spokesman for their small cause. Senator McCarran, according to the historian E. Louise Peffer, "initiated what was to become the lengthiest, most concerted, and in some respects, the most successful attempt made in the twentieth century by one person to force a reinterpretation of land policy more in accordance with the wishes of the using interests." McCarran had been lukewarm toward the Taylor Grazing Act, and although he rose on several occasions to speak on public land issues, his comments did not attract much attention until 1940, after he became a member of the Senate Committee on Public Lands and Surveys. McCarran introduced his sentiments by reading Resolution 241, a nine-point program lambasting public land administration that closed with a demand for a Senate investigation into the Service's operations. "I do not propose to legislate the trailblazers of the West out of existence," McCarran said, referring to the cattlemen and sheepmen who had suddenly found themselves under the heel, timidly placed to be sure, of the federal government.

McCarran took issue with Secretary Ickes's stated intention of retaining all grazing lands; with the Grazing Service's attempt at range conservation; with federal interference with water rights; and with attempts to raise the pathetically low grazing fees. Despite the repeated requests of Grazing Service Director Clarence L. Forsling, formerly of the Forest Service, the five-cents-per-animal fee could not be budged for ten years. Forsling argued unsuccessfully that the raise was needed to pay for the cost of administering the range and improving it. Moreover, the federal range was in better condition than privately owned lands, and was therefore worth more.

The fee controversy broke wide open in 1946, when a House subcommittee chaired by Representative Jed Johnson of Oklahoma declared that the Interior Department had been too easy on the stockmen. To force the Grazing Service to get its "untidy, mismanaged house in order," Johnson and others recommended that congressional appropriations be slashed further so that the Interior Department would have no alternative but to make up the difference among the rancher permittees. The Grazing Service, continued Johnson, had practically turned over the Taylor Grazing Act lands to "the big cowman and the big sheepman of the West. Why, they even put them on the payroll . . . and it's common knowledge that they [stockmen] have been running the Grazing Service. They did not choose to assess grazing fees that were anywhere comparable to the fees other people pay. . . . They have made a joke out of the Grazing Service." Appropriations for the Service's budget in the following year were slashed from an already meager $1.7 million to about $500,000.

The stated purpose of the budget cuts was to force an increase in the grazing fees, but McCarran was able to keep them down—and he would have been justified in considering the whole affair a clear victory for the interests he represented.

There was another victory that year. Taking advantage of an executive reorganization bill introduced by the Truman administration,

McCarran and his allies in the Senate simply obliterated the Grazing Service by combining it with the old General Land Office to produce a brand-new agency—the Bureau of Land Management, which assumed the administration of all public lands. McCarran hoped that, under this new setup, grazing regulation, made just one part of the new agency's many responsibilities, would be lost in the shuffle of paperwork awaiting a harried and understaffed administration. Generally speaking, he was correct. With its wings pinned and its budget trimmed at the outset, the BLM would be in no position to extract itself from the powerful grip of the stockmen. It was little more than a "modern administrative structure for handling the Nation's public land," blandly observed the agency's first director, Fred W. Johnson. And, blandly, the structure administered.

The stockmen, feeling as though they were back in the saddle again, had called a meeting during that summer of 1946 in Salt Lake City to discuss other ways they might rid the West of the federal intruder. The meeting, with more than 150 in attendance, was notable in that it was composed of two groups that had actively hated each other for years, the cattlemen and the sheepmen, and representatives of the American National Livestock Association and the National Wool Growers Association. McCarran addressed the meeting briefly before the conferees turned their attention to a shared objective: the acquisition of all 142 million acres of Taylor Act lands, as well as the national forests (see chapter 2), national parks, and the rights to all minerals buried beneath this vast surface. The ranchers set their own prices for the public domain, starting at about nine cents an acre and going up to less than three dollars an acre. They also voted to limit the number of rightful owners of all this land to those in the room, and a few like-minded friends.

This grotesque proposal, unanimously approved by the convention, was translated into legislation by Senator Allan Robertson of Wyoming. Although its ultimate goal was the same as that of the stockmen, the Robertson bill was slightly more devious; it called for a massive transfer of all the lands to the thirteen Western states, to let the states decide the best course of action. There was little question about what that course of action would be. But historian and social commentator Bernard DeVoto had gotten wind of the bill and of the stockmen's meeting in Salt Lake City, and exposed it in the January 1947 issue of *Harper's*. DeVoto, a native of Utah, was furious. He wrote:

> So, at the very moment when the West is blueprinting an economy which must be based on the sustained, permanent use of its natural resources, it is also conducting an assault on those resources with the simple objective of liquidating them. The dissociation of intelligence could go no farther, but there it is—and there is the West yesterday, today and forever. It is the Western mind stripped to the basic split. The West as its own worst enemy. The West committing suicide.

The public outcry raised by DeVoto quashed the takeover plan, and the stockmen retreated. For the moment, the Robertson bill was dead, and so was the movement.

A CAPTIVE OF HISTORY

Today the Bureau of Land Management, "an unconvincing Goliath," in the words of law professor Sally Fairfax, remains a captive of its own history. So far it has almost no tradition of its own to pass on. The agency had no high-minded iconoclast in the mold of the Forest Service's Gifford Pinchot, no devoted idealist like the Park Service's Stephen Mather. Nor was the BLM spawned from the indefatigable legions that pressed for wilderness preservation and for the Alaska national interest lands. No President has come forward to champion the BLM's cause, as did President Theodore Roosevelt on behalf of wildlife refuges. Its directors have for the most part reveled in their low profiles, and often have been indistinguishable from those they supposedly regulate—a vestige of the McCarran era.

Livestock leaders rushed in to fill the vacuum created when the BLM was established. They started by insisting that the agency's director meet with their approval, but not all BLM directors were made in the permittees' own image. When Interior Secretary Julius Krug appointed Marion Clawson to the top position in 1948, the stockmen accepted the appointment because Clawson, a Nevadan, formerly of the abolished Bureau of Agricultural Economics, seemed to share their interests. "It was difficult to attract a first-rate, top-

flight man to the job," recalled Clawson years later. "BLM was drift-
ing. So, somewhat in desperation, Krug offered me the job." Clawson
understood that the stockmen wielded power beyond their number,
but did not allow this to keep him from implementing new procedures.
Shortly after he became BLM's chief, Clawson wrote a booklet called
"Rebuilding the Federal Range," which was an affront to the stockmen. It included photographs, for comparative purposes, of overgrazed land and correctly grazed land, and sought significant reductions
in the number of animals permitted. Possibly the severest offense
against the stockmen was that the pamphlet used the word "privilege"
rather than "right" in describing the permittees' connection to the
federal range.

Nevertheless, Clawson, who served until 1963 and wrote many
valuable texts on the subject of federal land management, had inherited what has been called a "monopolitical structure." As palliative
as the Taylor Grazing Act was, it had established grazing as the
dominant use on much of the public domain. Adherence to the act
in its most basic form granted cattlemen and sheepmen an exclusive
interest in the land. Their use was framed as the highest, best, and—
in places—*only* use of rangeland. The only intervention tolerated
was by mineral and oil exploration outfits, since this did not seem
incompatible with grazing. As a result the federal range under Clawson and others was so closely identified with these two sectors that
cynics maintained the initials "BLM" stood for Bureau of Livestock
and Mining. The livestock interests had simply grown too proprietary
of the public land, and it was their best interests the BLM was
determined to serve.

"GRAB!—GRAB!—GRAB!"

While stockmen consolidated their effective control of a harassed and
understaffed BLM, Congress made one more major push to rationalize
the nation's perception and use of its public domain. In 1964 it passed
two basic pieces of public land legislation that pointed the way: the
Classification and Multiple Use Act and the Public Land Law Review
Commission Act.

The Classification and Multiple Use Act instructed the BLM to
classify the public lands according to those that were suitable for

disposal and those that were suitable for retention and management by the federal government under the principles of multiple use and sustained yield. By 1969 the BLM had obediently classified some 180 million acres, and recommended that of these almost 150 million be retained and managed; another six parcels, amounting to 146,694 acres, were recommended for inclusion in the new National Wilderness Preservation System (see chapter 5); less than 5 million acres were recommended for disposal. The response throughout much of the West was predictable outrage—in some cases, near derangement. "Grab!—Grab!—Grab!" rancher-lawyer Clel Georgetta wailed in *Golden Fleece in Nevada.* "Nine million acres here, ten million acres there, and twenty million acres somewhere else will soon withdraw all the public domain from the possibility of ever becoming privately owned. Thus the Bureau of Land Management is spreading its permanent control over the face of the earth in true bureaucratic, self-perpetuation style."

The Public Land Law Review Commission (PLLRC) was established by its act to study "all existing statutes and regulations governing the retention, management and disposition of public lands," to "review policies and practices of federal agencies administering these laws," and to "determine present and future demands on public lands." Colorado Representative Wayne Aspinall, a strong advocate of disposal and development, was appointed chairman of the committee, which included six senators, six congressmen, six presidential appointees, and a pool of twenty-five advisers. Aspinall ruled the committee, and those who testified before the PLLRC found it nearly impossible to sway the deliberations away from discussions of the need for intense development and consideration of economic returns only. Aspinall was too shrewd to campaign hard for the decidedly unpopular quest for large land transfers to the states, but he made much of dominant use over multiple use, and often ignored recreational or wildlife considerations.

The commission's report, entitled *One Third of a Nation's Land,* was published in 1970, and listed 137 recommendations for improved federal management. It managed to satisfy almost no one. The report left both developers and conservationists feeling shortchanged and grumbling that the other side had made out better than they had.

Nevertheless, the PLLRC's report set forth one tenet that could not be ignored. Despite recommendations for small land sales to continue, the commissioners stated that "we urge reversal of the policy that the United States should dispose of the so-called unappropriated public domain lands." It was the first, clear, official, and straightforward recommendation for retention of the public domain that had ever been made. At its weakest the recommendation merely restated what all rational observers already accepted. At its strongest, it definitively charted a new course for the BLM and for the nation.

AN ORGANIC SOLUTION

It was now established as public policy that the nation was going to retain and manage the great bulk of the public domain. But how manage—under what rules and regulations, with how much power? There were plenty of rules and regulations already, of course—principally those three thousand and more land laws that had accumulated over the course of the past two centuries. These were, as they always had been, a ghastly tangle of confusion. As for power, the BLM had precious little of it. Its authority was diffuse and confused, and for actual enforcement of federal law it was all but helpless. For example, if a BLM field man caught someone stealing a forbidden cactus or vandalizing a prehistoric petroglyph—both violations of federal law— his only recourse would be to hurry to the nearest town and contact the county sheriff and ask him to come out and arrest the culprit. Who would, of course, not be there.

The agency itself needed firm direction in a number of matters. Such as grazing. Although the condition of the range had improved markedly with passage of the Taylor Act, BLM researchers reported in 1975 that only 17 percent of the federal range was in good condition, 50 percent in fair condition, and the remaining 33 percent in poor condition. Despite its belated efforts and good intentions, the agency had not been aggressive enough in pursuing grazing cutbacks. Nor did it show much inclination to achieve them; to fulfill its responsibilities under the National Environmental Policy Act of 1970, BLM officials had decided to apply the broad brush to range considerations by lumping nearly 178 million acres of heterogeneous landscape into a single environmental impact statement on the effects of livestock grazing. In 1974 the Natural Resources Defense Council brought a suit to force the BLM to write individual impact statements for site-specific allotments, covering the impact of grazing on all resources—including wildlife and recreation. The NRDC won its point, and BLM officials agreed that 144 separate impact statements, reduced from 212, would be written by 1988.

For these and a number of other reasons, some of them outlined in *One Third of a Nation's Land*, it became increasingly clear to all concerned that the BLM needed its own organic act to facilitate the administration of its awesome responsibility of land—greater than that of any federal land-managing agency. "Despite the enormous responsibilities of the BLM," Interior Secretary Rogers C. B. Morton complained, "the definition of its mission and the authority to accomplish it have never been comprehensively enunciated by Congress." In 1976, Congress finally paid heed by passing the Federal Land Policy and Management Act (FLPMA), which placed the BLM on equal footing (on the face of it, at least) with the National Park Service and the Forest Service.

Among other things, the act repealed all public land laws (except the everlasting General Mining Law of 1872), and in its opening paragraph stated that the public lands were to be retained for the long-term use of the American people unless "it is determined that disposal of a particular parcel will serve the national interest." The lands were henceforth to be identified as the National Resource Lands, and the BLM was directed to pursue multiple-use, sustained-yield goals, with land-use planning as the cornerstone for management. The act also stipulated that the "United States receive fair market value of the use of the public lands and their resources," and that "areas of critical environmental concern" be designated to protect historic, cultural, and natural values. Although the BLM was allowed to retain its decentralized structure—a throwback to both the Taylor Act's advisory committees and the GLO's local land offices—appointment of the BLM's director was no longer left to the Interior Secretary. Instead, the director would be a presidential appointee subject to Senate approval. Finally, the FLPMA directed the BLM to study its lands for their wilderness qualities and to determine which of them ought to be included in the National Wilderness Preservation

System. The agency was given fifteen years to complete the task. (These wilderness study areas eventually included some 25 million acres.)

The Bureau of Land Management had finally been joined to the upper ranks of the administrative bureaucracy. It had no sooner achieved this exalted status, however, than a movement began to develop among its own constituency that would have obliterated it, given a choice.

THE SAGEBRUSH REBELS

On June 4, 1979, the Nevada legislature passed a resolution proclaiming that "all public lands in Nevada and all minerals not previously appropriated are the property of the State of Nevada." This empty declaration was the symptom of one more Western revolt against the federal presence on federal land—or at least the federal presence on federal land in the West. The people who espoused the state ownership of federal lands called themselves the Sagebrush Rebels and mounted a campaign that seemed too vigorous to be merely symbolic. The rebels were well-financed and spread their message to the other public-land states. Legislature after legislature passed resolutions similar to Nevada's, and where a sagebrush resolution was defeated it did not go down without a struggle. Even Ronald Reagan, a presidential contender in 1980, got mileage out of the Westerners' cause. "Count me in as a rebel," he shouted to a Utah crowd, while campaigning. Reagan won votes and the rebellion glowed brightly in the national limelight. It was the Hoover plan of the 1930s and the DeVoto-denounced land grab of the 1940s repackaged and delivered to the 1980s. But to those who did not know better, the Sagebrush Rebellion's goal of ridding itself of federal land administration seemed like a good idea. Shortly after his election in 1980, Reagan, for example, admitted to being puzzled about why so much public land was in the West anyway, and promised to appoint a commission to look into the matter. Before the election he had promised to work for a "sagebrush solution," which meant that he wanted "the states to have an equitable share of public lands and their natural resources."

Once elected, however, President Reagan did not hand over the

132

West to those who demanded it. At least not literally. Instead, he opted for "privatization," or the sale of so-called surplus federal land. A 1982 executive order established the Property Review Board to identify properties that ought to be sold. Four million acres of BLM lands and about 6 million acres of national forests were targeted for sale, until the program encountered opposition among even the strongest administration allies. Nevertheless, Reagan had placated the Sagebrush Rebels by appointing Wyoming-born James Watt Secretary of the Interior. Watt was a Sagebrusher in steward's clothing, and made no secret of his distaste for federal conservation programs. As an attorney for the Denver-based Mountain States Legal Foundation before being named Interior Secretary, Watt had opposed Interior Department rulings on stricter strip-mining controls and had sued to speed up applications for oil and mineral exploration in wilderness areas. Just as environmentalists turned to litigation, so did Watt, declaring that he would "fight in the courts those bureaucrats and no-growth advocates who create a challenge to individual liberty and economic freedoms." As head of the department he had fought, he often seemed vaguely regretful that he could not simply turn over the public domain to the few states in the West, and assuaged his brothers with a promise that his department would be a "good neighbor."

The energy crisis gave him the perfect opportunity to step up private development of public resources. Indeed, since the Arab oil embargo in 1973, every President including Carter had made U.S. energy self-sufficiency a top priority. But whereas the Carter administration had pursued energy conservation measures and the development of alternative renewable energy sources, the Reagan administration concentrated on exploiting public reserves as quickly as possible. "Because of the actions taken by extremists to stop the orderly development of energy resources," Secretary Watt said, "the nation is likely to suffer energy shortages and thus severe economic hardship." He played upon the natural divisiveness between East and West by telling Westerners that if they listened too long to "environmental extremists," Easterners would gouge the West to extract the oil, gas, and coal needed to "light and heat the East and to maintain jobs in the Midwest and on the East Coast."

133

Watt's eagerness to exploit the energy resources in the BLM's domain got him into trouble almost immediately. In April 1982, in what was called by his office the "largest coal lease sale in history," the BLM awarded bids for a little over 1.1 billion tons of coal in the Powder River Basin of Montana and Wyoming. The bids brought in $43.5 million. Five additional lease sales were planned immediately. Before they could get under way, the General Accounting Office issued a report that the Powder River leases had been sold for $100 million less than fair market value. The House soon passed a resolution ordering a six-month moratorium on any further lease sales, and while the Senate would not concur, it did require Watt to set up an independent commission to study the integrity of such sales. In the meantime, another huge coal lease sale was allowed in the Fort Union District of North Dakota and Montana. When it was soon revealed that this sale, too, went for prices far below what the coal should have brought in, the House Interior Committee asked a federal court to invalidate the sale; the court accommodated the wish of the committee. The Senate changed its mind about a moratorium and, by an overwhelming bipartisan vote, joined with the House to declare one.

Secretary Watt was more successful in other aspects of his program. By the procedure of bypassing local BLM offices altogether, he managed to concentrate most decision-making in Washington, where he could keep an eye on things. "The power is concentrated in the Secretary's office," one BLM field man complained, and he was not alone. Between 1981 and 1983, Watt altered agency regulations for everything from geothermal leasing to wilderness management. In situations where public participation had been authorized, he eliminated it or reduced it so that it could not be meaningful. "Through budget cuts, Watt reinforced a historically strong preference in the Bureau for commodity programs like minerals extraction," wrote James Baker in the Winter 1983 issue of *Wilderness* magazine. A Sierra Club analysis of the BLM budget revealed "almost universal cuts between 1981 and 1984 in noncommodity programs: wildlife habitat, down 48 percent; wilderness, 41.8 percent; soil, air, and water management, 47.5 percent; land use planning, 25 percent." Yet the budget for mandatory archaeological inventories prior to clearances for mineral exploration soared to 426 percent in one year. In 1981 the Interior Department also fired two highly respected state directors and packed key advisory boards with those seeking rapid development of resources. To show its determination to get mineral exploration under way, the BLM, in keeping with Secretary Watt's goals, reduced the backlog of lease applications from about 13,000 to fewer than 1,000 in less than a year. While such bureaucratic efficiency is often laudable, in this case it revealed devotion to one end rather than to the many mandated by law and led to damaging ecological impacts because of poor regulation.

Watt's distaste for the BLM's wilderness study responsibilities was especially pronounced. Not only were wilderness supervision and study reduced, the acres under consideration were also cut back. In 1982 Watt excluded 1.4 million acres of wilderness study areas from further consideration, and opened these to exploration and development. The Secretary claimed he had exercised his discretionary power in doing so, but in 1983 the Sierra Club filed suit to have the lands restored to study status and interim protection, and in April 1985 a federal district judge ruled that "in large measure" Watt "failed to follow the law" when he allowed the lands to be opened to development. (By the summer of 1985, the BLM had restored the so-called "Watt drops" and had begun to include them in the wilderness study process.)

After Watt's departure in October 1983, Interior officials persisted in their lack of appreciation for wilderness values. Neither William P. Clarke nor Donald Hodel, each of whom served as Interior Secretary in the Reagan administration, demonstrated any measurable commitment to wilderness values. Clarke, who once referred to the BLM domain as "the land no one wanted," professed to be "surprised . . . that we have been able to find, frankly, 24 million acres of this stepchild acreage that we can even study [for wilderness designation]." Manuel P. Lujan, who became Secretary of the Interior in the Bush administration, was no more enlightened on the subject than his three predecessors, but in spite of opposition from the Interior Department itself, the movement for the preservation of these lands picked up speed all through the decade, until by 1990 it could point to one major victory in Arizona, one coming near to fruition in California, and coherent wilderness proposals well established by conservationists in Utah, Oregon, and New Mexico. (For more on BLM wilderness developments, see chapter 5.)

The Sagebrush Rebels did not get the public domain placed in the hands of the western states, as they had wanted, nor did the privatization movement work out to any significant degree. By the middle of the 1980s the "Sagebrush Rebellion" had all but vanished as a movement —but the resentment against federal control that had driven it remained undiminished. Within a few years that resentment surfaced once again, healthier than ever. This time it was called the "Wise Use" Movement, an agglomeration of ranchers, miners, loggers, real estate entrepreneurs, and other development-minded folk who traveled under a number of individual banners—People for the West!, Center for the Defense of Free Enterprise, Multiple Use Land Alliance, National Wetlands Coalition, the Blue Ribbon Coalition, some 250 more, each and every one of which insisted that it was a genuine "grassroots" organization. Whatever their names, the groups and the individuals who comprised them shared a generally conservative ideology and a generalized contempt for environmentalists perhaps best expressed by Ron Arnold, co-director of the Center for the Defense of Free Enterprise. "Environmentalism," he said, "is the new paganism. It worships trees and sacrifices people." Environmentalists countered by challenging the legitimacy of the movement's claim to be a "grassroots" phenomenon, pointing out that most of its organizations were largely financed and controlled by mining, livestock, and other commodity interests. The largest group, People for the West!, for instance, listed most of the major mining companies in the West among its financial supporters, including Norco Minerals of Spokane, Washington, which in 1991 contributed $100,000 to this grassroots cause, while executives of the Canadian-owned Homestake Mining Company were among the organizers of various anti-environmental demonstrations around the West that year.

The Wise Use Movement could be found expressing itself on every issue from private-property disputes in New England to wetlands regulation in Florida, and most of the organizations it embraced were happy to endorse *The Wise Use Agenda*, a 1988 publication prepared by the Center for the Defense of Free Enterprise. The twenty-five goals set forth in this document included the removal of all restrictions on the development of private property; the opening of all national parks, national wildlife refuges, wilderness areas, and all other protected areas

136

to mining and oil and gas drilling; the encouragement of off-road vehicle use in virtually every area of the public lands where it was prohibited; the clearcutting and replanting of all ancient forests in the Pacific Northwest (thereby rendering them no longer ancient); and amending the Endangered Species Act to exclude "non-adaptive species such as the California condor and endemic species lacking the vigor to spread in range." Nevertheless, the movement reserved its greatest energy for two issues dominant in the BLM lands of the West, fighting reform of the General Mining Law of 1872 and resisting higher fees for public-land grazing permits and far more stringent regulation of grazing practices on those lands. Both issues, of course, were high on the agendas of most conservation organizations in the country, including such regional groups as the Southern Utah Wilderness Alliance of Salt Lake City and Moab, Utah, which wore the "grassroots" mantle with perhaps a little more authority than, say, the Center for the Defense of Free Enterprise.

The General Mining Law of 1872 was one of the oldest federal public-land laws on the books of the nation, one devised to satisfy the interests and perceived needs of the boom-and-bust frontier West whose idea of long-term thinking rarely got past the next big strike or dividend payment—a law, conservationists said, that continued to give away the public's land at preposterous prices and ensured environmental degradation that would cost generations to come billions of dollars to clean up. The indictment against the law was perhaps one of the most fully-documented of any environmental controversy of modern times. Everywhere, critics could point to examples where the law had enabled real estate and resort developers to file claims and obtain a "patent," or ownership, of federal land with no intention of ever mining it. There was, for instance, the man who paid the government $170 for a "mining patent" outside Phoenix, Arizona, where he promptly erected a golf resort valued at $60 million. Then there was the matter of royalties. There were none. There never had been any because the law did not call for any. Studies undertaken by the Mineral Policy Center and economists in The Wilderness Society's Resource Planning and Economics Department suggested the cost of this oversight to the taxpayers over the years. Between 1873 and 1988 (the last year for which complete figures were available), the study found, more than 289 million ounces of gold, more than 5 billion ounces of silver, and more than

137

82 million tons of copper ore had been taken out of western mines. The total value for these extractions, adjusted for inflation, was a shade over $363 billion, and if the government had imposed a royalty of 12.5 percent—as it did on coal, oil, and gas taken from public lands under the stipulations of the Mineral Leasing Act of 1920—the taxpayers could have collected more than $45 billion.

Finally, there was the matter of poisons—and in this regard, not even Wilderness Society economists could have come up with a figure that would accurately reflect what it would likely cost our own and future generations to clean up the ghastly mess left behind by more than a century of chemically dependent mining operations. The General Mining Law required no reclamation on the part of operators, and by the end of the 1980s many now-abandoned mining sites had fallen under the jurisdiction of the Environmental Protection Agency's Superfund program for reclamation. There was, for example, the Clark Fork River in Montana, where some 19 billion cubic yards of contaminated sediments were likely to cost as much as $1.5 billion to eliminate, or the Iron Mountain site of northern California, which could run to $1.4 billion for rehabilitation. The poisons continued to seep into soils, water tables, and rivers from thousands of abandoned sites all over the West, many of them not yet found, much less scheduled for any kind of clean-up. In the meantime, modern mining added its own burden of poison, particularly from gold mining, which had enjoyed several boom years in a row in the 1980s and early 1990s. The use of cyanide in the refining process continued to jeopardize wildlife and human health alike in scores of areas, and while some mining companies made a genuine attempt to contain their wastes, many did no more than what very inadequate existing regulations required them to do.

The only possible solution, it seemed clear, was to reform the law to remove the patenting clause (thus keeping the land itself in public ownership), institute royalties at least comparable to those stipulated by the Mineral Leasing Act of 1920, and impose severe restrictions on where mining would be allowed and even more rigorous requirements for reclamation once mining was done. Led by the Mineral Policy Center and the National Wildlife Federation, but fully supported by virtually the entire conservation community, similar bills to that effect had been introduced in both houses of Congress by the end of 1993. The legislation did not go unopposed by the Wise Use Movement, which launched a nationwide counterattack, claiming that reform would stifle industry and obliterate the entrepreneurial spirit of the West. The mining industry and its supporters began an attempt to so weaken the legislation as to render it toothless, while conservationists fought to retain its basic strengths. It was apparent as the second session of the 103nd Congress got under way in January 1994 that while some kind of mining reform might get passed before the Congress adjourned, it was not likely that it would satisfy either party to the question—even if the General Mining Law itself was given an official burial.

Even less could be said for the question of grazing reform, the other big management issue of primary environmental concern on BLM land. "Cattlemen and sheepmen," the old curmudgeon of conservation, Bernard DeVoto, had written in 1947, "want to shovel most of the West into its rivers." It would have been irresponsible to make so dramatic a charge by the 1990s, but the fact remained that the grazing lands of the West remained in no better condition at the end of the 1980s than they had been in the middle of the 1970s. A 1989 analysis published by the Natural Resources Defense Council and the National Wildlife Federation demonstrated that more than 100 million acres of public grazing land were in what ecologists would describe as an "unsatisfactory" condition, and the BLM itself reported in 1991 that only 36 percent of its grazing land was in "good" to "excellent" condition. Degradation could be found on all types of land, but of particular concern were riparian areas, those fragile strips of soil and vegetation that line the banks of the creeks, streams, and rivers of the arid and semi-arid West and provide the single most important habitat for the preservation of biological diversity. Most of the original riparian areas already were gone or badly deteriorated; in Arizona, for example, the Fish and Game Department said in 1988 that less than 3 percent of the state's original riparian habitat remained undamaged, and a 1990 report from the Environmental Protection Agency declared that "extensive field observations in the late 1980s suggest riparian areas throughout much of the West are in the worst condition in history."

For the privilege of placing so much public land at so much risk, some 24,000 livestock operators were paying bargain-basement fees for their grazing permits. By the spring of 1994, the fee was $1.93 for one

139

cow for one month (Animal Unit Month, or AUM). On private land, the fee charged was about $10.20, a difference that led environmentalists and taxpayer groups to point out that the livestock industry, like the timber industry and the mining industry, was benefitting from a federal subsidy of no mean dimensions; a Wilderness Society estimate in 1993 calculated that the industry had paid as much as $400 million less over the previous four years for federal grazing privileges than it would have had to pay on private land. That, critics said, was just as much of a subsidy as below-cost timber sales or the giveaway of gold.

As they had with regard to the General Mining Law of 1872, conservationists turned to Congress for a remedy, with mixed results. Widely supported the conservation community, scientists, and economists, appropriations-bill Amendments that would have raised grazing fees to levels more comparable to those charged for private land were adopted in the House in 1990. They were then blocked in the Senate by the same coalition of western political and economic interests that had so long controlled the management policies of the BLM—handsomely supported by the sophisticated and highly effective anti-reform campaign of the Wise Use Movement. A free increase was included in the President's budget proposals for fiscal year 1994, but ultimately was sacrificed to political expediency and budgetary considerations. Interior Secretary Babbitt promised to raise the fees administratively and to develop and impose strict new regulations for grazing management, but after a series of boisterous and often disruptive public meetings on the question in the West and a number of conferences with western governors, the Secretary's stern reform language grew increasingly less stern and more accommodating to industry desires with the passage of time. The degree of his commitment became even more clouded in February 1994 when Babbitt vaguely cited the problem of "differing management styles" and accepted the resignation of Jim Baca, his own choice as head of the BLM. Baca was a tough-minded former commissioner of public lands in New Mexico and a longtime advocate of significant grazing reform, and conservationists now wondered if the administration's credibility on the question had not been badly damaged. When the Secretary later came up with administrative recommendations to create regional "advisory councils" whose dominance by livestock and commodity interests was likely to be just about as complete as the old district

140

boards of the previous decades, then followed that by scaling back proposed fee increases to $3.96 and watering down proposed standards and guidelines for range management, environmentalists prepared for a continuing fight on the issue.

AN AGENDA FOR THE NATIONAL RESOURCE LANDS

The 236 million acres administered by the Bureau of Land Management are unique among the various national public land systems. Not only do they constitute the largest single unit of those systems, they embody within them many of the same natural qualities that distinguish our national parks, national monuments, historic sites, cultural sites, wilderness areas, wildlife refuges, even the national forests, and contain important deposits of such extractive resources as coal, oil, gas, and other energy materials. That very diversity—and the user conflicts that derive from it—has confounded us in our attempts to manage these lands intelligently. That we have done so badly in the past the most generous narrative of our history could not deny, and even passage of the Federal Policy and Management Act of 1976 was no guarantee that the future would see revolutionary change, however necessary.

The story consistently has been one of a confusion of values, but time no longer gives us the latitude for mistakes of a dimension comparable to those of the past. We must free the lands of that legacy. It is time to put forth a major new effort to assure that the natural values of this last and largest portion of the original public domain are pro-tected and that its exploitable resources are managed in such a way as to assure a sustained and balanced use in perpetuity—as the FLPMA intended.

To achieve this goal, there are a number of things that could and should be done in the near term that in aggregate would have significant long-term effects. Except in Alaska (see chapter 7), the BLM has now completed the review process of its lands required by the FLPMA; it passed its recommendations on to President Bush and he, in turn, made his recommendations to Congress. As noted in chapter 5, the recommendations consistently fell short of the amount of land that truly qualifies for preservation as wilderness—in Utah alone, by more than three million acres. Either the BLM or Congress itself should go back to the drawing board immediately, reviewing those recommendations with an eye toward increasing them dramatically; these wilderness lands include some of the most varied and important ecological, archeological, historical, and scenic sites left in the United States and to sacrifice them to a miserly vision would be unconscionable. As well, Congress should move immediately to rescind or otherwise render harmless a nineteenth century federal statute regarding rights-of-way (RS2477) that anti-wilderness factions in some BLM states (and Alaska, as noted in chapter 7) have been citing to justify the use and improvement of ancient trails and travel corridors through current or proposed wilderness areas. If such nearly invisible tracks are allowed to be raised to the status of roads, they will invalidate hundreds of thousands—perhaps millions—of acres of potential wilderness and harm the natural integrity of existing designated wilderness.

In addition, we should raise the funding and staffing levels of the BLM to something approaching parity with those of the Forest Service (which, after all, manages only a little over half as much land). When a single BLM officer is required to monitor hundreds of thousands of acres of land at a time, as is the case in many states, or when an entire district is provided with only a handful of biologists or other scientists, as also is the case in most districts, we cannot expect that the lands themselves are going to be given the care that law and common sense require. We should overhaul the entire grazing system, which still operates with the antiquated utilitarian procedures put in place during the years of the Grazing Service and remains utterly dominated by the livestock industry. Strict environmental regulations must be imposed and grazing fees raised. Even before that, the BLM itself must be prohibited from practicing the great euphemism called "range conversion," which is merely another way of describing the process by which BLM range managers destroy such natural habitat as juniper-pinyon pine forests in order to plant crested wheatgrass and other exotics designed for the bovine palate. Finally, the power of those whom Bernard DeVoto called the "Two-Gun Desmonds" of the West must be severely reduced by eliminating the district grazing boards and replacing them with bodies that, unlike those being proposed by the Interior Department, would be allowed to function in an advisory capacity only and be composed of those who represent a truly wide spectrum of

142

the public interest.   Of particular importance in this regard would be the inclusion of environmentalists of proven dedication to the principles of stewardship and of scientists who can help shape a grazing policy that is driven more by the requirements of the land than by the transient desires of the livestock industry.

Similarly, even if Congress does manage to reform or even gut the General Mining Law of 1872, as seems at least possible, it is not likely that reform will go far enough toward satisfying environmental needs. Congress must be prepared to consider further reforms in the future; only grazing is more harmful to the land, and the mining industry must be prevented from inflicting even more damage than it already has managed to accomplish.

More such actions could be taken, but, however necessary, they would by no means be enough to initiate the kind of sweeping change required to meet the needs of the next century and beyond. This kind of change will demand a major break with the past. Planning, obviously, is the key here. But what kind of planning—and how organized? The FLPMA throws considerable weight behind the concept of planning, including resource inventory. Indeed, the act declares at the outset that "the national interest will be best realized if the public lands and their resources are periodically and systematically inventoried and their present and future use is projected through a land use planning process." Yet the planning system that has evolved lacks the necessary coherence and firm direction to do the job properly. Furthermore, this inadequate planning is being undertaken at the same time that much of the land already is being used for various and potentially damaging purposes or is at least open to such use—a condition that further complicates an already demanding task. Finally, for the most part the planning process has all but ignored the ecological and biological resources of the land, emphasizing instead those resources presumed to be most economically valuable to human enterprise.

All of which has a lot of history behind it—but in that regard, it might be instructive here to recall the work of John Wesley Powell. In his seminal 1878 *Report on the Lands of the Arid Region of the United States*, Powell argued that the traditional system of rectangular cadastral surveys was an arbitrary device that imposed purely political boundaries on the land of the West, with no attention paid to geographical realities.

143

He maintained instead that the lands should be surveyed according to land types: timberland, mineral land, irrigable land, and pasture land. All such land not already appropriated, he said, should be closed to settlement or development until such surveys had been completed, boundaries carefully drawn, and the units classified as to type. They should then be opened only according to strict rules laid down to guide the proper use of each land type.

The political realities of his time defeated Powell and Congress largely ignored his recommendations. Should we attempt anything so ambitious now, the political realities of our own time almost certainly would defeat us, too, but after more than a century of the kind of waste and misuse that his ideas might have prevented, it is perhaps possible for us to revive at least some of his concepts and do with them what we can to institute a modern program designed to revolutionize the future utilization of the BLM lands. The passage of the FLPMA was itself a good step in this direction. Clearly, it was only the first step and in itself not sufficient to ensure the creation and performance of a long-range program. Congress should move to engineer new legislation—perhaps as a major amendment to the FLPMA—that will mandate that the intentions expressed in the FLPMA are indeed carried out. Such legislation should address itself to two major goals. First, inventory. Utilizing the authorization already established by the FLPMA, we should scrap the present system and institute a crash program to survey, map, and inventory the BLM lands with an eye toward determining as precisely as possible the type and condition of all land forms in the system and the location and extent of all resources available—with primary emphasis on soil, water, wildlife habitat, wildlife populations, and other information necessary to determine whether and to what degree the management of the land form in question is meeting its primary function: the preservation of biodiversity. The FLPMA states that the lands shall be managed "in a manner that will protect" such values—but we cannot protect that which we do not know, and today we do not yet have a comprehensive understanding of what the lands hold. The program should include those lands already set aside or recommended to be set aside as wilderness, but should embrace all other BLM lands as well, including those that should be reconsidered for wilderness designation and those that already are being used for such

144

things as grazing, mining, military exercises, the extraction of coal, oil, and gas, and other purposes.

To implement such a program, five separate resource surveys should be organized and firm deadlines established for their completion. They should include programs to determine the present known and potential sources of strategic minerals, with an eye toward setting aside strategic reserves of these essential materials for future needs, as well as surveys to discover the boundaries and estimated volumes of deposits of coal, oil, natural gas, oil shale, tar sands, and geothermal sites. Most importantly, however, the program should emphasize three major surveys:

A biological survey. Interior Secretary Bruce Babbitt has established a National Biological Survey to determine the nation's "natural capital"—that bank of living organisms on which the future ecological and economic economic health of the country depends. No such survey has ever been undertaken and is especially necessary for the BLM's lands, whose biological resources traditionally have been given short shrift—even though these lands almost certainly contain the greatest species variety and abundance of any of the public-lands systems. The survey should be adequately funded by Congress immediately and the BLM lands be made an immediate and important—indeed primary—part of the process.

A western water resources survey. In a program to rationalize future water use in the West, including the needs of land and wildlife, this study would work with the U. S. Geological Survey and other appropriate federal and state agencies to establish the precise quantity and quality of Western water resources and the overall ecological health of individual groundwater systems and watersheds; discover and clarify conflicts and present allocations among federal, state, local, Native American, and private rights; and determine which public-land water-development projects, planned or proposed, are justified on the basis of future available supplies and projected ecological impacts.

A soil and rangeland conservation survey. Like the other surveys, this would seek to discover the quantity and condition of its designated resources responsibility. One of its primary purposes, however, would be to investigate lands already in use to determine the degree of riparian habitat destruction that has taken place, as well as soil damage and loss through overgrazing and consequent erosion. Such investigations must be much more stringent and science-driven than the district-wide environmental impact statements that currently are in use. The importance of such studies was recently recognized by the National Research Council. "There is an urgent need to develop the methods and data collection systems at both the local and national levels to assess . . . rangelands," it declared firmly in *Rangeland Health: New Methods to Classify, Inventory, and Monitor Rangelands* (1994). "The importance of the values and commodities provided by rangelands, the history of rangeland degradation, the evidence pointing to ongoing rangeland degradation, and the inadequate data on current conditions at both the local and the national levels suggest that is unwise to neglect the nation's . . . rangelands." Such a survey should determine the condition of soil, plant, and water resources—especially riverine habitat—on all grazing lands, the Research Council recommends. "Soil stability, watershed functions, nutrient cycling, energy flow, and the mechanisms that enable recovery from stress should be assessed. . . ." This knowledge would then be used to establish standards of minimum ecological health that would provide the guidelines for future management. The council's recommendations concerned all American rangeland, federal and non-federal, but the summary remarks of the chairman of the study committee, F. E. Busby, should be kept near to hand by any BLM manager with a grazing allotment to administer, perhaps on the bulletin board for all to see: "An assessment of rangeland health should be made as a precursor to decisions about how we're going to use the land. Right now, we're making many of those decisions without really having a handle on the health of the land. If we knew that the integrity of the soil and ecological processes were being sustained, then we could make better decisions about how, when, and how much the land should be used."

In addition to these surveys, Congress should mandate the organization of a coordinated, centralized, and coherent planning process. This process should be designed to develop strict comprehensive guidelines governing the future use and protection of each of the landforms and

146

resources under investigation and to ensure that conditions are monitored regularly. It should be made as free as humanly possible of political or economic influences and be guided entirely by sound science. To avoid the pitfalls of inconsistency inherent in the present management planning structure, the law should establish overall standards and criteria to which all individual district management plans must adhere. Borrowing from the National Forest Management Act of 1976 (see chapter 2), the legislation also should stipulate that all plans developed would be subject to review and revision every ten to fifteen years in order to be certain, first, that management is indeed taking place as it should and, second, that the plans are compatible with the nation's needs as they develop over time. Finally, to ensure that the plans are actually accomplished, Congress should impose firm deadlines for their completion in the near future.

At the heart of both the survey and planning processes should be the goal of protecting biodiversity over ecosystem-wide areas, preserving the natural links between habitat and maintaining viable populations of plants and animals within those systems. As with the rest of the American public lands system, this "use" of the land and its resources must take precedence over all others. To that end, the Bureau of Land Management—at all levels, from district managers in the field to their superiors in Washington—must revolutionize its working relationships with the National Park Service, the Fish and Wildlife Service, and the Forest Service. These federal land-managment agencies have all operated for too long as if they had no one to answer to or work with but their own officials and the constituencies nearest to them, and the BLM—as probably the most thoroughly underfunded and understaffed of all—has been especially jealous of its territory and reluctant to coordinate its work with those of the other agencies. But if the term "ecosystem management" ever rises above the level of fashionable jargon, it will only be if all the federal agencies accept the fact that anything any one of them is likely to do on any given piece of its own land is likely to affect the integrity of any other given piece of land managed by any other given agency—to the land's detriment, more often than not. Such isolation of management practices must end, and since it has responsibility for the largest amount of federal land in the system—

147

virtually all of which is connected to one or more of the other land systems—the BLM in fact should take the initiative in an effort to develop
inter-agency planning for the management of all federal lands within
specific ecosystems.

It is often said that the lands administered by the Bureau of Land
Management constitute most of what is left when we speak of the "wide
open spaces" of the West. Such a patrimony deserves nothing less than
the best stewardship we can give it. Call it a space program.

*Butte on the Escalante River in southern Utah—one of the candidate areas
for BLM wilderness designation (T. H. Watkins).*

4

ISLANDS OF LIFE

The National Wildlife Refuge System

In the classic children's book *The Trumpet of the Swan*, by E. B. White, a father swan inspires his fledglings with a vision of their Promised Land:

"Montana is a state of the union. And there, in a lovely valley surrounded by high mountains, are the Red Rock Lakes which nature has designed especially for swans. In the lakes you will enjoy warm winter, arising from hidden springs. Here, ice never forms, no matter how cold the nights. In the Red Rock Lakes you find other trumpeter swans, as well as the lesser waterfowl—the geese and ducks. There are few enemies. No gunners. Plenty of muskrat houses. Free grain. Games every day. What more can a swan ask, in the long, long cold of winter?"

What more indeed? And Red Rock Lakes was not just a place in a storybook. It was and is quite real—a 44,158-acre unit of the National Wildlife Refuge System, and a remarkable place. Remarkable, too, that it even exists, considering the precedence human desires have traditionally excercised over those of other creatures nearly everywhere on the planet. There is simply no other entity in the world quite like America's National Wildlife Refuge System. Now 91.5 million acres, its size exceeds the National Park System, though all but about 15 million of its acres lie in Alaska. Of the 476 refuges outside Alaska, 65 percent are west of the Mississippi River. More than 92 percent of their lands were

President Chester A. Arthur with a day's take of ducks, 1882 (Indiana Historical Society Library).

151

withdrawn from the public domain while Congress authorized the purchase of much of the rest, or accepted them as gifts to the nation from private donors. The system operates in seven different biomes, distinct communities of soil types, vegetation, and animals. One official report described the refuges as "islands of habitat once widespread within each biome."

An "island" might be gigantic, like the 19-million-acre Arctic National Wildlife Refuge, which runs from the Arctic Circle north to the Beaufort Sea. Or it might be as small as a suburban back yard, like the six-tenths-of-an-acre Mille Lacs Refuge in Minnesota. In Alaska the system preserves refuge units the size of entire ecosystems, where man has barely intruded. Not all refuges are remote. The Great Swamp National Wildlife Refuge in New Jersey lies along a major commuting route well within Manhattan's sphere of influence. (Featuring the sort of landscape that people like to fill and wood ducks like to nest in, the Great Swamp became a refuge only after conservationists fought to keep it from becoming an airport.) Scores of smaller refuges, most on the coastlines, are close to other metropolitan areas.

The system is composed of 492 wildlife and waterfowl refuges, plus an assortment of related sites for waterfowl production. On and in these lands and waters dwell at least 220 species of mammals and 260 species of amphibians and reptiles, 178 of which are endangered. More than 600 of the 813 bird species found in the United States spend at least one season within the refuge system. This is no accident, since about three-fourths of the refuges were set aside primarily for the benefit of waterfowl and migratory birds.

Many of these refuges are along the four major north-to-south migratory routes: the Atlantic, Mississippi, Central, and Pacific flyways that carry tens of millions of birds every year. Other refuges have been established to preserve the habitat primarily for an individual species, such as the National Elk Refuge in Wyoming, or to reintroduce a species to an ancestral or otherwise suitable territory; in 1934, for instance, thirty-one musk-oxen from Greenland were released on Nunivak Island, part of Yukon Flats National Wildlife Refuge in Alaska. Now more than six hundred animals inhabit that refuge.

The refuge system has supported numerous extremely important wildlife recoveries. Tiny key deer numbered fewer than fifty in 1950, their population reduced by the conversion of their habitat into a resort development. Now there are hundreds of deer protected at the National Key Deer Refuge, in Florida. Perhaps the best known case of rejuvenation is occurring at the Aransas National Wildlife Refuge in Texas, where whooping cranes, mistakenly reported extinct in 1923 (they were only a few birds away), have made a comeback, with at least 138 now counted in the Aransas flock.

Refuge successes include the preservation of singular habitats of certain species, which, by virtue of their few but unalterable living requirements, have always been rare or endangered. The system also has recovered or aided many once-prolific, then drastically reduced species, such as the beaver, wood duck, sea otter, and dozens of shorebirds, which are once again very much in evidence in their native habitats.

Such success stories demonstrate the ideal for which the system was established. With the passage of the National Wildlife Refuge System Act in 1966, the Fish and Wildlife Service has earnestly set out to "provide, preserve, restore and manage a national network of lands and waters sufficient in size, diversity and location to meet society's needs for areas where the widest spectrum of benefits associated with wildlife and wildlands is enhanced and made available." This mission has spawned four key refuge goals. First, the refuges must preserve, restore, and enhance ecosystems of endangered species. Second, they must perpetuate migratory bird populations. Third, they must preserve natural diversity and abundance of all animals and nonmigratory birds that are present on the refuges. And, finally, they must engender an understanding and an appreciation of fish and wildlife, and of man's role in protecting the environment. This last purpose sounds like something straight out of the mind of Aldo Leopold, who declared that the hope of the future lay not in curbing the influence of human occupancy (it was already too late for that, he asserted in 1931), but in "creating a better understanding of the extent of that influence and a new ethic of its governance."

By all rational measure, this is a noble system with a noble purpose, and there is good reason to have pride in its existence as one of the major legacies this nation has had the foresight to preserve. But, like Aldo Leopold's Land Ethic, it was a long time developing out of a

153

complex welter of ideas and instincts—and again, like that ethic, it is still a long way from becoming all that it needs to be.

TIPPING THE BALANCE

Eons before the current refuge system was devised, another system of wildlife perpetuation flourished. Cycles of animal reproduction, birth, and demise revolved around tides, or the length of days and nights, or the phases of the moon and other gravitational exhortations—just as they do now. The fundamental difference between the old and the new systems is the changing role of the human species. Aboriginal societies had developed "an intimate understanding of the habits and ecology of other species," according to William Cronon, whose book *Changes in the Land* explores New England's ecological history through colonization. Indian societies were characterized by dietary flexibility and residential impermanence, Cronon says, thereby ensuring that the impact of the human presence on a particular place was minimal. Indians of New England and elsewhere in precolonial America lived according to the seasons, moving to wherever food was most heavily concentrated in the ecosystem. Whole villages, which varied in population density as well as in shelter type, congregated by a river in spring when fish were spawning, or moved into low-lying forests to track deer through autumn and winter. They shifted to where subsistence was easiest, taking whatever species were plentiful, then moved on when game grew scarce, thus giving it time to recover. And, since Indians traveled on foot, with no other means to bring down their game than bows and arrows, or snares and pits, they were discouraged from taking more than they could quickly transport. Even to the south, where tribes subsisted largely on cultivated foods such as corn and legumes, land and wildlife had time to recover from intensive farming. Fields remained fertile for as long as ten years because of mixed plantings of beans and corn, which preserved nitrogen in the soil. Indians moved on when their fields were exhausted, giving the soil ample time to recover its nutrients.

This unconscious ecological balance was not universally achieved, of course. Primitive cultures could and did manipulate nature when it suited their purposes. But for the most part, the native American maintained himself in a symbiosis, by his tradition, his limitations, or his instinct, and thus perpetuated his own kind in a healthy manner.

The impact of Europeans on this relationship was profound and immediate. Sweeping changes in how aboriginal people affected wildlife populations began to occur as early as 1540 in the Southwest, as the Spanish forged their conqueror's path out of Mexico. Coronado apparently was the first to import livestock: 6,500 sheep and cattle from Spain to the New World. It was not only a cultural preference for domestic meat that encouraged these importations; they were also useful in converting nomadic, hunting tribes such as the Navajo to a pastoral life so that they might be more receptive to Catholicism. Sheep and cattle multiplied rapidly, devouring ancestral rangelands of the bighorn sheep, pronghorn antelope, elk, and deer. Domestic breeds often carried deadly parasites to wildlife that had never been exposed to them before.

White settlement along the East Coast did not begin to entrench itself for another eighty years or so, but brought predictable changes. Domestic herds were introduced, and forests were cleared permanently, since more wood was needed to build roads, fences, and houses, and for fuel. Trees were also girdled and burned to make space for agriculture. Despite the existence of abundant game during the first years, as many as half the settlers died of starvation only months after they arrived. Here was what Cronon calls the "paradox of want in a land of plenty," for these people had been mostly tradesmen and professionals in England, and did not know how to live off uncultivated land.

Those who survived either brought provisions to last a year or learned what to do from the Indians. At the same time, the Indians were eager to hunt meat for the settlers in exchange for glass beads, steel knives, metal pots, and wool blankets. Wildlife historian James Trefethen noted that "while it lasted, this was probably the most rewarding trading relationship in history. Each side thought it was taking advantage of the other and obtaining priceless commodities in exchange for practically nothing." The problem was that trade was not restricted to New World settlers and Indians. The North American continent had turned into a supermarket, capable of meeting all the wants of European society.

Fur trading became a prime occupation, instituted by the Dutch in the 1620s. Beaver pelts were in such high demand that by 1650 the animals had been trapped out of all streams from Maine to South Carolina. But the pursuit of wildlife for commerce was doomed from the start, for it first depleted the exploited animal populations and then bankrupted the commercial exploiter. No matter; in the early years there were so many resources to be converted into finished products that depletion of one stock was an incentive to generate markets in others. Once whites took to hunting, they typically killed more than they needed, for there was always a demand for fresh game in the burgeoning settlements. This practice of taking more than necessary and then selling it affected Indian hunting patterns as well. More people turned out to kill more animals more often.

Increasingly, habitat disappeared under the implacable assault of the westward-moving pioneers, and with it went the wildlife, retreating inland until there was no place left to go. The Eastern beavers vanished, as did Eastern wolves when predation of domestic livestock brought eradication down upon their heads. Salmon runs were blocked by dams for gristmills and sawmills. The million-winged flocks of passenger pigeons dwindled, then disappeared. The heath hen, the Labrador duck, the great auk, the Carolina paraquet, the eastern cougar, grasses, plants, wildflowers, trees . . . gone or so depleted as to border on extinction.

BUFFALO RUN

Of all the life-forms put to the gun or driven out by a nation fulfilling its destiny, the fate of no creature so captured the imagination—and later the horror—of the country as did that of *Bison bison*—the American buffalo. In the beginning, buffalo herds had engulfed the land like a black sea, roaring and rolling in swells over the grasslands from the Canadian subarctic to as far south as central Mexico. Offshoots of the main herds spread as far west as the mountain valleys of Idaho and Montana and as far east as the banks of the Potomac. Aside from wolves, cougars, and grizzlies, the buffalo's only predators were Indians, particularly those Plains cultures that obtained their food, clothing, shelter, implements, and fuel from the herds that wandered into their territory. This required a great deal of effort

156

before the Spanish inadvertently introduced the horse in the sixteenth century. On horseback, Indians had an easier time hunting buffalo, but it was not until the white man discovered the sport that the slaughter really began.

Osborne Russell, a fur trapper who kept a journal of his life in the Rocky Mountains during the 1830s, reported the beginning of the end, and surmised that the insatiable demand for buffalo robes back East was contributing to the animal's destruction. In 1836, he noted, herds could be seen grazing almost every valley. Ten years later, Russell saw only their scattered bones, and remarked on how the wide swaths of earth that buffalo had worn bare during centuries of migration were becoming overgrown with weeds. To most people who saw them, the buffalo multitudes remained memorable for another fifty years. Herds were still large enough to feed the thousands of men laying down railroad track right through the heart of prime buffalo range. In 1867, Buffalo Bill Cody was hired by the Kansas Pacific Railway to provide fresh meat for the gandy dancers. In eighteen months he killed 4,280 animals. In a single day he slaughtered sixty-nine.

On May 10, 1869, the Central Pacific locomotive coasted to within handshaking distance of the Union Pacific's Number 119 locomotive at Promontory Point, Utah. East met West, making the country one, but cutting the last, best buffalo country in half. Now buffalo killing would begin in earnest, for the trains brought more people to the herds, which were confined to smaller and smaller ranges. Thanks to incentives created by the Civil War, ammunition for single-shot rifles such as the Remington and the Springfield, and for repeaters such as the Spencer, had been improved to the point that a hunter could get off twenty shots a minute with metallic cartridges, each packed with enough gunpowder to drop a buffalo. In less than a generation the millions of animals that had roamed Arizona, Colorado, Kansas, Oklahoma, and New Mexico had been processed into meat and hides.

Over time and under that country's blazing sun, the landscape became speckled with bright white buffalo ribs, femurs, and skulls. It made an impression, this graveyard of destiny, visible for miles and miles through the windows of the passing railroad cars—until

157

the bones, too, were gone, picked up and sold to be ground into fertilizer. As is often the case, the engines of progress are simultaneously vehicles for resurrection as well as destruction, and the scenes to be witnessed from the passenger trains sparked enough public concern to make Congress consider the plight of the buffalo. In 1874 it passed a bill outlawing buffalo killing in the territories. President Grant, however, had been counseled by General William Tecumseh Sherman that annihilation of the buffalo was a sure way to incapacitate hostile Indian tribes who subsisted on them. Grant, an astute military logician in his own right, pocket-vetoed the bill. With the utter defeat of George Custer's troops at the hands of Sioux and Cheyenne warriors two years later, a bill for the protection of buffalo would never have a chance to pass. Killing buffalo, as well as Indians, became an act of patriotism.

WHO OWNED THE WILDLIFE?

To its credit, Congress had at least tried to do something to save the buffalo. It is important to note, however, that it restricted its efforts to protecting the herds in the territories, since it was commonly accepted that the federal government had no business making decisions about wildlife within the states. Responsibility for wildlife at the federal level had not been expressly authorized by the Constitution, and therefore belonged to the states in which the animals were found. A Supreme Court decision reached in 1842 and written by Chief Justice Roger Taney reinforced that tradition. In *Martin v. Waddell*, a case regarding oyster-fishing rights in New Jersey, the Supreme Court ruled that "when the people of New Jersey took possession of the reins of government, and took into their own hands the powers of sovereignty, the prerogatives and regalities that belonged either to the crown or the parliament, became immediately and rightfully vested in the states." Wildlife law specialist Michael J. Bean notes that emphasis solely on this portion of Taney's ruling has always "ignored Taney's important qualifier that the powers assumed by the states were 'subject . . . to the rights since surrendered by the Constitution to the general government.' " No occasions arose on which Taney's decision could be read closely enough to consider this condition until the end of the century. Meanwhile, the doctrine of state ownership of wildlife proceeded apace, while the idea of federal jurisdiction nearly shriveled up and blew away.

The states did make some progress toward establishing a framework of game management by restricting certain hunting practices. When the Revolutionary War began, twelve colonies had closed hunting seasons; in 1850 Massachusetts and New Hampshire appointed the first game wardens; in that same year Connecticut and New Jersey passed laws protecting nongame birds such as songbirds, and Iowa introduced the first bag limit of twenty-five prairie chickens per person per day. Arkansas, in 1875, was the first state to outlaw commercial hunting. By 1880 all states had game laws of one sort or another, their necessity becoming apparent as civilization advanced. But belief in the doctrine of state ownership of wildlife did not produce much in the way of effective regulation or enforcement. The position of game commissioner was often awarded to a political hack whose outstanding qualification was that he loved to hunt, out of season as well as in. Biological training for the job didn't exist, so the game commissioner's foremost concern was to ensure the rights of his fellow citizens to hunt as much as or more than the citizens of another state. Particularly where migratory waterfowl were concerned, it seemed a good state policy to set liberal bag limits, if any were set at all. This had the unwelcome effect of reducing the size of flocks continuing their migration through other states, where citizens expected to exercise comparable rights over the quarry.

After Justice Taney's decision, the test for upholding the doctrine of state ownership of wildlife did not occur until an 1896 Supreme Court ruling. A man named Geer had shot birds in Connecticut in accordance with that state's game law, but then tried to ship them out of state. The question that needed answering was whether Geer's intent to transport birds out of Connecticut interfered with Congress's power to regulate interstate commerce. Justice Edward White wrote the majority opinion and concluded that states had the right "to control and regulate the common property in game," a right to be exercised "as a trust for the benefit of the people." States could name whatever conditions were justified in taking game, and these conditions also applied after the game had been killed. White asserted that because of the "peculiar nature" of game and the state's ownership of it, it

159

was doubtful whether interstate commerce was even created in the case. According to Michael Bean, Justice White's decision addressed the question too narrowly to rule out once and for all a federal role in wildlife matters.

Nevertheless, advocates for states took the extreme view, Bean says, that "the state ownership doctrine would render impossible the development of a body of federal wildlife law." Still, the federal government could not stay entirely out of wildlife issues any more than it could have stayed out of commerce or agriculture. In 1871, the post of Commissioner of Fish and Fisheries was created as a separate governmental entity, and was run as such until 1903, when it was included in the Department of Commerce and Labor and its name changed to Bureau of Fisheries. Its chore was to regulate ocean-based fishing operations, most taking place well beyond the borders of any state, often in international waters.

And in 1885 a far-reaching bit of work was given to the Department of Agriculture, which involved the completion of a national survey of birdlife initiated by the American Ornithologists Union. The union had asked ornithologists and birdwatchers around the country to survey the birds in their locale. The response had been so great that Dr. C. Hart Merriam, chairman of the Ornithologists Union, was forced to seek government funding to complete the survey. He explained that information about birdlife would be useful to agricultural programs. On that representation, Congress appropriated $5,000 for the survey, with Dr. Merriam as its head. In 1886, the new body became the Division of Economic Ornithology and Mammalogy, and in 1905 was renamed the U. S. Biological Survey.

SPORTSMEN TO THE RESCUE

Under pressure from farmers for "practical" information, the Biological Survey ultimately drifted away from mere survey efforts and toward more more "useful" work. The agency conducted numerous experiments in search of the best way to kill rodents and other large predators. The success of the effort was so remarkable that by 1917 the bureau's chief was announcing that he and his colleagues were confident that in five years they could wipe out "most of the gray wolves. . . ." In New Mexico alone, he was happy to report, the bureau had "destroyed fifty

160

percent of the gray wolves and expect to get the other fifty percent in the next two or three years."

Now here was federal intervention a farmer or stockman could appreciate, and as long as the government steered clear of hunting regulation, the states didn't mind the destruction either. Despite public concern over such examples as the buffalo, it was commonly accepted that the eradication of wild species was an inevitable part of the price of progress.

The only responsibility remaining, it seemed, was to catalogue and name every distinct animal form before it disappeared. This was the duty of the naturalists, and there was a sense of urgency attending their work because it was quite possible that a species could die out before a trained man could set eyes upon it. In 1875, for instance, the Labrador duck was eliminated from its territorial waters of northeastern Canada and the United States less than a year after its existence was dutifully recorded.

Ironically, the need to try to preserve wildlife was first recognized by those who most loved to kill it—the hunters. James Trefethen takes great pains to distinguish between two classes of hunters: sportsmen, who behaved honorably toward their quarry and enjoyed their interaction with nature whether they took down game or not, and market hunters, who killed for profit, using whatever means they could to bag the most game in the shortest time. This distinction is justified, although not always discernible, since many a good-hearted sportsman might kill more than he needed, certain he could dispose of it—if not profitably, then charitably. Nevertheless, few interest groups policed themselves as conscientiously as did sportsmen, for they divined that their avocation came a step closer to extinction with each species that was threatened. Conflicts between sportsmen and market hunters grew more severe as each favorite woodland or pond became gameless. Wealthy sportsmen formed groups to buy land that they alone could hunt, trying to preserve some places on the map from ambitious marketeers.

Some of the private reserves did not allow hunting of any kind, the grandest of these being the 12,000-acre Blooming Grove Park Association in Pennsylvania, created in 1871. The first state-designated sanctuary was created by the California legislature in 1870, eighteen years after a man-made lake in the city of Oakland had been expressly designed by Samuel Merritt for the protection of waterfowl. This tiny refuge attracted little public attention, and not much was done by the state to protect it. So the Merritt Lake sanctuary did not quite live up to its name.

Sportsmen, many of whom considered themselves the first conservationists, filled the void when it came to game law enforcement. The militant New York Sportsmen's Club was particularly strong in this regard. Organized in 1844, its wealthy and influential members pursued game violators on their own. Lawyers in the club sued poachers and restaurateurs who possessed game out of season. Colonial law had established the right of citizens to sue game violators, and often this was the only recourse left to official law enforcement, when state game wardens were either too scarce or too indifferent to uphold state regulations. Similarly disposed clubs sprang up in large cities, particularly after the Civil War, when hunting became leisure for the rich man rather than sustenance for the poor. The best known of these organizations was the Boone and Crockett Club, conceived by Theodore Roosevelt in 1887. The club sought to preserve large game animals and encouraged the "American hunting riflemen" to join its cause. One of Roosevelt's cofounders was George Bird Grinnell, an impressive spokesman for wildlife preservation on a national level. Grinnell was editor and publisher of *Forest and Stream* magazine, and he used it as a platform to denounce greedy hunters for their "sordid clutching after purses, gate money, entrance fees or prizes" in trophy competitions.

Grinnell, himself a hunter, was the son of a wealthy family in Brooklyn, New York. His father lost one fortune after the Civil War and made a second working for Commodore Vanderbilt. When Grinnell was eight years old, his family moved to an estate on the Hudson River near the home of John James Audubon's widow, Lucy. Under Lucy Audubon's tutelage the boy developed his love for natural subjects. One of Grinnell's fondest boyhood memories was of the passenger pigeons that flocked by the thousands near his house. By the time he was middle-aged, the pigeons were gone. The rapidity of their disappearance appalled Grinnell, who was also given to musing before two buffalo skulls that graced his hearth, thinking of the land they once commanded.

162

When careless readers of the magazine mistakenly sent him photographs of creatures they had shot, expecting praise for their bounty, Grinnell ran the pictures—above captions denouncing them by name for being "game hogs." He editorialized constantly for the creation of protective associations to halt the slaughter. The idea of such organizations appealed to Oliver Wendell Holmes, John Greenleaf Whittier, and other notables. It caught on quickly, and in honor of his childhood tutor, Grinnell in 1886 named the first association the Audubon Society—the first of many that spread throughout the country.

Forest and Stream launched attacks on every industry that abused game for profit. A favorite target was the fashion trade, which was then dictating that women wear colorful bird plumage and other bird parts in their hats. One of the magazine's first issues featured an essay by the poet Celia Thaxter, in which she attacked any woman who "goes her way, a charnel house of beaks, claws and bones and glass eyes upon her fatuous head." A major journalistic coup resulted in the passage of the Yellowstone Park Protection Act of 1894, which made it a crime to kill wildlife or remove it from the park. The act, which followed the creation of the park by twenty-two years, was the first federal law protecting wildlife and banned not only hunting, but any human activity that might upset the existence of wildlife.

Concerned by reports of epidemic poaching in the park, Grinnell had dispatched Emerson Hough, one of his top reporters, to Yellowstone to write a story on poaching. Hough's visit was fortuitous. He was on hand with a photographer the day Edgar Howell, the park's most infamous and uncaught poacher, was found skinning a buffalo. Five still-warm buffalo carcasses lay nearby. Moreover, Howell openly boasted to Hough regarding his killing exploits. Hough wrote it all up with a fine passion, and Grinnell added his own plea to readers to write their congressmen demanding some form of wildlife protection. The readers followed Grinnell's advice; within a year the Park Protection Act passed, making Yellowstone, and future parks, inviolate wildlife refuges.

In 1900 the federal government took a second step, albeit a tentative one, into the realm of wildlife regulation when Congress passed the Lacey Act. Based on congressional authority to regulate interstate commerce, the act prohibited the transportation of any wild animals or birds killed in violation of state law. Cautiously written, the act merely enlisted the aid of the federal government in enforcing state game laws. It also enhanced state prerogatives by allowing states to prohibit the export of game lawfully killed within their boundaries. This was an extension of the earlier *Geer* decision, although it differed in asserting that interstate commerce in wildlife did indeed exist. The Lacey Act authorized the Secretary of Agriculture to preserve, distribute, introduce, and restore game birds—subject, as always, to state laws.

THE FIRST REFUGE

Like his longtime friend George Bird Grinnell, Theodore Roosevelt's affection for wild things was forged in childhood. As a boy of twelve his passion was taxidermy, a craft he had learned directly from the man who taught Audubon. It was not a particularly saving pursuit, but at that time the only thing that separated the scientist from the sportsman and the market hunter was what he did with the quarry's carcass. Being first a science-minded boy and second a sportsman, young Roosevelt donated his collection of "one bat, twelve mice, a turtle, the skull of a red squirrel, and four bird eggs" to the American Museum of Natural History, which his father had been instrumental in establishing. He killed and "stuffed" as much wildlife as his parents would allow. In the two months he spent floating down the Nile with his family, he shot and mounted about 200 birds—he lost count of exactly how many. The practice made him an excellent marksman.

In 1884, after the tragic deaths of his young wife and his mother within hours of each other, the twenty-five-year old lit out for the frontier. A Winchester rifle and a "very enduring and very hardy" horse named Manitou were his constant companions; with them he dropped his first buffalo, numerous antelope, bighorn sheep, and bear, including a few grizzlies. After months of riding and tracking game, Roosevelt headed for the Badlands, where he bought some land and cattle and became a rancher. The experience nearly bankrupted him, but it left him with a deep understanding of how easily land could be abused—including his own. He returned home in 1887 to "do something in a public, and political way." In the public way he helped found the Boone and Crockett Club, for he had come to realize that preserving big game was a challenge as great as stalking it. Subsequently he made his political way and became Vice President and finally President of the United States, after President William McKinley was assassinated in 1901.

Two years later, Roosevelt created the first wildlife refuge. For years, the American Ornithologists Union had been trying to acquire 3.5-acre Pelican Island off the coast of Florida in order to protect egrets, herons, and brown pelicans from plume hunters. The island, dense with black mangroves, was a nesting place for about five thousand birds, one of the most important on the Atlantic Flyway. When the Ornithologists Union discovered that the island was federal property, its Committe on Bird Protection quickly requested federal protection by Roosevelt. The President had little or no precedent to go by, but this did not deter him (such matters rarely did). "Is there any a law that will prevent me from declaring Pelican Island a federal bird reservation?" he asked his advisors, with a forthrightness that was utterly characteristic of the man who carried sticks and walked softly. When he was assured that there was none, he replied, "Very well, then, I so declare it."

Roosevelt's action bestirred Audubon societies all over the country to locate other plots on federal lands appropriate as bird sanctuaries. But such sanctuaries, once created, did not receive any federal funding, although the Biological Survey was instructed to care for them. Audubon Society members were often caretakers, or else they paid refuge guardians from their own funds. The word "refuge" was interpreted strictly, and areas so designated often were fenced off and posted with signs to ward off human trespassers. Consciously, the Audubon Society's measures were meant to exclude hunting. Subconsciously, they recognized the important of habitat left in its natural state. Congress opened other possibilities with passage of the Antiquities Act of 1906, which affirmed the President's authority to withdraw lands for various purposes. Later that same year, Congress also declared it illegal to disturb birds on any federal lands "set aside as breeding grounds for birds by law, proclamation, or Executive Order."

Through such means, Roosevelt created fifty-one bird reservations before leaving office in 1909—most of the foundation of the present system. Nor did he stop at bird reservations. By the time he became President, only twenty-three American buffalo remained in the wild, and these had been isolated in Yellowstone National Park. In 1904 the Boone and Crockett Club and the new York Zoological Society launched a joint restoration effort. First they chose 59,000 acres of native grasslands in the Wichita National Forest Reserve in Oklahoma and then persuaded Congress to reserve the area for buffalo breeding. The New York Zoological Society gave the government fifteen of the thirty-three captive animals in exchange for the government's promise to fence the area against predation and poaching. On January 24, 1905, Roosevelt signed a law that authorized him to declare land in the Wichita reserve as sanctuary for game animals and birds. With this in hand, in June 1905 the President designated the Wichita Forest Reserve and Game Preserve.

The creation of the Wichita Preserve inspired the formation of the American Bison Society, headed by William Temple Hornaday, a big-game hunter who had recanted and turned virulently anti-hunting. Horaday became prominent in 1896 when he was made head of the New York Zoological Society and helped to create one of the world's leading zoological parks. Hornaday was a singularly righteous zealot whose views were often controversial, even a little peculiar; while denouncing the killing of most animals, for example, he excluded such "noxious predators" as bears, mountain lions, wolves, and coyotes. He also listed "several species of birds that may at once be put under the sentence of death for for their destructiveness of useful birds." Still, his commitment to buffalo was deep and abiding.

The American Bison Society scored its first victory in 1908, when Congress authorized the purchase of the National Bison Range on the Flathead Indian Reservation in Montana. Through public subscription the society raised $10,000 to purchase thirty-four buffalo from private owners. Its efforts were so successful that eventually the American Bison Society disbanded, its job finished.

JUSTICE HOLMES TAKES A HAND

The system was established by 1909, but wildlife was still in trouble. While the creation of refuges for plumed birds and the passage of the Lacey Act slowed the flow of supplies to milliners, populations of migratory waterfowl continued to decline sharply. Breeding grounds disappeared under farm fields, and many wetlands were absorbed by

166

growing cities. Spring shooting, still legal in most states, devastated flocks, as did each state's insistence that its hunters be allowed to take all of the state's allotment of birds as the flocks passed through. The idea of protecting live birds seemed, even to the most avid of wildlife conservationists, too far removed from Congress's authority to regulate interstate commerce. Senator Elihu Root, who had served as President Roosevelt's Secretary of State and was a Nobel Laureate, at last devised an ingenious approach. He introduced a resolution authorizing the President of the United States to seek international agreements for the protection of migratory birds. Slowed by World War I, the agreements between the United States and Great Britain on behalf of Canada were finally ratified in 1916. Under the conditions of the migratory bird treaty, the United States had to uphold its end by protecting birds as long as they resided in U.S. territory.

States' rights advocates viewed the treaty as a ploy by the federal government to interfere with state wildlife regulation, and decided to test the pact's constitutionality. They lost. In a landmark case, *Missouri v. Holland*, Supreme Court Justice Oliver Wendell Holmes rendered this decision:

> But for the treaty and the statute, there soon might be no birds for any powers to deal with. We see nothing in the Constitution that compels the government to sit by while a food supply is being cut off and the protectors of our forests and crops are destroyed. It is not sufficient to rely upon the States. The reliance is in vain, and were it otherwise, the question is whether the United States is forbidden to act. We are of the opinion that the treaty and statute must be upheld.

The Supreme Court having spoken, the Bureau of Biological Survey and its Canadian counterpart wrote regulations that restricted most of the destructive uses of migratory birds. The sale of game birds covered by the treaty was prohibited, spring shooting and night shooting were outlawed, and bag limits were reduced. Certain species, such as wood ducks and trumpeter swans, were off limits to all hunters, and the use of weapons of mass destruction was abolished. Considering all the opposition that had been mounted over the years against federal regulation of wildlife, all states eventually accepted the migratory bird treaty enthusiastically, promulgating their own regulations to toughen control.

As more was learned about flight patterns and nesting preferences of birds, treaties protecting other species were drawn between the United States and Mexico, Japan, and the Soviet Union. The vast territorial requirements of many birds dictated a global approach to their protection. Recognition of this fact was humbling, for wild things had long been considered the exclusive property of American states. Significantly, it was becoming more apparent that wildlife was not merely a special form of property, but an integral part of all life.

The conscientious enforcement of treaty restrictions on hunting and marketing dramatically increased migratory bird populations at the same time that habitat was disappearing at an alarming rate. More birds had fewer places to rest on their tiring north-south journey. This dilemma concerned visionaries among the game managers, who suspected that if the trend continued, the United States would not be able to uphold its end of the 1916 treaty with Great Britian. Most of the migratory bird refuges were in the West, where they had been carved out of public land. Unprotected was most of the Midwest, where wetlands and potholes had fallen into private hands and were being drained as quickly as possible for agricultural development. Birds would not deviate from their flyway patterns, so more refuges had to be created along the natural migration routes. This meant land would have to be bought, which seemed an unlikely prospect.

But as early as 1924, pressure from hunting groups and nonhunting groups alike finally persuaded Congress to appropriate $1.5 million to buy a ribbon of land along the Mississippi River—in all, 194,000 acres in four states were purchased to create the Upper Mississippi Wildlife and Fish Refuge, a 284-mile strip of riparian habitat. Much to the displeasure of the antihunting faction, however, this refuge allowed hunting; in fact, it was lauded as the first "public shooting ground." The accommodation of hunters seemed unavoidable. It spelled the difference between saving a key habitat and exploiting it for other purposes. As the need for more refuges along the Central and Mississippi flyways became apparent, Congress passed the Migratory Bird Conservation Act in 1929, which established a commission of Cabinet

168

members and congressional representatives to review and approve acquisitions of additional refuge lands. Unlike the Upper Mississippi project, these refuges were to be managed as "inviolate sanctuaries." All this was well and good except for the act's chief shortcoming: While it authorized the appropriation of funds necessary to buy the desperately needed lands, it did not specify *which* lands, and the early Depression years did not encourage Congress to hand money out. As a result, few new refuges were bought and the waterfowl situation deteriorated until the number of ducks in the fall migration sank to about thirty million from a previous population of about 120 million.

THE DARLING YEARS

With the coming of the first administration of Franklin D. Roosevelt and that patched-together system of emergency measures called the New Deal, the situation slowly began to change. These were the Dust Bowl years, when winds blew the fine grit of Kansas to Wall Street, and dust in Manhattan was so thick at times that cars drove with headlights on at noon. As bad as these years were for Americans everywhere, the peril they also posed for waterfowl could not be ignored. Under New Deal soil conservation programs and massive efforts to plant vegetation that would buffer wind and hold what topsoil remained, small mammals and insect-eating birds were enjoying a recovery. But refuges for waterfowl were still sorely lacking. In 1934, Roosevelt convened a committee to determine what to do about this. The committee consisted of wildlife biologist Aldo Leopold, magazine publisher Thomas Beck, and Pulitzer Prize–winning cartoonist J. N. "Ding" Darling, whose drawings in the *Des Moines Register* frequently pilloried the shortcomings of Roosevelt's wildlife policies. The committee discovered that about $50 million in new refuges was needed to save the waterfowl. The committee wielded considerable influence, and its recommendation that money be spent immediately reawakened an idea that had lain dormant for more than ten years. The idea was to require waterfowl hunters to buy a "duck stamp" each year, in much the same way Americans had been encouraged to purchase war savings stamps after World War I. Proceeds from stamp sales would be used to buy lands for refuges, thereby relieving Congress of the responsibility to appropriate funds for land purchases every year. The

Duck Stamp Act passed in 1934, although it was not to go into effect until 1935. In exchange for the right to hunt on non-refuge lands, hunters would pay one dollar for the stamp (the first one of which was illustrated by Darling himself). Proceeds would be used to purchase new refuge lands authorized in the 1929 Migratory Bird Act.

Hunters backed the stamp act because they believed the protected habitats would produce surplus game, and this would spill into adjacent shooting areas. (In practice this did not always happen, since many species develop an acute sense of what is safe habitat and what is not.) One of the far-reaching consequences of the Duck Stamp Act was that it encouraged hunters' support for refuges but did not similarly encourage nonhunter support. Since money talks—and loudly—nonhunters seldom had an equal say in the formation of refuge management policy.

Meanwhile, Roosevelt made the startling appointment of Darling as head of the Bureau of Biological Survey. It was a shrewd way of telling Darling that since he complained so much about the government's wildlife programs, he ought to do something constructive about them. Reluctantly, Darling accepted the challenge. "Darling was an extreme extrovert," one of his coworkers on the *Register* recalled. He was "awed by nobody, overflowing with self-confidence." With such leadership characteristics the bureau gained as powerful and able a director as the Park Service and Forest Service had first had. For the first time in the bureau's lusterless history it was devoted to refuge matters, and its director was committed to the bureau's own particular cause.

Darling, "a kind of visual Will Rogers," according to author Stephen Fox in *John Muir and His Legacy*, grew up in Iowa. He claimed his hobbies were "Roquefort cheese, dairy farming, rock gardening, black bass fishing, ornithology and duck shooting." Despite his passion for the last of these, he had been a close ally of Hornaday's in the 1920s. At one point conservationists accused Darling of knowing "nothing but ducks, if indeed he knows them," but he was a tireless advocate for more waterfowl refuges. Having served on the Leopold Committee, he knew he needed money before the Duck Stamp revenue would start flowing, so he took to the halls of the Agriculture Department, demanding funds to begin his purchases. By his own ad-

170

mission he used "a straw to suck funds from the other fellow's barrel," and explained to those he pressured that "ducks can't lay eggs on a picket fence."

His persistence paid off, for within a few months he had amassed $8.5 million for wildlife from drought relief funds, land retirement funds, and Work Projects Administration funds. Roosevelt teasingly accused Darling of robbing the U.S. Treasury—and getting away with it. He added that "the Federal Courts say that the United States Government has a perfect right to condemn millions of acres for the welfare, health and happiness of ducks, geese, sandpipers, owls and wrens, but has no constitutional right to condemn a few old tenements in the slums for the health and happiness of the little boys and girls who will be our citizens of the next generation! Nevertheless, more power to your arm!"

With the WPA money, Darling planned to buy worn-out agricultural land for wildlife habitat. The only problem was that all the WPA money he had sucked out with a straw had to be spent by April 1, 1935, which was less than a year away. To find suitable lands, Darling hired a young wildlife biologist named J. Clark Salyer, with whom he had worked on the Iowa State Conservation Commission. In his book, *Sign of the Flying Goose*, George Laycock describes how Salyer, determined to do more for waterfowl than anybody had ever done, crisscrossed the country for months in a battered black Pontiac that was also his home, office, and laboratory. He located 600,000 acres of new refuge lands, but as his March 31 deadline drew nigh, he was horrified to realize that he had committed—without authorization from Agriculture Secretary Henry Wallace—all but $250,000 of the millions of WPA dollars. Salyer drove back to Washington like a maniac, only to discover that the deadline for Wallace's authorization fell on a Sunday, and Wallace could not be reached until Monday. Seeing all his work inching closer to utter ruin, Salyer signed the authorizations for Wallace. "I could have gone to prison," Salyer recalled later. But he did not. Wallace heard Salyer's confession, then sent him back to his refuge-buying work.

With the joint effort of Darling and Salyer, refuges began to evolve into a respectable system. Salyer's time on the road led to the creation of fifty-five new refuges, and he was instrumental in the establishment of some of the system's most impressive units: the Red Rock Lakes Refuge for trumpeter swans in Montana, the Agassiz Refuge in Minnesota for the largest moose population in the lower forty-eight states, and the Upper Souris Refuge in North Dakota, where great blue herons and black-crowned night herons nested by the hundreds. As he had promised from the outset, Darling stayed with the Biological Survey less than two years. He was angered by the administration's refusal to accept a $10 million endowment for wildlife protection in exchange for a repeal of the existing 10-percent excise tax on guns and ammunition. "I know of no other way to accomplish the necessary reversal from downhill slide to upward climb for wildlife resources," he said. In September 1935, Darling wrote to Wallace that "it now seems the strategic moment to demand my resignation for insubordination, murder, incest and the good of the service." He left to head the National Wildlife Federation and was replaced by Ira Gabrielson, a biologist with the bureau since 1915.

COORDINATION, CONSOLIDATION, CONFLICT

While the Biological Survey pursued its goals, Congress was beginning to interject itself into questions of animal welfare. In 1934 it passed the Fish and Wildlife Coordination Act, which required public works administrators to assess the impact on wildlife of such projects as dam-building and reclamation. In practice the requirement was feebly met, since the only mandatory provisions were consultation with the Bureau of Fisheries and impoundment of some water for fish culture and migratory-bird resting sites. The consultation concentrated on whether fish ladders were necessary and "economically practicable," narrowing the focus of fish and wildlife welfare measures to less than meaningful assistance. A series of increasingly stringent Endangered Species acts would have to be passed years later to make up for the Coordination Act's shortcomings. Another important boost for wildlife was the passage of the Pittman-Robertson Act of 1937, which gave the states funds to establish their own refuges, and perpetuated the two-tiered approach to wildlife management. All told, New Deal land conservation programs resulted in "the greatest upsurge of the wildlife populations the nation had ever seen," historian James Trefethen asserts.

172

Matters appeared to improve still more with the Reorganization Act of 1939, when the Bureau of Fisheries in the Department of Commerce and the Bureau of Biological Survey in the Department of Agriculture were consolidated into a single agency and transferred to the Department of the Interior. The new agency was called the United States Fish and Wildlife Service, and refuge administration was made one of its primary responsibilities. But the consolidation did not strengthen the position of refuges as was hoped. A new ethic evolved in which refuges were manipulated to yield more game species, often at the expense of other species. This overt favoritism led in 1949 to a Faustian bargain: Fish and Wildlife Service officials lobbied to raise the price of the Duck Stamp from one dollar to two, promising to open 25 percent of each refuge to hunting and later, in exchange for a three-dollar stamp, to open 40 percent to hunting. The policy, developed within the Service, signified a major turning point in the philosophy of the refuge concept.

Neither World War II nor the Truman and Eisenhower administrations that followed were strong on conservation measures. During the Eisenhower years, car dealer Douglas McKay was Interior Secretary, and morale at the Fish and Wildlife Service sank especially low. Among other things, McKay wanted to open refuges to oil and gas drilling to make them more economically attractive, and issued sixty-four permits for this work in three years. He often sided against his own agency in conflicts about the use of refuge lands. Cabeza Prieta Game Range in Arizona, for instance, a refuge for desert bighorn sheep, had been used during World War II for pilot and weapons testing. Fair enough, given wartime necessities—but when the war was over, the Air Force wanted to continue using it. McKay saw nothing wrong with this idea and promptly approved it, an act that appalled the Service.

In 1956, under a new Interior Secretary, the Service mutated again. Its name was changed to the Bureau of Sport Fisheries and Wildlife, and responsibility for commercial fishing was vested in the Bureau of Commercial Fishing. The two agencies were given equal billing *within* a third entity called the Fish and Wildlife Service, which many conservationists felt diluted the federal commitment to wildlife preservation. Meanwhile, the Bureau of Sport Fisheries and Wildlife would have more aptly been named the Bureau of Sport Fisheries and *Sport* Wildlife, since emphasis in the refuges was definitely on increasing popular game species. A refuge's success was often measured by the number of huntable animals it hosted, an emphasis that sometimes produced unhappy consequences.

As a result of this policy, the number of huntable Canada geese at Horicon Marsh in Wisconsin, for example, grew from 2,000 in 1948 to about 208,000 in 1975. Through a vigorous program of artificial planting, the refuge had attracted most of the geese in the Mississippi Flyway, not only depriving other refuges in other states of their fair share, but creating tenement conditions at Horicon. Other waterfowl were driven out, and without enough food on the refuge to support the new population, flocks of geese dined in the grainfields of neighboring farms, stripping them bare. Only by adjusting Horicon's food and habitat could refuge managers force many geese farther south. The Horicon situation was a by-product of the circle in which refuge administration had been traveling, at least at the upper levels of management. (Many local managers sturdily fought the trend, to little avail.) Political support for the refuge system was strongest among hunters and fishermen; the system's primary concern was to produce the species these supporters preferred. Economic development via hunting was the chief measure of progress, and, while refuge officials were willing to go to bat against other economic developments such as logging or grazing, they would usually only do so for the benefit of hunters.

A FLOCK OF LEGISLATION

Ironically, while the Fish and Wildlife Service during these early years (and later) never produced a nationally known leader to plead its cause or enhance its image—another Stephen Mather or Gifford Pinchot, say—it did, deep within its institutional structure, harbor perhaps the most influential environmentalist of the twentieth century. Her name was Rachel Carson, and she worked as an editor for the Service during the 1940s, becoming the first woman in the agency to hold a nonclerical position. Carson, who was born in 1907, was a writer and biologist who combined her talents exceedingly well. One of her chores at the Service was the production of a series of booklets under the general title "Conservation in Action," each of which examined the natural wildlife and habitat of a single refuge, and each of which was unabashedly devoted to the promotion of an ecological conscience. That interest and conviction, fostered and supported during her years with the Service, came to its fullest expression, of course, in her own 1962 book, *Silent Spring*—which many have called the single most important conservation manifesto since George Perkins Marsh's *Man and Nature* in 1867.

The alert raised by *Silent Spring* began a period in which ecological concern blossomed. Congress enlarged upon the federal role in environmental protection, passing legislation that mandated the cleanup of the country's air and water, recognized the value of wilderness, and expressed the intent that all species—birds, fish, reptiles, or mammals—would endure. This new national consciousness also held the promise of better days for the National Wildlife Refuge System. But hope and good intentions were consistently undermined by a combination of structural inadequacies within the Fish and Wildlife Service, a tortuous confusion of national priorities and public policy, and, in recent years, the influence of a presidential administration that often demonstrated either indifference or open antagonism toward the purposes for which the refuges were established.

To begin with, repeated legislative efforts designed to fix agreement on central issues turned out to dodge them neatly instead, resulting in many laws but little guidance. Preceding the publication of *Silent Spring* by one year was the Wetlands Loan Act, passed by Congress to speed acquisition of wetlands for the refuge system. The act authorized an advance appropriation of up to $105 million (later increased to $200 million) to buy essential wetlands over a seven-year period. (To encourage nonhunters to buy stamps also, the name of the Duck Stamp was ultimately changed to the Migratory Bird Hunting and Conservation Stamp.) Amazingly, the Wetlands Loan Act, given the interest-free use of money to buy land and have done with it in seven years, nevertheless has yet to reach the goal set twenty-four years ago. Only about half the land targeted for purchase has been acquired, while many acres have been lost to commercial development. Since it was the responsibility of the Fish and Wildlife Service to find the land and request the funding already authorized, it is obvious that other jobs rated a higher priority.

Another act designed to strengthen the refuge concept was the

175

Refuge Recreation Act, passed in 1962. The act stated that refuges could permit secondary recreational activity so long as such acitivity was compatible with the primary purpose of the refuges and there was money available to administer it. Out of this act arose the "dominant use" doctrine of the refuges. But the act's stipulations were not clear enough to prevent types of recreation detrimental to wildlife. At the Ruby Lake Refuge in Nevada, for instance, the seven-thousand-acre lake had become a haven for some thirty thousand motorboats a year, with an alarming impact on the nesting sites of canvasback and redhead ducks, before a lawsuit resulted in court-ordered restrictions. In 1964 the passage of the Wilderness Act (see chapter 5) brought hope of a slight measure of relief, since it provided the means to gain an extra layer of protection for the relatively small number of refuge areas qualifying for wilderness designation. But the Wilderness Act was the only congressional guarantee that even a fraction of a refuge would be kept sacrosanct.

Similarly ambiguous aid came with passage of the National Wildlife Refuge System Administration Act of 1966. On the face of it, this act may have sounded like the much-needed organic act for the system, but it was not. Companion legislation to the Endangered Species Preservation Act of that year (see below), it provided only broad statutory guidance, while failing to define the basic purposes of the system or establish clear, strong measures for protection. In actuality, the Administration Act merely brought all types of wildlife areas and game ranges under one overreaching and weakly supported roof. Trouble arose because of the act's vagueness on how the lands were to be managed. Areas known as game ranges, for example, were managed jointly by the Bureau of Land Management and the Fish and Wildlife Service.

The potential conflict inherent in such joint management was problem enough, but many conservationists were stunned when Secretary of the Interior Stanley K. Hathaway transferred three game ranges entirely over to the BLM. This was a precedent that many found alarming, not only because it would place these specific ranges in the hands of an agency that had not formerly exhibited that much interest in managing its lands for wildlife values, but because it might suggest that the Interior Secretary could, at his discretion, create more game ranges out of wildlife refuges by simple administrative action, then turn, these too, over to the BLM. The Wilderness Society filed suit in the U. S. District Court for the District of Columbia to stop the transfer, and in *The Wilderness Society vs. Hathaway*, the court ruled in The Society's favor on the grounds that "The Secretary is required to exercise his discretion and authority with respect to the administration of game ranges and wildlife refuges through the Fish and Wildlife Service." In other words, the distinction between game ranges and wildlife refuges was artificial, and in either case lands should be managed primarily for wildlife. Those principles were embodied in an amendment to the Administration Act in 1976, and all units, whether game ranges or refuges, were consolidated under the Fish and Wildlife Service.

THE CONUNDRUM OF COMPATIBILITY

There remained plenty of "windows of opportunity" provided by the Refuge Administration Act—particularly the window that granted the Interior Secretary broad discretionary authority to "permit the use of any area within the System for any purposes, including, but not limited to hunting, fishing, public recreation and accommodations, and access whenever he determines that such use is compatible with the major purposes for which such areas were established." Although specific standards to determine compatibility did not exist, many optimistic observers felt that no secretary was likely to exceed common sense by emphasizing logging or other commercial uses at the expense of wildlife needs. That optimism was sorely tested in 1981 when James Watt was appointed Secretary of the Interior, for in the fall of 1981 his Deputy Director of the Fish And Wildlife Service, E. Eugene Hester, sent out a memorandum asking all refuge managers to supply his office with a list of potentially commercial operations that could be put in place on their lands in addition to those already existing.

The refuge managers did not reply with proper enthusiasm, for in July 1982, another, more pointed memorandum was issued. "Last fall," it complained, "we asked each region to identify expansion potential. The response we received was not satisfactory. . . . We believe that there is potential to expand economic uses in such areas as grazing, haying, farming, timber harvesting, trapping, oil and gas extraction, small hydroelectric generation, concessions, commercial hunting and fishing guides, guided interpretive tours, and commercial fishing. We believe if you use innovation and creativity and, if necessary, a redirection of effort, these as well as other uses can be expanded." Outside Alaska, it would have taken more than "innovation" to open the refuges to oil and gas operations, since such uses were prohibited by law in the refuges of the Lower 48 states. That inconvenience was alleviated in June of 1983, however, when the Interior Board of Land Appeals ruled that any refuge land acquired through purchase or by donation of private land (and not withdrawn from the public domain) could be used for the extraction of oil and gas. Watt immediately accelerated the leasing program, until by the time he was forced to resign in October 1983, 144 lease applications had been received by the Interior Department involving 614,876 acres on forty-six refuges in twenty-four states. Meanwhile, Watt had even attempted to give away part of Alaska Maritime National Wildlife Refuge in a swap for other land interests. About four thousand acres of St. Matthew Island, the site of one of the largest sea-bird nesting populations in North America and one of the few known nesting grounds for McKay's bunting, was destined by this scheme to be turned over to the Atlantic Richfield Company for an airfield, seaport, and support base for its oil and gas operations. The fact that the island was a wildlife refuge unit and a designated wilderness area did not stop Watt—although an Alaska court decision in 1984 would declare that the Secretary's act was a "misapplication of the law."

The frenzy to develop the commercial possibilities of the refuge system swiftly declined after Watt's removal, and while the law has remained ambiguous and vulnerable to misuse ever since, no Interior Secretary that has followed him has attempted anything quite so far-reaching. Which is not to say that the refuges as a whole have been managed substantially better, or that problems have vanished. Administrative anomalies and policy confusions remain legion throughout the system, but in some areas *people* have posed the biggest problem. Refuges record more than 30 million visits a year. Spread out over the entire system, this may not seem like much, but nearly 80 percent of the visitation takes place on only forty refuges.

Chincoteague National Wildlife Refuge, part of a fragile barrier island off the coasts of Maryland and Virginia, for example, has received more than a million visitors annually for many years, more than any

178

natural area that size should be asked to absorb. Until off-road access was barred and a permit system established at Virginia's Back Bay National Wildlife Refuge in 1972, for another example, proper administration of the refuge for the protection of nesting birds and other wildlife was virtually impossible. "In the summertime," remembered Dennis Holland, the manager at the time, the refuge "was packed with people pouring onto the beach. In that first north mile of beach, we had swimming, surfing, fishing, sunbathing, plus a constant flow of bumper-to-bumper traffic. With all of these uses and children wading in the water and running up and down the beach, it was just a frightening experience to feel that I had the responsibility for their safety. And my conservation upbringing to that point told me that this was a refuge and, by golly, you're not supposed to be doing all these things. . . . We were not wildlife enforcement officers, hell, we were city policemen."

At Parker River National Wildlife Refuge on Plum Island near New-buryport, Massachusetts, the population of human visitors became such a problem that the Fish and Wildlife Service was forced to close the narrow refuge beach during the nesting season of the threatened piping plover and endangered least tern. Unsurprisingly, this caused an uproar of objection from those citizens of Newburyport who wanted to keep the beach open as one of the town's summertime tourist attractions—even though there were other beaches available. The refuge managers so far have resisted several years of pressure to open the area and have utilized a cadre of volunteers to help monitor the beach until the young plovers have fledged every year, while the Friends of the Parker River National Wildlife Refuge, a local conservation group, has launched an educational campaign to inform the local citizenry and vistors alike of the necessity to keep the beaches off limits to human use in the crucial nesting months. Meanwhile, partly in an effort to counter the effect of the beach closing, the refuge has expanded recreational facilities and built so many hiking trails in the areas behind the beach that some critics fear that the natural habitat has been fragmented beyond recognition and maybe beyond repair.

Then there is the question of hunting, a use tolerated, even encouraged, on more than half the refuges ever since passage of the Migratory Bird Hunting Stamp Act (the so-called "Duck Stamp Act") in 1934—so much so that scores of refuges, like many of those in the Mississippi

179

River Valley, seem to function as little more than enormous duck blinds during hunting seasons. The Fish and Wildlife Service argues reasonably enough that hunting has replaced natural predation on many refuges, and to have neither could lead to habitat destruction and overpopulation. "Nature habitually maintains a wide margin of overproduction," wildlife biologist Durwood Allen has written. "She kills off a huge surplus of animals whether we take our harvest or not." The Fish and Wildlife Service welcomes the funding that the Duck Stamp Act provides, too, but not everyone is convinced that hunting is an unalloyed good. The concentration of effort on preserving various game birds for hunting, some conservationists worry, takes time, money, and effort away from the preservation of other wildlife values. Some wildlife biologists also say that too much hunting has been allowed in too many refuges where it is simply biologically unsound. In Kenai National Wildlife Refuge in Alaska, for example, wolves have been so depleted by hunting and trapping programs undertaken by the state that humans are indeed now the chief predators of the moose. But human hunters are selective predators who take the biggest and best of the animals, unlike wolves, which customarily take the slowest or weakest—the ones most easily run down. The consequent damage to the genetic "pool" from which future populations of moose will come if the healthiest animals are eliminated is a cause for concern.

Still, if population pressure and hunting problems are shared by some refuges, most continue to be threatened more by commercial exploitation and other clearly "incompatible" activities taking place inside and outside their boundaries. In 1981, even as James Watt's Interior Department was stepping up its commercial program, a Fish and Wildlife Service task force undertook to investigate problems facing the system. Its report, issued in draft form as "Field Stations Threats and Conflicts" in August 1982, cited no fewer than 7,717 internal and external resource threats throughout the system. "These threats will continue to degrade certain fish and wildlife resources until such time as mitigation efforts are implemented," it concluded. "In some cases, this degradation or loss of resource is irreversible. It represents a sacrifice by a public that, for the most part, is unaware that such a price is being paid." The report, politically discomforting, was not formally released to the public until July 1983; by then, it had been refined somewhat: now, the terms "threats" and "conflicts" were downgraded to "problems" and "resource problems" (and the report was now titled "Fish and Wildlife Service Resource Problems"). The particularly incendiary comment about continuing degradation and an uninformed public did not survive the revision, but the report now listed 7,718 "problems," 5,228 of which it classified as "documented."

Seven years later, The Wilderness Society made its own investigation and concluded that not much had changed. "Today many of the national wildlife refuges are refuges in name only," writer Ben Beach noted in *The Ten Most Endangered National Wildlife Refuges.* "Migrating water-fowl are landing in poisoned marshes, development is destroying vital wetlands, and dams and irrigation projects are choking off essential sources of water." In New Jersey, the report said, Great Swamp National Wildlife Refuge was on the receiving end of polluted runoff from a fast-growing suburban area, while in Florida's Key Deer National Wildlife Refuge as much as 20 percent of the dwindling population of little key deer were being slaughtered by automobile traffic every year. At the Chincoteague refuge, beachgoers, many of them in off-road vehicles, were still threatening areas vital to endangered shorebirds, and in the Lower Rio Grande Refuge in Texas a proposed resort threatened critical habitat. At Stillwater in Nevada, toxic runoff from nearby agricultural enterprises threatened fish and waterfowl; at Yazoo in Mississippi, the largest land-fill project in American history damaged already troubled waterfowl wintering grounds; at Upper Mississippi River, agricultural wastewater, sedimentation, and inappropriate public use were impacting habitat for all species. Oil companies still wanted to open the Coastal Plain of Arctic National Wildlife Refuge in Alaska (see chapter 7), and a waste disposal company wanted to build an enormous processing plant on the edge of Loxahatachee National Wildlife Refuge just north of the Everglades.

The tenth of the "Ten Most Endangered" refuges listed in The Society's report was Kesterson National Wildlife Refuge in the San Joaquin Valley of California, one of the few threatened refuges that had caught the attention of the national media. The problem here was agricultural wastewater that had been dumped into the refuge from nearby farms (almost all of them using subsidized irrigation water provided by the Bureau of Reclamation's Central Valley Project). In that water were a number of contaminants, chief among them selenium. In concentrated amounts, selenium is toxic and grows more deadly the farther up the food chain it goes. In Kesterson, it had gone far enough to inflict terrible harm, a fact that began to become apparent by the early 1980s. Tests discovered the highest levels of selenium ever found in living fish. Dead and deformed birds were found in increasing numbers. Some had no eyes. The average concentration of selenium in the livers and kidneys of birds collected from the refuge's ponds were about ten times those from birds in a nearby control area. "In 1984," Beach wrote, "Fish and Wildlife Service crews began to spread out over the refuge with shotguns and explosive devices to scare away wildlife that was headed for Kesterson's tainted ponds. In March 1985, a few days after CBS' "60 Minutes" ran a story on Kesterson, Interior Secretary Donald Hodel ordered it closed. In June 1986, the U. S. Bureau of Reclamation finally closed the agriculture drains sending contaminated water to the refuge." (Since then, the federal agencies involved have been engaged in a massive cleanup program whose final cost to the taxpayer has yet to be determined.)

Many of the situations reported by The Wilderness Society echoed those in a 1990 Fish and Wildlife Service survey of refuge managers, who identified 133 individual "incompatible" uses that were still being allowed on these sanctuaries in violation of the law. This prompted a lawsuit on the part of The Society and other conservation organizations, and at the end of 1993 the Fish and Wildlife Service negotiated a settlement with the plaintiffs, pledging to modify or eliminate within one year most incompatible uses. "Settlement of this lawsuit clearly signals the Interior Department's intent to protect our National Wildlife Refuges," Interior Secretary Babbitt declared in announcing the agreement.

A QUESTION OF BIOPHILIA

For nearly thirty years, the continuing struggle to protect the viability of the National Wildlife Refuge System has been given an added measure of urgency by the fact that federal law requires the protection and recovery of species listed by the Fish and Wildlife Service as endangered or threatened—although the law had to be born again twice before reaching its present state. In 1966, Congress passed the Endangered Species Preservation Act, which officially recognized the right of other species to share in the glory of the planet. The act directed all federal land-managing agencies to preserve the habitats of native vertebrate species found by the Secretary of the Interior to be in danger of extinction. (As noted earlier, companion legislation that same year, the National Wildlife Refuge System Administration Act, institutionalized the National Wildlife Refuge System for the first time, linking these two ideas neatly and permanently.)

Unfortunately, critics said, the Endangered Species Act of 1966 was a pretty toothless affair, with few solid guidelines for the identification of endangered species and little enforcement authority. In 1969 it was replaced with the Endangered Species Conservation Act, which extended protection to invertebrate species and authorized the Secretary of the Interior to maintain a list of species "threatened with worldwide extinc-tion" and allowed him to prohibit the importation of most such species and their products (furs, feathers, etc.). That was better, but still fell short of protecting domestic species sufficiently, and in 1973 a more ecologically correct Congress passed yet another Endangered Species Act. This version—still on the books today, though in need of reauthorization—ordered the protection of "endangered" species, those in immediate danger of becoming extinct throughout all or a significant part of their range, and "threatened" species, those likely to become endangered in the foreseeable future. Once a species was placed on either list, the law mandated the designation of critical habitat and the preparation of plans for the species' recovery; it also prohibited the killing and capturing of fish and wildlife on the lists, and the destruction and collecting of plants on the lists, prohibited the importation of any foreign endangered species and the exportation of any domestic endangered or threatened species, and, finally, enjoined any federal agency from taking any action or allowing any action to be taken—including the destruction or damage of habitat—on federal lands or by federal projects that would jeopardize the continued existence of any listed species.

Like many laws, the Endangered Species Act did not become widely known until it engendered controversy, largely over conflicts between what the act stipulated and what some human wanted to do to some piece of land or water occupied by some endangered or threatened species. In the 1970s, there was a noisy controversy raised over the fact that the listing of a subspecies of the tiny snail darter would have blocked the construction of Tellico Dam on the Tennessee River; when additional numbers of the little fish were later discovered elsewhere, critics of the act pointed to what they described as its muddleheaded fallibility. (That the dam also turned out to be one of the great boondoggles of the age and might legitimately have been rejected on those grounds alone does not ordinarily enter the discussion among those who bemoan the arbitrary nature of the Endangered Species Act and maintain that it stifles enterprise and cripples industry.) When the act was invoked for the protection of the northern spotted owl during the fight to save the Ancient Forests of the Pacific Northwest (see chapter 2), similar complaints could be heard, most of them insisting that the government, in league with anti-development environmentalists, was costing the region tens of thousands of jobs. Agitation in and out of Congress began to call for amendments that would significantly weaken the act, or obliterate it altogether; among those calling for such amendments was Presi-dent George Bush's Interior Secretary, Manuel Lujan, who, he said, did not understand why *every* species should be saved and suggested that the economic impacts that might result from the act's enforcement be given equal weight when a species was considered for preservation.

The law has so far survived without being significantly maimed, and with good reason. Among other things, it has been solidly demonstrated that the economic impact of the act has been minuscule. While it prohibits federal actions that would jeopardize a species, it also stipulates that the federal agency involved—the U. S. Army Corps of Engineers, say, wanting to issue a dredging permit, or the Bureau of Reclamation wanting to build a waterwork—must consult with the Fish and Wildlife Service or, in the case of marine species, the National Marine Fisheries Service, to identify "reasonable" and "prudent" alternatives to a proposed action that would allow it to go forward. Out of more than 71,000 such consultations between 1987 and 1991, there were only 18 projects stopped because no alternatives could be worked out. Clearly, the act is no monkeywrench tossed into the clattering machinery of progress.

What it is, however, is a safety net that is our last best hope of saving species that continue to disappear at a terrifying rate. Critics say such statements are alarmist and exaggerated, pointing out the indisputable fact that the engine of evolution continues moving along, changing ecosystems, altering the mix of diversity, building new species every day; nature is bountiful, productive, and never, ever stops. Why should we worry, they ask, if we wipe out a single species here or a habitat with a lot of species there? Defenders of the act reply that so are we *humans* bountiful, productive, and we never ever stop either. What we are doing, they say, is not altering species but obliterating them, not changing the character of diversity but destroying it by wrecking functioning ecosystems that have taken eons and eons to evolve in all their complexity—and doing so at a rate whose speed we cannot even decently measure yet, except to say that no other force in the history of the planet has accomplished so much damage in so short a time: Half the number of species known to have become extinct in all of recorded history were done away with in this century alone, and we are driving other species to extinction at the rate, some say, of three a day; some predict the loss of as many as one *hundred* species a day by the year 2000. The Endangered Species Act, its supporters insist, has demonstrated its competence by rescuing local populations and sometimes the last remaining individuals of such species as whooping cranes, American alligators, California sea otters, peregrine falcons, blackfooted ferrets, bald eagles, brown pelicans, fringe-toed lizards, and desert pup-fish, as well as sundry varieties of butterflies, salamanders, flowers, and other plant and animal species.

Most Americans appear to agree with professional environmentalists. A bipartisan national poll taken at the height of the 1991 recession, when jobs and economic opportunity were much on everyone's mind, revealed that 66 percent of the Democrats and 65 percent of the Republicans interviewed expressed support for the act; 73 percent overall said that a political candidate's stand in favor of protecting endangered species was a reason to vote for him or her; when asked specifically to choose between jobs and wildlife, most chose wildlife.

Biologist and natural philosopher Edward O. Wilson probably would not have been surprised at the outcome; it was he who coined the phrase "biophilia" to describe what he believed to be an innate sense of connection, even love, that ties human beings to all other forms of life. If such a connection does in fact exist, then perhaps it can be said that the Endangered Species Act is the relationship's sacred compact.

THE CURSE OF ANONYMITY

Without habitat in which to harbor protected species, of course, the Endangered Species Act would be useless, and while the country's national parks, national forests, and even its Bureau of Land Management lands all provide substantial habitat, the National Wildlife Refuge System is the only one of the public-land entities that was specifically *designed* for the protection of the creatures that lived on and in its hundreds of individual units. Its preservation, even expansion, is crucial to the task of preserving those creatures, yet it still wallows in a slough of anonymity that seriously hampers the system's ability to function on an equal basis with the national park or national forest systems. If most Americans can name at least one or two national parks or national forests, few even know that the refuge system exists; only the lands of the BLM are as little known. Lynn Greenwalt, once director of the Fish and Wildlife Service, painfully noticed this while reviewing public comments following a 1978 task force report on proposed plans for the entire National Wildlife Refuge System. "If there is any part of this very productive exercise about which I am disappointed," he commented, "it is in the sense that there was so little broad public reaction." The report had engendered more than two thousand public responses, but Greenwalt's disappointment was understandable when those two thousand responses were compared to the more than sixty thousand the Yosemite Master Plan—just one park, not the entire National Park System—brought forth (see chapter 1).

"One outdoor traveler of my acquaintance—a person familiar with the scenic wonders of our national parks," environmental journalist John G. Mitchell wrote in the Fall 1983 issue of *Wilderness*, "confesses that he is yet to set foot in a national wildlife refuge. Never got around to it, he says. For the record, I asked him to name a few of the refuges he might like to visit, when he got around to it. He could not name *one*." Part of the problem, Mitchell believed, was "rooted in the way we look at wild things. The unfortunate fact of the matter is that most of us, like my friend, are collectors of waterfalls. We lean toward the bold and romantic. . . . Beneath our abiding affection for wildlife lurks a subconscious twinge of regret at the critters' indifference to any sense of human aesthetics. Why do so many of the most admirable beasts so often prefer the blandest or scratchiest settings on earth? For that matter, why can a refuge not look more like a park?"

Wildlife biologist Robert Giles found the blame for the system's regrettable anonymity in the management priorities of the Fish and Wildlife Service itself. The refuge system, he has written, "is the most underdeveloped public wildlife resource in the nation." He was not, we should note, speaking of commercial exploitation but of managerial structure, which was, he said, "an administrative no-man's land—a prime example of how failure to provide consistent leadership can prevent a system from achieving its potential." Above all, Giles continued, "the Fish and Wildlife Service has tended to treat refuges as unwanted responsibilities rather than build them into a land management agency fully as productive of public benefits as the national forests and the national parks." Within the Fish and Wildlife Service, Giles and other critics have charged, the administration of the refuges has lain buried beneath layers of bureaucratic sediments and has no direct link to the Secretary of the Interior. Until 1984 there was not even a line on the national budget showing how much money was spent on the third-largest public lands system in the country. An informal survey once taken by an agency administrator revealed that fewer than a thousand people were actually stationed on the refuges. Many refuges do not even have on-site managers, but are managed as a group.

In its defense, the Fish and Wildlife Service has had much to occupy it besides the administration of the refuge system. It runs the national fish hatcheries, conducts law-enforcement programs for the prevention of poaching and the importation of exotic species, administers the Endangered Species Act along with more than 150 other acts of Congress (or portions thereof), manages migratory birds in association with international treaties, evaluates the impacts of public works projects on wildlife, administers grant programs for state wildlife agencies, provides technical assistance on wildlife matters to nearly anyone who asks for it. As a consequence, refuges themselves are considered just one function among many in the agency, not a program with its own needs and purposes.

All of which makes it difficult to attract a broad, loyal constituency like that enjoyed by the National Park System or to some extent even the National Forest System. As a result, the system's growth has been called opportunistic rather than planned, expanding where it could instead of where it should. Considering the concentration of refuges in some parts of the country and their notable scarcity in others, considering their emphasis on game birds rather than all creatures, considering the seemingly contradictory allowance for non-wildlife uses, and considering the system's bureaucratic fragmentation and near invisibility in the public mind, the National Wildlife Refuge System brings to mind Voltaire's eighteenth-century evaluation of the Holy Roman Empire as being neither holy nor Roman nor an empire.

Amid such confusion, it might be well to remember some words of Rachel Carson written nearly fifty years ago, long before her powerful expose of the chemical industry, *Silent Spring*, showed us all what the ultimate environmental consequences of our actions could be. At the time she was still a writer and editor with the U. S. Biological Survey and her assignment was to produce a series of descriptive booklets celebrating the hundreds of refuges established during the reign of J. N. "Ding" Darling. "We in the United States have been slow to learn that our wildlife, like other forms of natural wealth, must be vigorously protected if we are to continue to enjoy its benefits," she cautioned in her introduction to the series. "Like the resource it seeks to protect, wildlife conservation must be dynamic, changing as conditions change, seeking always to become more effective. We have much to accomplish."

AN AGENDA FOR THE NATIONAL WILDLIFE REFUGE SYSTEM

The proper mission of the refuge system was succinctly outlined in the *Refuge Manual* issued by the Fish and Wildlife Service as a management handbook. That mission, the manual states, is "to provide, preserve, restore, and manage a national network of lands and waters sufficient in size, diversity, and location to meet society's needs for areas where the widest possible spectrum of benefits associated with wildlife and wildlands is enhanced and made available." More specifically, the various objectives of this diverse land-management system were to preserve, restore, and enhance in their natural ecosystems all species of animals and plants that are threatened or endangered; to perpetuate the migratory bird resource for the benefit of people; to preserve natural diversity and abundance of mammals and nonmigratory birds; to provide an understanding and appreciation of fish and wildlife ecology and man's proper role in his environment; and to provide high-quality recreational experiences oriented toward wildlife.

As we hope this chapter has made clear, the implementation of that otherwise perfectly appropriate mission is seriously hampered on a number of levels. As an entity within the Fish and Wildlife Service, the refuge system's management priorities are confused by the lack of a clear bureaucratic identity and self-sufficiency. Federal funding and personnel are inadequate to carry out proper scientific research, law enforcement, planning, habitat preservation and acquisition, employee training, and on-site wildlife-education programs necessary to the development of a supportive public constituency. Serious abuses have arisen from a too-careless accommodation with commercial and recreational uses at the expense of wildlife and habitat values.

All of this will have to change or be significantly modified if the system is to be given proper stewardship. At the heart of our concern should be the ongoing "domino effect" that now characterizes the human impact on the natural world: The destruction of habitat that leads to the extinction of species that results in the loss of biological diversity that ultimately impoverishes the quality of all life—including human life—and limits its ability to sustain itself. The preservation of biodiversity is the motivating factor in The Wilderness Society's current "Lifelands" program outlined at the end of chapter 5, and it is the paramount motive behind the recommendations that follow. The protection and preservation of the National Wildlife Refuge System inevitably will be essential to the protection and preservation of most large coherent systems of natural landscapes and all the life—human and wild—that they nurture.

Passage of organic legislation for the National Wildlife Refuge System. Of all the difficulties attending the refuge system today, none is more onerous than the lack of any single overall guiding body of law for its administration. It is the only major federal land entity that does not have such law. The National Park System acquired its direction with passage of the Organic Act of 1916; the National Wilderness Preservation System was *created* by its law, the Wilderness Act of 1964; the national forests received the National Forest Management Act of 1976; and the Bureau of Land Management's land was given the Federal Land

189

Policy and Management Act of 1976. By comparison, the refuge system basically operates under the administration of a loose and confusing amalgam of individual laws and legal authorities, fragments of responsibility that never quite come together to produce a coherent management program.

For the past several years, The Wilderness Society has been working with other conservationists and members of Congress to craft legislation that would give the refuge system its fair measure of identity and authority. The resulting bill, the "National Wildlife Refuge System Management and Policy Act," sponsored and introduced by Senator Graham of Florida in the Senate and by Representative Gibbons in the House, was placed before Congress in 1993. Elaborating on and expanding the official mission for the refuges, the act's purposes are, first, to "provide a national network of lands and waters with respect to which the size, variety, and location are designed to protect the wealth of fish, wildlife, and plants of this Nation and their habitats for present and future generations"; second, to "provide healthy, naturally productive, and enduring food, water, and shelter to fish, wildlife, and plant communities and to ensure naturally diverse, healthy, and abundant populations of fish, wildlife, and plant species in perpetuity"; and to meet international treaty obligations "with respect to fish, wildlife, and plants, and their habitats." No mention here of economic development or military necessities; the emphasis is on the protection of these resources as essential to the preservation of biological diversity. The legislation also calls for a strict "compatibility" standard; limits the discretion of the Secretary to interpret that standard; provides that permits for current uses must be revoked within five years unless the Secretary of the Interior, in consultation with the Director of the Fish and Wildlife Service, determines that the use does in fact meet the new compatibility standards; and calls for the preparation of unit-by-unit long-range refuge management plans to be completed within ten years of the act's passage, such plans to be designed to meet specific goals and to be reviewed and revised at least every fifteen years.

Reauthorization and sufficient funding of the Endangered Species Act of 1973. Since 1992, when the Endangered Species Act was scheduled for reauthorization, Congress has floundered in indecision, the act remaining in force only through successive continuing resolutions while those who oppose the act have proposed amendments that would strip it of any real power to protect species and species habitat. The Wilderness Society and the Endangered Species Coalition, a gathering of conservation organizations and individuals formed to defend the act, have asked Congress not only to reauthorize it but to provide the Fish and Wildlife Service with funds sufficient to implement it at necessary levels. While the agency has promised to accelerate its listing of the tremendous backlog of species identified as potentially endangered— more than 3,700 species in this country, at last count—some 40 percent of those species already listed have not yet been given recovery plans, nor have habitat recovery areas been identified.

A recent report from the Interior Department's Office of Inspector General estimated that it would take as much as $4.6 billion to get all currently listed species on the road to recovery (and this does not include species not yet on the list), yet funding for this program has traditionally been authorized at less than $10 million a year. That is not enough by far to ensure that this program can function in full partnership with the National Wildlife Refuge System for the preservation of species and species diversity.

The immediate designation of recommended wilderness areas in the National Wildlife Refuge System. Even when more coherent and stringent management legislation is put in place, the best way to protect any given part of any given wildlife refuge still must be designation as wilderness. More than two million acres of wildlife refuge wilderness in the Lower 48 states have been designated since passage of the Wilderness Act, but that still leaves more than 1.8 million acres that the Fish and Wildlife Service has identified and recommended for wilderness—while neither the Executive Branch nor Congress has acted on these recommendations. From a low of six-tenths of an acre in Mille Lacs National Wildlife Refuge, Minnesota, to a high of 1,588,779 acres in Desert National Wildlife Range, Nevada, the twenty-six areas involved cover a broad and valuable spectrum of habitat types, including coastal, riverine, and inland wetlands, Sonoran and Great Basin deserts, mountainous regions, and High Plains grasslands. The designations should either be made on a state-by-state basis or as part of an omnibus

191

wildlife refuge wilderness bill.

In Alaska, the Alaska Lands Act established sixteen new wildlife refuges that totaled 76 million acres and stipulated that these lands be studied for possible inclusion in the National Wilderness Preservation System. Those studies resulted in the recommendation of wilderness designation for about 54 million acres, but, as in those for the Lower 48 states, the recommendations have not yet been sent to Congress. This should be done immediately.

Begin an aggressive expansion program for refuge habitat. The 91.5 million acres currently in the National Wildlife Refuge System (only 13 million of which lie outside Alaska) are not enough to sustain the habitat needs of the near future, much less those of the next century. From the "pothole" country of North Dakota to the Louisiana coast, from the San Joaquin Valley to the Ohio River Valley, habitats for many species are under great pressures from urban, industrial, and agricultural expansion, recreational use, and economic development. Particular emphasis should be placed on the acquisition of critical wetland habitat. There is no more urgent need today than the protection and preservation of the nation's fast-vanishing resource of wetland habitat, as many as 350,000 acres of which are destroyed every year, square miles sucked dry, filled, planted on, built on, poisoned, vandalized. Finally, the acquisition of lands for many existing refuges remains to be completed; such units should be expanded by the addition of enough surrounding land to provide the preservation of functional ecosystems.

Annual appropriations from the Land and Water Conservation Fund, which traditionally have been preposterously low (in the federal budgets for 1984, 1985, 1986, and 1987 no money at all was appropriated for refuge purchases), must be significantly increased. Another avenue of expansion could be through an inventory of all appropriate federal land that might qualify for refuge classification. More than 97 percent of the current National Wildlife Refuge System was originally established with land already in federal ownership. Many of the millions of acres now under the management of the Defense Department, the Forest Service, and the Bureau of Land Management could appropriately be transferred to the refuge system—certainly, no better or cheaper method exists to expand the system quickly to meet the present and future needs of all

192

forms of wildlife.

Above all, expansion should be governed by a long-range plan subject to public review. During the administration of President Jimmy Carter, the Fish and Wildlife Service authorized the drafting of a ten-year acquisition plan. The target date for completion of the plan was February 6, 1981. It was neither completed nor released during the Reagan and Bush years, although it recently has been revived and is currently under completion. The scope of such planning should be raised from ten years to at least twenty. Further, the acquisition plan should be more thoroughly incorporated into refuge programming and master planning; the size of the refuge system should always be considered open-ended and subject to growth as future requirements dictate.

We created the National Wildlife Refuge System because over millennia a profound change had taken place in the way in which human beings viewed the rest of life on the planet. We learned that the concept of stewardship had implications far beyond simple human use for simple human needs. We learned that all forms of life have an individual integrity that should be respected and protected. We are learning still, which is why the continuing existence of a healthy, expanded, and revered National Wildlife Refuge System is so essential: this is where the lessons reside, and with them a viable future for all that is embraced within the community of life.

5

THE FREEDOM OF
THE WILDERNESS

The National Wilderness Preservation System

In 1893, Frederick Jackson Turner, a young man recently out of graduate school, read his doctoral thesis to a gathering of the American Historical Association in Chicago. Turner, who was thirty-two at the time, told his audience that democracy flourished in America not in spite of the obstacles posed by its native landscape but because of them. He said that this landscape—or frontier—was nothing more than a wilderness that irradiated opportunity and encouraged freedom, mobility, and the development of free institutions. The frontier, he said in what became known as the Turner Thesis, was "the line of most rapid and effective Americanization." His interpretation was so convincing and extraordinary that it dictated the course of historical analysis for the next thirty years, and his thesis remains, after nearly a century, the most widely known historical essay explaining America to Americans. He wrote:

> The wilderness masters the colonist. It finds him a European in dress, industries, tools, modes of travel, and thought. It takes him from the railroad car and puts him in the birch canoe. It strips off the garments of civilization and arrays him in the hunting shirt and the moccasin. . . . Little by little he transforms the wilderness, but the outcome is not the old Europe, not simply the development of Germanic germs. . . . Thus the advance of the frontier has meant a steady movement away from the influence of Europe, a steady growth of

Robert Marshall (left) on one of his endless wilderness hikes, this one with friend and guide Ward Shepard in 1925 (The Wilderness Society).

195

independence on American lines. And to study this advance, the men who grew up under these conditions, and the political, economic and social results of it, is to study the really American part of our history.

In his thesis, as in his subsequent writings, Turner's affection was for the frontier and its social institutions, and he mourned their passing—as described in the official 1890 Census, which declared that the "frontier line of settlement" had finally disappeared. For the wilderness itself he held little more regard than did most people of his time and place. Nevertheless, he had legitimized wilderness by writing about it and outlining what he believed its influence had been on the shaping of the American character. There were those after him who mourned not just the passing of the frontier but of the wild country that had given it form, and some of these—not many at first, but a recognizable vanguard—began to wonder if some wilderness could not be saved as a living reminder, so long as it endured, of the place from which the American civilization had emerged.

They stood firmly in a long tradition, those who thought about such things—one that stretched back through John Muir to Henry David Thoreau and beyond, one that held, as Thoreau had put it, that "a town is saved, not more by the men and women in it than by the woods and swamps that surround it." The final expression of that tradition is today's National Wilderness Preservation System, an administrative classification now placed on 95.3 million acres of national forest, national park, Bureau of Land Management, and wildlife refuge lands in the lower forty-eight states and Alaska—the Great Land holding more than any other state, with 56 million acres. It comes in all shapes and varieties—as alpine wilderness, desert wilderness, tundra wilderness, swampland wilderness, coastal wilderness, forest wilderness. It is there for its own sake and for ours, protected in perpetuity from all that there is in us that would destroy it. There is nothing in any country in the world to match it—and there are those who say it is not yet complete, may never be complete, even while they concede that this Wilderness Preservation System is already among this country's best accomplishments.

But before there was a system, there was an idea.

TWO MEN AND A SINGLE STARTING POINT

One of the people who was beginning to do some serious thinking about wilderness and its preservation early on was a landscape architect named Arthur Carhart. In the summer of 1919, the Forest Service had hired him to work at its Region 2 headquarters in Denver. He had been turned down once before because he had no experience or education in building roads and dams, two activities in which agency officials had a large interest in those days. Between his first and second applications for a job, however, recreational use in the national forests had picked up considerably, thanks to the automobiles that visitors were now able to drive almost anywhere they dared. In many places, national forest scenery rivaled that of the national parks. Forest Service officials wanted this to become more widely known, and spread the word via posters and billboards that proclaimed the national forests as the "People's Playgrounds" (much to the irritation of Director Stephen Mather and other National Park Service people, who believed the nation's proper playgrounds were its parks). In 1915 the Secretary of Agriculture had issued special-use permits—at ten to twenty-five dollars a year—to anyone who wanted to build a cabin, store, or lodge in certain remote parts of the national forests. The response was so good that Carhart, calling himself a "beauty engineer," was hired to landscape new roads, disguise sanitation problems at ranger cabins, and plan for the development of summer communities.

Carhart was dispatched first to Trappers Lake in Colorado's San Isabel National Forest, about thirty miles from Glenwood Springs. He was told to design a through road that might show off the scenery to its best advantage, and to plan a vacation settlement on the lake. Carhart spent several days hiking around the three-hundred-acre lake. He marveled at the eleven-thousand-foot peaks tiered like wedding cakes, and thought about how a road might go through the area, how cabins could be arranged. After thinking, and thinking some more, he returned to Denver with a novel suggestion: squelch the entire project. Not far into his career with the Forest Service, then, Carhart had uncovered his own true feelings and spent the rest of the time bombarding his superiors with letters and long memoranda on the subject. He even began to write magazine articles about the need to preserve natural areas. "Individuals naturally desire to help themselves to the best home sites they [can] obtain," he wrote in one of his Forest Service letters. "This very greed indirectly defeats our purpose." The time would come, Carhart prophesied, when "the scenic spots where nature has been allowed to remain unmarred will be some of the most highly prized scenic features in the country."

If the Forest Service encouraged the total exploitation of the forests for both recreational and commercial purposes, it would be severely criticized later, Carhart believed. Steadily he built a case for the retention of some areas "to which the lover of the outdoors can return without being confronted by a settlement, a country store, telephone pole, or other sights of civilization." Man-made improvements on backcountry lands had to stop—of this Carhart was sure. "How to do this, is perhaps the real question, rather than shall it be done," he wrote.

Carhart's persistent rejection of the vacation-home syndrome was so unusual at the Forest Service that it caught the attention of Aldo Leopold, at that time assistant district forester in Albuquerque. On his own, while surveying a remote ridge for "some fool road," Leopold had reached the same conclusion as Carhart. To Leopold it seemed that man's encroachment on the wildest places had reached the speeds traveled by motorized vehicles. He was beginning to see an insidious connection between roads and automobiles and the destruction of wildlife habitat in the national forests. "Who wants to stalk his buck to the music of a motor?" he asked. "Or track his turkey on the trail of a knobby tread? Who that is called to the high hills for a real *paseo* wants to wrangle his packs along a graveled highway? There's car sign in every canyon, car dust on every bush, a parking ground at every watering hole, and Fords on a thousand hills."

Leopold, an enthusiastic hunter who later would write the first treatise on game management, was born in Burlington, Iowa. His passion for wildlife developed from a boyhood spent along the Mississippi, prowling its banks for a closer look at birds and other creatures that concentrated there. Leopold went East to prep school, after which he enrolled in the Yale School of Forestry. He graduated in 1908 and joined the Forest Service the following year as a forest assistant in the Arizona Territory. It was here that the comprehensive meaning of wilderness first touched him. He and friends had been out "pumping lead" into a pack of wolves bounding down a mountainside, he later wrote. An old she-wolf went down, and in the dying green fire of the wolf's eyes Leopold saw something he had never seen before—"something known only to her and to the mountain." He spent the rest of his life, which ended in 1948 with a heart attack while he was fighting a fire on a neighbor's farm, trying to comprehend what the wolf and the mountain knew. In *A Sand County Almanac*, Leopold's last and best-known work, he put it all together:

> Ability to see the cultural value of wilderness boils down, in the last analysis, to a question of intellectual humility. The shallow-minded modern who has lost his rootage in the land assumes that he has already discovered what is important; it is such who prate of empires, political or economic, that will last a thousand years. It is only the scholar who appreciates that all history consists of successive excursions from a single starting-point, to which man returns again and again to organize yet another search for a durable scale of values. It is only the scholar who understands why the raw wilderness gives definition and meaning to the human enterprise.

These ideas were still germinating when Leopold went to Denver on a winter day in 1919 to meet Arthur Carhart, who had been prating himself—in government memoranda, no less—about the same sort of things. Their meeting must have been productive; Carhart immediately dashed off a "Memo to Mr. Leopold," in which he restated their shared views regarding permanent alterations in wild places. In 1920 the Forest Service accepted Carhart's Trappers Lake recommendation, the first time the Service had ever denied a project because of the threat it posed to an area's natural integrity. In his short tenure with the Forest Service (he quit after four years because he did not like the direction it was taking in spite of his efforts), Carhart also influenced the denial of road funds for Superior National Forest in Minnesota. The forest consisted of more than one million acres of lakes and pine forests, and to Carhart keeping Superior in primitive condition was of prime importance; it was the only national forest in the nation where lakes dominated the landscape.

Meanwhile, Leopold had returned to his Southwest region determined to hold the line on encroachments. When he had first arrived, in 1909, there were six roadless areas, each of one million acres or more, in the national forests. In 1922 the only large tract that remained was in New Mexico's Gila National Forest, created in 1906. A 540,000-acre section at the headwaters of the Gila River contained a maze of red canyons that had thwarted railroads earlier and still presented problems to roadbuilders. Its stands of ponderosa pine, ancient juniper, piñon, and scrub oak were not considered commercially valuable. Leopold proposed that the area be preserved intact and designated as a special primitive area. State game protection associations and local stockmen saw preservation as a way to serve their own interests and supported the idea. Game protection advocates thought it would safeguard wildlife habitat, and stockmen figured that if the area remained roadless, tourists could not drive in and harass the sheep and cattle still allowed to graze there.

The Gila received its unique designation from the Forest Service in 1924. Two years later, L. F. Kniepp, chief of the division of lands and recreation, began to survey other national forests, looking for additional roadless areas to preserve along the lines set out by Leopold. Kniepp and his staff spent months squinting at quarter-inch topographical maps "upon which were recorded each forest supervisor's wildest flights of fancy as to the ultimate road and trail system for the forest." Through this scrim of dream-roads, Kniepp's survey identified seventy-four wilderness tracts unsuitable for roading, totaling 55 million acres, with the largest single unit covering 7 million acres. In 1929 this survey's findings led to an administrative regulation called L-20. It gave the chief of the Forest Service official authority to do what had already been done in the Gila—to establish "primitive areas" that were to remain primeval in their "environment, transportation, habitation and subsistence." Still, L-20 was not genuinely protective. Logging was still allowed, because it was believed that, if properly regulated, it would not be incompatible with the ultimate purpose of the reservation. Nor was L-20 strictly enforced. The fact is, most public land historians have viewed the L-20 regulation as merely a stalling measure to keep the most scenic lands within the national forests from being transferred to the national parks, which had often been the case.

200

THE MAN WHO WALKED

The L-20 regulations fell short of satisfying the more wilderness-minded foresters like Leopold, who had transferred to a forest products laboratory in Madison, Wisconsin, in 1925. And they certainly did not satisfy a young man named Robert Marshall. Marshall, born into a wealthy family, was raised in New York City but spent his summers at Knollwood, his family's summer home on Saranac Lake in the Adirondacks. His father was Louis Marshall, a prominent attorney, civil libertarian, and wilderness advocate. The elder Marshall was one of those responsible for inclusion of a clause in the 1885 New York State constitution that "forever kept as wild" forestlands in the Adirondacks. Bob Marshall climbed his first Adirondack peak when he was fifteen, and he and his brother George climbed all forty-six together, becoming the first people ever to do so. By the time Bob was sixteen he knew he wanted to be a forester. "I love the woods and solitude," he wrote during his junior year in high school. "I like the various forms of scientific work a forester must do. I should hate to spend the greater part of my lifetime in a stuffy office or in a crowded city."

Ironically, many wilderness enthusiasts had been of the armchair variety—for them, simply knowing that wild places existed was stimulation enough. But Marshall felt incomplete anywhere but in the back of beyond, and would gladly expend all his energies getting there. When he was enrolled at the New York State College of Forestry in Syracuse, he decided to walk thirty miles in every state of the union, covering that distance in a single day in each state. He started in New York. A classmate remembers driving by Marshall and stopping to offer him a ride, which Marshall accepted, thinking he had walked his allotment. Studying the map as they rode together, Marshall realized he had fallen just short of the distance and leaped from the car to end the day properly. He was a powerful hiker. In college he once covered sixty-two miles in a day. Later, in Arizona, to break his own record, he walked for thirty-six hours and covered seventy miles. During forest tramps, friends who joined him fretted about getting their feet wet, but Marshall, always in sneakers for these occasions, started out by sloshing straight through the first puddle he came to.

After receiving his doctorate in plant pathology from Johns Hopkins

University in 1930, Marshall went to work for the Forest Service in the Wind River Mountains in Wyoming. Despite the L-20 regulations, he was disturbed by the rapid disappearance of wilderness from national forestlands and articulated his concern for the February 1930 issue of *Scientific Monthly* in an article that later came to be called the "Magna Carta of wilderness." Wilderness, he explained, was a region containing no permanent inhabitants, possessing "no possibility of conveyance by mechanical means and . . . sufficiently spacious that a person in crossing it must have the experience of sleeping out. The dominant attributes of such an area are: first, that it requires anyone who exists in it to depend exclusively on his own efforts for survival; and second, that it preserves as nearly as possible the primitive environment. This means all roads, power transportation and settlements are barred." Marshall's definition permitted the occasional temporary shelter, since this was common "long before the advent of the white race." He also softened his stance on wilderness purity by permitting fire-protection "infringements" such as telephone lines, trails, and lookout cabins.

To Marshall the wilderness offered the best chance to discover self-sufficiency. "Toting a fifty-pound pack over an abominable trail, snowshoeing across a blizzard-swept plateau, or scaling some jagged pinnacle which juts far above timber will develop a body distinguished by a soundness and stamina and élan unknown amid normal surroundings," he preached. He thought civilization's coddling gave nations the time to go to war: "People become so choked by the monotony of their lives that they are readily amenable to the suggestion of lurid diversions."

Sheer size had to be part of the wilderness spell. Marshall once compared wilderness to the Mona Lisa and said, "If you cut it up into little pieces one inch square and distribute them among the art galleries of the world so millions might see it where hundreds see it now, neither the millions nor the hundreds would get any genuine value."

Marshall's article called for the immediate identification and rescue of remaining wilderness, and for a thorough study of the country's future wilderness requirements, all of this to be carried out by those who firmly recognized the innate worth of land in its natural state.

"There is just one hope of repulsing the tyrannical ambition of civilization to conquer every niche on the whole earth," Marshall wrote. "That hope is the organization of spirited people who will fight for the freedom of the wilderness."

Within the Forest Service, Marshall had a reputation as an eccentric; he was not "of the family." His socialist convictions, among other things, made him stand out. Congressman Hamilton Fish of New York accused Marshall of being the single largest contributor to an unnamed "Communist veteran organization whose main purpose is to spread class hatred and propaganda for the destruction of American institutions." "I've been out in the woods and up in the arctic a good part of the past five years," Marshall responded. "It may be that the Bill of Rights was repealed without me hearing of it."

Yet, because he was bright and worked extremely hard, Marshall rose quickly in the ranks. And as he gained stature, so did his most fervent interests. As director of forestry for the Bureau of Indian Affairs in the Department of the Interior, Marshall created sixteen new wilderness areas on the reservations, with the full support of BIA chief John Collier and Interior Secretary Harold Ickes. Later, as head of the Division of Recreation and Lands in the Forest Service, Marshall restricted roads and development on 14 million acres. The work took him two years. During this time he personally financed out-of-pocket expenses for a new map inventorying remaining roadless areas larger than 300,000 acres. Doing the surveys himself, Marshall identified forty-six areas, thirty-two of which were in the Western national forests. He had in mind the eventual protection of nearly 45 million acres, constituting about 9 percent of the national forest system.

But there arose another impediment to the establishment of the fragile wilderness preservation system he was assembling. This time it was the generally progressive make-work industriousness of the Civilian Conservation Corps, in which a job often was created regardless of whether the work needed to be done. A good part of this work was roadbuilding. The CCC paid no special attention to administrative wilderness areas, so Marshall wrote to Ickes in 1934, pleading with the Secretary to keep the CCC highway work out of undeveloped areas in his jurisdiction, to "preserve a certain value of the timeless, mysterious, in a world overrun by split-second schedules, physical certainty and man-made superficiality." But President Roosevelt, ardent conservationist though he was, took special delight in being able to wheel his own specially equipped roadster through the countryside in spite of his paralysis. Through Ickes, he made it known that parkways would not be kept out of wilderness, and that was that.

A WILDERNESS WAY

One of those parkways—intended for the wildest region of the Great Smokies—would have torn through portions of the two-thousand-mile-long Appalachian Trail. This possibility mobilized the trail's founder, Benton MacKaye, a forester who worked for the Tennessee Valley Authority, and his two friends, Harvey Broome and Harold Anderson. MacKaye had proposed the trail in 1921 to save a ribbon of wilderness between Maine and Georgia, calling the path "a wilderness way through civilization, not a civilized way through wilderness" (see chapter 7). The highway plans would have turned that around, MacKaye and his colleagues feared. Ironically, they had worked to bring the area of the proposed highway under the protection of the National Park Service, and it was now the Park Service that was suddenly pushing for construction of the new parkway. Anderson wrote to MacKaye that there had been enough rhetoric about the need for an organization of friends of the wilderness. The time had come to act. MacKaye met with Marshall, Broome, and Bernard Frank, another TVA forester, at a forestry convention in Knoxville in October 1934, and the four men drove out to look at a CCC camp. On the way they discussed—or rather, disagreed about—Marshall's version of a constitution for this "friends of the wilderness" group. The argument grew so heated that they pulled off the road, climbed an embankment, and haggled until they all agreed on what needed to be done to save wilderness, "that extremely minor fraction of outdoor America which yet remains free from mechanical sights and sounds and smells."

Selected others were asked to join them in a group that came to be known as The Wilderness Society. Additional charter members, in January 1935, were Aldo Leopold and Robert Sterling Yard, former publicity chief for Park Service Director Stephen Mather. At seventy-four, Yard remained a vigorous spokesman for wilderness and had become one of the Park Service's sternest critics. Months after The Wilderness Society's founding, Yard edited and distributed the first issue of The Society's magazine, *The Living Wilderness*. On the cover appeared Yard's "Summons to Save the Wilderness," a manifesto that described the organization's objectives:

> The Wilderness Society is born of an emergency in conservation which admits no delay. It consists of persons distressed by the exceedingly swift passing of the wilderness in a country which recently abounded in the richest and noblest wilderness forms, the primitive, and who purpose to do all they can to safeguard what is left of it. This is for transmission, a sacred charge, to its preservers of the future.

In closing, Yard denounced the "craze" to "build all the highways possible everywhere while billions may yet be borrowed from the unlucky future. The fashion is to barber and manicure wild America as smartly as the modern girl. Our duty is clear."

The Wilderness Society grew slowly at first, because its founders wanted no straddlers: "We want those who *already* think as we do," MacKaye told Marshall, "not those who have to be shown." Four years later, The Wilderness Society suffered a harsh personal blow. The kinetic Bob Marshall, just thirty-eight, died while traveling on a train from Washington to New York. For much of his life he had had a heart condition, and recently it had begun to show. On a hike in Oregon a month before he died, he had ended the day uncharacteristically breathless and exhausted. An autopsy found that he had succumbed to "thrombosis." But the Indian guides, foresters, fishermen, and park rangers who knew him from the mountains agreed that he had simply walked himself to death. Marshall left his personal fortune of $1.5 million to his favorite causes. To The Wilderness Society he bequeathed $400,000. The only bequest to a single person was $3,000 to his old Adirondack guide, Henry Clark.

In 1940 the Forest Service created the Bob Marshall Wilderness Area in Montana, in recognition of Marshall's many contributions to the preservation of wilderness. One of those contributions was the adoption of stricter regulations to replace the flimsy L-20 rules of 1929. The new regulations had been devised largely by Marshall and were promulgated by his successor and close friend John Sieker. This time they were called U Regulations, and defined three categories of wilderness. The first and largest of these were wilderness areas that consisted of tracts larger than 100,000 acres, designated for protection by the Secretary of Agriculture, based on Forest Service recommendations. Next in size were wild areas consisting of tracts between 5,000 and 10,000 acres. In the third category were roadless areas, to be managed primarily for recreation and left "substantially in their natural condition." Good enough, but still a little vague as to precisely what *kind* of land qualified as wilderness. Even within The Wilderness Society, members were having trouble agreeing on a universally acceptable definition. To straighten things out, The Society's Robert Sterling Yard wrote to the National Park Service for the agency's definition of wilderness, but was told that the one person who knew it was away, indefinitely. Some Wilderness Society members believed that a delineation of true wilderness could be achieved by subtracting all the roadless areas from the total area; one member believed that wilderness ought to be the national park for the poor; Aldo Leopold stressed that any wilderness designation should include "scientific research in ecology," along with programs in history, education, and recreation; Robert F. Griggs of the National Research Council insisted that wilderness must not be open to grazing because if it were, "there will be no wilderness areas"; and in a letter responding to Griggs's concern, wildlife biologist Olaus J. Murie allowed that grazing wasn't so bad, but road construction of any sort was the most serious threat and must be strictly prohibited. And so it went. With some reservations, Society leaders finally accepted the Forest Service definition that wilderness areas "provide the last frontier where the world of mechanization and of easy transportation has not yet penetrated. They have an important place historically, educationally and for recreation. The National Forests provide by far the greatest opportunity for wilderness areas. Suitable provision for them is an important part of the National Forest land use planning."

UNTRAMMELING THE WILDERNESS

On the face of it, then, the Forest Service appeared ready to keep faith with Marshall's vision. In practice, this was not always the case. During World War II, when the exigencies of a nation at war gave increasing rein to industrial extraction and use of all natural resources, the utilitarian philosophy of forest use once again grew dominant within the Service. New wilderness designations nearly ceased, while other areas were withdrawn from protection and were roaded and logged. At times the agency seemed openly antagonistic toward the wilderness idea, causing Wilderness Society cofounder Bernard Frank to lament conditions in a letter to MacKaye in 1946: "Wilderness affairs are in serious shape. Just between us two, I don't think the Forest Service is really concerned." Postwar economic growth accelerated this shift through the Truman administration and on into that of Dwight D. Eisenhower. It was during the Eisenhower administration, it will be remembered (see chapter 1), that the utilitarian doctrine was given one of its most dramatic expressions with the Interior Department's support of a plan to build two major dams within the confines of Dinosaur National Monument. That unenlightened project was squelched by the coalition of conservation sentiment against it, but it stood as an ominous talisman for the future of wilderness preservation—whether on Forest Service lands or anywhere else.

The experience gave Howard Zahniser, executive secretary of The Wilderness Society and one of the most effective opponents of Dinosaur, pause for thought. Unless there was a strong national program of wilderness protection, Zahniser concluded, the conservation community would exhaust itself repulsing project after project. Worse, inevitably it would lose some of its battles. Zahniser was a bookish, polite, and, as it turned out, unflaggingly persistent man. Like Marshall, he had learned to love wild country during his long acquaintance with the Adirondacks. A journalist by training and an editor for the U.S. Biological Survey, he went to work for The Wilderness Society in 1945, became its editor and executive secretary, and eventually its executive director. Zahniser had always been impressed by the simplicity and power of the words in the New York constitution regarding the Adirondacks. The "forever wild" clause, as he called

207

it, was all that stood between their grand beauty and their not-so-grand exploitation.

In 1956, a week after Dinosaur had been secured, Zahniser sat down to draft a bill to protect wilderness. "We must recognize that all our lands are destined to be put to some human use," he said. "If any of it is to be preserved in its natural condition it must be as the result of a deliberate setting aside of it for human use of it in a natural condition." By the end of May, his first draft of a wilderness bill was completed. The gist of the bill was that a federal umbrella of perpetual protection would be given to a small lot of federal lands that met approved standards of wilderness. Such designations would be made by executive order from recommendations of various land-managing agencies and a presidentially appointed citizens committee. Each agency would be responsible for managing the designated wilderness areas within its jurisdiction. Zahniser emphasized that no new bureaucracy was needed, nor would additional lands be purchased for inclusion in the system. The wilderness law, as he saw it, would only redefine the future of some lands already retained by the federal government. He outlined his idea first in a speech to the American Civic Planners Association, then gave Senator Hubert Humphrey a copy of the proposed legislation. Humphrey introduced it formally in 1957. As expected, opposition to the bill was loud and strong. Many commercial interests with political clout wanted to retain their "right" to enter and exploit any piece of public land. Both the National Park Service and the National Forest Service flatly opposed the bill. To the Park Service it was a slap in the face; was not the agency congressionally mandated to preserve wilderness from exploitation for profit? Forest Service officials rejected the proposal because participation by the citizens council would limit the range of their administrative judgments and keep them from making land-use decisions that, so they maintained, only Forest Service personnel were trained to make.

Finally, the Forest Service paraded its homegrown U Regulations to show that the agency was already doing something—that it had, in fact, pioneered the doing of something. Yet the record did not speak well for the Forest Service, and only supported Zahniser's conviction that a dose of something stronger was needed. Since 1939 the vaunted U Regulations had added only 350,000 acres to the administrative system—compared with the 14.2 million acres to which Bob Marshall alone had granted protection in the Bureau of Indian Affairs and the Forest Service from 1930 to 1937. A common complaint outside the Service was that permanent wilderness designation would "hamstring economic development in the West, leaving this vast area as a playground." So said, among others, Senator Arthur Watkins of Utah, one of the bill's most bitter antagonists. "Out our way millions of acres are already adequately preserved and reserved in the wilderness state," he asserted at a hearing in July 1958. They "probably always will be because nature has made it that way."

The battle over the wilderness bill divided along regional lines. The South and Northeast were generally for it, but the West, with its history of opposition to federal land management in any form, was generally against it. Oddly, even those who opposed wilderness legislation always explained that they had nothing against saving some wilderness per se. It was just a matter of how much, and where. "Wilderness has its place, but it mustn't destroy the economy," said W. D. Hagenstein, executive vice-president of the Industrial Forestry Association. "Conservationists want to build a wall with 'verboten' signs at 150-foot intervals completely around the wilderness system," he added. "This limits its use to the handful who have time, resources, and stamina to invade its depths by foot or on horseback." Hagenstein admitted that the idea of wilderness was appealing, "but so are three squares a day, money to pay monthly bills, with some left over to provide junior's education, and to have a cushion against catastrophe. We who are engaged in providing raw materials for our basic industries do not do so because we enjoy harvesting century-old trees, building roads up beautiful creeks, exploring the earth for its mineral and petroleum riches . . . but because the public demands it."

The wilderness bill was rewritten sixty-six times. The words in each version were mostly Zahniser's, and he fretted over each one. He did not like "bill language," and said he wished he could write legislation in iambic pentameter. Particularly troublesome to him was the bill's lack of a single word to convey the unique quality of wilderness. The words "undeveloped" and "undisturbed" were lusterless, he believed. One day Zahniser was talking with a friend who used the word "untrammeled" to describe what she loved about the seashore in Olympic National Park. It was exactly what he had been looking for, and he stuck by it. Zahniser steered each new version through eighteen public hearings in ten states, despite lung surgery and a heart problem. At times the struggle seemed so long and hopeless that Wilderness Society council members urged Zahniser to pour his declining energy into something else. But Zahniser would not let go. At every opportunity he drove home three main points: first, that wilderness was necessary for human health, welfare, knowledge, and happiness; second, that wilderness preservation concerned lands that were already largely unsuitable for economic exploitation; and third, that the wilderness system at its fullest would cover only about 60 million acres in the lower forty-eight states, or 2.5 percent of the total land area—this would be all the wilderness there could ever be on the American continent.

As time and Zahniser wore on, support for the wilderness bill grew in unexpected places. In the May 1961 *Journal of Forestry*, for example, one forester wrote that "there are a goodly number of us who like the forest exactly as Nature made it. We know we are a minority, like the Negroes and Jews, and I suppose we should naturally expect to some degree the same treatment." Testimony at the hearings ran into the thousands of pages, and speakers came forward by the hundreds. The proceedings were generally dull and predictable, but many of the most eloquent statements in favor of the bill were delivered by individuals who were not professional conservationists. During hearings in McCall, Idaho, a college student named Michael V. Mahoney, who had traveled from Portland, Oregon, addressed those who complained that any wilderness protection was a "lockup," that it was too nebulous and high-sounding, and that only a few people were able to partake in its pleasures anyway. Congress held the key to wilderness if it was needed in a national emergency, Mahoney reminded opponents, and continued:

As for the privileged few, this phrase represents a misconception of the way things are done in this country. What is privilege? Birth? Rank? Age? None of these. All you need to become "privileged" is the desire for wilderness. The American way is not to distribute everything equally. We do not, for instance, distribute wealth equally. Instead, we distribute opportunity equally and let wealth be the reward for the successful endeavor. Similarly, there is nothing un-American about distributing wilderness experience only to those who seek it. For the opportunity is available to us all.

At last it seemed certain that there would be some sort of federal protection of wilderness. The final form of such a system was not clear, except that Zahniser's definition of what qualified for preservation stuck: "A wilderness," he had written, "in contrast with those areas where man and his own works dominate the landscape, is hereby recognized as an area where the earth and its community of life are untrammeled by man, where man himself is a visitor who does not remain." This language survived each legislative revision and emerged intact in the final version in 1964. Otherwise, that version was a collection of compromises. Among other changes from Zahniser's original, the citizens advisory committee had vanished, a concession to the Forest Service's territorial imperatives. Also gone was the President's power to create wilderness by executive fiat; instead, the land-managing agencies were directed to review their holdings and recommend those that qualified for wilderness designation, for which the President would request Congress to pass enabling legislation. (It was not until the passage of the Federal Land Policy and Management Act of 1976, however, that the more than 300 million acres of Bureau of Land Management lands would be placed in wilderness review—as discussed in chapter 3.) Moreover, Congress could now act independently to create new wilderness designations.

Many conservationists were not especially pleased with this aspect of the bill, fearing that it would delay the process. It did slow things down, but it also encouraged wider public participation in the designation process, and in the end probably contributed to the designation of more wilderness acreage than would have been established otherwise. But the most troubling compromise of all had to do with mining, prospecting, and oil and gas drilling. Exploration and possible development of all of these were permitted to continue until December 31, 1983, at the discretion of the Secretary of the Interior.

In previous drafts of the bill there had been no cutoff date at all for exploration, so in this twenty-year deadline conservationists at least gained a compromise of the compromise. Any mining claim established during this period, however, could be developed at any time in the future, as long as it was done in a manner vaguely defined as conforming to wilderness aesthetics.

On April 27, 1964, Zahniser testified for the last time in favor of the bill, confident now as he read his statement that it would pass.

> Civilization's ambition can encompass wilderness protection. And so sublimated, it can make preservation a prevailing purpose. We maintain the gallery of art, even though few use it. . . . The wilderness system that has come to us from the eternity of the past we have the boldness to project into the eternity of the future. It seems presumptuous for men and women who live only forty, fifty, sixty, seventy, or eighty years to dare to undertake a program for perpetuity, but that surely is our challenge.

When the Wilderness Act was signed into law by President Lyndon Johnson on September 3, 1964, Howard Zahniser did not attend the ceremony in the Rose Garden. He had died in his sleep a week after his last congressional testimony.

THE BUREAUCRATIC BALK

At its signing, the Wilderness Act immediately designated as wilderness 9.1 million acres of national forest, national park, and wildlife refuge land. In the lower forty-eight states, the great bulk of land that might qualify for addition to this embryonic National Wilderness Preservation System lay under the administration of the Forest Service. To its credit, the Service diligently and constructively prepared regulations for the protection and management of areas already classified as wilderness under the provisions of the act. In the matter of studying and recommending additions to the system, however, it dragged its numerous feet. Between 1964 and 1973 it made not a single such recommendation. All proposals made during this period came from the swelling ranks of professional conservationists and

212

interested citizens. Steadfastly committed to the principles of multiple use—which, by agency interpretation, wilderness preservation defied—the Service was institutionally reluctant to move on wilderness designation and, many conservationists maintained, erected obstacles where there had been none.

One of these obstacles was an extremely narrow interpretation of the law regarding an area's suitability as wilderness. By agency standards, few places (if any, it seemed) were pristine or "untrammeled" enough to be classified as wilderness—at least as foresters were given to understand the word. If the ground showed evidence of any past alteration, such as an overgrown road or an abandoned mine shaft, chances were good that the entire tract would be eliminated for its lack of purity. Adhering to its high standards, the Forest Service declared it next to impossible to find wilderness areas east of the Front Range of the Rockies. Land in the East had been too long and too thoroughly disturbed by man and his commerce. Of 256 areas surveyed in the East, the Forest Service identified only three as potential wildernesses. To remedy this situation, Congress passed the Eastern Wilderness Act in 1973. The new law added sixteen parcels in thirteen states, for a total of 207,000 acres, and made it clear that in the opinion of Congress, if an area had recovered significantly from prior abuse—as was often the case in the fast-growing forests of the humid East—it was on its way back to a pristine condition and could be included in the National Wilderness Preservation System.

The agency showed similar disinclinations toward wilderness in the West. In 1968 the Gore Range Primitive Area in the White River National Forest in Colorado had been slated for inclusion in the wilderness system. Conservationists wanted the primitive area enlarged so that it would include forest cover and meadow as well as the "rocks and ice" that made up so much of wilderness acreage. But the area conservationists thought should be included in the eventual wilderness designation was also wanted by the Forest Service for timber-cutting. The Service had planned to sell 4.3 million board feet of the area's timber, and had dismissed its wilderness potential because an abandoned road less than a mile long marred a portion of the terrain.

213

Wilderness supporters ultimately sued the Forest Service in the U.S. District Court for the District of Colorado on the ground that if the agency went ahead with the logging, it would effectively remove the East Meadow Creek area from further wilderness consideration. In 1969, in a landmark decision, the court ruled against the Forest Service. In his opinion, Judge William E. Doyle wrote that the Forest Service action "thwart[ed] the purpose and spirit of the Act" because it prevented presidential or congressional involvement. "Decisions regarding the classification [of] areas which are predominantly of wilderness value must be left open through the presidential level," wrote Judge Doyle. The U.S. Court of Appeals for the Tenth Circuit later affirmed the lower court's decision.

The National Park Service was still finding the Wilderness Act difficult to digest. It had opposed passage of the act because it believed that the legislation was designed to duplicate or even supersede its own efforts. But while the Park Service had once been the unquestioned leader in natural preservation, its recreation development policies, especially after World War II, had weakened its claim to sovereignty in the eyes of many conservationists. In 1965 this view gained even more credence when some 400,000 acres of Great Smoky Mountains National Park came up for consideration as wilderness under the 1964 act. Almost simultaneously, national park officials announced plans for a new highway that would accommodate summer traffic jams, and fulfill an old Park Service promise to the town of Bryson City, Tennessee, to give it a new road.

When the officials unveiled their highway plans they noted that less than half of the park was recommended for inclusion in the wilderness preservation system, and the lands that were to be included had been broken up into chunks of from 5,000 to 110,000 acres each. Local businesses and the chamber of commerce heartily praised the new roadway. Scientists, conservationists, and concerned citizens opposed it just as heartily and in greater numbers. "The Park Service has put forward a roadbuilding project that transgresses the spirit of the Wilderness Act," moaned *The New York Times*. It would "bring heavy automobile traffic streaming through the very area that needs to be protected. The proposal for this trans-mountain road reflects weariness rather than foresight and clear thinking." Drawing constant fire from such quarters, the road plan was finally shelved five years later in favor of a scenic loop highway around the perimeter of the park, as had been urged by citizen groups. (Wilderness classification, however, has not yet come to the park.)

Similar public pressure persuaded the Forest Service to launch a more ambitious survey of its "de facto" wildernesses—roadless areas that might be included in the National Wilderness Preservation System. In 1972, Chief Forester Edward Cliff announced an agency study of 56 million acres, known as the Roadless Area Review and Evaluation, or RARE. RARE's results two years later were disappointing because only 12.3 million acres, or 19 percent of the roadless areas surveyed, were recommended for wilderness protection. Conservation organizations ridiculed this recommendation, and the Sierra Club brought suit. The Forest Service quickly capitulated so far as to agree that it would comply with the stipulations requiring environmental impact statements mandated by the National Environmental Protection Act of 1969 before developing any roadless areas. Such compliance effectively slowed roadbuilding and timber-cutting, and in 1977 the Forest Service attempted another nationwide review.

This second review, called RARE II, was far more comprehensive than its predecessor. It identified almost three thousand potential wilderness areas in thirty-eight states, for a total of 62 million acres. But RARE II recommendations also raised conservationist protests. This time, only 15 million acres of national forest lands were to be set aside as wilderness, so little that, as one Sierra Club member put it, "the fact that timber operators complained was pro forma, for the record; they have been secretly delighted." A key part of the RARE II determinations were public hearings so that the Forest Service could be made aware of local and corporate sentiment regarding wilderness preservation in each locale. In the summer of 1977, remarks from 47,000 people were tabulated. Nevertheless, many foresters claimed that public participation was dominated by elitist professional conservationists, not ordinary citizens. "Those sought-after folks, the moms and pops who give their disinterested opinion on wilderness, are as mythical as unicorns," grumbled one forester in the *Journal of Forestry*. The magazine also carried the opinion that RARE II was "largely a political exercise masquerading as a profes-

215

sional study," and sarcastically referred to the whole wilderness designation system as a way to determine "where the hand of man has never set foot." Still, in 1980 the process resulted in statewide bills for Colorado, New Mexico, Missouri, Louisiana, and South Carolina, all passed by Congress.

The anti-wilderness contingent took heart when the Reagan administration came into office and began to cast covetous glances westward to all that underutilized land—especially with regard to what it might hold in the way of oil, gas, and other energy resources. As noted earlier, the Wilderness Act had specified that designated wilderness areas would be open to leasing for oil, gas, and mineral exploration until December 31, 1983—at the discretion of the Secretary of the Interior. Out of respect for the idea manifest in the Wilderness Act, one Interior Secretary after another had declined to exercise this discretion. President Reagan's Secretary of the Interior, James Watt, felt no such compunction; indeed, he went so far as to announce that the act *obligated* him to begin leasing.

The Arab oil crisis of the 1970s had made the federal government eager to locate and develop substantial domestic resources of oil, and the discovery of new oil and gas deposits along the "Overthrust Belt"—a geological formation that runs through much of Montana, Idaho, Utah, Wyoming, and Arizona, and cuts a swath as much as a hundred miles wide—seemed to be the answer to a lot of prayers. In the oil-drilling business the region was called "elephant country" because of the potential size of the deposits that might be found there, and beginning in 1981 the BLM and the Forest Service were under great pressure to process the backlog of lease applications for exploring wilderness areas in the region. Coincidentally, a 1980 U. S. District Court decision on a lawsuit that Watt had brought years before, when he was head of the Mountain States Legal Foundation in Denver, ordered the government to accept or dismiss industry applications forthwith. As Interior Secretary, Watt found himself in the happy position of being able to accelerate the processing of applications to abide by the very court ruling he had prompted.

Seismic exploration commenced in several wilderness areas. Although the least intrusive part of oil and gas development, seismic exploration can have some notable impacts. Above all, there is dynamite, which must be exploded to ricochet shock waves off deep strata and give a reading, by the nature of the echo, of what might be buried there. In one seismic crew member's account of working near the Bob Marshall Wilderness Area, fifty pounds of dynamite were exploded every 220 feet, for a total of fifty to one hundred detonationss a day.

Conservationists and their allies in Congress, believing this clearly to be an incompatible use of wilderness, attempted to halt Watt's move, arguing that industry should explore other lands first. "There are only so many drill rigs available for exploration," said Andrew F. Weissner, counsel to the House Interior Subcommittee on Public Lands and National Parks. "It will take years to explore the Overthrust Belt, so why not explore less fragile areas first?" In the meantime, The Wilderness Society commissioned a study by economist Leonard L. Fischman that would determine the amounts of important minerals, oil, and natural gas within wilderness areas, designated or proposed. The study, issued early in 1982, and whose conclusions were later confirmed by the General Accounting Office, found that designated wilderness contained only about 1 percent of the nation's potentially producible onshore oil and gas reserves. The Fischman report also concluded that about 77 percent of the potential oil and 81 percent of the potential gas reserves were not on federal lands at all, but on private or state lands. Additionally, some 130 million acres of federal land outside the wilderness system already were leased for oil and gas exploration or development—with only a fraction of these ever having been seriously exploited, or even explored.

For this and other reasons, public disapproval of Watt's plans to speed up oil and gas exploration in wilderness ran so high that in 1982 the Secretary formulated what he called a compromise. He proposed a "Wilderness Protection Act," which critics quickly revealed to be something closer to a "Wilderness Destruction Act," since buried in its high-toned language were stipulations that would have made it more difficult to add lands to the National Wilderness Preservation System, would have made it easier to open existing wilderness to development, and would have removed *all* protection after the year 2000. The public was outraged again, at least if newspaper editorials could be believed: The Wilderness Society counted more than three hundred editorials that appeared in response to the proposal over several weeks, virtually all of

217

which were dead against it.

Congress refused to take Watt's legislation seriously, and in August the House passed its own version, one that would have banned all oil and gas leasing immediately. The Senate did not go that far, but during a lame-duck session in December the two houses did tack on an amendment to the Interior Appropriations Bill that prohibited the Forest Service from processing lease applications for wilderness during fiscal 1983. Finally, in July 1983, the administration capitulated. "That's it," said Gary Carruthers, then-Assistant Secretary of the Interior for Land and Water Resources. "We quit. What we wanted was exploration. But it has become so politically explosive that we determined that you can't jeopardize all our leasing programs on exploration in a limited number of areas." In October, James Watt resigned. Congress renewed the leasing ban until the end of the year, during which time the December 31 deadline came and went with no further commotion—at least from the Interior Department.

Meanwhile, a 1982 federal court of appeals had complicated the wilderness designation process itself by upholding a challenge to the validity of RARE II; in *California* vs. *Block* the court ruled that the RARE II environmental impact statement covering several areas in California —produced in compliance with the National Environmental Policy Act— was inadequate. This decision forced the Forest Service to jettison RARE II. Assistant Secretary of Agriculture John Crowell announced that another study, "RARE III," would have to begin, but this time it would be incorporated into the forest-by-forest management plans called for by the National Forest Management Act of 1976 (see chapter 2).

SOME MILESTONES ON THE WILDERNESS ROAD

While the Forest Service went back to the wilderness drawing board, Congress continued to use the RARE II study as the basis for further state wilderness bills, and in 1984—on the twentieth anniversary of the Wilderness Act—the Ninety-Eighth Congress designated 8.6 million new acres of wilderness in twenty-one states. It was the largest amount of acreage allotted to the National Wilderness Preservation System since the Alaska Lands Act of 1980 (see chapter 6). Numerous additional proposals were in the works by then, although for many the road to designation was both long and rugged—and for some of the biggest proposals, the journey continues.

By 1993, Alabama, Illinois, Georgia, Maine, South Carolina, Oklahoma, Virginia, and West Virginia all received new or enlarged wilderness designations, most of them on national forest lands. In 1988, Washington got more than 1.7 million acres of new wilderness in Olympic, Rainier, and North Cascades national parks, while in 1989, Nevada was blessed with over 733,000 acres of national forest wilderness and in 1990, with passage of the Tongass Reform Act (see chapter 6), Alaska's Tongass National Forest received six new wilderness areas totaling more than 1.2 million acres.

Two years later, California got more than 500,000 acres, including the enormous 219,700-acre Sespe Wilderness in Los Padres National Forest. In November 1993, Colorado got 612,000 acres of new forest wilderness—more than a third of it in the spectacular Sangre de Cristo Range in the southern part of the state—but the success came only after years of contention and negotiation over the question of whether or not the federal government could exercise water rights on streams flowing through wilderness areas to the potential expense of state and private rights that might be claimed outside the wilderness. "We got around that contentious issue," said Darrell Knuffke of The Wilderness Society's Central Rockies office in Denver, "by including language stating that a water right was neither implied nor denied." (For particulars on the state-by-state wilderness additions made since 1986, see Appendix B at the end of the book.)

By far the most gratifying success in these years for wilderness advocates was passage of the Arizona Desert Wilderness Act in October 1990, largely engineered by local, regional, and national groups that had gathered under the banner of the Arizona Wilderness Coalition and, especially, by the ailing Arizona Representative, Morris K. Udall, an ardent environmentalist who was determined to get wilderness legislation passed for his state as the crowning conservation achievement of his political career. He accomplished his goal, but here, too, success came only after a compromise regarding water rights (in this case, however, federal rights were specified in all but two wildlife refuge wilderness areas), as well as the equally difficult question of grazing. It would not be opposed, environmentalists finally conceded, so long as it was managed in accordance with the meaning and purpose of the Wilderness

219

Act and under stiff guidelines established by the House of Representatives in a special report ten years earlier. In brief, the Arizona Desert Wilderness Act designated 1.3 million acres of wilderness in Havasu, Imperial, Kofa, and Cabeza Prieta national wildlife refuges, then went on to add 1.1 million acres of Bureau of Land Management wilderness to the 250,000 BLM wilderness acres established in 1984. The bill also added 12,710 acres to the existing Aravaipa Canyon Wilderness and established a 20,900-acre Gila Box Riparian National Conservation Area (though conservationists had pushed for wilderness designation for this important and beautiful place). More than 2.4 million acres of wilderness was nothing to scoff at, but the state's conservationists could take particular pride in the fact that at 1.35 million acres, Arizona was now the preeminent BLM wilderness state.

California, Arizona's erstwhile competitor in that regard, had not enjoyed similar bounty, although the campaign for wilderness designation in the California Desert region was even older than that which had brought victory to Arizona's deserts. The Federal Land Policy and Management Act of 1976 had specifically recognized the 12.1 million acres of California Desert that bordered on the greater Los Angeles Metropolitan Area as special, calling it "a total ecosystem that is extremely fragile, easily scarred, and slowly healed" and mandating that the Bureau of Land Management develop a comprehensive management plan for what it called the "California Desert Conservation Area." In 1980, the BLM issued its proposed plan, which was endorsed by then Interior Secretary Cecil Andrus. Conservationists were not happy: The plan called for the wilderness designation of only 2.1 million acres out of the 5.7 million acres of BLM land that were eligible. They were even less happy in 1981, when Interior Secretary James Watt's BLM reduced its wilderness recommendations to 1.8 million acres—while authorizing damaging activities on many Wilderness Study Areas (WSAs), including roadbuilding, exploratory drilling for minerals, and cyanide storage for mining operations, in spite of the fact that the FLPMA specifically prohibited such actions. In 1984, led by The Wilderness Society, the Sierra Club, and such local conservation organizations as the California Desert Protection League, wilderness advocates began working with Senator Alan Cranston's staff to develop wilderness legislation for the California Desert that would include much more than what the BLM had in mind. The result was the California Desert Protection Act, introduced by Cranston in 1986.

This time, it was the anti-wilderness crowd that was unhappy. Not only did the bill call for the wilderness designation of 4.5 million acres of BLM land, it would have taken 1.5 million acres of the East Mojave National Scenic Area away from the BLM and given it to the National Park Service as a brand new national park—East Mojave National Park, to be precise. It also would have enlarged both Death Valley and Joshua Tree national monuments and raised *their* status to that of full-fledged national parks. Finally, it would have designated several million acres of wilderness within all three new national parks. In spite of the fact that he could never get his fellow California senator, Pete Wilson (later to become California's governor), to co-sponsor his bill—an unwritten but no less rigid necessity for passage in the Senate—Cranston faithfully reintroduced sundry versions of it over the next several Congresses, while the conservation community kept up an ever-louder drumroll of support. By the beginning of 1994, although Senator Cranston had left office, it seemed that the California Desert Protection Act—modified here and there by compromises, but still an ambitious piece of legislation—finally might move. A strong version had passed the House of Representatives and both of California's new senators, Dianne Feinstein and Barbara Boxer, had endorsed and helped promote a similar version in the Senate. Odds were that before the end of the year California would take Arizona's place as the state most handsomely endowed with BLM wilderness—not to mention the extra added attraction of three new national parks.

While the long campaign to bring wilderness and park protection to the California Desert seemed nearing an end, other wilderness proposals of comparable size and importance around the country continued to wallow in a state of limbo. In Idaho and Montana, state wilderness bills and proposals for the undesignated and so far unroaded forest lands of the northern Rocky Mountain region remained stalled in a tangle of opposition that featured consistently antagonistic state congressional delegations, stubbornly resistant timber, logging, and mining interests, off-road vehicle enthusiasts who objected to the "lockup" of lands to which they wanted to introduce their dirt bikes, snowmobiles, and all-terrain vehicles, and a vocal contingent of warriors for the "Wise

Use"movement (see chapter 3). In Utah, Congressman Wayne Owens, one of the few national politicians in the Rocky Mountain region who was willing to challenge similar kinds of opposition in his state, introduced legislation in 1985 that had been crafted by the Southern Utah Wilderness Alliance in partnership with The Wilderness Society, the Sierra Club, and the National Parks and Conservation Association. The bill called for the designation of 5.1 million acres of BLM land in the glorious canyon country of southern Utah, but after more than eight years of effort—during which the wilderness proposal increased to 5.7 million acres and Wayne Owens lost a bid for a Senate seat—the bill, bitterly resisted by the BLM itself, remained in a mire of legislative indifference. Much the same could be said for more than 1.8 million acres of wilderness proposals offered up by the members of the New Mexico BLM Wilderness Coalition as long ago as 1982, or for the six million acres proposed for the Oregon High Desert in eastern Oregon by a consortium of conservation groups under the leadership of the Oregon Natural Resources Defense Council in 1991.

Arizona, California (potentially, at least), and other states aside, it grew more and more difficult every year to establish new wilderness, as regional and political interests seemed to congeal in a pudding of opposition. For its part, the "Wise Use" movement increased its noisy resistance to all environmental notions and called for county governments to "take back" the federal public lands, among other equally preposterous (and almost certainly illegal) proposals, while Congress demonstrated a declining leadership on and growing disinterest in the issue. Still, those "spirited people" who had fought—and continued to fight—for wilderness could and did take pride. By the time The Wilderness Society led a nationwide celebration of the twenty-fifth anniversary of the Wilderness Act in 1989, the National Wilderness Preservation System had topped 90.7 million acres, and by the end of 1993, the system had grown to more than 95 million acres in 591 individual wilderness areas. However short of what it still could be, it was now truly a *system*, a reality that extended far beyond Arthur Carhart's appreciative gaze across Trappers Lake or Aldo Leopold's hope for the Gila more than seventy years before, a reality that would have challenged even the obsessive tramp, tramp, tramp of Bob Marshall, had he lived to see it. The ultimate physical and philosophical dimensions of the wilderness system now had given weight to a dictum laid down by novelist and historian Wallace Stegner in 1960. He was not saying anything that anyone who esteemed wilderness did not already know, but no advocate had ever said it better: "We simply need that wild country available to us, even if we do no more than drive to its edge and look in. For it can be a means of reassuring ourselves of our sanity as creatures, a part of the geography of hope."

AN AGENDA FOR THE NATIONAL
WILDERNESS PRESERVATION SYSTEM

What next, then, for the future of that great "geography of hope" that is the National Wilderness Preservation System? Expansion, surely; even when the California Desert Protection Act is passed, bringing the grand total of wilderness in the system to a shade over 100 million acres, there still will remain as much as 100 million more potential acres available for designation from the holdings of the three great public-land agencies. As 1994 began, in fact, the National Park Service, under Director Roger Kennedy, had decided to actively accelerate long-dormant recommendations for millions of acres of new wilderness in the National Park System, while urgings from the conservation community for concrete refuge wilderness recommendations from the Fish and Wildlife Service and for Alaska and Nevada BLM wilderness recommendations from the Bureau of Land Management seemed more likely to be heeded in the Clinton administration than they had been during preceding administrations. Those recommendations should be made and acted upon by Congress as soon as possible, and current proposals under consideration for Idaho, Montana, Utah, Oregon, and New Mexico should be moved to passage in the near future.

These specific expansion efforts should be accompanied by a serious change in the common perception of the National Wilderness Preservation System. Ever since passage of the Wilderness Act, there has been a tendency, particularly among opponents of wilderness designation, to think of the system in static terms: This much and no more. But for so long as important wild country remains unprotected and susceptible to no other absolutely compelling national interest, it must be considered candidate material for the National Wilderness Preservation System. We must establish an open-ended view of wilderness designation as permanent national policy. Regular and continuing wilderness review must be made an integral part of the planning process among *all* federal land-managing agencies.

Setting aside wilderness is one thing; the question of how best to manage this preserved inheritance is quite another—even though some critics are persuaded that the term "wilderness management" is an oxymoron. A wilderness, to remain a wilderness, they say, should be left alone. It is not that simple. Whatever the long-term ecological reasons for setting aside wilderness, however necessary this ethical gesture to the needs and priorities of a protected natural world, the fact is that wilderness also is for human use, however restricted, however transient. And the uses of human beings need to be managed. As a general rule, the management stipulations in the Wilderness Act can be viewed as a kind of overlay on the present rules and regulations of the various agencies that administer wilderness within their larger responsibilities. The act itself generally lays down no specific regulations for any given wilderness, but its intent is clear and its central principle unmistakable: The purpose of wilderness management is the maintenance and, if need be, the restoration of a dynamic equilibrium of natural forces; the fundamental purpose for designating and subsequently managing wilderness is the preservation of wilderness character in perpetuity.

That is the meaning of the law, but its application and enforcement are complicated by confusions and conflicts over everything from whether to fight a natural fire to whether to allow a commercial backcountry packer to establish seasonal "caches" of supplies for the use of his business, or whether to establish a reservation and permit system to limit the numbers of individuals who are allowed to hike any given wilderness during any given period of time. In some designated wilderness areas, recreation is a concern that is only likely to get more pointed as the popularity of backcountry hiking grows, as it surely will. If popularity provides clear justification for the continuing expansion of the National Wilderness Preservation System, it also can lead to abuse of the land by too many people using it badly and without proper guidance by wilderness managers. Visitor freedom should be a management goal, and wilderness management must recognize "unconfined" recreation as one of the major appeals of wilderness. But user impacts should be closely monitored to prevent resource deterioration and maintain a high-quality wilderness experience. If and when some sort of visitor management becomes necessary in a wilderness area, it should be designed to accomplish resource protection objectives with as little regulation of and interference with visitors as possible.

To that end, wilderness managers in the Bob Marshall Wilderness of Montana have initiated a management technique they call "Limits of Acceptable Change," or LAC. At the heart of the LAC process is a system of land-use classification that divided "the Bob," as it is generally known, into four categories, ranging from Class I—most pristine—to Class IV—least pristine. Use regulations were then determined for each category. In Class I land, for instance, there can be only one campsite for every mile of travel route and no campsites can be established within sight or sound of a trail. Designed for high levels of solitude, Class I lands must further provide an 80 percent likelihood that a hiker will not meet another living soul during his travels. Class IV lands, on the other hand, accept higher levels of use; as many as six campsites per mile are allowed, and as many as six meetings. The middle two land categories are a variation on this theme, but all four are monitored closely to see that use within them does not exceed the "Limits of Acceptable Change" that managers have determined each can tolerate, whatever its individual category.

While such a system is admittedly less than perfect even in the Bob Marshall Wilderness (among other things, much depends upon available funding and staffing), this and other techniques being developed there and elsewhere should be studied closely by managers in other wilderness areas to determine what can and cannot be usefully transplanted to their lands.

Above all, wilderness management training must be greatly accelerated at all levels. All agencies—the Forest Service, the National Park Service, the Fish and Wildlife Service, and the Bureau of Land Management—should be required, by congressional directive if necessary, to institute extensive training programs in wilderness management. Further, such training should go beyond the agencies themselves to the public at large; wilderness managers should be encouraged (and given whatever necessary money and personnel) to develop innovative public education programs.

Finally, a system, if it is to be called a system at all, must have something more than size. It must have context, a distinct and calculated purpose that makes it more than the sum of its parts. For wilderness, one significant purpose—in addition to such traditional justifications as the protection of watersheds, wildlife habitat, scientific research, air quality, medical materials, scenic beauty, spiritual satisfaction—must be the protection of ecological integrity. And in that regard, the present system, as impressive as it is, as necessary as it is, still is inadequate. Unless they are of a size to encompass entire ecosystems themselves— and only 81 of the 233 separate ecosystems identified in the United States are found within currently designated wilderness—existing and proposed wilderness areas are too small and widely separated to protect coherent systems of land of a size sufficient to ensure the protection of biological diversity. Alone, designated wilderness cannot do the job of ecosystem protection. Neither can parks or wildlife refuges or wild and scenic rivers systems, for that matter, even those in which major portions have been protected as wilderness. For the most part, the best that wilderness and these other reserves can do under present conditions is to preserve isolated portions of coherent systems.

That is not enough. Nor is the Endangered Species Act enough; the single most useful tool we now have for the preservation of biological diversity cannot do the job alone, either, as noted in chapter 4. There are those who have likened the operation of the Endangered Species Act to that of a metropolitan hospital's emergency room during a terrible disaster—mortally injured patients are carried in one-by-one, patched together, then wheeled off to intensive care units, while the sirens keep screaming, the ambulances keep disgorging patients, and the lines of misery-laden gurneys lengthen in the hallways beneath the heartless glare of corridor lights.

There are a lot of patients out there. As discussed earlier, the list of "candidate" species for listing as endangered or threatened has grown to more than 3,700. And those are just the species that managed to survive; some died while lying on the gurneys, waiting. Assuming that the number of unlisted species that we know about is much lower than the total of those that should be listed but have not yet been discovered, it seems clear that we are in no position, financially, logistically, or logically, to rush from one disaster area to another, setting up Endangered Species M.A.S.H. units and attempting to save every life that is threatened.

What to do, then? Save the land—not merely pieces of it, as we always have done, but whole, large units of federal, state, local, and private lands that, whatever their invididual uses, comprise functioning ecosystems within which there remains undeveloped land sufficient to provide for the survival and nurturing of enough varieties of plants and animals to keep biodiversity flourishing. We can save grizzly bears in the Lower 48 if we give them enough room in which to forage, enough wildness in which to breed. We can save salmon if we keep their rivers free as uncorrupted, unsilted arteries of ecosystem-wide watersheds. We can save the spineless hedgehog cactus if we give it ground to grow and expand its range. We can save not one species, but many species, species we do not even know yet that we have to save, if we learn to think as Aldo Leopold would have us think: of land, from soil to tree-tops and the air above that, as whole communities of life and ourselves a part of it all. If we learn to save the communities, we can save the lives within them.

The Wilderness Society, like many other conservation organizations— and to some extent, the federal government—is thinking in such terms now. The Society is beginning a long process of planning for the articulation of what we have chosen to call "Lifelands." This thinking is still in its infancy, but we already know some things: We already know that what such a program will need is the development of enough scientific knowledge to accurately determine just what it is that truly defines an ecosystem, as well as how it works; that it will need leaders to develop the political will to decide that the preservation of such systems must be one of the most important tasks of the federal government; that it will need the ingenuity of planners from all levels of public and private life to develop legal and administrative structures with which to establish functioning relationships among many different kinds of ownership in the lands to be protected; and, above all, that it will need the support of an informed and committed public.

It will take a long time. So did the creation of the National Wilderness Preservation System, whose individual units, whether as big as the wilderness of Arctic Refuge or as tiny as that on Passage Key, whether old, new, or still to come, will provide the foundation on which this new vision must be built.

The New York Mountains, one of many proposed wilderness areas in the proposed East Mojave National Park, California (T. H. Watkins).

6

INLAND PASSAGES

The National Wild and Scenic Rivers and National Trails Systems

The 1960s were a time of turmoil and trouble in America, and it is sometimes too easily forgotten that this decade also was one of the most environmentally enlightened in our history. It saw, among other conservation highlights, publication of Rachel Carson's *Silent Spring*; passage of the Endangered Species Act, the Wilderness Act, the Clean Air and Clean Water acts, and the National Environmental Policy Act; the designation of Redwood National Park; and the creation of the Land and Water Conservation Fund, the Outdoor Recreation Resources Review Commission, the Environmental Protection Agency, and the President's Council on Environmental Quality—all of this capped off in 1970 by the nation's first Earth Day.

A busy and productive period, and near the end of it, on October 2, 1968, President Lyndon B. Johnson signed into law two bills particularly dear to him—one creating the National Wild and Scenic Rivers System, the other the National Trails System, linear variations of the National Wilderness Preservation System established four years earlier. Johnson, who wanted to originate the best ideas himself, or at least take credit for them, was so fond of the trails legislation that initially his administration delayed its progress so that it would come from his office rather than from that of its actual sponsor, Senator Gaylord Nelson, a Wisconsin Democrat.

The advocates for both of these systems cherished a grand design for them: they would span the continent. The Wild and Scenic Rivers

Shooting the rapids with a lumber raft on the Wisconsin River in 1886 (H. H. Bennett Studio).

231

System, intended to preserve to varying degrees free-flowing waterways, began with eight river segments totaling 789 miles, all part of the original legislation, but was anticipated to grow much larger. Another one hundred or so rivers were slated to be added to the system within ten years; in fact, it took more than twenty years to reach that total and more than another five years for the system to scratch and claw its way up to where it is today: 212 designated river segments totaling 10,574.1 miles. Impressive as it seems, this still represents only about one-third of one percent of the nation's total river mileage.

However small, the system still encompasses an impressive network —from the Noatak, sweeping 330 miles along the southern base of the Brooks Range in Alaska to the tiny (33 miles) segment of the Little River in eastern Ohio; from the Allagash of Maine (95 miles) to the Eleven Point of Missouri (4.4 miles); from the Skagit (157.5 miles), emptying into Puget Sound, to the Rio Grande (191.2 miles), emptying into the Gulf of Mexico). These segments, incorporating a wide variety of riverine ecosystems, are to be kept forever free of development—they are not to be channelized, canalized, dredged, filled, or dammed along their designated lengths, and their banks are similarly protected to a width of half a mile on either side. They are remnants of the free rivers that once laced through the landscape, at once the most precious and the most fragile of the natural preserves established by law. "The degradation of America's riverine systems, and the depletion of their biodiversity, have reached alarming levels," write the authors of *Entering the Watershed: A New Approach to Save America's River Ecosystems*, a 1993 publication of the Pacific Rivers Council. "Not one river system in the United States has been spared." So we save what we can, each segment administered by the federal agency responsible for the land that borders it—the National Park Service, the U. S. Forest Service, the Fish and Wildlife Service, or the Bureau of Land Management.

The National Trails System, meanwhile, has come somewhat closer to realizing its potential—at least on paper. The 1968 act authorized the designation, after proper study, of scenic and recreation trails, and imdiately designated the 2,000-mile Appalachian Trail from Mount Katahdin in Maine to Springer Mountain in Georgia, and the 2,350-mile Pacific Crest Trail meandering through Washington, Oregon, and California from the Canadian border all the way down to the Mexican border, as the first scenic trails. The act also named another fourteen trails as worthy of study for designation and authorized the secretaries of Agriculture and Interior to designate recreation trails on land within their jurisdictions (all others could only be made by Congress). Later, a 1978 amendment established historic trails as an additional category.

To date, more than 23,650 miles of scenic and historic trails have been designated, the most recent of which—the 694-mile Natchez Trace Trail, the 704-mile Potomac Heritage Trail, and the 1,300-mile Florida Trail—were named as late as 1983. (For a complete list, see Appendix A at the end of the book.) In addition, the Interior and Agriculture departments have established 752 miles of recreation trails comprising more than 8,000 miles. All but one of the thirteen existing scenic and historic trails—the Iditarod of Alaska, administered by the Bureau of Land Management—are under the management of either the National Park Service or the U. S. Forest Service. Of the 752 National Recreation Trails, 499 are under federal management, twelve are jointly administered by federal, state, and local governments, 78 are administered by the states, 138 are administered by local governments, and 26 are managed by private organizations.

One of the major problems shared by both the Wild and Scenic Rivers and the National Trails systems is a powerful confusion of responsibility. From creation to administration, both are tangled in a bureaucratic and political snarl that has hampered their continued growth and intelligent management. There has been a consistent lack of funding for both systems, and for the most part Congress and the Executive Branch both have displayed only intermittent concern—and sometimes downright antagonism. As a result, the growth of the Wild and Scenic Rivers System has been sporadic at best. Similarly, the National Trails System remains incomplete—not only as a system but in regard to the existing designated trails themselves. Nine years later, it is not necessary to revise significantly a statement first issued by the National Park Service in March 1985: "Except for the Appalachian and Pacific Crest Trails, which are usable for much of their lengths, the remaining trails are proposed routes and are not necessarily available at this time for long-distance, continuous trips. In some cases, the original route has been obliterated by commercial, industrial, residential, agricultural, and transportation development."

233

The confusion and incompleteness of both systems are regrettable, for any number of reasons, among them the fact that the demand for the recreational use of both is growing and can only increase even more markedly as the end of the century draws near, and the further fact that each system in its own way is capable of preserving significant portions of the national estate overlooked or impossible to administer by other conservation measures. Finally, no other conservation units in the country speak so eloquently or so directly to the narrative of our history.

CONDUITS OF ADVENTURE

From the beginning, the rivers beckoned with promise. Along the river that would later bear his name, the English navigator Henry Hudson in 1609 reached into the country, did not find what he was looking for, turned his eighty-ton vessel *Half Moon* around, and sailed back out to sea. The waterway was not, as he had hoped, the legendary Northwest Passage through the continent to the Pacific—and from there to the riches of the Orient—and was therefore of no use. Still searching for the Northwest Passage 167 years later and three thousand miles to the west, Captain James Cook just missed the mouth of the Columbia River on the Northwest coast. He kept sailing north until he entered the Bering Strait, then pressed on to the Arctic Sea before turning back.

For these two and the dozens of similarly motivated explorers by land and sea who came and went in the years between, the rivers of America were a sore disappointment. But for those with smaller ambitions, who wished only to settle the new land and take what it had to give them, the rivers lacing down to the sea all along the Eastern Seaboard were a godsend and a necessity. They provided power for mills and, with them, the beginnings of industry. They were the first avenues of commerce, the best means at hand of moving people and goods from the interior to the coast and back again. Their valleys held soil so rich and moist a man could mold it in his fist. And with a little imagination, they could be made even more useful— or so it often was hoped. George Washington chose the site for the United States capital on a slough of the Potomac River largely because he anticipated that river's development as an avenue running deep into the Appalachian interior, and his own Potowmack Canal Company constructed canals to bypass the river's wild places and make it navigable by mule-drawn barge. The project—later called the Chesapeake and Ohio Canal—got as far as Cumberland, Maryland, falling far short of Washington's intended junction with the Ohio River, along which he had been promoting settlement on some land he happened to own there.

River country was plowed into farmscapes and citified, and as settlement spilled over the Appalachians into the valley of the Ohio (too late to do Washington any good), and then the broad, river-rich valley of the Mississippi from Canada to the Gulf of Mexico, it was the rivers again that both inspired and made possible the exploration of the trans-Mississippi West. The United States had hardly purchased the immense Louisiana Territory from France in 1803 when Jefferson, as President, ordered its exploration. He chose Captain Meriwether Lewis, a fellow Virginian who had served as his secretary, to head the expedition. Lewis chose Captain William Clark, also a Virginian, to share his command. "The object of your mission," Jefferson wrote to Lewis, "is to explore the Missouri River, & such principal stream of it, as by its course & communication with the waters of the Pacific Ocean, may offer the most direct and practicable water communication across this continent, for purposes of commerce." Again, the search for a shortcut, the old dream of a Northwest Passage.

On May 14, 1804, the thirty-five-member expedition launched its fifty-five-foot keelboat and two flat-bottomed boats called pirogues from their winter base just above St. Louis and began the ascent of the Missouri River—thus entering the "Big Muddy" in the list of what Bernard DeVoto called "the conduits of national adventure." This adventure could have, and even should have, ended tragically. Not only were the men heading into rough, uncharted country, but what they had expected to find—a short portage between the Missouri's eastward-flowing source and the next river's Pacific-bound source—did not exist. The Rocky Mountains stood in the way. If not for the help of a Shoshone Indian girl named Sacajawea who had joined the expedition at Fort Mandan in Montana, the party may have been doomed. Sacajawea had been captured from her tribe and taken

235

east by Minnetarees several years before, but she still remembered landmarks of her childhood, and correctly identified the Missouri's headwaters at the junction of three rivers, which the expedition named after Albert Gallatin, James Madison, and Thomas Jefferson. Her presence among the company also assured them safe passage through hostile Shoshone country, and she stayed with the expedition all the way to the mouth of the Columbia River.

Although the Lewis and Clark Expedition failed to substantiate the myth of an easy river passage across the continent, it did bring back a great deal of useful information about the country and its native inhabitants. Fur trappers and traders were the first to seize the opportunities laid open by Lewis and Clark. The Hudson's Bay Company, the Rocky Mountain Fur Company, and the American Fur Company all conducted operations on the watershed systems of the Missouri, Yellowstone, Columbia, and Colorado rivers, among others, for two decades. To go west before the 1840s was, in large part, to travel over water in the company of fur trappers. By the end of that period, however, the beaver—the primary item of the trade—had been trapped out of its ancestral waters, and rivers were invested with a new kind of romance.

Throughout the middle period of the nineteenth century—and to a lesser extent right up to the beginning of the twentieth—the heartland rivers of America were the great highways of the Industrial Revolution. The greatest of them all, of course, was the Mississippi. This was the home of Mark Twain's heart and the setting of his greatest books, *Huckleberry Finn* and *Life on the Mississippi*. In *Mark Twain's America*, Bernard DeVoto gave us the best capsule description of the river that called to Twain:

> There were barges, the broadhorns and the scows—the slow freight of the world moved by creatures of terror and romance. There were rafts of timber and of lumber floating from the forests to build the houses of democracy by the half-million. And the steamboats. Boats of the Cairo line and the Memphis line tied up daily at the wharf. So did boats from the Illinois River, the Red River, the White River, the Missouri, the upper Mississippi, the Ohio, the Monongahela, the Tennessee, the Cumberland, the Arkansas, the Yazoo.

236

And there were the travelers, the "traders, drovers, farmers, home-steaders, tinmen, miners, masons, shipwrights, actors, minstrels, mesmerists, phrenologists, bear leaders, circus men, gamblers, pros-titutes and prophets." Duplicated in its parts—though nowhere on so grand a scale—this was river life in Victorian America.

In the years following the Civil War, this turmoil of life began to subside, increasingly affected by the rise of the railroad as the nation's principal transportation network. Which is not to say that we suddenly had no use for the rivers. We used them, right enough—used them badly, too many of them. Rivers had been and remained for a long time the open sewers of the nation. All the rubbish of industry and city life was dumped into them. The current, it was hoped, would simply carry the mess away. By the mid-nineteenth century, water pollution was a serious problem in Chicago and other major cities built along rivers. Between 1840 and 1860 the population of Illinois soared from 5,000 to nearly 110,000 and the Illinois River absorbed this growth poorly. Waterborne diseases, spread by the release of raw sewage into the source of drinking water, were rampant.

Near Chicago, wrote a researcher in 1911, the Illinois River reached its "lowest point of pollutional distress, becoming, when very hot weather coincides with a low stage of water, a thoroughly sick stream."

Its oxygen is nearly all gone; its carbon dioxide rises to the maximum; its sediments become substantially like the sludge of the septic tank; its surface bubbles with the gases of decomposition escaping from sludge banks on its bottom; its odor is offensive; and its color is gray with suspended specks and larger clusters of sewage orga-nisms. . . . On its surface are also floating masses of decaying debris, borne up by the gases developing within them, and covered and fringed with sewage fungus . . . the vegetation and drift at the edge of the stream are also everywhere slimy with these foul-water plants and minute, filth-loving animals.

Such sights and stenches were common to all rivers on whose banks cities and industry flourished; dead fish were a good sign of a suc-cessful papermill. Those who could afford to do so abandoned the stinking metropolises in summer and headed out to country estates, often to where a stretch of river flowed by, still cold, clear, and odorless.

"TURNING OUR DARKNESS TO DAWN"

While the conservation of forests and wildlife was gaining influential adherents at the turn of the century, rivers in their wildest forms found few defenders. Even the intense battle over the flooding of Yosemite National Park's Hetch Hetchy Valley in 1913 was not so much a fight to keep the Tuolumne River running freely, as to preserve the integrity of the national park system. Rivers were understood not as organisms but as receptacles, to be filled or emptied as circumstances required. Waterways that seasonally flooded or dried up were of no use to people; in fact, they were a threat to health and prosperity. Hence, a conservationist in the Gifford Pinchot or Theodore Roosevelt tradition could agitate eloquently for the saving of forested land on the one hand and the calculated destruction of rivers on the other. There was no contradiction in these beliefs. Both were well-meaning. Rivers flowing freely for miles and miles through thirsty country were as wasteful, according to some, as cut-and-run logging methods. Water that could be put to immediate use but was not only wound up in the sea. Almost any way a person looked at it, a wild river was not considered as good a neighbor as a tamed one. Though the doctrine of utility was applied vigorously to forests, on the federal level perhaps its most ingenious expression was applied to rivers. Put plainly, the rivers were "engineered" from one end of the country to the other— dammed, turned into canals, dredged, burdened with flood-control works—much of this at the hands of the U.S. Bureau of Reclamation and the Army Corps of Engineers and almost all of it with the full and enthusiastic approval of the public. Engineered rivers have been among the proudest technological achievements of mankind. They have saved lives, spread electric power throughout the land, raised living standards, and reclaimed deserts. This was democracy in action. During the 1930s, when the Columbia River was being harnessed to generate the cheapest publicly owned electricity in the nation, Woody Guthrie could sing with a clear social conscience, "Roll on, Columbia, roll on. Your power is turning our darkness to dawn."

Between 1933 and 1963, ten dams were built on the Columbia, with large dams constructed on its major tributaries in that same period. And the Columbia was not the only river being restructured. All along the nation's major streams, massive projects were being undertaken for water storage, flood control, electric power generation, recreation, and irrigation. In 1933, Congress established the Tennessee Valley Authority to rejuvenate one of the most economically hard-pressed, river-ravaged regions of the country. The Tennessee River had always been destructive, periodically flooding Chattanooga and wiping out small towns located at its bottlenecks. The TVA engineered hope, and conservationists, believing in the authority's goals of land restoration, were proud to help. "What we are doing down there is taking a watershed with about 3.5 million in it, almost all of them rural, and we are trying to make a different type of citizen out of them," explained President Franklin Roosevelt. "TVA is primarily intended to change and improve the standards of living of the people in that Valley."

The TVA was comprehensive. Hills were reforested to check the massive erosion caused by the bad logging practices of the previous century. New farming techniques were introduced. The Tennessee's 652-mile main stem was made commercially navigable, and its flooding was checked. The river itself was reorganized into sixteen lakes covering more than 600,000 acres of land, forming links in a chain of water.

Far to the west, the Colorado River, beginning in the 1930s, was also being put to dramatic use. The 1922 interstate Colorado River Compact and later amendments apportioned the river's waters so that the dry states of Wyoming, Colorado, Utah, Nevada, Arizona, New Mexico, and California all received their share. The terms of that compact and other agreements have made the Colorado River "the most used, the most dramatic, the most highly litigated and politicized river in the nation, if not the world," according to Philip L. Fradkin in *A River No More*. Because of the demands placed on its changeable flow, the Colorado River is also the river that comes closest to having its last drop of water used; not for twenty years has the Colorado's water reached its natural outlet in the Gulf of California. To fulfill the demands on it, the Colorado was systematically dammed, beginning with Hoover Dam, which started backing up the river's waters along the Arizona-Nevada border in 1936, forming the serpentine Lake Mead. Thirty years and seven major dams later, the seven-hundred-foot-high Glen Canyon Dam at Lee's Ferry, Utah, was the Colorado River Storage Project's crowning glory. In 1963 it began impounding the Colorado's waters to form Lake Powell, the nation's largest man-made reservoir, named after the river's key nineteenth-century explorer—though it is not likely that he would have approved of the reservoir (see chapter 3). Lake Powell is a popular recreation site for thousands. Hundreds of feet beneath its surface, however, lie the canyons Powell himself had loved. Below the great dam, the river's level rises and falls with the flip of switches in the bowels of the dam, proving that even a river can be fully automated.

Perhaps many of the massive river projects undertaken during the first half of the twentieth century were worthwhile. Perhaps others were unavoidable. Perhaps they were even inspirational, for the way in which they pitted human wits against raw power. With the number of major dams now in excess of fifty thousand, and with several hundred thousand smaller ones, the job of remaking rivers had been tackled too zealously, and before all the consequences were understood. Examples of wretched excess abound. Take, for instance, the 1934 Pick-Sloan Plan, authorizing the construction of more than one hundred dams in the Missouri River's watershed, at a cost of $5 billion (in 1934 dollars). The plan was a compromise between the Army Corps of Engineers, which favored the Pick plan's dams for flood control and navigational purposes in one part of the river system, and the Bureau of Reclamation, which urged the Sloan plan's dams for irrigation and hydroelectric power in another. At the time it was passed, the Pick-Sloan Plan was described as a "loveless, shameless shotgun marriage of convenience" and the projected number of its dams nothing less than a gigantic boondoggle. Only a few—like the Garrison Dam in North Dakota—were in fact ever built.

The idea that there was no limit to the things one could and should do with a river was implanted as dogma. But for a lack of humor, some of the reasons given for damming, diverting, and dewatering began to sound almost like Dr. Seuss in their exuberance. *The Cat in the Hat* comes most readily to mind:

Look at me! Look at me! Look at me NOW! It is fun to have fun, but you have to know how. I can hold up the cup and the milk and the cake! I can hold up these books! And the fish and the rake! I can hold the toy ship and a little toy man! And look! With my tail I can hold a red fan! I can fan with the fan as I hop on the ball! But that is not all. Oh, no. That is not all. . . .

AGAINST THE CURRENT

There are, as it turns out, a number of good reasons to question the propriety of water projects. Often the cost-benefit analysis written to justify impoundment or diversion ignores the fact that some of the benefits are already being supplied. Recreation, for example, does not require a lake. Free-flowing water offers even more chances for enjoyment than does placid water, and in one survey conducted in the West, public use of natural rivers was found to be twelve times greater than that of man-made lakes and reservoirs. The typical cost-benefit statement also fails to weigh the values inherent in the existing natural conditions; often it was assumed that there simply were not any. On thousands of rivers the alteration of the water's flow via dams or diversions has destroyed commercial as well as recreational fishing, and has thus resulted not in the addition of river-derived benefits, but in the displacement of long-established ones.

"Dams have no consideration for fish," says Verne Huser, a mediator in natural-resource disputes who specializes in water issues. Anadromous fish such as salmon, which must swim upriver to spawn, are cut off from their ancestral waters. Fish ladders can correct some of that problem, but dams and spillways confront fish with other perils. High flows through turbines are the prime killers of young fish, which may get caught in them or be suctioned against the fish screens designed to keep them out. Sudden changes in water temperature, in the form of thermal plumes at the points of water discharge, cause instant death, while temperature increases can delay fish migration, foster the growth of fungus and debilitating bacteria, and change the food situation. High nitrogen levels, which are found in the spillway portion of a dam, cause gas-bubble disease in salmon, also hindering their spawning. Young salmon require a strong current to push them out to sea, but a dam might hold back too much water at the wrong

241

time, reducing the current so much that smolt are not able to reach their destination.

These are a few of the problems that dams cause for fish. The California planner for the Bureau of Reclamation who once remarked that "when the going gets tough, people will get the water, not fish," was no doubt correct, although it should be pointed out that dams can be a problem for people, too. Often they do not prevent floods, they merely move them someplace else—upstream, for example. And even along the most painstakingly controlled rivers, devastating floods have occurred, such as that on the lower Colorado in 1983, confirming Mark Twain's early skepticism about the value of making a river over again—"a job transcended in size only by the original job of creating it." (Speaking of the Mississippi River, Twain wrote that one who knows it "will promptly aver—not aloud but to himself—that ten thousand river commissions with the mines of the world at their back, cannot tame that lawless stream, cannot curb or confine it . . . cannot bar its path with an obstruction which it will not tear down, dance over and laugh at.")

The tendency to turn lawless streams into a chain of quiet lakes shortens by a millennium or so the waterway's natural lifespan. "The very nature of a lake is death," says Huser. "With their silt and vegetation lakes are the dying portions of water, and by creating more and more reservoirs we are increasing the number of dead parts." Indeed, siltation is a major and inescapable problem in all reservoirs. To postpone the inevitable, one dam must be built after another, as impoundments begin to fill with silt and are able to hold less water. Lake Powell, for instance, is expected to be completely filled with silt in less than three hundred years, while Arizona's Lake Mead is already well on its way to being incapacitated. Excessive salinity also plagues rivers where man's tinkering is apparent. Half of the Colorado River's burden of 11 million tons of salt each year is caused by evaporation from man-made reservoirs; evaporation leaves the naturally occurring salt behind, making the water progressively more salty. Waters used over and over again for irrigation also pick up salt from minerals in the ground. In some places the excessive salt has ruined the land for cultivation purposes.

For these reasons and others, major water projects, particularly

242

those involving dams, have become the symbol, for most conservationists, of all that is reprehensible about our technocratic society. In the words of John McPhee, dams themselves represent "something disproportionately and metaphysically sinister" to conservationists. As McPhee wrote in his book *Encounters with the Archdruid*:

The outermost circle of the Devil's world seems to be a moat filled mainly with DDT. Next to it is a moat of burning gasoline. Within that is a ring of pinheads each covered with a million people—and so on past phalanxed bulldozers and bicuspid chain saws, into the absolute epicenter of Hell on earth, where stands a dam. The implications of the dam exceed its true level in the scale of environmental catastrophes. Conservationists who can hold themselves in reasonable check before new oil spills and fresh megalopolises mysteriously go insane at even the thought of a dam. The conservation movement is a mystical and religious force, and possibly the reaction to dams is so violent because rivers are the ultimate metaphors of existence, and dams destroy rivers.

This theory certainly would explain the intensity of the conservation movement's reaction to the proposal to erect Echo Park Dam in Dinosaur National Monument in the 1950s (see chapters 2 and 5), a proposal defeated largely because it inspired the first major conservation coalition effort in our history. The victory sparked the wilderness preservation movement, and led almost nine years later to the establishment of the National Wilderness Preservation System. To a lesser extent it also bestirred a concern for all free-flowing rivers, which, if the past was any indication, would continue to be viewed by the government as little more than dam-building opportunities. Separate opposition would have to be mounted on hundreds of separate water projects. Driving that point home was the fact that while Dinosaur National Monument was saved, the exquisite Glen Canyon was lost to another Colorado River Storage Project dam. It was only as the floodgates closed that conservationists began to realize what had been sacrificed by a momentary lapse in their vigilance. David Brower of the Sierra Club, who had been the principal spokesman

243

against the Echo Park Dam, called the Glen Canyon Dam the greatest failure of his life.

Brower did not let down his guard again. That there are no dams within the Grand Canyon is largely his doing—and also his undoing. In the mid-1960s, the Bureau of Reclamation requested a portion of the Colorado River in the Grand Canyon for its use. Without authorization of the Sierra Club board, Brower spent funds to buy a full-page ad in *The New York Times* asking, "Should we also flood the Sistine Chapel so tourists can get nearer the ceiling?" That ad and similar applications of public pressure killed the plans. It also cost the Sierra Club its tax-exempt status, for the Internal Revenue Service had determined that its tactics smacked of lobbying. Shortly thereafter, Brower was dismissed as executive director but went on to found Friends of the Earth and continued his opposition to the dam-builders. In the course of John McPhee's long profile of him in *Encounters with the Archdruid*, Brower tells an audience that "I hate all dams, large and small."

"Why are you conservationists always against things?" came a question from the back of the room.

"If you are against something, you are for something," Brower replied. "If you are against a dam, you are for a river."

BEING FOR A RIVER

In 1960, while the furor over dam construction still ran high, National Park Service officials quietly recommended to the Senate Select Committee on National Water Resources that federal steps be taken to spare some of the nation's free-flowing rivers. Senate committee members accepted the notion. Support for national river preservation also filtered in from the Outdoor Recreation Resources Review Commission in 1962. The commission's final report proposed that "certain streams be preserved in their free-flowing condition because their natural scenic, scientific, aesthetic, and recreational values outweigh their value for water development and control purposes now and in the future." The commission suggested that those rivers deserving to be left alone be identified. For that purpose the Wild Rivers Committee, composed of people from the Departments of Interior and Agriculture, was formed. Twenty-two rivers were judged to be immediately worthy of federal protection, and it was agreed that a system be developed to encompass them.

The timing could hardly have been better. President Johnson supported the creation of such a system, for it fit in well with his stated commitment to the preservation of natural beauty. In 1965, Johnson told Congress that rivers "occupy a central place in myth and legend, folklore and literature. They are our first highways, and some remain among the most important. . . . We will continue to conserve their water and power for tomorrow's needs with well-planned reservoirs and power dams, but the time has come to identify and preserve free-flowing stretches of our great scenic rivers, before growth and development make the beauty of the unspoiled waterways a memory."

During congressional hearings to install a national river system, Interior Secretary Udall expanded on Johnson's theme. He reviewed the nation's largest river programs, specifically those for irrigation, championed by Theodore Roosevelt, and those for flood control and hydropower, pushed by Franklin Roosevelt. "We need to give further balance to these programs, and to systematically single out those rivers and segments of rivers that have not been developed. . . . We are not just talking about protecting our premier trout streams, as important as that is. We are not just talking about rivers to float. One of the things I would like to stress is what we will be doing for water quality and water conservation."

Despite the administration's strong backing of river-preservation bills, however, the first measure offered by the Wild Rivers Committee was deemed inadequate by conservationists. Pennsylvania Congressman John P. Saylor, who had served on the ORRRC, was particularly disappointed. "They must not have been listening to the President," he said during river hearings in 1967. "Or they were so fainthearted that they beached their canoe before they got to the water, because I can tell you that the bill they sent up left so much to be desired that some of us wondered whether or not those two secretaries were trying to support the President in his program of conservation." The bill Saylor was objecting to started the system with only seven designated rivers, and mentioned seventeen for further study. Saylor said he could think of at least sixteen rivers eligible for immediate protection, and could name another sixty-six candidates for study. Saylor and others began working up their own legislation.

One problem they faced was that many sections of river and land were not on public property. They would have to be acquired before protection could be assured. And, as popular as the concept of a national river-preservation system had grown, private landowners objected when it was their property being mentioned for acquisition. Federal jurisdiction where local control was long ensconced was "gall and wormwood" to many river frontage owners. Some felt that federal involvement was unnecessary, since they had willingly provided public access across their land. Past permission, however, was no guarantee of future access. There was no telling what would happen from one generation to the next. The federal agencies approached the issue of condemnations gingerly. "We don't come in here waving a flag, and say, 'Give us the power to condemn' " said Agriculture Secretary Orville Freeman. "We use it very charily, because it is always a bloody business, and we get hurt in the public image."

Nevertheless, the issue was so sensitive that many rivers had to be withdrawn from consideration. People who had lived along the Shenandoah River in West Virginia were particularly incensed by the proposed usurpation of their land, some of which had been in families for two hundred years. "I am truly appalled by the lack of safeguards afforded to innocent citizens whose only fault is being on land some other citizens covet," Dr. Barbara Moulton of Charles Town testified. "There is nothing the U.S. Government could give me that would make up for my losing that property if I lost it. And I don't think there is anything the rest of the country would gain from my losing it. Free citizens owning their own land, free to grow their own food, to enjoy the fruits of their labor—this is more a part of the American heritage than is a wilderness." Because of such persuasive opposition, the portion of the Shenandoah under consideration was cut.

Of course, many local groups also lobbied hard for the inclusion of their favorite rivers in a national system, because it was the only way to ensure their free-flowing existence. "The wild river concept in your bill is a great thing," declared Glenn Thompson, editor of the Dayton, Ohio, *Journal Herald*, who came to Washington to campaign for the preservation of the Little Miami River in his state. "I hope you capture them all. But the real urgency is on the hundred little rivers. The government owns the land along the dramatic western streams; the subdividers are after ours," he said. Federal protection was essential, Thompson asserted, because states and local governments "are not geared for this job. We are organized into counties which are big enough so you can drive to town in a wagon in one day. That is not big enough to manage a river."

When the Wild and Scenic Rivers Act finally passed, the Little Miami was not among those immediately preserved. Congress agreed instead to designate portions of the Middle Fork of the Clearwater and the Middle Fork of the Salmon in Idaho, the Eleven Point in Missouri, the Feather in California, the Rio Grande in New Mexico, the Rogue in Oregon, and the St. Croix and Wolf in Wisconsin, for protection. But the Little Miami and the hundreds of "little rivers" like it would at least have the opportunity to be considered for inclusion later. The act declared it to be "the policy of the United States that certain rivers, which, within their immediate environments possess outstandingly remarkable scenic, recreational, geological, fish and wildlife, historic, cultural, or other similar values, shall be preserved in a free-flowing condition, and that they and their immediate environments shall be protected for the benefit and enjoyment of present and future generations." The act stipulated that future rivers could be added either by Congress or by individual state legislation submitted for the Interior Secretary's approval, after study had been completed; during the study period of five years, no development was to be allowed. The responsibility for preservation was assigned to whichever federal land-managing agency happened to have the closest jurisdiction. The act, through negotiated purchase, condemnation, and various easements, also protected a half-mile corridor on both sides of the river. Depending on the degree of protection, rivers were defined as either recreational, which allowed the most development along the banks, or scenic and wild, for more pristine conditions. On these rivers the Army Corps of Engineers, the Bureau of Reclamation, and the Federal Power Commission (later the Federal Energy Regulatory Commission) were not allowed to perform their works.

As mentioned earlier, Congress expected the number of protected rivers to rise to one hundred within ten years. By 1990, another one hundred river segments were to be added. Instead, the system expanded at a snail's pace. Much of the problem, some felt, was that river-protection efforts were left largely in the hands of scores of local conservation groups, like Rivers Unlimited in Ohio or Friends of the River in California, whose energy and commitment were prodigious but whose influence outside their immediate areas was limited. Representation at the national level was lacking, not least because the general conservation organizations did not have specific river-protection programs. "The rivers have taken short shrift," Brock Evans of the National Audubon Society conceded in 1970. "The [national] conservation groups budget their work on rivers within the category of public lands, and as a result, the rivers don't get the attention they deserve." In 1972, Jerry Meral, an Environmental Defense Fund scientist, called for the creation of a national organization devoted entirely to river protection, and in March 1973 the leaders of various grassroots organizations from around the country joined together to form the American Rivers Conservation Council (ARCC). While the old national groups steadily increased their own efforts, from then on the ARCC (which in 1984 changed its name to American Rivers, Inc.) led the fight for river protection nationwide. Among the most useful devices it developed was the annual publication of "The Ten Most Endangered Rivers" list, a heavily documented sum-mary of abuse that soon became one of the most effective and best-publicized conservation documents available.

Still, the system expanded slowly. On the tenth anniversary of the 1968 act, there were only only forty-three river segments totalling 2,299 miles. Part of the difficulty was the process itself. New river segments can be designated only after a lengthy and convoluted process of proposal and study. Typically, it takes five or six years for a river to be added, from the moment local supporters rally around the idea, convince their congressional delegation to introduce the proposal, and see it through public hearings and congressional committees, which may or may not report it to the House and Senate for full consideration. The bill may then pass, or it may languish. If it passes and the President signs it, either the Department of Agriculture or the Department of the Interior studies the river and assesses the environmental impacts of designation. The study recommendations are then sent to the Congress, the President, and the Office of Management and Budget, which then arrive at a final decision. At the very best, such a system is cumbersome and time-consuming, as well as especially susceptible to political expedience and ideological relcalcitrance, as events would demonstrate.

LOW-HEAD AND HIGH RISK

In December 1980 President Jimmy Carter signed the Alaska Lands Act (see chapter 7), which added segments from thirty-three rivers totaling 3,284 miles—although conservationists were disappointed that this represented less than half the number of rivers agency planners had recommended. In that same year, 125 miles of the Salmon River in Idaho had been designated, and in 1981, the day before officially leaving office, Interior Secretary Cecil Andrus authorized designation for nineteen California rivers (challenged by water development interests, the Andrus designations were finally upheld by the courts in 1984). Many rivers had been studied and recommended by the end of 1980, waiting only for the next step in the path to designation. But Reagan and his people did not share the Carter administration's passion for river protection. None of the recommended rivers was granted protection until 1983, when pressure for additions could no longer be ignored. In the meantime, funds for river study were cut to the bone, while appopriations to the river-wrecking Bureau of Reclamation were increased. Shortly after becoming Secretary of the Interior, James Watt abolished the Heritage Conservation and Recreation Service, which had managed the wild and scenic rivers program and the national trails program at the national level. Watt's own feelings regarding the recreational and inspirational value of rivers were revealed in comments he made to national park concessioners shortly after a river-rafting trip through the Grand Canyon. The first day, he said, was "thrilling." The second day was "a little tedious." By the fourth day, he said, he was "praying for helicopters" to rescue him. "I don't like to paddle and I don't like to walk," he explained.

When the Reagan administration at last submitted eight new river segments for protection, they were drastically reduced in scope from what had been recommended by the agencies during the Carter years. Furthermore, tacked on to the Reagan contribution to the rivers system were several potentially destructive amendments. Mandated protection for rivers under study was cut from five years to three, and state legislatures were given the opportunity to cancel protection of any wild and scenic rivers designated in their states. These amendments did not fly, but the administration discovered other ways to weaken the process: it requested a measley $1.5 million for river acquisition (Congress raised it to $5 million). It also successfully opposed legislation introduced in 1983 (and again in 1984 and 1988) by Minnesota Republican Senator Dave Durrenberger that was designed to enhance state-initiated preservation systems.

As long ago as 1905, when the state of Wisconsin banned dams on the Brule River, various states have protected some of their rivers—Oregon stopped dams on portions of the Rogue in 1915, California did the same on portions of the Klamath in 1924, and by 1993 thirty-two states had designated a total of about 13,000 miles of segments on 303 rivers. The degree of protection, of course, varied from state to state. Some were content merely to place a descriptive plaque by the river's edge; others, such as Minnesota, California, and Wisconsin, specifically banned such projects as dams. Durrenberger's failed legislation would have provided federal grants of as much as $5 million a year for state river-conservation programs, banned federal water pro-jects on any state-protected river whose governor submitted an objection, and clarified tax laws to ensure that donors of riverside land for preser-vation purposes would receive appropriate tax breaks.

Even if the Durrenberger legislation had become law, however, it would have done little to interfere with one of the most consistent threats to river protection: The Federal Energy Regulatory Commission (FERC), whose licensing system controls all applications for the development of water projects, large and small. By the 1980s, many said, the age of the "mega-dams" was over, though it had been something to see when it was in its glory, particularly in the West. By 1977, the seventy-fifth anniversary of its creation, the Bureau of Reclamation had constructed no fewer than 322 storage and hydropower dams and another 345 diversion dams on western rivers, from the Colorado to the Columbia, the Missouri to the Sacramento. That time, it was said, was now gone. "These days," historian Donald Worster wrote in the Fall 1987 issue of *Wilderness*,"anyone seeking to build a new dam anywhere in the United States (or for that matter in most other nations) must anticipate a long, discouraging battle, rather like that involved in constructing a new nuclear power plant; he must be prepared for immense cost over-runs and, when finished, fend off potential saboteurs." In 1986, the Gunnison Diversion Project of North Dakota had been severely cur-tailed, and three years later the proposed Two Forks Dam (619 feet high, 1,700 feet wide) on the South Platte River in Colorado was de-feated by a combination of conservation pressure and an unfavorable decision from the Environmental Protection Agency. (The presumed end to the age of the big dams would be provided with a particularly intri-guing footnote in 1993, when the Interior Department made a serious recommendation that an old federal dam on the Elwha River in Washington be *torn down*—this from the agency whose Bureau of Reclamation had proudly built so many dams, to the cheers of millions.)

Nevertheless, if mega-dams were no longer likely, there remained smaller existing and proposed "low-head" hydropower projects devel-oped at the local level, and the FERC had demonstrated its willingness to approve such efforts—hundreds of them all over the country, in fact. Moreover, the FERC also had the power to exempt from its major envi-ronmental provisions any project designed to deliver less than five megawatts of power; here, too, it had been generous, granting more than nine hundred such exemptions. While federally designated wild and scenic rivers, and those under study for such status, were generally pro-tected from FERC's licensing authority, state-designated rivers were not, and the agency cheerfully authorized projects on many state rivers in spite of frequently energetic opposition from the state governments themselves.

The threat from the FERC was compounded by the provisions of ano-ther federal law, the Public Utilities Regulatory Policies Act (PURPA) of 1978. This act, designed to enhance the nation's energy indepen-dence, required public utilities to purchase power from small developers at a price equal to what it would have cost the utilities to build their own facilities to produce the same amount of power. PURPA, too, inspired a boom of applications, many for the reconstruction of of now-unused hydropower projects, some of them decades old. In Washington, Oregon, and California alone, 1,300 such applications were made by middle of the 1980s.

It did not necessarily follow that every appropriate unprotected river

251

in the land was going to be stoppered by such projects. "The economics of this business are very shaky," one developer remarked in 1984. "In California, the Corps of Engineers compiled a list of thousands of projects. Applications were filed on several hundred of those. More than ninety have made their way through the permitting and licensing process. How many do you see being built? Hardly any. This is a capital-intensive business. You're talking about borrowing a lot of money at high interest rates and getting a low rate of cash flow. In most cases, you plot out your investment and interest costs next to your anticipated cash flow and the two lines never meet. It's a case of slow, controlled bankruptcy."

Still, the possibilities of hydropower development on at least some potential additions to the Wild and Scenic River System colored the movement for their protection with a certain urgency, and gradually, though sometimes in breathtaking spurts, the system managed to add segment after segment, even during the anti-preservationist years of the Reagan and Bush administrations. Indeed, one of the best years for wild and scenic river protection since 1980 and the Alaska Lands Act was 1992, the last year of President Bush's term, when 520 miles of twenty-four rivers in fourteen major river systems in Michigan were designated, together with Sespe Creek and the Big Sur and Sisquoc rivers in California and 85 miles of the Allegheny in Pennsylvania.

There remained astonishing gaps in the singularly disconnected network of 10,574.1 protected miles that had accumulated by the end of 1992, however. If the Snake, the Columbia, and the Missouri rivers, three of the interior West's four most important rivers, had achieved partial protection, not a single mile of the fourth, the Colorado, had been designated wild and scenic. While Idaho possessed nine protected river segments, three other Rocky Mountain states—Montana, Colorado, and Wyoming—could count only seven among them, and Utah, the fourth, had *no* wild and scenic rivers at all. What was more, by the end of 1993 only 34 rivers out of the 132 Congress had authorized to be studied had received designations; some, like the Wallowa of Oregon or the Menantico in New Jersey, were still under study; a few—from the Elk in Colorado to the Priest in Idaho, from the Red in Kentucky to the Snake in Wyoming—remained unacted upon in spite of recommendations that they be designated, and others, like the Porcupine and the Coleville

252

in Alaska or the Salt and the San Francisco in Arizona, even while not recommended, almost certainly qualified for inclusion.

Clearly, the Wild and Scenic Rivers System fell short of completely justifying its title as a system. This did not discourage river advocate Tim Palmer. "In spite of all that," he wrote in his definitive 1992 study, *The Wild and Scenic Rivers of America* (from which much of the information in this chapter has been taken), "the system has clearly saved many rivers, and . . . has contributed to the change in public attitudes and thus to the protection of *all* rivers. The debates over individual streams have served to heighten awareness and delineate the arguments implicit in all river conservation. The national status and the efforts to designate rivers flowing through public lands have pushed river conservation closer to the mainstream of . . . thinking on conservation, closer to par with wilderness and national park concerns that had ranked prominently for decades."

Exactly. Today, for all the gaps that remain, for all the weaknesses and rickety bureaucratic machinery that hampers its process, the Wild and Scenic Rivers Act remains a powerful and important tool for the preservation of some of the most important wild habitat left in the nation. And with that necessary task, it also can help us nurture the magic described by former National Park Service planner John Kauffman in his book, *Flow East*: "Take a child to a river. Acquaint him with its wonder, its beauty, and its power; let him enter into the joy of running water, and it will not only be a playmate and playground but a teacher and classroom as well."

A WALK IN THE COUNTRY

In the beginning, the trails were all business. The Indians put their feet where the animals had gone, and established a network that laced through the woodlands and mountains of the East for the purposes of hunting and trading. When the Europeans came, they put the same network to their own purposes, which included not only hunting and trading, but settlement, the footpaths gradually widening into horse trails, then wagon roads, interconnecting with the rivers to form a transportation system that serviced the needs of the loose coalition of colonies that became an adolescent nation between the Atlantic and the Mississippi.

And then into the West, some of the trails blazed now instead of followed—Lewis and Clark heading over the High Plains to the Rocky Mountains from their camp on the upper Missouri in 1804. Two decades later, the first trading caravans began rumbling southwest from St. Louis to the settlements in a foreign land called New Mexico, along the Santa Fe Trail, and from there north along the Taos Trail. In the 1830s and 1840s, the promise of rich land and richer opportunity in the Pacific Northwest and California called the wagons west from "jumping-off" points on the Mississippi and Missouri rivers, up the valley of the Platte River to Fort Laramie, through South Pass to Fort Bridger, then north up the valley of the Snake River, if you were bound for the Oregon country, or west by southwest across the Great Basin and the Sierra Nevada if you were bound for California. Depending upon where you were headed, it was called the Oregon Trail or the California Trail, and tens of thousands wore a tracery of ruts into both over the course of nearly thirty years. The Mormons, too, the definitive settlers, cutting off from the main stem in 1846 to the Great Salt Lake, then sending from there shoots of settlement all the way to San Bernardino in southern California, on what came to be known as the Mormon Trail.

The Natchez Trace, up from the Mississippi River through Mississippi and Tennessee, the Tamiami Trail across Florida, the Goodnight-Loving and Chisholm trails up through Texas to the cattle towns of Kansas, the Camino del Diablo west from Santa Fe to San Diego. We were a nation of trails that became roads, then highways, and even in some cases railroads, and over most of them was carried the baggage of our history. It was traffic with a purpose, most of it, but at an astonishingly early period there were those with little but the pleasure of a walk in the country in mind.

Up in the White Mountains of New Hampshire, in 1819, Abel Crawford and his son Ethan cut a trail to the top of Mount Washington. It was soon known as the Crawford Path, and it was the first route to the mountain's summit, where there seemed little reason to go, except for the pleasure of being there. Mount Washington was, after all, not only the highest peak in New England, but the windiest one in the world, with gusts later clocked at 235 miles an hour. No commerce or industry thrived there. Yet the Crawford family may have been the first in the nation to profit from those out for a mere hike in the hills.

Their taverns furnished food and warmth, while their knowledge of the mountains was sought by such illustrious visitors as Daniel Webster and Nathaniel Hawthorne. The Crawford Path, a portion of which is now used by the Appalachian Trail, is the oldest continuously used recreational footpath in North America.

In New England the tradition of taking to a path through the woods for the sheer pleasure of it runs deep, though educational benefits were not overlooked. In 1876 the Appalachian Mountain Club (AMC) was formed by a professor at the Massachusetts Institute of Technology "to explore the mountains of the Northeast and the adjacent regions, for both scientific and artistic purposes, and, in general, to cultivate an interest in geographic studies." Since then the group has built and maintained almost four hundred miles of trails through the White Mountains. By 1888, hiking in the Whites had become so popular that the club decided to build a hut in a high col for shelter, since many who ventured out were not prepared for the exigencies of mountain weather. The AMC eventually built seven more high huts along its trails, offering hot meals and beds to the stream of hikers—this in addition to maintaining another twenty shelters in New Hampshire and Maine. (The AMC is now not only the oldest mountain club in the United States, but the largest, with 35,000 members.) The trail tradition was picked up by James P. Taylor, associate principal of a boy's school in Vermont, who was disappointed by the lack of access to Vermont's Green Mountains. Following the AMC's example, Taylor formed the Green Mountain Club in 1910, and set its members to work cutting a 265-mile "footpath in the wilderness" between the Canadian border and the Massachusetts state line. They called it the Long Trail.

One man who had earlier visited the Green Mountains and decided the Long Trail was only the beginning was Benton MacKaye, son of the prominent dramatist Steele MacKaye. At the age of fourteen, MacKaye, descended from generations of New Englanders, decided that he would specialize in "geotechnics," which he defined as the "applied science of making the earth more habitable." He worked for the U.S. Forest Service from 1905 to 1916, then for the Labor Department for three years before turning to free-lance writing and consulting work. In 1923, he, Clarence Stein, Lewis Mumford, and others formed the Regional Planning Association of America. At various times he served as a consultant in planning programs for the Commonwealth of Massachusetts, the Tennessee Valley Authority, the Bureau of Indian Affairs, and the Forest Service; became one of the principal founders (and later a president) of The Wilderness Society in 1935 (see chapter 5); and worked on the staff of the Rural Electrification Administration before his "retirement" after World War II. For the rest of his long life (he died in 1975 at the age of 96), he lived and worked in his hometown of Shirley Center, Massachusetts.

Precisely when the glimmer of the idea that became the Appalachian Trail first came to him MacKaye could never quite remember. "It may have been in 1891," he wrote in 1972, "while I was listening to bearded, one-armed Major John Wesley Powell recount to an enthralled audience in Washington City his historic trip through the Grand Canyon. . . . It may have been in 1897, in the White Mountains of New Hampshire, as Sturgis Pray and I struggled through a tangled blowdown. . . . Or it may have been in 1900 when I stood with another friend, Horace Hildreth, viewing the heights of the Green Mountains." Whenever its genesis, the idea simmered in him for a long time, until 1921, when he outlined it for Charles H. Whitaker, editor of the *Journal of the American Institute of Architects*. Whitaker asked for an article. "An Appalachian Trail: A Project in Regional Planning," which the journal published in October of that year, offered the blueprint for a hiking trail that eventually followed the crest of the Appalachian Mountains from Maine to Georgia, covering two thousand miles. As one of its justifications, MacKaye noted that

we have neglected to improve the leisure which should be ours as a result of replacing stone and bronze with iron and steam. . . . The customary approach to the problem relates to work rather than play. Can we increase the efficiency of our *working* time? Can we solve the problem of labor? If so we can widen the opportunities for leisure. The new approach reverses this mental process. Can we increase the efficiency of our *spare* time? Can we develop opportunities for leisure as an aid in solving the problem of labor?

A WILDERNESS WAY

In 1930, MacKaye offered some additional reflections on what his trail concept could mean. It presented, he said, "a wilderness way through civilization . . . not a civilized way through the wilderness. It is a real trail. A path and not a road . . . the foot replaces the wheel, the cabin replaces the hotel, the song replaces the radio, the campfire replaces the movie. It is the trail of the *new* pioneer, not the old pioneer." By then, a substantial number of people agreed with him. The work of building the Appalachian Trail began not long after his 1921 article, when volunteers from Georgia to Maine began cutting and marking it. Miles of existing sections of local trail systems established by such groups as the Dartmouth Outing Club, the Appalachian Mountain Club, and the Green Mountain Club were incorporated into the new trail. In seven years, five hundred miles of the trail had been established, and it was first completed for its entire length in 1937.

In 1925, MacKaye and a few of his compatriots founded the Appalachian Trail Conference (ATC) to act as a monitoring and coordinating body for volunteer efforts in the development and maintenance of the entire trail. Some such organization was necessary, for it was not long before this unique idea began to present some unique problems. Since most of the trail crossed private lands, its integrity depended upon the cooperation of various landholders, and a change of ownership could force the relocation of a section at any time. Worse, over the years, second-home real-estate development encroached upon the route. In 1938, at the urging of ATC leaders, the National Park Service and Forest Service agreed to establish a "recreation zone" wherever the trail entered federal lands, prohibiting any sort of development deemed incompatible with trail objectives. But not even the generally conservation-minded New Deal government could always be depended upon to preserve the trail's integrity. During the 1930s, as an anti-Depression measure, the Roosevelt administration gave approval for the construction of the Blue Ridge Parkway linking Great Smoky Mountains National Park and Shenandoah National Park—and cutting into the heart of pristine trail country. Benton MacKaye fought the proposal (it was one of the reasons he helped found The Wilderness Society), but to no avail.

257

During the ATC meeting of 1937, Edward B. Ballard of the National Park Service offered at least a partial solution to the vulnerability of the trail. He proposed that "trailway" agreements be made with federal and state agencies to secure inviolable rights-of-way. Myron Avery, chairman of the ATC, jumped at this idea and over the next several years negotiated agreements with the federal government that allowed for an inviolable right-of-way for a distance of one mile on either side of the trail through federal lands, and with state governments that established a similarly protected right-of-way one-half mile on either side through state-owned lands. Although a stipulation did allow logging to take place up to two hundred feet on each side of the trail on national forestlands, these government agreements at least established the concept that the trail's environment, wherever possible, should retain a wilderness character.

The trail way agreements did not, of course, alleviate the situation in regard to private lands, on which about half of the trail still remained vulnerable to development. In 1945, Avery persuaded Congressman Daniel Hoch of Pennsylvania to introduce an amendment to the Federal Highway Act of 1944 that would have mandated the creation of a nationwide federal system of foot trails, with provisions for the purchase of land and easements wherever necessary. The proposal died in committee, and it would be nearly two decades before the idea of federal protection could be revived. In 1963, during a meeting in Maine, ATC chairman Stanley A. Murray and a group discussed the possibility of legislation devoted to the protection of the Appalachian Trail specifically. At about the same time, at a cocktail party in Washington, D.C., an advocate of the trail mentioned his concern to Senator Gaylord Nelson, who had once proposed a 1,500-mile trail system for his home state of Wisconsin. Nelson had never set foot on the Appalachian Trail at that time, but, as he said in an interview years later, "I didn't have to be on it to know it was good!" and in 1964 he introduced the first of several bills for its protection.

WHY NOT HERE?

By the time Gaylord Nelson's first bill for the protection of the Appalachian Trail entered the legislative process, a movement to establish similar trails all over the country had slowly gathered momentum. As early as 1932, the idea had leaped across the continent to emerge on the Pacific Coast, where Californian Clinton C. Clark proposed the establishment of an intermountain footpath running from Canada to Mexico across the Cascade and Sierra Nevada ranges. It was called the Pacific Crest Trail. Out in Wisconsin in the 1950s, Ray Zillmer, an attorney, began to promote the idea of a trail that would follow the traces of the great moraines that marked the deepest penetration of the last glaciers. This was called the Ice Age Trail. A few years later, citizens in Ohio conceived a trail running from Cleveland to Cincinnati, and later extended it northward to Toledo then back to Cleveland in a kind of great circle, 1,200 miles in length. They called it the Buckeye Trail. In upstate New York, in the Finger Lakes country, Wallace Wood and a few other enthusiasts began cutting a path from Allegheny State Park in western New York to the Catskills in the southeastern portion of the state—the Finger Lakes Trail.

After passage of the Wilderness Act of 1964, Benton MacKaye, well into his eighties by now, conceived of a "Cordilleran Trail" that would traverse the Rocky Mountains along the Continental Divide, linking one newly created wilderness with another. To him, both the trail and the areas served the common purpose of preserving wilderness in what he called the "French" strategy in a report for The Wilderness Society in 1966: "In order to hold the Mississippi Valley as part of *L'État Français*, the French established a series of forts held together by a winding river. In order to hold the Cordilleran Range as part of original America, let Americans establish a series of 'original' areas (wilderness areas) to be held together by a winding trail. As once a line of military posts defended the Great River, now a line of wilderness posts can defend the Great Divide."

These efforts and others found comfort in a 1962 report of the Outdoor Recreation Resources Review Commission, which lamented the fact that in this country very little had been done to encourage the healthful pastimes of walking and cycling, and a good deal had been done to discourage them. The commission stated:

We are spending billions for our new highways, but few of them being constructed or planned make any provision for safe walking and cy-

259

cling. Europe, which has even greater population densities, has much to teach us about building recreation into the environment. Holland is constructing a national network of bicycle trails. In Scotland, the right of the public to walk over the privately owned moors goes back centuries. In Scandinavia, buses going from the city to the countryside have pegs on their sides on which people can hang bicycles. Car ownership is rising all over Europe, but in the planning of their roads and the posting of them, Europeans make a special effort to provide for those who walk or cycle. Why not here?

Why not indeed? It was a question more and more people began to ask—including Senator Nelson, who in 1965 introduced another trails bill, which, going beyond protection for the Appalachian Trail alone, would add footpaths across the nation. The idea was suddenly so attractive that the Johnson administration seized it and began preparing legislation of its own out of the Department of the Interior. After three years of the kind of compromises and bickering typical of any sort of environmental legislation, a National Trails Act emerged from Congress in 1968 and was signed into law by President Johnson. It was the intent of Congress, the act stated, that "in order to provide for the ever-increasing outdoor recreation needs of an expanding population and in order to promote public access to, travel within, and enjoyment and appreciation of the open-air, outdoor areas of the Nation, trails should be established primarily, near the urban areas of the Nation, and secondarily, within established scenic areas more remotely located." As noted at the beginning of this chapter, the act immediately established the Appalachian Trail and the Pacific Crest Trail as the first components of the National Scenic Trails System, authorized the study of fourteen additional trails, and empowered the Secretaries of the Interior and of Agriculture to establish the shorter, urban-oriented recreation trails. It also established the category of Connecting and Side Trails (although no such routes have yet been designated). In 1978, because many of the trail studies were identifying extensive historic features and values on trails that did not quite qualify as "scenic," the Secretary of the Interior requested an amendment to the 1968 act that would establish Historic Trails as a separate category. In November, Congress complied with his request—and in the same amendment designated the Lewis and Clark, Mormon Pioneer, Oregon, and Iditarod as the first Historic Trails. In that same year, Congress also named the Continental Divide (MacKaye's "Cordilleran" concept) as the third Scenic Trail.

There now was, at least on paper, a National Trails System. But there were those in 1968 and later—as there are today—who questioned whether what we had could realistically be called a national system at all.

DRAWING-BOARD DREAMS

Not a single designated Scenic or Historic Trail in the present system is complete. Even the Appalachian—the venerable AT—still needs the acquisition, through purchase or easements, of almost three hundred miles to finally make it the unbroken "footpath *of* the wilderness" dreamed of by Benton MacKaye. Furthermore, of the twenty-nine studies authorized by the act of 1968 and subsequent amendments, only ten of the trails involved have even been designated. Eight that were under study were found "not to qualify" for designation by the Park Service (although those who supported these trails would still be willing to offer arguments for their revival as candidates), and two—the 265-mile Long Trail of Vermont and the 1,000-mile Pacific Northwest Trail of Washington and Idaho—were "not recommended" for designation, a decision vague enough to leave room for hope. The nine remaining candidates are still under study.

Finally, as mentioned above, no Connecting or Side Trails have been designated, even though heavy recreational use on many trails— however incomplete—suggests a significant need for these. More than 4 million people use portions of the Appalachian Trail every year, for example. Designation of Vermont's Long Trail, extending from the Massachusetts border to the Canadian border, was seen as one way of relieving this pressure on the AT, while in Georgia, Tennessee, and North Carolina volunteers have been working for several years to construct the Benton MacKaye Trail, a 250-mile-long loop off the AT that would wind through scenic and remote portions of Great Smoky Mountains National Park and Cherokee, Nantahala, and Chattahoochee national forests. The Long Trail, as noted, was not recommended for designation by the Park Service, and the MacKaye

Trail has not yet been seriously considered, though it clearly is a strong candidate.

At the heart of the problem has been a lack of money and commitment from the goverment itself. It was, in fact, ten years after the 1968 legislation before Congress appropriated *any* money specifically for the trails system. By the middle of the 1980s, the situation was summed up nicely in a National Park Service internal memorandum: "Inadequate funding for trails at all levels of government has made it impossible to meet the growing public demand for trail opportunities." The attitude of the Reagan administration toward the trails system was an echo of its policies with regard to other conservation programs—no support at all, if possible, and minimal support when it could not be avoided. And when James Watt abolished the Heritage Conservation and Recreation Service, he left the trails, like the wild and scenic rivers, without any federal agency primarily responsible for planning, development, and management. "There are probably no more than twenty people in the service who understand trails," a National Park Service employee told journalist Donald Dale Jackson in 1988. "It's no high road to promotion here, it's more like a cul-de-sac."

Such sluggish bureaucratic attitudes were compounded by a designation process nearly as time-consuming and onerous as that for river designation; by a lack of proper communication, interest, and cooperation among individual agencies on whose land any given trail or proposed trail might fall; by a confusion of regulations issued by various federal, state, and local entities—many of which often conflict and all of which require mounds of paperwork—and by a lack of public awareness of the needs and indeed the very existence of the National Trails System that sometimes bordered on plain igonorance. There was little significant pressure placed on government from the private sector to improve the situation—and what there was tended to be fragmented and inadequate. As was the situation with the National Wild and Scenic Rivers System until American Rivers filled the vaccuum, the trails system did not have a true national voice. "It's a serious problem," Ron Tipton, a longtime leader with the Appalachian Trail Club and at the time National Parks Program director for The Wilderness Society, told Donald Dale Jackson. "Trails lack a rallying point, they're not national by nature, their support groups are local. And trails have been a lower priority with conservation organizations as well as government."

Little has changed since Tipton's evaluation in 1988. The Appalachian Trail Conference, composed of independent hiking, camping, and trail clubs, remains the largest private organization devoted to trail concerns, with a total membership of about 80,000 scattered among its member organizations. It has long been the model for volunteer involvement in long-distance trail development and management and has been imitated—though never on so large a scale—by such groups as the Finger Lakes Trail Conference, the Buckeye Trail Association, the Ice Age Trail Council, the Benton MacKaye Trail Association, and the North Country Trail Association. On the national level, the tiny staffs of the American Hiking Society and the National Trails Coalition attempt to monitor not only the National Trails System but the condition and management of *all* public-land trails in the national forests, national parks, and Bureau of Land Management lands. No major conservation organization—not even The Wilderness Society, whose co-founder Benton MacKaye was the "father" of the trails system—has any kind of significant program devoted to the trails.

As a conservation issue, then, the trails lack national strength—the power of a single voice—necessary to force the government of the United States to the invest the National Trails System, which it created, with a semblance of reality and the financial and bureaucratic support sufficient to make it something more than what most of it sadly remains: dreams on a drawing-board.

AN AGENDA FOR THE NATIONAL WILD AND SCENIC RIVERS AND THE NATIONAL TRAILS SYSTEMS

THE RIVERS

Since its creation in 1968, the National Wild and Scenic Rivers System has taken on the character of a neglected stepchild—while it has managed to grow, it is neither as large nor as healthy as it should be. The more than ten thousand miles of 212 river segments currently included are still but a portion of all that could be included; at best, they constitute no more than the disarticulated skeleton of a system. Part of the reason behind this fitful and retarded growth lies in the inadequacies and confusions of the very law that created the system, but an equally significant obstacle has been the absence of any clear, organized, and coherent constituency for its continued health and growth—a deficiency unfortunately true not only of the public at large, but of the conservation movement generally, the American Congress, and, most particularly, the current administration (whose interest in wild and scenic rivers, when demonstrated at all, has been plainly antagonistic). And, while the system lies in a state of arrested growth, the fate of hundreds of America's remaining free rivers—many of them prime candidates for preservation—is shadowed by the rapid development of small-scale hydropower technology whose potential impact may outstrip all the megadams and diversions of the past.

Clearly, this moribund situation cannot be allowed to continue if the system is to take its proper place in the full web of this country's legacy of public lands—resources whose future is vital to the future of the nation itself. It is equally clear that in order to change things significantly, it is the responsibility of the conservation community at large to begin to build the necessary base of widespread support. The piecemeal defense of individual rivers is not enough; local support of local rivers is not enough; state systems of protection are not enough. We must create national support on a national scale for a truly national system, just as we did for the National Wilderness Preservation System, just as we did for the national interest lands of Alaska. Achieving this may require the kind of formal cooperation among national conservation groups that was demonstrated so successfully by the Alaska Coalition of the 1970s. However such a community of effort is structured, it should be put into motion swiftly in full recognition of the dimensions and significance of the tasks that await it. We offer the following as the most important immediate goals:

Passage of an omnibus wild and scenic rivers bill. At present, there are 4,425 miles of rivers and tributaries on which studies have been completed, including the Priest of Idaho, the Youghiogheny of Pennsylvania, the Wisconsin of Wisconsin, the Dolores of Colorado, and many other segments. Yet these rivers are victims of political inertia, and there is no reason to expect that they will soon be placed in the federal system of protection if they are acted on one river at a time.

264

These rivers and river sections should be included in a single bill that will give them immediate designation with broad-based congressional consent. The passage of such a bill should be the first step in a continuing program aimed at accelerating and expanding the current study process (see below) and the designation by the year 2000 of at least fifty additional river segments on federal land and another fifty (through acquisition and easement) on nonfederal land.

Completion of already authorized acquisitions and easements. The incorporation of ridge-to-ridge "buffer zones" on either side of designated rivers flowing through private lands is a device essential to the protection of watershed and riverine habitat, and authorization for the purchase of this land through outright acquisition or easement procedures was included in the acts that designated each of the segments now in the system. Yet there is a large backlog of unacquired land (some of it on rivers designated as long ago as 1968). Sufficient Land and Water Conservation Fund money should be allocated for the completion of these unresolved purchases over the next five years.

Initiation of a program of regular congressional oversight hearings. Congress has been particularly dilatory in its responsibility to monitor the development of this important resource system. Since passage of the Wild and Scenic Rivers Act in 1968, there has not been a single oversight hearing on the rivers system by any committee or subcommittee in either branch, yet such hearings are the principal means Congress has of determining how any law it has created is being administered—whether the intent of Congress is being carried out faithfully, whether programs are being properly funded, whether interpretation and implementation need to be refined or substantially revised. The Wild and Scenic Rivers System is in serious need of such attention, and hearings should be scheduled as soon as possible— in the House, by the Subcommittee on Public Lands and National Parks; in the Senate, by the Subcommittee on Public Lands and Reserved Water.

Moving swiftly to accomplish the three goals listed above would go a long way toward putting the Wild and Scenic Rivers System on a better footing in the near future. But as we have emphasized in each of these "agenda" statements, the management of America's public lands cannot be left hostage to the near-term syndrome; that very phenomenon is why the future of so much of the American land is in jeopardy today. In regard to the nation's rivers, then, as with all other units of the public lands, we must learn to think in the range of decades, indeed, of scores of years, if we are to properly maintain and even improve a legacy we have no right to neglect, and to that end we believe that three major long-range programs should be put into effect.

Mandate a national rivers study program. Under current procedures, an individual river is placed under study as a possible candidate for wild and scenic designation only after passage of a specific act of Congress. This ponderous approach is time-consuming and fraught with the possibility that many important rivers will not be seriously studied for inclusion before hydropower or other development renders them ineligible. Instead, we call for a nationwide study program for *all* currently eligible candidate rivers (a list that could easily be derived from the National Park Service's excellent "National Inventory of Rivers"); during a specified period of time for study (we recommend five years), no hydropower, real-estate, or any other kind of development that might affect the ecological integrity of a river or its wildlife or habitat would be allowed; after completion of the study, recommendations for individual rivers would then be passed on to Congress for designation where it is deemed appropriate. Such a program (similar in some respects to the National Forest Service's Roadless Area Review and Evaluation process) could be initiated by executive order, by separate legislation, or (as noted below) by amendment to the National Wild and Scenic Rivers Act of 1968.

Establish a permanent administrative body for river policy and planning at the federal level. At present, as many as fifteen government agencies at the federal, state, and local levels can be involved at one time or another in planning, policy, and management decisions affecting any given river. This is a confused and confusing business and must be simplified and clarified if we hope to produce any sort of long-range planning. Furthermore, the wild and scenic rivers need

266

a constituency of support *within* the federal government as well as outside it. The nearest thing to such a body was the Interior Department's Heritage Conservation and Recreation Service (before being abolished by James Watt), and even it had only six staff people in Washington, D.C., dealing with river programs. While day-to-day management decisions for any given river in the system should be left to the appropriate agencies—the U.S. Forest Service, the National Park Service, and the Bureau of Land Management—an Interior Department office of river planning should be created with adequate funds and staffing to take responsibility for the system as a whole in all matters of overall planning and policy—including the monitoring of a continuing study program and inventory, the supervision of all purchase procedures (including the allocation of funds), and technical assistance to individual states in the planning and development of their own wild and scenic rivers programs (a service now offered only by the National Park Service in a limited fashion). This Interior Department office should become the recognized government "voice" for American rivers.

Encourage the development of meaningful state wild and scenic rivers programs. Although the federal system of rivers is the best opportunity for preservation on a coherent national scale, this basic protection should be augmented by state programs to achieve the widest possible diversity and comprehensiveness. Only twenty-eight states now have river programs. A few of these—as in California—are comparable to the federal system in their scope and goals. Many others are little more than casual lists with little or no regulation or protection to give them weight. Through the agency described above, the federal government should vigorously promote the creation of substantive river programs in all fifty states. A major step in this direction would be swift passage of a bill similar to that introduced by Senator Dave Durenberger in 1984, the proposed State and Local Rivers Conservation bill. Such a measure would not only encourage states to designate rivers for special management, it would offer matching federal funds to help states develop river conservation efforts. Equally important, it would block the present autonomous power of the Federal Energy Regulatory Commission by declaring all state-designated rivers off-limits to hydropower development if the governor of a state so determines. Another measure introduced by Senator George Mitchell (D-Maine) in 1984 would have encouraged states to prepare comprehensive plans for their rivers to determine which should be available for hydropower development and which should be reserved for other purposes, such as recreation. The Federal Energy Regulatory Commission would be required to approve such comprehensive plans. Versions of both bills—or a combination of the two—should be acted upon by Congress as soon as possible.

The Wild and Scenic Rivers Act of 1968, like much conservation legislation, has revealed significant weaknesses and omissions over the years that were not sufficiently anticipated at the time of its passage. It needs to be refined and strengthened in a number of areas to aid and implement the kind of long-range proposals we have been discussing. First, as noted above, if it cannot be accomplished in any other manner, a nationwide study program for all eligible rivers on federal lands should be mandated by amendment of the act, eliminating the need for individual acts of Congress before any river or river segment can be placed under study. In addition, we recommend amendment of the act in three other areas:

Management planning. One of the greatest difficulties in properly administering the units of the rivers system as it now exists has been the lack of comprehensive management plans. To alleviate these problems in the future, the act should be amended to require each federal agency charged with the administration of each component of the system to prepare such a comprehensive management plan within three years after the component has been designated. In providing for the protection of river values, each plan should address the costs and effects of resource protection alternatives, the necessary development of lands and facilities, and appropriate user capacities, including provisions for the issuance of user permits, if deemed necessary. Further, this amendment should require similar plans to be drawn up by the appropriate agencies for those rivers already in the system.

Acquisition. Under the provisions of the present law, acquisition procedures through outright purchase or the purchase of easements are strictly limited to an area one-quarter mile from the ordinary high-water mark of both sides of a river. This rigid limitation does not properly take into account requirements for habitat protection that can vary considerably from river to river—and even portion to portion of any individual river. In addition, local landowners often want to sell their entire property, rather than just the portion that is contiguous to a river. For the purposes of intelligent planning, the act should be amended to allow the acquisition of land, where it is considered necessary to the purposes of the act, beyond the quarter-mile limits up to a maximum of one mile from the normal high-water mark on either side. Further, this amendment should stipulate that such acquisition authority extends to those wild and scenic rivers that already have been designated, so that refinement and improvement of riverine habitat protection can be made where necessary during the continuing planning process and so that landowners may convey to the government those portions of their property not previously eligible for sale. In addition, the Alaska Lands Act should be amended to increase to a mile the current half-mile width limitations on all protected streamside corridors on those Alaskan rivers designated wild and scenic by the act—as well as on those rivers that should be added to the system in Alaska.

Finally, the National Wild and Scenic Rivers System must be made an integral and recognized part of the interagency management of large natural systems, not just an incidental management matter of concern only to the agency directly responsible—when even that level of management is practiced. "The Wild and Scenic Rivers Act is far from perfect," Beth Norcross, director of legislative programs for American Rivers, remarked on the occasion of the twenty-fifth anniversary of the act in 1993. "But we have at our disposal a river protection tool that Congress embraces and understands. It has successfully protected over ten thousand miles of outstanding rivers and streams. It has the flexibility to address myriad land management issues if we are creative and thoughtful in using it." This "tool," thoughtfully and creatively implemented, can become essential to ecosystem protection. Designated rivers and the corridors of land they embrace can become a hugely important means of linking blocks of both public and private land across ecosystem-wide units of natural landscape. Future designations, as well as the management plans prepared for existing designated rivers, should be made with the needs of the whole system through which such rivers and their tributaries flow kept at the forefront of the planning process.

If they could be reduced to a single goal, the recommendations we make here are designed to provide the still-young National Wild and Scenic Rivers System with the stature and commitment long since given to such other units of the public lands system as the national parks or the national forests. Our rivers are no less important and should be treated with the same care so that, as Tim Palmer has written, they may play a commensurate role in the future resource planning of the nation: "Rivers, being everywhere important in natural areas and communities alike, constitute an inexhaustible frontier for environmental action. Long after debates over national parks and wilderness have simmered down, river protection will likely be going strong simply because there are so many important streams. They are at both the periphery of civilization and at its center, lending power, complexity, and difficulty to this movement. The goal of protecting rivers may become a prominent extension of other conservation agendas running far into the future and touching virtually everyplace where water flows."

THE TRAILS

As should be readily apparent, many of the problems—hence, many of the solutions—that relate to the National Wild and Scenic Rivers System also apply to its "twin," the National Trails System. In some cases, the problems that afflict the trails system are more serious than those that now hamper the rivers system. Take, for example, the matter of a coherent public support network. The rivers system has American Rivers, Inc., to speak for it at the national level, with at least varying degrees of significant support being provided by various other national conservation organizations. The trails of our country have not a single adequately staffed and funded national organization equipped to do the same, and the contributions made by the national conservation organizations to trail designation, maintenance, and protection has ranged from little to less over the past several decades. A nationally significant coalition of support for the trails must be fashioned in the near future if the system is to survive in anything approching a healthy state, much less grow. As with the rivers, this may require the formation of an inter-organizational group similar to the Alaska Coalition or the Ancient Forest

Alliance—a conservation task force with the funding, resources, and expertise to study the system's needs and problems and formulate specific recommendations that can then be translated into administrative action or, where necessary, new legislation. The beginning of such a group effort exists in the National Trails Coalition, which includes most of the national conservation organizations, but it has never been invested with either the money or the staffing necessary to become a genuine force in the movement. That should be rectified.

Certainly, one of the most immediate challenges of any coalition effort will be to cut through the present condition of apathy that enwraps both Congress and the federal land-managing agencies whenever trail needs appear. Influence should be applied at all government levels to per-suade policymakers that it is in the best interests of the nation to establish a truly realistic National Trails Systems that possesses both the prestige and the authority of other public-land units; the system must be given weight within the government. To accomplish this, the Secretary of the Interior should create an administrative body within the Interior Department whose only function is to coordinate with other federal, state, and local agencies, as well as the conservation community and local volunteer groups, and generally administer the National Trails System—with the staffing and funding necessary to the task. The trails system has never had its own supervisory structure; it should be given one as soon as possible, and the new agency should move at once to outline, establish, and promote a trails program designed to meet the following immediate and long-term goals:

A comprehensive survey of trail needs, now and in the future. One of the tasks assumed by the Heritage Conservation and Recreation Service before it was abolished was to initiate a grassroots effort to assess the needs of the trails system throughout the nation. The objectives of this assessment were to define the scope of the existing National Trails System and develop suitable amendments that would better implement the intent of the National Trails System Act of 1968; to determine the number of trails now in use, their proximity and availability to users, and their deficiencies; and to report the concerns, perceptions, strengths, and recommendations of trail-user groups all over the country. After the Heritage Conservation and Recreation Service was eliminated,

271

the task was turned over to a tiny group within the National Park Service. The resulting report was a noble effort produced under very difficult circumstances, but fell far short of being the detailed and comprehensive document it might have been. An entirely new effort must be initiated, with sufficient funding and personnel—both in Washington, D. C., and the field—to accomplish the goals of such a survey properly.

Completion of the existing trails system by the end of the century. It is now more than twenty-five years since passage of the 1968 act and with the exception of the Appalachian and Pacific Crest trails, both of them now relatively near completion, little has been done to fill in the gaps that have existed since the system was established. A classic example is the North Country Scenic Trail, designated in 1980. This unique trail, 3,200 miles in length, is designed to run through portions of eight states, beginning at the Vermont-New York border and meandering west to the Missouri River in North Dakota, where in theory it will link up with the Lewis and Clark National Historic Trail. But except for a few hundred miles within various national forest lands, this exciting trail experience remains almost entirely a phantom more than fourteen years after its designation. It is not alone in this distinction. Congress must allocate enough Land and Water Conservation Fund money to acquire the land necessary to complete this and and all other unfinished trails and, where negotiated purchases are impossible and condemnation proceedings inhumane or impractical, appropriate conservation easements and other agreements must be reached.

Addition of new scenic trails to the system, with the objective of adding these new trails to the existing network by the end of the century. The emphasis here should be on scenic trails rather than historic trails, for the paramount need in terms of providing a true sense of the nation's rich and various natural heritage through a trails system is for pathways that offer the closest and most immediate contact with the environment itself. By their very nature, most historic trails are designations on maps that largely follow highways; just as in the past, these routes are used to get from one place to another. Only scenic trails can provide some idea of what it was once like to walk out into new wilderness

272

country for the first time.

Of numerous proposals that have been offered up as candidates for addition to the trails system, five have been on the drawing boards for years. They encompass an impressively varied and extensive spread of territory and would, it seems clear, significantly enhance the present system. But after a long evaluation of four of the proposals, the government concluded that it could not recommend them for designation—and it has never studied the fifth (the Benton MacKaye). The government, we respectfully suggest, should change its mind:

The Pacific Northwest Trail. This proposed trail would offer the hiker the possibility of something no other existing or proposed trail can match—the chance of encountering a grizzly bear at one end and a pod of whales at the other. Beginning at a point on the Continental Divide just south of the Canadian border in Glacier National Park, Montana, and ending at the Pacific Ocean on the edge of Olympic National Park, Washington, the trail would cover about one thousand miles on the ground and include in its itinerary everything from the forget-me-nots of alpine meadows in the Northern Rockies to carpets of ferns in the temperate zone rainforests of the Olympic Peninsula. Together with segments in seven national forests in three states, one national recreation area (Ross Lake in Washington), and North Cascades and Olympic national parks, the trail also would feature a long trek through forests of lodgepole and ponderosa pine, Engelmann spruce, and old-growth Douglas fir in the two enormous units of the spectacular Pasayten Wilderness Area of Washington.

The Desert Trail. This proposal might be characterized as the Great BLM Trail, for it would utilize Bureau of Land Management lands for most of its considerable length. Indeed, it is by far the most ambitious of all the proposed trails, crossing through portions of four states in a 2,500-mile journey from the Centennial Mountains on the Idaho-Montana border to the town of Jacumba on the California-Mexico line. Among its principal features would be the Snake River plains and Craters of the Moon National Monument in Idaho; Malheur National Wildlife Refuge and Steens Mountain in Oregon; High Rock Canyon, the Black Rock Desert, and the Excel-

273

sior Mountains in Nevada; and Death Valley National Monument, East Mojave National Scenic Area, Joshua Tree National Monument, and Anza Borrego State Park in California.

The Dominguez-Escalante Trail. While essentially scenic in character, this proposed trail has historic significance as well. In July 1776, Francisco Atanasio Dominguez and Silvestre Velez de Escalante, Franciscan missionaries, set out to establish a land route between Santa Fe below New Mexico's Sangre de Cristo Range and Monterey on the California coast. They had little more than myth, instinct, and a few sketchy Indian directions to guide them, and consequently found themselves becoming increasingly lost as they wandered vaguely north-west through Colorado and Utah. By the time they reached Utah Lake in Utah it was near the end of October, and, still lost, they turned back, moving through the canyon country of southern Utah and northern Arizona, finally cros-sing the Colorado River north of the Grand Canyon and staggering east to Santa Fe. The route was a great ragged circle some two thousand miles long. The proposed trail addition would follow the original as closely as modern circumstances permit and would expose the hiker to an abundance of truly wild country, from the Uncompahgre Plateau of Colorado to the Uintah Basin of Utah, from the valley of the Sevier River to the redrock canyons of the Escalante River (named after the friar himself) and the Pariah River. Along the way, the route would traverse or at least pass within sight of Carson, San Juan, Ashley, Fishlake, and Dixie national forests; Bryce, Capitol Reef, and Arches national parks; and Glen Canyon National Recreation Area.

The Benton MacKaye Trail. It is fitting and proper that this proposed trail—already virtually completed by volunteers, though not in the system—would be attached to the trail of MacKaye's own invention—the Appalachian Trail (AT). Attached for the relief of the AT, in fact, for this venerable pathway is one of the most thoroughly used public-land units in the United States and the addition would provide more than 250 additional miles in much of what is left of some of the wildest portions of the Southern Appalachian forest country. The trail would link up with the AT just a little north of the older trail's terminus at Springer Mountain in Georgia, then wind along ridgelines through Chattahoochee, Cherokee, and Nantahala national forests, then form a "loop" through Great Smoky Mountains National Park before finally hooking up with the AT again at the northern border of the park.

The Long Trail. Like the Benton MacKaye Trail, the proposed Long Trail addition is generally completed already and would also serve as a relief measure for the well-trodden AT. It would branch off from the AT halfway across Vermont and run north to the Canadian line through 150 miles of some of the wildest country left in New England—the Northern Forest, a landscape of trees, streams, bogs, ponds, and lakes that still possesses much of the character that the original European settlers encountered and set out to obliterate as best they could.

Other trails that have been proposed at one time or another—the Daniel Boone Trail through North Carolina, Tennessee, and Kentucky, for example, or the Nez Perce Trail through Oregon, Idaho, and Montana—should be seriously considered as well. But another potentially important means of expanding the trails system lies in the conversion of old railroad rights-of-way. Each year, more than three thousand miles of railroad track are abandoned by companies as they discontinue service on various lines through the country. The Railroad Revitalization and Regulatory Reform Act of 1976 included a stipulation giving private citizen groups and local, state, and even federal park authorities the right to petition for the public use of any such abandoned corridors. A 1983 amendment to the National Trails Act carried the idea even further: in what is called a "railbank" system, the ownership of abandoned roadbeds can be retained and the rails and ties themselves sold by railroad companies; however, until such time as a company can demonstrate a need to reopen the abandoned line to rail service, it also can be managed as a public trail by any private group or government park agency, providing such groups maintain the trail, assume all liability for its use by the public, and pay any applicable taxes. Already, many "rails-to-trails" conversions have been made successfully in Iowa,

Wisconsin, Illinois, Virginia, California, Washington, Maryland, and elsewhere. In 1985, to promote this idea, the Rails-to-Trails Conservancy was formed in Washington, D. C.

The emphasis in the recommendations above has been on the government's role in the future of the National Trails System. This is only as it should be, for it is time that the federal government began to play a role commensurate with that performed by the private sector for nearly three-quarters of a century. While the importance of the participation of such organizations and coalitions as the Appalachian Trail Conference and other citizen groups as well as the public at large is crucial, if we continue to allow the federal government to abdicate its responsibility—as it plainly has done over most of the past twenty-five years—then we can never hope to achieve a lasting system of national trails that will enlarge the wilderness experience for the generations to come.

Noatak Wild and Scenic River in Gates of the Arctic National Park and Preserve, Alaska (T. H. Watkins).

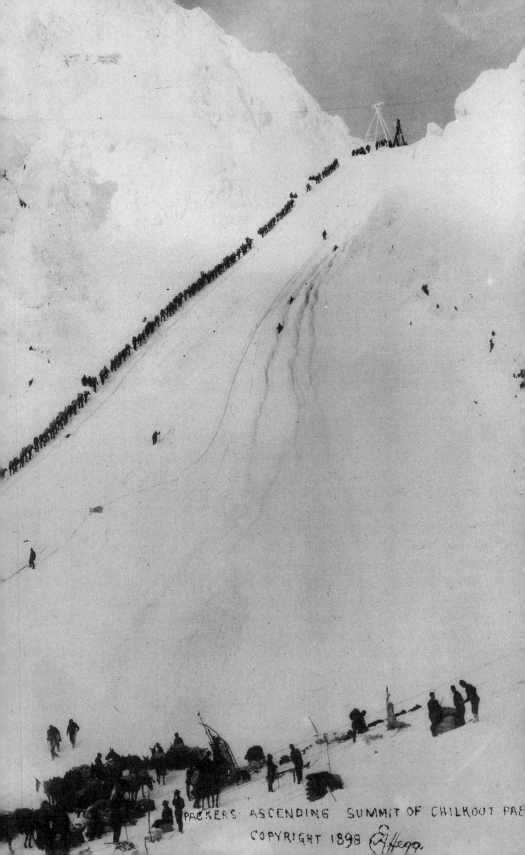

PACKERS ASCENDING SUMMIT OF CHILKOUT PAS
COPYRIGHT 1898 Hegg.

7

THE STATE OF NATURE

The National Interest Lands of Alaska

Koyukon Natives of north central Alaska who have not broken with tradition consider it impolite to admire a mountain's size or a scene's beauty at the moment of observation. "Don't talk, your mouth is small," comes the hushed reprimand from an elder when a child misspeaks. Later, in less splendid surroundings, it is all right to show appreciation. In detail, then, the elder re-creates the scene, savoring the play of light and grandeur. Through such humble articulations, says anthropologist Richard K. Nelson, Koyukons, along with other Alaskan Eskimos, Indians, and Aleuts, express their devotion to lands that are, for humans, among the most inhospitable on earth. And among the most beautiful, with a sweep of variety, majesty, and richness matched nowhere else. It is perhaps for this reason that Native peoples speak carefully, reflectively, when attempting to describe what lies before them every day. It is perhaps for this reason that the Aleut people gave the place its name—Alaska, meaning, in their language, "Great Land."

When a map of the forty-ninth state is superimposed on a map of the coterminous United States, its southeastern tip reaches the Georgia coastline. The Aleutians meander into California. Alaska's northern edge runs through northern Wisconsin and Minnesota and its interior bulk throws a shadow across all of Illinois and Iowa, together with most of Nebraska, Indiana, Oklahoma, and Kansas. Its 35,000 miles of convoluted coastline is half that of the whole United States. From Alaska's western extremity you can see the Soviet Union, and

Goldseekers climbing up Chilkoot Pass on the way to the Klondike mines, 1898 (Bancroft Library, University of California at Berkeley).

Japan lies within one thousand miles of its remotest Aleutian island. Author Joe McGinniss aptly titled his best-seller on Alaska *Going to Extremes*, with the climate being but one example. In summer, temperatures can hit one hundred degrees. In winter, readings plunge to seventy-five below zero, with temperatures remaining at about forty below zero for weeks of darkness. North of the Arctic Circle, the Kobuk sand dunes shift in the wind; farther south, glaciers, one bigger than the state of Rhode Island, calve into deep bays and inlets. Alaska's Mount McKinley is the highest mountain in North America, and its eighteen-thousand-foot rise from base to summit makes it one of the most impressive vistas in the world. Thousands of miles of rivers course through Alaska, and its lakes number in the tens of thousands, though much of the state is arid, receiving less than twenty inches of precipitation a year—except in the southeast panhandle, where precipitation is heavy enough to produce rain forests of giant Sitka spruce and hemlock.

Given such extremes, the diversity of wildlife is unexcelled. Alaska supports more than three hundred species of birds that come to nest or feed from six continents. Walruses and sea lions haul themselves up by the thousands on rocks worn smooth by the uncounted ancestors who were there before them. At least thirteen distinct herds of caribou roam Alaska's tundra; polar bears, grizzlies, moose, wolves, and Dall sheep are everywhere. At times certain rivers run red with salmon, and where salmon spawn and die, the sky clouds over with the bald eagles who come to feed on them. "Anybody who says the ecology is fragile is an ignoramus or liar," declared Joe Vogler, one of the most vociferous objectors to the Alaska National Interest Lands Conservation Act. Yet the teeming vigor of wildlife in Alaska is open to misinterpretation. Alaska is delicate precisely because it *still* holds the lives of so many creatures in the balance. They depend on Alaska for the survival of their kinds, which is the nature of any ecosystem that is intact.

The northern land, deprived of sun and moisture, vegetates slowly. Outside the rain forests, trees can take a century to grow as high as a man's knee; a campfire ring on the tundra remains visible for decades. The animal species that make their living here need space. A grizzly bear often requires one hundred square miles to sustain itself, and does not tolerate many intruders. Still, there are those who insist that Alaska needs no special looking after, that it can take care of itself. If anything, some would say, it is man who needs protection from the land. "The cold can kill you," said former Alaska governor Walter J. Hickel, in support of Alaska's resilience. "The beautiful sky can kill you. . . . It's a tough place up here. . . . This country can kill you."

Although Alaska's harshness has always been its best defense, human resolve to accomplish the impossible is often implacable; no sooner is a technology pronounced too costly or difficult to undertake than money and motivation conspire to undertake it. The greater challenge in the current age will be not how to engineer the subduing of Alaska, but how to save it from the weight of our whole history. This is the place, conservationists like to say, where we have the chance to do it right, to rise above and move beyond the misuse and ignorance that have so often governed our occupation of this continent. If so, we have a lot of tradition to overcome in this Great Land.

"THE TSAR IS FAR AWAY"

Although rumors of its existence had been circulating for at least a generation, Alaska was not discovered until 1741, when a Danish sea captain named Vitus Bering, along with his Russian crew, glimpsed the peaks of the St. Elias Range. Bering, who never set foot on Alaska and died on an island named for him far to the west of its mainland, had no interest in exploring unknown new worlds. He represented Peter the Great of Russia, whose curiosity about his empire's eastern reaches triggered Bering's mission. First, Bering was ordered to determine once and for all whether Asia and America were land-joined, thereby settling a long-standing dispute. Next, Bering was instructed to explore Japan and map the western end of the American continent as far as Mexico. He did neither. Wracked by scurvy and short of food, Bering was anxious to return to St. Petersburg before winter. But he died in December, leaving his men to the long, frigid winter. The survivors sustained themselves on the meat and skins of sea otters. When spring came they headed back to civilization with great bundles of otter pelts—and became rich men. Alaska, or Russian

America as it was called, was soon a major source of furs for Russian royalty as well as for the sovereigns of Europe.

Aside from plundering Russian America for its furs, the Russians did some colonizing, although their numbers probably never exceeded twelve thousand throughout the territory. The colonizing effort entailed the massacre of resistant Aleut Indians and the establishment of about forty onion-domed Russian Orthodox churches. Guidance for colonial deportment in this backwash of a backward empire was summed up in the saying, "Heaven is high and the tsar is far away," according to historian Hector Chevigny. One Russian American governor had more devout intentions toward his realm, as indicated in the anthem he wrote: "The will of our hunters, the spirit of trade / On these far shores a new Muscovy made / In bleakness and hardship finding new wealth for fatherland and tsardom." The Russian presence in Alaska lasted 126 years. It was gently undermined by the vestiges of Manifest Destiny that a few American statesmen were clinging to. Chief among the holdouts was William Henry Seward, a powerful Secretary of State under President Lincoln, with presidential aspirations of his own. Seward did not accept the notion that Manifest Destiny had achieved its aims at the Pacific Coast. He thought American democracy quite suitable for numerous distant islands, as well as for the great mass of land on Canada's western border, Russian America. In 1860 he said:

Standing here and looking far off into the northwest, I see the Russian as he busily occupies himself by establishing seaports and towns and fortifications, on the verge of this continent, at the outposts of St. Petersburg, and I can say, "Go on, and build up your outposts all along the coast and up even to the Arctic Ocean—they will yet become the outposts of my own country—monuments to the civilization of the United States in the North West."

Seward's aspirations were not encouraged by his compatriots. He had lost much prestige by deciding to serve Andrew Johnson, whose enemies in Congress were plentiful enough to almost succeed in impeaching him. But the Russians took Seward more seriously. "The

282

United States are bound to spread over the whole of North America," predicted one Russian diplomat as early as 1853. "Sooner or later we shall have to surrender our North American possessions." Although America and Russia were on excellent terms at the time, the Russians feared that if they were not willing to surrender Alaska peaceably, they would one day have to go to war over it, judging from previous examples of American inclinations where land was concerned. Great Britain, with dominion over Canada, was the more obvious successor, but Russia and England were estranged during the Crimean War. In 1867, negotiations over Alaska proceeded despite enormous opposition. The treaty was negotiated secretly but still needed to be ratified by the Senate. The agreement, with its $7.5 million price tag, would have died in the Foreign Relations Committee but for the efforts of committee chairman Charles Sumner of Massachusetts, who, in a speech that lasted three hours, spoke movingly of the nation's duty to uplift the immense country that would otherwise remain "without form and without light." He based his argument for its purchase more on the need to keep Russia happy than on Alaska's worth to the United States. "Even if you doubt the value of these possessions," he said, "the treaty is a sign of amity. It is a new expression of that *entente cordiale . . .* which is a phenomenon of history." The Senate finally ratified the treaty by three votes, making it possible for the United States, which did not really want to buy Alaska, to acquire it from Russia, which did not really want to sell it. Ironically, after the sale, relations between the two nations worsened, and Russia had to wait more than eighteen months to be paid for its good intentions.

In the United States, Alaska was called many things: Walrussia, Icebergia, and—most enduringly—Seward's Folly. Despite the cost of about five cents an acre, Alaska was called a "swindle" and "utterly worthless." Alaska, declared Congressman Benjamin Loan of Missouri, was an "inhospitable and barren waste," and would "never add a dollar to the wealth of our country or furnish any homes to our people." Upon hearing that the United States had bought land on which every foot of soil was frozen, New York Congressman Dennis McCarthy observed that soon America would "hear that Greenland and Iceland are on the market." The ridicule did not abate. Government policy toward Alaska, what there was of it, became thoroughly ingrained with the belief that a region one-fourth the size of the lower forty-eight states was utterly, irrevocably worthless.

For the first seventeen years there was no government in Alaska, and therefore no law. Alaska was nothing more than a customs district. If a person moved to Alaska, he could not expect to be able to marry there, buy land, build a cabin, or draw up a will, since there were no laws permitting the execution of such routine matters. For ten years the navy ruled the district, overlooking drinking and Native-debauching sprees by the enlisted men stationed there.

Finally, in May 1884, Alaska was granted a greater semblance of government when Congress passed Senate Bill 153, sponsored by Indiana Senator Benjamin Harrison. The act gave Alaska a governor, a district judge, a district attorney, and a skeletal court system. Mining laws were put into effect, although general land laws were specifically excluded. Twenty-five thousand dollars was appropriated for the education of school-age children in the district, but there was no other revenue for government, aside from a fraction of the fees taken from seal hunting. Possibly the most significant provision of the 1884 act was its concern for Native Alaskans. Ironically, the campaign against Indians and their ancestral ways was still being brutally waged in the West when Congress generously stipulated that in Alaska, "Indians or other persons in said district shall not be disturbed in the possession of any lands actually in their use or occupation or now claimed by them, but the terms under which such persons may acquire title to such lands is reserved for future legislation." As long as Alaska seemed valueless to whites, such magnanimity posed no hardship to them.

THE TOIL OF GIANTS

Spring came on once more, and at the end of all their wandering they found . . . a shallow placer in a broad valley where the gold showed like yellow butter across the bottom of the washing-pan. They sought no farther. Each day they worked earned them thousands of dollars in clean dust and nuggets, and they worked each day. The gold was sacked in moose-hide bags, fifty pounds to the bag, and piled like so much firewood outside the spruce-bough lodge. Like giants they

284

toiled, days flashing on the heels of days like dreams as they heaped the treasure up.

It was the summer of 1897, and the discovery of gold near the junction of the Yukon and Klondike rivers stirred an international sensation. More than eighty thousand seekers streamed northward into Canada and Alaska, although few reaped the legendary bounty of John Thornton, Jack London's hero in his 1906 novel, *The Call of the Wild*, from which the excerpt above is taken. Alaska's gold rush was the last in which a poor man could become rich, or so it has been said, but only if he was first and could withstand brutal deprivation and loneliness. Most could not. The trail of optimism was littered with the log cribs of dreamers, in towns they named Arctic City or Beaver or Peavey or Jim Town. The wildness appealed to some and they stayed on. "We didn't have no time for prospecting," reminisced one German miner. "We was just running around wild, stampeding."

Injustices began to surface. Native Alaskans who joined the search for gold and who were lucky enough to find it were not entitled to stake their claims because they were not considered U.S. citizens. Worse, the infiltrators depleted native supplies of caribou, moose, and small game animals, putting settlements on the verge of starvation.

By 1906 the easy metal had been sifted from the creeks and rivers, leaving them silted and stocked with dead salmon. Gold extraction could no longer be left to the poor sourdough, loosely defined as any prospector who had been in Alaska long enough to see the Yukon's tributaries freeze up in fall and break up in spring. Hydraulic machinery owned by large mining concerns began to replace simple placer operations, powerful jets of water cutting away whole riverbanks and exposing the skeletons of prehistoric animals in the permafrost. But even the heavy-duty operators were forced to look for their wealth in less accessible regions, and the cost of discovery eventually became prohibitive.

Alaskan fish and wildlife suffered a frenzy of exploitation, and their depletion triggered some of the nation's first federal conservation measures. American ownership of Alaska had produced a flurry of sealing, trapping, and canning enterprises, and contributed hundreds of millions of dollars to the nation's wealth. Historian (and former Alaska governor and senator) Ernest Gruening measures the excessive attention by appropriations: in 1887 the entire budget for civil government in Alaska was $25,000, while Congress spent $43,000 on the supervision of such seal islands as the Pribilofs. Despite this attention, the fur seal population declined drastically, from more than 3 million at the time of Alaska's purchase to about 350,000 thirty years later. Walrus, whale, and otter were hunted nearly to extinction.

Salmon also declined precipitously, because of overfishing and illegal obstructions of streams and rivers. Canning soon became Alaska's first industry, and the number of canneries went from two in 1878 to thirty-seven ten years later. In that time their annual output climbed from eight thousand cases packed and shipped a year, to more than 700,000.

Fortunately the dramatic shrinkage in Alaska's fish and game populations coincided with the ascendance of wildlife preservation sentiment in the United States. Many felt that Alaska was a good place for the federal government to dabble in the conservation of species, notably the salmon. In the 1880s Livingstone Stone, head of fish hatcheries in California and Oregon, suggested that "national salmon parks and salmon reservations" be established in Alaska. "Not only is every contrivance employed that human ingenuity can devise to destroy the salmon of our West Coast rivers," he said, "but more surely destructive, more fatal than all is the slow but inexorable march of destroying agencies of human progress, before which the salmon must surely disappear, as did the buffalo of the plains and the Indian of California." Editor George Bird Grinnell took up Stone's idea and popularized it in his magazine *Forest and Stream.* On December 24, 1892, President Benjamin Harrison obliged the preservationists by proclaiming the Afognak Forest and Fish Culture Reserve on Afognak Island, off Alaska's southeast coast. Harrison's was the first cautious exercise of executive privilege granted when Congress passed the Forest Reserve Act ten months earlier. (The Forest Reserve Act also extended homestead laws into Alaska.)

The naturalist John Muir was the first to exalt Alaska's landscape for its own sake. He made his first trip there in 1879, when kind words about the district were virtually unrecorded. While sailing through the Inland Passage, Muir wrote along the way that "every view of islands and mountains [seemed] ever more and more beautiful; the one we chanced to have before us seeming the loveliest, the most surpassingly beautiful of all." Muir had probably seen more of America than anyone else of his day, but he declared he had never seen vistas "so hopelessly, overabundantly beautiful for description" as those of Alaska. Muir's articles helped change public opinion regarding Alaska, but its best promotion came in 1899 when Edward H. Harriman, owner of the Union Pacific Railroad, assembled scientists and artists for an appreciative cruise to Glacier Bay and other points on a 250-foot steamboat he had chartered. Muir was a member of the expedition, as was Henry Gannett, a surveyor of the Wyoming Territory in the 1870s and director of the U.S. Geological Survey. Gannett carried back with him a strong impression of where Alaska's enduring strengths could be found. "The Alaska coast is to become the showplace of the earth," he predicted in an essay in a 1901 issue of *National Geographic.* "Pilgrims, not only from the United States but from far beyond the seas, will throng in endless procession to see it." To Gannett, Alaska's economic good was grandeur, its worth "measured in direct returns in money received from tourists." Its scenery, he insisted, "is more valuable than the gold or the fish or the timber, for it will never be exhausted." He concluded his essay with advice that has been much quoted since: "If you are old, go by all means, but if you are young, stay away until you are older. The scenery of Alaska is so much grander than anything else of the kind in the world that, once beheld, all other scenery becomes flat and insipid. It is not well to dull one's capacity for such enjoyment by seeing the finest first."

THE CONSERVATION FACTOR

In less than fifty years, Alaska went from being overlooked by the federal government to being over-federalized by it, with no pause in between for the orderly development of entrepreneurial freedom—at least, according to those who have always resented the government's presence there. By 1915 there were twenty-three separate Alaskan bureaus or offices of the Departments of Agriculture, Interior, Commerce, Navy, War, and Justice. Despite such "obstacles," fortunes had already been made in gold, copper, coal, salmon, seals, and timber—most by absentee corporations that contributed precious little to the welfare of Alaska or its citizens. Had it not been for the federal presence, particularly in the form of Theodore Roosevelt's gang of conservationists, much of the same kind of rampant exploitation that had brought ruin to so much Western land in the lower forty-eight states would have flourished in Alaska, too. In Alaska, foresight reared its intelligent head early on, and if it was not a permanent condition, it at least gave Alaska a better start in this direction than any other region of the country had enjoyed.

The establishment of Alaskan forest reserves, beginning with Afognak in 1892 and greatly increased during the Roosevelt years, is an obvious example of a priori protection. The cost of transportation discouraged wholesale logging for export, but President Theodore Roosevelt did not want to leave the continuance of this impediment to chance. First, he set aside the Alexander Archipelago and Tongass forest reserves on a chain of islands in the southeast. In 1907 he proclaimed the 4.9-million-acre Chugach National Forest, and a year later combined the Alexander Archipelago reserve with the Tongass reserve to form one entity of 6.7 million acres called Tongass National Forest. These reserves had been recommended by F. E. Olmsted, Chief Forester Gifford Pinchot's main inspector. Olmsted believed that if the reserves were not created there would soon be a scramble to acquire them from the public domain by Pacific Northwest lumbermen who were facing depletion closer to home. Also, Olmsted discovered, timber fetched higher prices when it was cut from forest reserves rather than from unreserved public-domain land. As usual, protests dogged Roosevelt's proclamations, some of them exceedingly strange. "It is well known that rainfall is attracted by large bodies of timber," explained a part-owner of a sawmill on Prince of Wales Island in the Alexander Archipelago. "The rainfall in southeastern Alaska is excessive. If the commercial timber on Prince of Wales Island were cut off, the miners would have wood they needed for their operations, the ground would be rid of its encumbering trees, the climate would become more livable, and prospecting would be easier."

The main problem faced by the Forest Service in Alaska, which for the first six years consisted of exactly one man, was in persuading people to accept the need for supervision. This was hardly different from the resistance met around forests of the West, though in some ways administration in Alaska was actually easier. Grazing, a major issue of conflict in the West, did not exist in Alaska. "Foxes are the only livestock on the reserve," reported Olmsted after a tour of the southeast. "They graze on salmon at the rate of four cents an acre. There is a trespassing mule somewhere in the Klawak region but he cannot be located." More embarrassing was the Forest Service's trouble with prostitutes and bootleggers who set up shop within Forest Service jurisdiction, since agents of the General Land Office occasionally allowed such types to file for land under the special Alaska Homestead Act, knowing full well how they meant to use it.

Dissension between Pinchot's Forest Service and the General Land Office broke out frequently around the country, but the rift over Alaska led to the sensational dismissal of Gifford Pinchot in 1910. While serving as land office commissioner under Roosevelt, Richard Ballinger, a quiet former mayor of Seattle and confidant of timbermen in the Pacific Northwest, had objected to the creation of the Tongass and Chugach national forests. To Ballinger, Alaskan forest reserves were unnecessary, and he saw in their establishment the influence of the empire-hungry Pinchot. Trouble between the two men led to Ballinger's resignation, but it began brewing again in 1909, when William Howard Taft appointed Ballinger Interior Secretary. Since 1907, rumors of questionable coal claims within the Chugach National Forest had been circulating among foresters. Even though the claims lay within Forest Service territory, the General Land Office was responsible for their administration. Meanwhile, between his term as General Land Office commissioner and his appointment as head of the Interior Department, Ballinger had returned to Seattle and served as attorney to the claimants of the clouded mining patents. Several years before, an Idaho miner named Clarence Cunningham had secretly been given the power to file claims on behalf of the Alaska Company, a syndicate controlled by the Morgan and Guggenheim banking interests. Such filing on behalf of absentee speculators was routine in Alaska and in remote regions of the lower forty-eight states, but syndicate control violated the stipulations of the Coal Mining Act of 1873, which limited the number of claims any one corporation could own. It was for this reason that Roosevelt had withdrawn 100,000 acres of coal-bearing lands in Alaska in 1906 (see chapter 3).

When Ballinger assumed his Interior post, he ordered that the Cunningham claims be allowed to go to final patent, without further investigation into their legitimacy. Louis Glavis, an unusually vigilant young land office agent in Seattle, became suspicious of Ballinger's eagerness to proceed with the claims and recommended a field examination. He wanted to pursue the rumor that the claims violated coal-mining laws, and that in truth the syndicate behind them was using mining laws to obtain not coal but marketable timber. Glavis went to Pinchot with his suspicions and was promptly dismissed for discussing the case with a rival department. Pinchot publicized his long-lived mistrust of Ballinger and land office procedures by publicly accusing the Secretary of conspiring with the syndicate, and of trying to cover up his association with it. President Taft fired Pinchot for gross insubordination, and a subsequent Senate investigation exonerated Ballinger—even though the suspected taint of corruption finally caused his second resignation. The highly visible case harmed the Forest Service's standing in Alaska, according to Tongass supervisor William A. Langille. Afterward, Langille noticed "a biased antagonism toward the Forest Service which is the outgrowth of the more or less radical anti-conservation movement in Alaska . . . conceived to be so radically unjust to Alaska and its development. . . ."

The national park system, limping along before the arrival of Stephen Mather in 1915, did not incorporate any Alaskan lands until 1910, when President Taft invoked the 1906 Antiquities Act to establish Sitka National Monument. Sitka, or New Archangel as the Russians had called it, was the first "capital" of Alaska. It was also the site of numerous Tlingit Indian relics and artifacts. The village of Old Kasaan was another obvious candidate for national monument designation. Although Old Kasaan was designated a monument in 1916, much of what had made it qualify for such recognition had been burned the summer before. In 1917, National Park Director Mather brought Mount McKinley National Park (now Denali National Park and Preserve) into the park system, largely as a result of naturalist Charles Sheldon's ten-year campaign to obtain national park

290

status for his beloved mountain and its wildlife. Sheldon, who had been a companion of Muir's on Alaskan treks, lived in a cabin through a winter at the base of Denali, Mount McKinley's Indian name. By 1927, Katmai and Glacier Bay national monuments were added to the 'park system.

It was to become customary for Alaskan lands to join the national park system by executive proclamation rather than by congressional act, though the areas were larger and surpassed in grandeur the parks in the lower forty-eight states. Although the National Park Service's presence in Alaska was quite meager, the antifederal sentiment pervading the territory was aroused by the monument proclamations. In 1924 the *Juneau Empire* labeled the establishment of the Glacier Bay reserve "a monstrous proposition." An editorial railed that "the suggestion that a reserve be established to protect a glacier that none could disturb if he wanted and none would want to disturb if he could, or to permit the study of plant and insect life is the quintessence of silliness. It leads one to wonder if Washington has gone crazy through catering to conservation faddists."

Since Director Mather and his successors devoted themselves to promoting the parks with the highest visibility, Alaska's parks functioned without guardians. Mount McKinley National Park, for example, did not record a park visit until 1922. Appropriations for visitor comforts were channeled to other park properties. It was, according to national park historian Frank Williss, "because of the remoteness of the areas and the relative lack of population and developmental pressures that administrative neglect of the Alaska parks and monuments was not as serious as it might have been. External factors, not design, served to buffer the areas from serious and irreversible encroachment."

The largest withdrawal of land from Alaska's public domain was made in 1923 by President Warren G. Harding. This time the area, which lay on the North Slope of the Brooks Range and was approximately the size of Indiana, was reserved for its oil potential and placed under the supervision of the Navy Department. Estimates of the recoverable reserves in Naval Petroleum No. 4, or Pet-4, ranged between 10 billion and 100 billion barrels. The navy, which supervised three other reserves including the infamous Teapot Dome in

Wyoming (see chapter 3), was constantly on guard to ensure that its emergency rights to the oil in the reserves were not abrogated. "I have been compelled to fight almost every day of my incumbency in office to prevent the dummy entrymen and illegal operators from taking the Naval Reserves," stated Josephus Daniels, Navy Secretary under President Woodrow Wilson. These reserves were "the only hope for the Navy when the all too rapid use of American oil will leave [the reserves] the only available supply." Particularly in Alaska, the major oil companies fought this arrangement for years, insisting that all exploration and extraction ought to be governed entirely by the needs of the private sector.

THE PRESERVATIONISTS MUSH IN

In the summer of 1929, wilderness enthusiast Robert Marshall boarded a small plane and flew where no plane had ever landed before, to the town of Wiseman, population eighty-one, on the Middle Fork of the Yukon River near the Arctic Circle. Ostensibly, his reason for venturing into the Alaskan bush was to study Arctic plants. Aside from his desire to serve science, however, Marshall simply wanted to live among Eskimos and to explore country no white man had ever seen. He balanced restful periods in Wiseman with ambitious forays into the Central Brooks Range, the northernmost mountain chain in the world, extending six hundred miles across the Arctic. On his several trips by dogsled and on foot, he climbed twenty-eight peaks, many of them first ascents, and named a delicate valley bordered by steel-gray peaks decapitated by a low sky, calling it Gates of the Arctic. One of Marshall's expeditions was arranged simply to settle an argument about the source of the Clear River. "I had more work planned already than I could possibly ever accomplish, but the chance of following an unknown river to its source in mid-winter seemed more important than anything else," he wrote in his journal. Shortly before his death in 1939, Marshall devised a blueprint for Alaska's future that would come to bear on future legislation.

Because the unique recreational value of Alaska lies in its frontier character, it would seem desirable to establish a really sizeable area, free of roads and industries, where frontier conditions will be preserved. Fortunately, this is peculiarly possible in northern Alaska, for economic and social reasons. Economically, the population is so scattered that airplane transportation is the only feasible means of mechanical conveyance, and auto roads could not possibly justify their great cost. Sociologically, the country of northern Alaska is inhabited chiefly by native populations which would be much happier, if United States experience is any criterion, without either roads or industries.

During the 1930s, other travelers and scientists publicized the need to preserve vast parts of Alaska, for the sake of its wildlife as well as its people. It was an era when wildlife biologists were in ascendance and Alaska lay before them, a ripe field for scrutinizing. Writer-photographer John M. Holzworth produced his moving account of grizzlies and bald eagles on Admiralty Island and campaigned for its designation as a wildlife refuge or national park; Olaus Murie followed caribou through Arctic valleys and over mountains, in awe of the animals' "roaming freedom shared by no other creature"; his brother, Adolph Murie, wrote a precedent-setting monograph on Alaska's wolves, and promoted a deeper understanding of the synergism of species. Economic depression shrank Alaska's human population and industry. But scientific recognition of its incalculable worth had begun to rise.

STATEHOOD AND THE CONSERVATION MOVEMENT
Until World War II, it was easy for many people inside and outside Alaska to ignore the territory's ties to the United States. Congress repeatedly refused entreaties by Alaskan boomers and boosters for admission to the Union on the grounds of its transient population (meaning its *white* population, the only one that counted politically). But then came the Japanese invasion of the Aleutian Islands in 1942, which strengthened the bonds with home as nothing else. During the spring of that year, 2,500 American soldiers died in combat on the islands of Attu and Kiska; it was the only time in the war that American soil in the Western Hemisphere was invaded and occupied by enemy troops. The task of defending this northwest corner of the United States introduced about 300,000 American soldiers to Alaska's beauty

293

and resulted in the territory's first airfields, radio stations, sewers, schools—all those things Alaskan boomers had failed to get during peacetime.

After the war, the quest for statehood gained new momentum, though not without opposition from some politicians and not without giving concern to conservationists. Southerners were the foremost opponents of Alaska's admission—largely because of its nonwhite population, some critics said. In 1952, Senator John Stennis of Mississippi gave a more civic-minded explanation for his objections: "The county is the great training ground" for self-government, he said. "With all deference to the fine people of Alaska the main essential training element for American citizenship would be totally lacking," since Alaska had no counties. To Stennis, the fact that "only three-tenths of one percent of privately owned land" existed in Alaska was also a problem—the rest of it belonged to the federal government. In the growing clamor for statehood, that fact had not been lost on two agencies—the National Park Service and the Fish and Wildlife Service—which had been exploring the possibilities of preservation on a grand scale, once all the conditions of statehood had been decided. It was a nervous time for preservationists in and out of government, for the tone of Alaskan rhetoric, and its emphasis on unbridled development, did not further their own aims.

During the 1950s, George Collins and Lowell Sumner of the Park Service recommended that a substantial portion of the northeastern Arctic be protected as wilderness for "perpetual preservation as a scientific field laboratory and also for the education, enjoyment, and inspiration of outdoor-minded people." Olaus Murie and his wife, Margaret, who had lived off and on in Alaska since she was nine, pursued this recommendation for the establishment of the 9-million-acre Arctic National Wildlife Refuge. "There is a great gift to be won in places like the Arctic Wildlife Refuge," Mrs. Murie testified in one of many congressional hearings she attended for Alaska's sake. There was, she said, "the gift of personal satisfaction, the personal well-being, purchased by striving, by lifting and setting down legs, over and over, through the muskeg, up the slopes, gaining the summit—man using himself." Support for the designation of this refuge from the local statehood movement was one of the conditions Alaska's conservationists demanded in exchange for *their* support of statehood.

Both sides got their wish. In 1958, Alaska became a state, and in 1960 the refuge was designated. To make up for its "unique neglect" of Alaska for eighty-three years, Congress displayed unusual generosity in the statehood bill. First, the new state was allowed to choose, for its own use, 104.6 million acres from the public domain administered by the Bureau of Land Management, and was given twenty-five years to make its selections. This grant surpassed the total acreage of all federal lands transferred to seventeen Western states on their admission. Second, Alaska could retain 90 percent of the royalties generated from oil and mineral leases on the remaining public domain. In all other states, income from subsurface federal leases in their midst could not exceed 25 percent of the royalties earned.

Flushed with new hopes of growth, Alaskan boomers were now eager to extend American civilization into the farthest reaches of their state. The key project intended to do this was the construction of a dam about one hundred miles from Robert Marshall's beloved Wiseman. Rampart Dam, as proposed by the Army Corps of Engineers, would have flooded the Yukon flats with a body of water larger than Lake Erie—for hydroelectric power generation. "Search the whole world and it would be difficult to find an equivalent area with so little to be lost through flooding," claimed an assistant to Senator Ernest Gruening. The entire site being considered was larger than New Jersey and contained "not more than ten flush toilets," the assistant boasted, without bothering to add that it did not *need* ten flush toilets (a closer count revealed none). The Rampart Dam controversy erupted in the 1960s, with memories of the Echo Park and Split Mountain dam proposals for Dinosaur National Monument still vivid in the public's mind (see chapters 1 and 5). It was easy enough for the growing conservation community to become exercised about the Alaskan proposal—and defeat it.

As another sort of statehood gift, in 1958 the Atomic Energy Commission offered to demonstrate the civilian use of nuclear power by exploding a device to make a harbor at the western edge of the Brooks Range. This notion was called Project Chariot, and it appalled Native Alaskans, who feared that the blast would ruin their traditional hunt-

295

ing and ceremonial grounds, and thereby undermine their subsistence living. This project, too, was defeated.

The submission of such plans to promote an assumed prosperity caused more and more Alaskans to wonder whether they really wanted to create their state in the image of Los Angeles or Detroit. Somehow, the routine strivings of the rest of America did not seem to belong in Alaska. Quietly, the Park Service and the Bureau of Sport Fisheries, later known as the Fish and Wildlife Service, had been preparing alternative scenarios. The chief hope of Alaska wilderness preservationists lay with these two agencies, which, unlike the Forest Service and the BLM, did not, in theory at least, have to strike bargains and work trade-offs among eager multiple-users. Land and wildlife would remain their top concerns.

During the 1950s and 1960s the Park Service drew up a "wish list" of thirty-nine areas that might be added to the Alaskan park system. The Fish and Wildlife Service identified a comparable number for the refuge system.

In 1965, after traveling to Alaska in the company of top national park officials, Interior Secretary Stewart Udall became infected with their zeal for new parks there. The problem was how to get them. The state of Alaska was busily selecting its lands according to its charter, Natives were beginning to agitate for their fair share, and Congress was loath to step in and start preserving vast areas from the Arctic to the southeast and possibly thwart the whole state selection process. In 1968, Udall persuaded President Lyndon Johnson, who had shown little prior interest in Alaskan protection, to invoke the 1906 Antiquities Act and create a grand sweep of national monuments to rival even Theodore Roosevelt's dramatic withdrawals. At the same time Udall would establish two new wildlife refuges, each exceeding one million acres. The entire package would be billed the "President's Christmas conservation gift to the nation" and would send Johnson into history as the greatest conservation President since T.R. Christmas came and went, but the President's commitment was eroded by a brief illness and other executive business. Meanwhile, National Park Service officials had done their work. Necessary proclamations for a 4-million-acre Gates of the Arctic National Monument, a 2-million-acre addition to Mount McKinley National Park, and several

296

other key areas in Alaska and other states were drawn up for the President's signature. Johnson agreed to do all this, and even alluded to his intentions in his departing State of the Union Address in January 1969, but his consent was based on the assumption that Secretary Udall had informed House Interior Committee Chairman Wayne Aspinall of the presidential prerogative as a matter of courtesy. Udall, however, had not done this. He knew the Colorado congressman was vehemently against the freewheeling establishment of monuments by presidential proclamation because it circumvented congressional authority to create new parks. It was feared that if Aspinall was told too far in advance, he would marshal his considerable influence against the conservation package. As predicted, Aspinall was furious when he heard about it, and Johnson in turn flew into a rage at Udall—although he still agreed to go through with the proclamations. His signature on them seemed so certain that Park Service officials had already mailed out press releases announcing the new monuments.

Hours before Richard Nixon's inauguration, Johnson changed his mind and did not sign all the proclamations set out for him. In the end he added 94,000 acres to the existing Katmai National Monument, and agreed to let Udall go through with his new wildlife refuges. "Lyndon Johnson did the conservationists a favor," wrote journalist Robert Cahn, although at the time nobody saw it that way. "Johnson's negative action served to stimulate both Alaskan and national conservation groups to more vigorous activity." Had Johnson fulfilled all his intentions, chances are that the greater allotments of the future would have been impossible.

THE NATIVE CONTINGENT

When Johnson left office, the state of Alaska had selected only about one-quarter of the lands to which it was entitled. State picks were largely oil and gas lands, for these were considered the highest revenue producers. But some of the lands wanted by the state were also wanted by Native Alaskans. In 1964 they formed the Alaskan Federation of Natives and began developing the political clout they had always lacked. At the request of the federation, Secretary Udall slapped a moratorium on state selections in 1966 so that all the

297

overlapping claims could be straightened out. Udall's moratorium was still in effect two years later, when the Atlantic Richfield Company and the Humble Oil and Refining Company struck an immense pool of oil in Prudhoe Bay, north of the Arctic Circle, not far from Pet-4. The companies needed transportation corridors and rights-of-way before production could begin, but no one could say for certain who owned what land. Within a month of the discovery, a consortium of oil companies consisting of ARCO, Humble Oil, and British Petroleum announced plans to build an eight-hundred-mile pipeline from Prudhoe Bay to Valdez, a fishing village on Prince William Sound.

Suddenly the settlement of Native claims became urgent—to both the Natives and the oil companies. The odd alliance resulted, in 1971, in passage of the Alaska Native Claims Settlement Act (ANCSA). ANCSA awarded Alaska Natives—defined as any Alaskan-born persons at least one-quarter Eskimo, Aleut, or Indian—a land grant of 44 million acres plus a cash payment of $962 million for renouncing all claims to the rest of the state. The financial compensation was prorated so that half of it would be paid by oil royalties and the other half by the federal government. The Natives were required to form corporations for the ownership and management of the land and the administration of the money, which was to be viewed as corporate assets; only Natives could hold shares in these corporations and no shares could be sold or exchanged for a period of twenty years. All of this seemed fair enough, even generous, and most Natives signed up. Indeed, the settlement was so generous and arrived at so quickly that author John McPhee, in *Coming into the Country*, labeled it "the great, final and retributive payment for all of American history's Native claims—an attempt to extinguish something more than title. The settlement suggests not only principal but interest as well on twenty decades of national guilt."

Some Natives were more cynical about their good fortune. Joe Upicksoun, president of the North Slope Native Association, surmised that guilt had less to do with the arrangement than greed. "By accident of nature, right now the eyes of the nation and the world are centered on the North Slope," he said. "Without intending to belittle your land, the real reason for the entire settlement is oil, which by accident is on our land, not yours." Most non-Native Alaskans were downright

298

jubilant. They truly believed the words of Governor Keith H. Miller, uttered back in September 1969: "Tomorrow we will reach our birthright. We will rendezvous with our dreams."

SOMETHING FOR EVERYONE

The development of the Prudhoe Bay oil discovery and the construction of the pipeline to Valdez inspired an economic boom to rival that of the Gold Rush nearly eighty years before. Alyeska, as the pipeline consortium was called, employed more than twenty thousand people in 1975 and 1976, two years before the line's completion. At Prudhoe Bay, men were paid $2,000 a week plus room and board, and (according to Joe McGinniss, who witnessed the event) rioting reportedly broke out when employees were told that steak and lobster would no longer be served in the same meal, but only on alternating nights. Valdez's population bloated from four hundred to eight thousand. The city was so proud of its role in receiving the Arctic oil that the local newspaper urged that Valdez's main street be renamed "11:02 Boulevard," after the exact moment of the first oil's arrival eight years after pipeline construction had begun.

The discovery of mammoth oil reserves in Alaska carried with it something for everyone. The Natives secured their birthright (presumably), Alaskan boosters achieved their ultimate boom, and oil companies found something to sell. Conservationists found a way to save some land for the future, too. For, once the state and Natives had selected their lands, something had to be done with those that remained in the unreserved public domain. The solution to this third dilemma was drafted into ANCSA, under Section 17(d)(2). This section provided for the Interior Secretary to "withdraw from all forms of appropriation under the public land laws, including the mining and mineral leasing laws . . . up to, but not to exceed eighty million acres of unreserved public lands in the State of Alaska . . . which the Secretary deems are suitable [to study] for addition to or creation as units of the National Park, Forest, Wildlife Refuge, and Wild and Scenic River Systems. . . . " The act also stipulated that the Secretary would have two years to make his recommendations. If Congress did not ratify or otherwise act on them by the end of 1978, the "d-2" lands would revert back to commercially exploitable public domain.

A few days after ANCSA was enacted, the Interior Department met with its agencies to brief them on the "d-2" lands. Theodor Swem, a National Park Service veteran and assistant director to Hartzog, was appointed head of the Park Service's planning effort. For Swem it was the career opportunity of a lifetime. As a boy growing up in Iowa, he had become enchanted with Alaska after he read John Holzworth's account of the grizzlies. Swem would retire from the Park Service in 1976, having made about forty visits to Alaska in fifteen years to study places he had previously seen only in his youthful imagination. There are two things Swem remembers about the initial ANCSA meeting at the Interior Department. "One was the real lack of knowledge as to what the law contained," he said. "The other was Under Secretary Bill Pecora's statement that Interior Secretary Rogers Morton saw in Alaska a great opportunity 'to do things right the first time.'" Swem and his colleagues would invoke those words many times over the next few years to ward off routine assaults on superb areas. At last, as Robert Cahn put it in *The Fight to Save Wild Alaska*, his account of the struggle, "The door to new parks, wildlife refuges, and wilderness in Alaska had been flung open." But constant vigilance was demanded to ensure that that door did not slam shut.

THE ROAD TO ANILCA

Despite Secretary Morton's expressed commitment to the expansion of parks and refuges in Alaska, interdepartmental pressure built to keep as much land as possible in multiple-use classifications so that hunting, logging, and mining would be guaranteed. The National Park Service and Fish and Wildlife Service scrambled to identify all the areas where multiple use should not prevail. The first phase of study took two years. It was hobbled when the state of Alaska filed land selections on 72 million acres (including some "d-2" lands) and when it threatened to bring suit against the Department of the Interior for its 1966 moratorium. Forest Service demands for its share of the resource pie also proved a difficult obstacle. Agriculture Secretary Earl Butz had demanded that the Interior Department be generous to his agency. Specifically, he wanted 42 million acres of additional national forests, much of it in areas proposed for parks and refuges. At last Secretaries Morton and Butz compromised, and Morton offered 18.8 million acres to the Forest Service, most of it in central Alaska. Then he submitted his legislative recommendation for 83.6 million acres of parks, forests, refuges, and wild and scenic rivers.

Morton's proposal reached Congress at the end of 1973, a time when the country was becoming too preoccupied with President Nixon's Watergate indiscretions to pay attention to Alaskan conservation. Besides, according to ANCSA, Congress had until December 1978 to decide what to do with the public domain in the forty-ninth state. There was no rush. Not until Jimmy Carter was elected President in 1976 did the "d-2" lands begin to assume greater importance. The deadline for Congress to act on the recommendations was now less than two years away, and Carter had appointed numerous conservation-minded officials who saw in Alaska the chance for momentous decisions. Interior Secretary Cecil Andrus made his intentions clear at one of his first briefings on Alaska. Andrus remarked that since Republicans had recommended the preservation of about 80 million acres, Democrats would have to recommend more. He made good on his promise.

January 1977. Twenty-three months to go. The day Congress convened, Representative Morris Udall, the new chairman of the House Interior Committee, introduced H.R. 39, a bill for the protection of 110 million acres, cosigned by Ohio Representative John Seiberling, an ardent preservation advocate, and seventy-five other cosigners. Many of the House cosigners had been buttonholed by members of the Alaska Coalition, a grassroots citizens lobby that had picked up the fight for parks, wildernesses, and refuges where Interior Department officials left off. The coalition, chaired by Charles Clusen of the Sierra Club and later The Wilderness Society, was a consortium of fifty-five organizations that devoted itself to building broad public support for Alaska preservation. The future of Alaska, coalition leaders asserted, was a national issue, not a local one. The Alaska Coalition kept congressional hearings on Alaska well stocked with citizens from all over the country. The hearings, held at various sites around the country, were consistently packed. In Chicago, on a Saturday morning in May, three hundred people had come to speak on Alaska's behalf. In Atlanta the following week, two hundred people gave statements. "Those of us here in the great public land desert of the eastern United States know better than anyone what happens when the public domain is frittered away," said a woman who had come from Auburn, Alabama, to give her statement. "We need to communicate to Congress and to the people of Alaska what it is like to be living in a place a hundred and fifty or two hundred years after the public domain has been unloaded into private hands." In Denver, another three hundred people crowded the hearing room. In Alaska, one thousand residents of twenty towns and Native villages were heard, about half of whom were in favor of H.R. 39. This division disproved the assertion of Alaska's three congressmen that virtually all of their constituents opposed any preservation effort as dramatic as the one described in the Udall-Seiberling bill.

Although H.R. 39 substantially increased the acreage for the highest order of preservation, much of the land it encompassed had been classified as "preserves," which allowed for hunting and other activities that were typically anathema to parks. The "preserve" classification had been added to make the vast land designations more palatable to people who did not favor parks and wilderness. In addition to these concessions, when drawing all the boundaries for the national interest lands, great pains had been taken to exclude the areas with the highest estimated reserves of oil, gas, and minerals. Government documents indicated that only about 3 percent of lands with known oil reserves had been withdrawn by H.R. 39, and only 5 percent of those with various minerals. One geologist who testified for the preservation measure asserted that no more than a thirty-eight-day supply of oil lay beneath the Arctic Wildlife Refuge.

Nevertheless, antifederal feeling still ran high in Alaska, where many felt they were being deprived of their frontier heritage by meddlesome bureaucrats. In the late 1970s, for instance, when the Park Service temporarily increased its ranger power to administer new national monuments created by President Carter, outbreaks of violence were not uncommon. In some stores, rangers were refused service. One Park Service employee went to a dentist in Anchorage who refused to treat his impacted tooth because of the ranger's affiliation. Others received bomb threats at their lodgings, or death threats—

302

one accompanied by a spray of bullets into an office window. In Lake Clark, an arsonist burned an airplane that had been chartered by three rangers.

Back in Washington, Alaska Senators Mike Gravel and Ted Stevens were engaged in their own political sharpshooting to prevent what they saw as Alaska's "lockup." Senator Gravel repeatedly threatened to filibuster if H.R. 39 got as far as the Senate floor. It did. In April 1978, H.R. 39 passed the House by a vote of 277 to 31. Suddenly, in May, just seven months before the deadline set by ANCSA, Gravel changed his mind. In a letter to his fellow senator, Gravel stated that he had canvassed Alaskans in his area and found they were not strenuously opposed to the "d-2" legislation. He had decided to support it. This good news resulted in a negotiating session between jubilant House bill proponents and the Alaskan delegation, so that further agreements could be worked out. At the end of the long meeting, Udall stood up and began to leave. "Gentlemen," he said, "we've done something historic here today. Let's get it resolved on paper and go to the floor with it." Then Gravel spoke up, for the first time that day, though he had been present through the whole session. "Just a minute," he said. "I've got a few things I want to raise." His "few things" turned out to be serious. One of his demands was for five transportation corridors through the heart of several parks and refuges, which would have negated all efforts put into their preservation. No agreements could be reached before the Ninety-fifth Congress adjourned, and Gravel threatened to filibuster if anybody tried to submit a bill to extend the deadline for "d-2" consideration. The Senate adjourned, and Alaska's future again seemed uncertain.

The dissolution of H.R. 39 at the last minute prompted President Carter to keep a promise he had made. To ensure that the lands covered in H.R. 39 would not revert to unreserved public domain, he used the Antiquities Act to create 56 million acres of national monuments. Carter's proclamation, according to author David Rains Wallace, was "the most daring executive action for conservation since Theodore Roosevelt withdrew the national forests." Carter also directed Secretary Andrus to set aside 40 million acres of wildlife refuges, using authority granted in the 1976 Federal Land Policy and Management Act. "As the steward of these lands, I feel a responsibility to protect them until Congress legislates their future," Andrus said. The Alaska Coalition had not lost its momentum, despite the disheartening turn of events in May. To show its still-vigorous support for Alaskan protection, the coalition sent a telegram to the President that included the names of one thousand citizen groups with an aggregate membership of 10 million. The telegram overflowed onto the floor.

In the Ninety-Sixth Congress, work began anew when Morris Udall introduced a new H.R. 39 to open the session. However, the oppositon had gained some strength and, following a series of actions in committee, a substitute bill, which was a considerably diluted version, made it to the House floor in May 1980. It passed, 268 to 157. The Alaska delegation continued its delaying tactics in the Senate, hoping that it could be weakened. It was; the compromise bill that emerged from the Senate in July reduced the acreage of new parks and wildlife refuges, mandated timber cuts in Tongass National Forest, reduced the width of land corridors along the designated wild and scenic rivers, put the Coastal Plain of Arctic National Wildlife Refuge at risk of oil and gas development, and included other stipulations that thoroughly displeased the Alaska Coalition. It prepared to fight the newest version.

Circumstances dictated otherwise. In November 1980, Ronald Reagan achieved a stunning upset victory over Jimmy Carter. Conservationists correctly assumed that the chances for an improved bill under Reagan were slim at best. They decided to stick with what they had. On November 12, Congress passed the Alaska National Interest Lands Act (ANILCA, though more simply referred to as the Alaska Lands Act), and in one of the last acts of his administration, Jimmy Carter signed it into law. He could (and did) take considerable pride in the fact that the law had come to reality on his watch. It set aside 104.3 million acres, and out of this reservation it designated twenty-five new wild and scenic rivers; established twelve new national parks, monuments, and preserves; eleven new national wildlife refuges; the Steese National Conservation Area and the White Mountains National Recreation Area (both administered by the Bureau of Land Management); added 12.3 million acres to existing national parks, national forests, and wildlife refuges; and, in perhaps the most dramatic stipulation of all, designated more than 56 million acres of the 104.3 million acres as wilderness.

Taken together, the Alaska Lands Act was the most sweeping piece of public lands conservation legislation in American history.

THE FRUITS OF COMPROMISE

"What we have achieved in this legislation, imperfect as it is," Edgar Wayburn of the Sierra Club told reporters after the signing of the Alaska Lands Act, "marks a great milestone in the history of American conservation. The body politic has acknowledged the supreme values of one hundred million acres of primeval land and wildlife. It signals, in part, the coming of age of our country's environmental conscience." Nevertheless, the greatest conservation act in our history had, at the last instant, become hostage to political expedience. "Our joy," Alaska Coalition leader Theodor Swem remembered, "was tempered by the uncertainty of what would come next." They did not have long to wait. "We are not finished, Mr. President," Senator Ted Stevens told Carter after the signing. "We've really just started. We know that the time will come when those resources will be demanded by other Americans."

The psychology of conflict was still in place, then, when President Reagan took office in January 1981 and began assembling the members of his administrative team. The reputations of people like Interior Secretary James Watt and Assistant Secretary of Agriculture John Crowell as pro-development conservatives preceded them, and three months later Rebecca Wodder, The Wilderness Society's Alaska specialist, succinctly outlined those things the conservation community would be watching out for in the Reagan-Watt-Crowell era: "Three major questions are of immediate concern. First, will the Reagan administration issue the rules and regulations needed for properly implementing the act? Second, will the administration put enough money and personnel into Alaska to carry out those regulations? And third, in applying the many sections of the act which allow administrative discretion, to what degree will the administration lean to development rather than preservation?"

Within a matter of months, the answers were apparent. "Under the guise of implementing the law," Senator Paul Tsongas declared in June 1982 in remarks aimed at Watt, "the secretary is, in fact, undoing the law. Through calculated use of the budget, selective enforcement of some provisions of the law but no enforcement of others, and by suspect

305

interpretation of statutory provisions—the Alaska National Interest Lands Conservation Act is being transformed into the Alaska National Interest Lands Development Act." Rough words, but the relentless management directives of Watt and Crowell (most of which would be endorsed by their successors for more than twelve years), had justified strong language. These two men, together with their subordinates and the successors who faithfully upheld their decisions, burdened the Alaska Lands with a record of nonfeasance, misfeasance, and malfeasance whose long-range effects would be felt far beyond their vagabond years in office.

Here is just a little of that record:

Year after year, the administration requested too little money to accomplish the specific requirements of the act to develop and submit management plans for parks, forests, wild and scenic rivers, wildlife refuges, and the BLM's two conservation areas; consequently, necessary planning mandated by the act fell hopelessly behind schedule even when it could be performed at all.

The administration was just as miserly when it came to financing the study of potential park, forest, and wildlife refuge additions to the National Wilderness Preservation System—studies that the act ordered be undertaken; in 1982, as a matter of fact, the administration requested *no* money for wilderness studies in Tongass National Forest. Consequently, wilderness planning, like other planning, moved ahead at glacial speed.

The administration refused to assign a sufficient number of people to administer all the new conservation units; by the middle of 1983, for example, there had been only twenty full-time employees added to national park and preserve staff to manage more than 50 million acres.

If the administration was hard put to find sufficient funding for planning and wilderness studies and management staffing, it consistently requested and received generous allotments for such practical matters as minerals management, timber-sale administra--

306

tion, and road-building; for Fiscal 1983, for instance, the largest single planning budget item the administration requested was for $9.4 million to finance the Alaska Minerals Resource Assessment called for by the act—a million dollars more than the total requested for planning for *all other Alaska departments combined.* As a result, the government soon knew—or at least suspected—more about potential sources of gold, silver, oil, and gas than about the habitat and wildlife the full development of such commodities would destroy or irreparably damage.

In June 1981, the U. S. Fish and Wildlife Service issued interim management regulations for the Alaska wildlife refuges established by the Alaska Lands Act. "The Fish and Wildlife Service in Alaska," the regional director told his personnel, "will permit energy development on refuges whenever and wherever development can be accomplished without thwarting the achievement of the major purposes for which each refuge was established." In the political temper of the times, it was a dense refuge manager indeed who did not understand that "thwarting" was a more flexible term than "incompatible." Most proceeded accordingly, and to a measurable degree, "anything goes" became an unspoken watchword for the Alaska refuge system.

In a related move, each of the federal land-managing agencies negotiated a "Memorandum of Understanding" with the Alaska Department of Fish and Game that gave the state agency broad and too often unchallenged authority over the wildlife resources of the federal lands.

Finally, the administration frustrated wilderness review for the lands under the aegis of the Bureau of Land Management by direct action. Except for the lands of the Central Arctic Management Area (CAMA) on the North Slope, the Alaska Lands Act did not order a wilderness review for BLM lands in the state. Neither did the act *prohibit* such review, however; in fact, its language gave the Secretary latitude to do so if he wished. Interior Secretary Watt did not wish, and just to be certain that no wilderness reviewing got done while he was in charge of things, he issued a policy directive in March 1981 stating that "no further inventory, review, study or consideration by the BLM is needed or is to be undertaken in Alaska." Policy became order when the BLM itself soon directed that except for the CAMA lands, "all work related to designation of public lands as wilderness in Alaska is to stop immediately." So it did, and so it remained.

The ponderous inheritance of directives, decisions, interpretations, misinterpretations, and acts of omission so mutilated the structure of land management in Alaska that the highest purposes of the Lands Act, like the highest purposes of a wildlife refuge violated by oil rigs and drilling muds, were thwarted to a fare-thee-well. But not all that was wrong in the Great Land could be blamed on the legacy of the Reagan years. Some of the problems were built into the act itself, the residue of those desperate weeks in the fall of 1980 when those who had been fighting for so long to get a law with muscle, purpose, and power were forced to accept less than they had hoped for.

Such was the case with regard to the future of the Coastal Plain of Arctic National Wildlife Refuge—known more simply as Arctic Refuge—the second largest and the northernmost unit in America's National Wildlife Refuge System. There is no place like Arctic Refuge anywhere on earth, and no part of its unique ecosystem is more important than the Coastal Plain, which provides habitat for at least 142 species of birds, millions of which are migrants that return to the plain every spring and summer, as well as for grizzlies and polar bears, wolves, wolverines, arctic foxes, arctic ground squirrels, thousands of Dall sheep dotting the mountain slopes like tufts of cotton, hundreds of musk oxen moving around like big hairy sofas.

And caribou. The Coastal Plain has been called "America's Serengeti," and not without reason. In addition to the Central Arctic Herd, a population of the big ungulates that resides in the central and western portion of the Brooks Range and on the broader portions of the North Slope west of the Canning River, there is the Porcupine Caribou Herd, whose numbers can vary between 160,000 and 180,000, depending upon the health of the herd in any given year. The annual wanderings

308

of the Porcupine Herd takes it from the sheltered winter valleys of the Porcupine River on the South Slope of the Brooks Range and the Ogilvie Mountains of Canada to the Coastal Plain in the summer to drop calves and stuff themselves with the nutrient-rich forage of the tundra grasses, lichens, and sedges before gathering in enormous aggregations and returning to the mountains in the early fall.

Clearly, a place worth the saving, but the huge oil discoveries at Prudhoe Bay, just across the Canning River to the west, provided an impediment. For years, the state of Alaska had been receiving 85 percent of its revenue from Prudhoe Bay oil royalties. This had been enough not only to make it unnecessary for a state income tax but to establish an oil-revenue trust fund that would grow to $11 billion by the end of 1989 and pay annual "dividend" checks to every living Alaskan. The dividend was nothing to sneeze at; it ranged between $800 and $1,000 in any given year. But what to do when the Prudhoe Bay oil gave out? If there were nine billion barrels of oil in Prudhoe Bay, many reasoned, there might be at least that many under the Coastal Plain farther to the east. That dream had been enough to enable Senator Ted Stevens and the rest of the Alaska delegation to engineer one of the most troublesome of the compromises in the Alaska Lands Act: Section 1002. This section ordered that 1.5 million acres of the Coastal Plain of Arctic Refuge be placed in a kind of limbo, studied by the Interior Department to determine whether it should be put in the National Wilderness Preservation System, as the Alaska Coalition had urged (and as two unsuccessful House bills already had proposed); opened up for oil and gas exploration and development, as the Alaska delegation, the state government, and the oil companies fervently wished; or left as "de facto" wilderness and managed as such, an alternative favored by no one.

The "Coastal Plain Resource Assessment" was released to the world under the imprimatur of Interior Secretary Donald Hodel in August 1987. Hodel's covering letter was forthrightly optimistic: "The Arctic Refuge coastal plain is rated by geologists as the most promising onshore oil and gas exploration area in the United States. It is estimated to contain more than 9 billion barrels of recoverable oil. . . . [Therefore] I have selected as my preferred alternative . . . making available for consideration the entire Arctic Refuge coastal plain for oil and gas leasing." Even before the issuance of the report, the conservation community—particularly a revived and expanded Alaska Coalition—had readied itself for the expected assault on the refuge. In 1986, with the full support of the Coalition, Congressman Morris Udall had introduced a bill (deliberately titled HR 39 to echo the Alaska Lands Act) that would have given the Coastal Plain wilderness designation immediately, and while the bill did not move any distance to speak of, it provided a rallying point for the conservationists as they systematically began to eviscerate Hodel's assumptions.

Hodel's claim that development had taken place without significant harm in and around Prudhoe Bay was categorically denied, the conservationists citing abundant evidence regarding air pollution, oil spills (at least 17,000), leaking waste pits, and severe impacts on wolves, grizzlies, and other wildlife. A good many of the necessary facts to counter Hodel's pellucid hopes for the Coastal Plain could be derived from the report itself. The claim that 9 billion barrels of recoverable oil would be found, for example, flew in the face of the report's own "mean" average estimate of 3.2 billion barrels. Similarly, Hodel's assurances that development would be relatively harmless to habitat and wildlife populations was contradicted by a nightmarish scenario of potential harm to all wildlife outlined in exquisite detail by the report's own scientists. No wildlife would be more dramatically impaired, however, than the caribou of the Porcupine Herd, which depended absolutely on the presence of an undisturbed calving ground and the freedom of movement to graze and to escape the maddening concentrations of mosquitoes, botflies, and other insects that torment the creatures in July and August. The impact of oil-field development on as many as 180,000 animals trying to move and feed in a narrow band of territory between the mountains and the sea could be devastating.

Notwithstanding logic, the promoters of drilling attempted to persuade Congress that oil and wilderness could be made to mix in the Arctic Refuge, with some success. The lines of opposition were soon drawn with precision. Udall's bill in the House was matched by similar bills in the Senate, while Senators Murkowski and Stevens and Congressman Don Young all fashioned and introduced development bills.

OIL ON TROUBLED WATERS
The debate among the supporters and opponents of preservation

simmered along without resolution until March 24, 1989, when the oil tanker *Exxon Valdez*, outward bound from the Valdez Marine Terminal, ran aground on an underwater reef in Prince William Sound, spilling 11 million gallons of Prudhoe Bay crude into the water. Aided by a combination of corporate and governmental ignorance, incompetence, confusion, cupidity, and evasion of responsibility, the oil quickly did its work, contaminating tidal flats, estuaries, and hundreds of island and mainland beaches from Storey Island in Prince William Sound to Aniakchak National Monument on the Alaska Peninsula four hundred miles away. It was the worst oil spill in American history, and it killed at least one thousand otters, an undetermined number of seals and whales, and anywhere from 100,000 to 350,000 birds of all species, including bald eagles, peregrine falcons, swans, puffins, murres, cormorants, loons, and 2,927 birds that were so cloaked in oil that no one could accurately identify them.

Suddenly, the oil companies and the Alaska delegation temporarily suppressed their cries for the opening of the Coastal Plain of Arctic Refuge; ARCO and the other companies even went so far as to pull all local magazine and television advertising. "This was a textbook public relations move," Art Davidson noted in his 1990 study of the spill, *In the Wake of the Exxon Valdez* "—even positive messages would have reminded people who they were mad at." This sudden shyness did not last long. In March 1990, almost precisely one year after the *Exxon Valdez* disaster, the Alaska Coalition for American Energy Security, an industry-supported "citizen's group," petitioned the state legislature to finance what it described as a "national grass roots and advertising strategy in targeted congressional districts in the Lower 48 states to educate the American public on the benefits of ANWR oil development." The petitioners thought that about $11.2 million would be a good figure to start with. Alaska Governor Steve Cowper, while not unsympathetic, thought that a more likely figure was just a little over a million dollars, and introduced legislation to that effect. In a rare demonstration of independence, the legislature balked at both proposals.

Notwithstanding the passage of time, public sentiment regarding the development of Arctic Refuge remained an open question that Congress did not feel compelled to address during most of 1990—it was, after all, an election year, and who needed the grief of environmental agitation?

311

Then, in August 1990, President Saddam Hussein of Iraq lurched into Kuwait, seized its government and hundreds of hostages, and with brute force changed the positions of all the pieces on the board of global oil politics. Oil imports to the United States seemed suddenly threatened, per-barrel prices for oil immediately shot up, and the Coastal Plain of Arctic Refuge once again was threatened, itself hostage to an eruption on the other side of the world.

Oil companies immediately revived their claims that the only solution to America's dependence on oil from the uncertain Middle East was to exploit all available domestic sources. At the top of the list again was the legendary and probably mythical pool of 9 billion barrels lying beneath the tundra of the Coastal Plain. The campaign for development was beefed up The American Petroleum Institute commissioned a study in 1990 from the WEFA Group, Inc., claiming that not only would the recovered oil enrich the oil companies, the state, and the state's citizens, as Prudhoe Bay oil had done, but that development of the Coastal Plain between 1997 and 2010 (the assumed life of the so far undiscovered field) would produce no fewer than 735,000 jobs nationwide. The Wilderness Society would later counter with an economic analysis of its own from the Tellus Institute that would indicate that the WEFA projections were off by at least 600,000 jobs even if oil were discovered, and that over the same period of time as many as 1.3 million jobs could be created in the nation through the development of energy-efficient automobiles and other energy-saving policies.

In November, 1991, a few months after Saddam Hussein had been booted back to Iraq, the industry and its supporters launched their most effective effort in Congress, getting a development bill so close to passage in the Senate that only a last-minute vote to impose cloture kept it from success. Among the weapons the Alaska Lands Coalition used to garner opposition to the bill was a series of newspaper advertisements admitting that the oil industry did have a history of providing jobs, all right—most recently, by providing a need for clean-up crews after the *Exxon Valdez* incident. The industry and its supporters in Congress did not appreciate the sarcasm, but after oil prices stabilized and the situation in the Middle East appeared to calm down, pressure for immediate development of the plain eased off somewhat. So matters stood when President Bill Clinton took office in January 1993. He had supported

312

the protection of the Coastal Plain during his campaign and lived up to that pledge when he declared that his administration's policy would be to leave it undrilled. Conservationists applauded that decision, but continued to push for a wilderness bill, knowing full well that without such protection, future circumstances almost certainly would once again place at risk the mutely glorious landscape that lies on a fringe of tundra between the looming magnificence of the Brooks Range and the glimmering ice of the Beaufort Sea.

OF BUFFERS AND BOARD FEET

Another major loophole in the Alaska Lands Act through which the engine of development could be driven was Section 705, a part of the act codifying ruinous Forest Service timber policy in the 16.8 million-acre Tongass National Forest. Encompassing most of the southeastern Alaska panhandle, the Tongass is the largest national forest in the country, the richest portion of an ecological system that runs from Glacier Bay in Alaska to southern Oregon and the tip of northwestern California, a band of temperate-zone rainforests of Sitka spruce, Douglas fir, western red cedar, hemlock, and other tree species that has no counterpart anywhere on the continent—and possibly the world. Further, the Tongass is home to the world's greatest concentration of bald eagles and grizzlies, and generous populations of Sitka black-tailed deer, black bears, moose, wolves, mountain goats, many varieties of birds, and extraordinarily productive spawning grounds for five species of salmon.

All this abundance was threatened by the continuation of logging practices that had ripped through too much of the forest already, and in this regard the Alaska Lands Act was almost no help at all. First, it had designated only 5.4 million acres of wilderness in the forest, about half what the Alaska Coalition had called for, and most of the designations were made on tundra, mountain peaks, and glaciers—what critics called "wilderness on the rocks." Most of the virgin old-growth forests of the river valleys and lower mountain slopes were left vulnerable to logging. Basically, the act ratified the land-use allocations and management directives that had been adopted in 1979 and devoted almost entirely to a policy of timber extraction over virtually all other uses. This validation carried on the traditions established by the Tongass Timber Supply Act of 1947, a postwar boom measure that had set in motion the

313

development of a large-scale timber-and-mill economy for southeast Alaska—and the signing of fifty-year contracts with just two corporations: the Ketchikan Pulp Company (KPC, later to become a subsidiary of the gigantic Louisiana Pulp Company), which signed its contract in 1951, and Alaska Lumber and Pulp (ALP—which later became the Alaska Pulp Company, or APC), a Japanese firm financed by a loan from the U. S. Import Bank, which signed its own Forest Service contract in 1956.

This was not an economic boon to the federal treasury. In 1980, the timber harvest on the Tongass amounted to 452 million board feet, supporting a work force of about 2,700 loggers and millworkers, bringing in a little under $32.5 million in receipts to the U. S. Treasury, and cost-ing the Forest Service nearly $45.6 million to plan and administer sales and build the logging roads necessary to timber production (some of the most difficult of which to build, as noted in chapter 2, cost as much as $250,000 a mile). That year alone, then, it cost the taxpayers more than $13 million to subsidize two lumber companies and keep approximately 2,700 people employed in southeast Alaska. (By comparison, the federal government spent only a little over $9.5 million on the General Assistance portion of the Aid to Families with Dependent Children program that year.) The subsidy, critics said, amounted to a very expensive welfare program, but this did not deter the ordinarily conservative Senator Ted Stevens, or his equally conservative colleagues, Senator Mike Gravel and Congressman Don Young, or the timber industry, or the timber unions, all of whom pressed for a stipulation in the proposed Alaska Lands Act that would perpetuate the timber program in the Tongass. They got it with Section 705, which mandated a ten-year cut of 4.5 billion board feet—or 450 million a year—together with guaranteed funding of no less than $40 million every year to finance the Forest Service's work there. Finally, the act left untouched the fifty-year contracts with KPC and APC, which continued to enjoy virtual monopolies in their bailiwicks.

It was a enough to give good conservationists the galloping fantods. Among them were scientists at the Auk Bay Laboratory of the National Marine Fisheries Service in Juneau, the state's capital, and what they were worried about was the destruction of streamside habitat, a condition that by 1990 had put several populations of salmon and other spaw-

314

ning fish at considerable peril. "All these fish—salmon, steelhead, and char—have the same basic requirements for migration, reproduction, and rearing," noted biologist K. V. Koski. "There have been a variety of studies throughout the Pacific Northwest on all aspects of timber management—road construction, rate of reforestation after logging, etcetera—but what's been really important is the streamside habitat. That's been crucial." At issue was the Forest Service's habit of allowing cutting to take place right to the edge of streams. Trees that once provided cool, shaded places and deadwood that formed natural pools and eddies had been stripped from riverbanks, and consequent erosion had dumped silt over gravel beds. Shade, cool temperatures, pools and eddies, and abundant gravel beds were all necessary to the production of healthy fish, and such habitat was rapidly disappearing, threatening not only the fish themselves but the $100-million commercial fishing industry they supported. After twenty years of on-the-ground research, the scientists of the Marine Fisheries Service were convinced that the minimum width of streamside habitat required to maintain fish populations was no less than one hundred feet on each side.

The Forest Service disagreed, maintaining that its own field monitoring could determine just how wide streamside buffers should be in any given case; many streams, it said, required much less than one hundred feet. Robert Pennoyer, Director of the Marine Fisheries Service's Alaska Region, had his doubts. "The Forest Service," he wrote in January 1990, "has done very little monitoring to measure the impacts of timber activities in Alaska on fish habitat and water quality, or to measure the effectiveness of Forest Service streamside management practices in protecting fish habitat." In fact, investigations by his agency and others, he said, "have shown . . . that certain Forest Service practices in Alaska have likely caused irreparable damage."

Such destruction was taking place, economists at The Wilderness Society continued to point out, at a cost to the taxpayers that continued to grow with each passing year, each clearcut mountain, each wrecked streamside. By 1990, the return to the Forest Service for every dollar invested in its timber production program had dropped to as little as two cents. The economists soon added their calculations to the body of evidence that supported an increasingly powerful move to repeal Section 705. That movement began its most durable legislative journey on February 2, 1989, when Senator Tim Wirth introduced his version of a Tongass Reform Act. He was followed later that month by Congressman Robert Mrazek, who introduced his own bill in the House. While differing in some particulars, each bill proposed the repeal of Section 705, with its mandated annual cut and its mandated $40 million yearly appropriation, as well as the repeal of the fifty-year contracts with KPC and APC. Furthermore, the legislation would have given five-year protection for 1.8 million acres of critical habitat.

This legislation, sniped at by the Alaska delegation all the way, survived into 1990 and was finally passed as the Tongass Timber Reform Act in December. It did not go unscathed. While it eliminated the mandated $40 million subsidy and the mandated cut of 450 million board feet a year, the new law contained a clause stipulating that the Forest Service had to supply local industry with enough timber to meet "local demand," providing that it did so in a manner consistent with sound management of all the forest's natural resources. Given the agency's history in the area, conservationists took little comfort in so vaguely worded a directive. Nor did the law cancel the fifty-year contracts. Among its good points, however, the law protected a little over one million acres of habitat. This was a good deal less than the 1.8 million conservationists had asked for, but it did include a little under 300,000 acres of designated wilderness and removed the remaining 700,000 acres or so from the timber-supply "pool" for five years. It also established hundred-foot buffers along many of the most important salmon streams.

AN OPPRESSION OF DETAIL

As the chronicles of Arctic Refuge and Tongass National Forest demonstrate, the issues and interests and worries at work in Alaska are not merely numerous, they are so complex and embrace so wide an expanse of threatened land, water, and wildlife that they become overwhelming, an oppression of detail that it sometimes seems cannot adequately be comprehended, much less resolved. Consider, for example, the fate of Alaska's rivers. For years, they have been subjected to decades of a destructive gold-mining technology that, in the words of Allen Smith, The Wilderness Society's Regional Director for Alaska, "tears the guts out of the bottom of the river, runs all the gravel through a sluice operation, and leaves it in piles like ice cream scoops in and around the river." In such places as Denali, Gates of the Arctic, Yukon-Charley Rivers, and Wrangell-St. Elias national parks and preserves, the National Park Service has at least instituted an attempt to purchase and reclaim old abandoned mining sites, although the level of funding and staffing remains too low to get the job done as well and as swiftly as it should be.

The Bureau of Land Management, which supervises most current mining operations in the state, has never even shown much interest in reclamation, and although current law requires it to prepare individual environmental impact statements for every mine it approves, the funding provided for such purposes, like that for the National Park Service's purchase and reclamation program, is minimal at best. Meanwhile, the state of Alaska, led by its development-minded governor, Walter Hickel, muddied the waters even more, so to speak, when in 1990 it declared that it was going to claim ownership of the beds of all "navigable" streams in the state, as constitutional law stipulates. One particular stream it had in mind was Moose Creek in Denali National Park and Preserve, and shortly after the state asserted ownership, thirty-seven gold claims were filed. Russell Berry, superintendant of the park, promised that he and the Park Service would use every legal tool at their command to prevent Moose Creek from being destroyed. The state responded with uncommon meekness, withdrawing all park waters from mining entry and deciding that it would "restudy" even the Moose Creek claim. Conservationists took little comfort in the state's reversal, fearing that such proposals inevitably would rise again, putting virtually every stream in the state, including those in parks and wilderness areas, in jeopardy of river mining—a spectacularly slipshod industry whose adherence to water quality and other environmental standards imposed by the Environmental Protection Agency and other federal bodies would be monitored by a BLM that has never indicated the slightest enthusiasm for the strict regulation of much of anything in Alaska. And, as Allen Smith's remark above suggests, a riverbed whose stream has been dammed and diverted, then worked over by bulldozers and earthmovers and jets of highpowered water and flatboat suction dredges and other equipment is as thoroughly wrecked a piece of ground as one is likely to find anywhere north of Mount St. Helens.

On another front, both the conservation community and the National Park Service are worried about an ancient federal law, Revised Statute 2477, referred to as RS2477 (as we note in chapter 3, this statute also is a matter of concern on some BLM lands in the Lower 48 states). The law states that the builder of a road on non-reserved federal land owns the right-of-way over which the road travels. The Alaska Roads Commission, as it happened, built a number of "roads"—though most were little better than primitive tracks that have long since nearly vanished with disuse—before the Alaska Lands Act established all those national parks, wildlife refuges, and other federal reserves. Some of the tracks even predated the designation of Denali National Park (then McKinley) in 1917. At Governor Hickel's prodding, the state of Alaska currently has made several hundred assertions of RS2477 ownership out of a possible 1,400-1,700. (With a certain mischievous glee, it also has encouraged private citizens to discover and perhaps lay claim to other, privately built tracks and trails.) Eleven of its assertions are in Wrangell-St. Elias National Park and Preserve, and while it has not yet made assertions in Denali, there is no question but that it has designs on the state's preeminent park as well, where tourism promoters have dreams of building an ambitious system of state-owned off-road vehicle trails. In addition, the state has started planning for the construction of a 300-mile highway from McGrath on the north side of the park into a resort area on the Kantishna River. It might also assert ownership of the present Denali Park road itself. The park road already is badly overcrowded with visitor traffic, and should the state succeed in any such claim, it doubtless would widen the road and perhaps even attempt to extend it all the way through the park—all of which would profoundly stress a wildlife population already feeling the effects of more than 600,000 visitors every summer. "The Hickel administration," Allen Smith believes, "is using transportation policy to crack open the national parks of Alaska."

AN AGENDA FOR THE ALASKA LANDS

The litany continues: Overcrowding, a proposed utility corridor, and extensive commercial fur-trapping operations threaten the already over-crowded habitat of Kenai National Wildlife Refuge; bear-human con-

318

flicts and proposed commercial development of a portion of Kodiak National Wildlife Refuge threaten brown bear populations; oil spills—there were at least thirty in 1989 alone, including, of course, that from the *Exxon Valdez*—constantly imperil bird and mammal species in hundreds of the tiny units that make up the Alaska Maritime National Wildlife Refuge System; mining proposals, commercial fishing, tourist "love boats," and conflicts over whether commercial and subsistence fishing should be allowed to threaten the natural integrity of Glacier Bay National Park and Preserve; river mining has brutally degraded hundreds of miles of streams in Steese National Conservation Area and White Mountain National Recreation Area, while future operations threaten more; and mining, hunting abuses, off-road vehicles, and conflicts over subsistence questions have threatened Wrangell-St. Elias National Park and Preserve in the southeastern corner of Alaska's great "fist" and Gates of the Arctic National Park and Preserve in its northwestern corner. With these and scores of other problems still unresolved, it becomes clear that more than a decade after the passage of the Alaska Lands Act, the future of Alaska's landed patrimony is uncertain. Overcome by the economies of scale, the bewildering snarl of issues that greet them at every turn, the intransigence of a local population of boomers, a congressional delegation that appears to have learned next to nothing from two hundred years of American history, and agency doubletalk and stubbornness, even the most dedicated grassroots environmentalist might succumb to darker moments of reflection that suggest that saving Alaska may be impossible.

The solutions exist, however, and for the most part are not so different from—and certainly no more revolutionary than—those we have offered up here for the preservation of the rest of the nation's inheritance of public lands Properly committed, we can substitute the litany of destruction with a litany of salvation:

> Funding must be allocated to increase staffs so that adequate regulations and study of wildlife and habitat use can be carried on by all public land agencies;

> Wilderness recommendations must be made where they have not yet been made. There is the potential of another 100 million acres

319

of wilderness designations in Alaska. The National Park Service, the Forest Service, and the Fish and Wildlife Service have all completed their studies and prepared their environmental impact statements, but not a single wilderness recommendation has been forwarded to Congress. Those recommendations should be made an acted upon as soon as possible. As for the the BLM, it should immediately revisit the non-CAMA lands and prepare wilderness recommendations for these as well—and above all, the Coastal Plain of Arctic National Wildlife Refuge must be given wilderness designation immediately, so that it never again is threatened by oil and gas development;

Public money from the Land and Water Conservation Fund and other sources must be used to purchase all inholdings and mining claims that threaten the future integrity of rivers and other natural areas;

The Memoranda of Understanding that have manacled the federal agencies and kept them from managing the wildlife on the public lands must be rescinded and replaced, for if they are not, hunting pressures on moose, bears, and other creatures will become intolerable and, furthermore, the world will continue to be treated to such primitive exercises in mindless destruction as the massive wolf hunts endorsed and promoted by Alaska Governor Hickle in recent years;

A careful path must be steered between the call to satisfy the legitimate subsistence needs of the Native and rural populations and the cry for development on public lands as a panacea for all the ills that plague Native communities;

In Alaska, even more vigorously than elsewhere, the Bureau of Land Management must be yanked bodily into the twentieth century and forced to abandon its love affair with the boom and bust economy of the mining industry, replacing that sordid passion with a suitably faithful dedication to the protection of biological diversity;

Similarly, the Forest Service must cease its longstanding and ruinous concubinage with the timber industry and begin to prepare for the preservation of some of the last temperate-zone rainforests left on the planet with the sense of stewardship that is its own highest inheritance;

The Alaskan national parks and refuges must remain primitive, as *wilderness* enclaves, the last opportunity we have to establish permanently protected coherent land systems on such a scale;

And finally, in Alaska as elsewhere, all four public-land agencies must begin the bureaucratically painful process of cooperation that is essential to intelligent ecosystem protection, reflecting sentiments expressed by Russell Berry, superintendant of beleaguered Denali National Park and Preserve, in 1993: "We need to be looking fifty, a hundred years ahead. All the land management agencies need to work together now to identify wildlife corridors that connect their lands, to talk about how to preserve those crucial linkages intact—so the grizzlies and caribou and wolves have room to roam, so the gene pools stay ample and diverse."

To say that the solutions above are not significantly different from or more revolutionary than the recommendations we make for the rest of the American public lands is not to suggest that the task of implementing them is not every bit as huge as the dimensions of beauty, diversity, and living fragility that are at stake in Alaska. It will take a level of commitment that the United States has not often achieved short of war. But it is by remembering the dimensions of the place itself that the vision possibly can be achieved. For Alaska is not merely unique to the United States; it is not merely unique to North America or even to the Western Hemisphere; it is unique to all the world. In its wholeness and its vulnerability, Alaska must be looked upon by all of us as not just another state but as an international responsibility it has fallen upon

321

this nation to embrace and honor. It is not a marketplace for bargaining, for trading a little development here for a little natural beauty there, or an arena in which we can safely act out the old adventure of killing the future for the sake of present gain. If we sacrifice Alaska to the machinery of abuse, we will have violated the honor of having had the Great Land in our care; if we move to save it, however, if we have the strength to throw off the weight of our own history, we will have the regard of the family of nations and at least one living reason to describe this as indeed the American century.

Looking toward the Brooks Range from the Coastal Plain of Arctic National Wildlife Refuge, Alaska (T. H. Watkins).

APPENDIX A

The Public Lands and Major
Public Land Legislation of the United States

THE FEDERAL LAND-MANAGING AGENCIES

Agency	Founded	Responsibility	FY1994 Budget	FY1994 Employees
National Park Service	1916	National Parks and Monuments	$1,061,823,000	14,771 permanent 3,794 seasonal
U. S. Forest Service	1905	National Forests and Grasslands	3,251,753,000	34,056 permanent 18,030 seasonal
Bureau of Land Management	1946	National Resource Lands	599,860,000	11,860 permanent
Fish & Wildlife Service	1940	Wildlife Refuges	484,313,000	6,247 permanent

THE NATIONAL PARK SYSTEM
NATIONAL PARKS

	State(s)	Acreage
Acadia	Maine	38,523
Arches	Utah	73,378
Badlands	South Dakota	243,302

El Capitan, Yosemite National Park, California. Photograph by Carleton E. Watkins (Bancroft Library, University of California at Berkeley).

325

NATIONAL PARKS (*cont'd*)

	State(s)	Acreage
Big Bend	Texas	708,118
Biscayne	Florida	180,275
Bryce Canyon	Utah	35,835
Canyonlands	Utah	337,570
Capitol Reef	Utah	241,904
Carlsbad Caverns	New Mexico	46,755
Channel Islands	California	249,353
Crater Lake	Oregon	160,290
Denali	Alaska	4,698,583
Everglades	Florida	1,398,800
Gates of the Arctic	Alaska	7,498,066
Glacier	Montana	1,013,594
Glacier Bay	Alaska	3,220,396
Grand Canyon	Arizona	1,218,375
Grand Teton	Wyoming	310,515
Great Smoky Mountains	North Carolina, Tennessee	517,368
Guadalupe Mountains	Texas	76,293
Haleakala	Hawaii	28,655
Hawaii Volcanoes	Hawaii	229,177
Hot Springs	Arkansas	5,826
Isle Royale	Michigan	571,796
Katmai	Alaska	3,678,929
Kenai Fjords	Alaska	676,667
Kings Canyon	California	460,139
Kobuk Valley	Alaska	1,749,037
Lake Clark	Alaska	2,633,933
Lassen Volcanic	California	106,372
Mammoth Cave	Kentucky	52,128
Mesa Verde	Colorado	52,085
Mount Rainier	Washington	235,404
North Cascades	Washington	504,780
Olympic	Washington	908,720
Petrified Forest	Arizona	93,492
Redwood	California	109,225
Rocky Mountain	Colorado	263,790
Sequoia	California	403,023
Shenandoah	Virginia	194,801
Theodore Roosevelt	North Dakota	70,344

Virgin Islands	Virgin Islands	14,708
Voyageurs	Minnesota	219,128
Wind Cave	South Dakota	28,292
Wrangell–St. Elias	Alaska	8,331,406
Yellowstone	Idaho, Wyoming, Montana	2,219,822
Yosemite	California	760,917
Zion	Utah	146,546

NATIONAL MONUMENTS

(of 20 acres or more in size)

Agate Fossil Beds	Nebraska	3,055
Alibates Flint Quarries	New Mexico, Texas	1,332
Aniakchak	Alaska	136,955
Aztec Ruins	New Mexico	27
Bandelier	New Mexico	36,971
Black Canyon of the Gunnison	Colorado	13,672
Buck Reef Island	Virgin Islands	880
Cabrilla	California	143
Canyon de Chelly	Arizona	83,840
Cape Krusenstern	Alaska	636,685
Capulin Mountains	New Mexico	775
Casa Grande Ruins	Arizona	472
Cedar Breaks	Utah	6,154
Chiricahua	Arizona	11,088
Colorado	Colorado	20,449
Congaree Swamp	South Carolina	15,200
Craters of the Moon	Idaho	53
Death Valley	California, Nevada	2,067,627
Devils Postpile	California	798
Devils Tower	Wyoming	1,346
Dinosaur	Colorado, Utah	211,060
Effigy Mounds	Iowa	1,346
El Morro	New Mexico	1,278
Florissant Fossil Beds	Colorado	5,998
Fossil Butte	Wyoming	8,198
Gila Cliff Dwellings	New Mexico	553
Grand Portage	Minnesota	709
Great Sand Dunes	Colorado	38,951
Hohokam Pima	Arizona	1,690

APPENDIX

NATIONAL MONUMENTS (cont'd)

	State(s)	Acreage
Homestead National Monument of America	Nebraska	194
Hovenweep	Colorado, Utah	785
Jewel Cave	South Dakota	1,274
John Day Fossil Beds	Oregon	14,100
Joshua Tree	California	559,959
Lava Beds	California	46,821
Lehman Caves	Nevada	640
Montezuma Castle	Arizona	849
Mound City Group	Ohio	67
Muir Woods	California	553
Natural Bridges	Utah	7,779
Navajo	Arizona	360
Ocmulgee	Georgia	683
Oregon Caves	Oregon	473
Organ Pipe Cactus	Arizona	330,688
Pecos	New Mexico	364
Pinnacles	California	16,221
Pipe Spring	Arizona	40
Pipestone	Minnesota	281
Rainbow Bridge	Utah	160
Russell Cave	Alabama	310
Saguaro	Arizona	83,576
Saint Croix Island	Maine	35
Salinas	New Mexico	1,079
Scotts Bluff	Nebraska	2,987
Sunset Crater	Arizona	3,040
Timpanogos Cave	Utah	250
Tonto	Arizona	1,120
Tuzigoot	Arizona	848
Walnut Canyon	Arizona	2,249
White Sands	New Mexico	144,419
Wupatki	Arizona	35,253

THE NATIONAL FOREST SYSTEM

FORESTS

	State(s)	Acreage
Allegheny	Pennsylvania	510,406
Angeles	California	653,862
Angelina	Texas	154,244
Apache	Arizona	1,187,685
Apalachicola	Florida	558,737
Arapaho	Colorado	1,024,980
Ashley	Utah, Wyoming	1,384,699
Beaverhead	Montana	2,128,798
Bienville	Mississippi	179,394
Bighorn	Wyoming	1,107,670
Bitterroot	Idaho, Montana	1,578,330
Black Hills	South Dakota, Wyoming	1,235,411
Boise	Idaho	2,645,938
Bridger	Wyoming	1,733,555
Cache	Idaho, Utah	679,333
Calaveras Bigtree	Arkansas	380
Caribou	Idaho, Utah, Wyoming	987,187
Carson	New Mexico	1,391,355
Challis	Idaho	2,463,633
Chattahoochee	Georgia	748,663
Chequamegon	Wisconsin	847,954
Cherokee	North Carolina, Tennessee	625,606
Chippewa	Minnesota	661,218
Choctawhatchee	Florida	675
Chugach	Alaska	6,122,949
Cibola	New Mexico	1,635,510
Clearwater	Idaho	1,688,687
Cleveland	California	420,590
Coconino	Arizona	1,835,767
Coeur d'Alene	Idaho	722,571
Colville	Washington	945,120
Conecuh	Alabama	82,826
Coronado	Arizona, New Mexico	1,779,297
Croatan	North Carolina	157,054
Custer	South Dakota, Montana	2,173,506
Daniel Boone	Kentucky	529,121

FORESTS (*cont'd*)

	State(s)	Acreage
Davy Crockett	Texas	161,500
Deerlodge	Montana	1,196,547
Delta	Mississippi	59,518
Deschutes	Oregon	1,604,705
DeSoto	Mississippi	501,724
Dixie	Utah	1,883,736
Eldorado	California, Nevada	672,784
Fishlake	Utah	1,424,527
Flathead	Montana	2,350,439
Francis Marion	South Carolina	250,008
Fremont	Oregon	1,197,012
Gallatin	Montana	1,738,056
George Washington	Virginia, West Virginia	1,055,568
Gifford Pinchot	Washington	1,253,585
Gila	New Mexico	2,704,781
Grand Mesa	Colorado	346,219
Green Mountain	New York, Vermont	307,842
Gunnison	Colorado	1,662,839
Helena	Montana	975,088
Hiawatha	Michigan	879,593
Holly Springs	Mississippi	152,174
Homochitto	Mississippi	188,994
Hoosier	Indiana	187,523
Humboldt	Nevada	2,527,938
Huron	Michigan	428,669
Inyo	California, Nevada	1,861,540
Jefferson	Kentucky, Virginia, West Virginia	698,846
Kaibab	Arizona	1,556,432
Kaniksu	Idaho, Montana, Washington	1,616,201
Kisatchie	Louisiana	597,933
Klamath	California, Oregon	1,707,104
Kootenai	Idaho, Montana	2,224,717
Lassen	California	1,060,001
Lewis and Clark	Montana	1,843,587
Lincoln	New Mexico	1,103,490
Lolo	Montana	2,112,597
Los Padres	California	1,752,523

Malheur	Oregon	1,459,422
Manistee	Michigan	522,167
Manti–La Sal	Colorado, Utah	1,265,254
Mark Twain	Missouri	1,453,743
Medicine Bow	Wyoming	1,093,667
Mendocino	California	884,231
Modoc	California	1,654,527
Monongahela	West Virginia	848,879
Mount Baker	Washington	1,280,972
Mount Hood	Oregon	1,060,092
Nantahala	North Carolina	515,287
Nebraska	Nebraska	141,553
Nezperce	Idaho	2,221,816
Nicolet	Wisconsin	656,248
Ocala	Florida	382,318
Ochoco	Oregon	843,721
Oconee	Georgia	114,248
Okanogan	Washington	1,499,462
Olympic	Washington	649,975
Osceola	Florida	157,379
Ottawa	Michigan	928,221
Ouachita	Oklahoma	248,965
Ozark	Arkansas	1,119,639
Payette	Idaho	2,314,379
Pike	Colorado	1,107,946
Pisgah	North Carolina	495,730
Plumas	California	1,154,610
Prescott	Arizona	1,237,061
Rio Grande	Colorado	1,851,296
Rogue River	California, Oregon	629,191
Roosevelt	Colorado	788,268
Routt	Colorado	1,127,291
Sabine	Texas	188,220
St. Francis	Arkansas	20,937
St. Joe	Idaho	866,500
Salmon	Idaho	1,771,180
Sam Houston	Texas	161,150
Samuel R. McKelvie	Nebraska	115,707
San Bernardino	California	657,975
San Isabel	Colorado	1,115,754
San Juan	Colorado	1,860,728

FORESTS (*cont'd*)

	State(s)	Acreage
Santa Fe	New Mexico	1,567,389
Sawtooth	Utah, Idaho	1,802,715
Sequoia	California	1,125,693
Shasta	California	1,133,519
Shawnee	Illinois	253,378
Shoshone	Wyoming	2,433,029
Sierra	California	1,303,032
Siskiyou	California, Oregon	1,083,488
Sitgreaves	Arizona	817,338
Siuslaw	Oregon	628,175
Six Rivers	California	987,920
Snoqualmie	Washington	1,225,748
Stanislaus	California	889,478
Sumter	South Carolina	359,648
Superior	Minnesota	2,054,022
Tahoe	California	391,970
Talladega	Alabama	371,850
Targhee	Idaho, Wyoming	1,642,755
Toiyabe	California, Nevada	3,195,400
Tombigbee	Mississippi	66,457
Tongass	Alaska	16,815,703
Tonto	Arizona	2,873,759
Trinity	California	1,045,441
Tuskegee	Alabama	10,925
Uinta	Utah	812,760
Umatilla	Washington, Oregon	1,402,500
Umpqua	Oregon	984,797
Uncompahgre	Colorado	943,894
Uwharrie	North Carolina	47,069
Wallowa	Oregon	985,980
Wasatch	Utah, Idaho	848,609
Wayne	Ohio	177,485
Wenatchee	Washington	1,620,031
White Mountain	Maine, New Hampshire	728,623
White River	Colorado	1,961,539
Whitman	Oregon	1,263,879
William B. Bankhead	Alabama	180,615
Willamette	Oregon	1,675,470
Winema	Oregon	1,034,915

THE NATIONAL RESOURCE LANDS (BLM)

GRASSLANDS

Black Kettle	Oklahoma, Texas	31,300
Buffalo Gap	South Dakota	591,700
Caddo	Texas	17,784
Cedar River	North Dakota	6,717
Cimarron	Kansas	108,177
Comanche	Colorado	418,870
Crooked River	Oregon	105,224
Curlew	Idaho	47,658
Fort Pierre	South Dakota	116,001
Grand River	South Dakota	155,170
Kiowa	New Mexico	136,412
Little Missouri	North Dakota	1,027,922
Lyndon B. Johnson	Texas	20,320
McClelland Creek	Texas	1,449
Oglala	Nebraska	94,332
Pawnee	Colorado	193,060
Rita Blanca	Oklahoma, Texas	92,989
Thunder Basin	Wyoming	571,885

THE NATIONAL RESOURCE LANDS (BLM)

State	Acreage	Wilderness Study Areas	WSA Acreage
Alabama	3,100	none	none
Alaska	65,000,000	none	none
Arizona	12,283,541	62	1,521,000
Arkansas	1,820	none	none
California	17,158,098	185	6,829,000
Colorado	8,365,552	60	801,000
Florida	1,937	none	none
Idaho	11,906,806	61	1,913,000
Illinois	12	none	none
Kansas	728	none	none
Louisiana	3,962	none	none
Michigan	766	none	none

State	Acreage	Wilderness Study Areas	WSA Acreage
Minnesota	60,615	none	none
Mississippi	597	none	none
Missouri	400	none	none
Montana	8,093,612	42	437,000
Nebraska	8,002	none	none
Nevada	48,591,143	83	4,381,000
New Mexico	12,850,966	43	892,000
North Dakota	68,104	none	none
Ohio	120	none	none
Oklahoma	6,231	none	none
Oregon	15,694,891	85	2,312,000
South Dakota	274,599	none	none
Utah	22,166,755	81	3,139,000
Washington	312,451	one	5,518
Wisconsin	589	none	none
Wyoming	18,410,441	36	550,000

THE NATIONAL WILDLIFE REFUGE SYSTEM

	State(s)	Acreage
Agassiz	Minnesota	61,052
Alamosa	Colorado	10,352
Alaska Maritime	Alaska	3,551,783
Alaska Peninsula	Alaska	3,500,000
Alligator River	North Carolina	120,000
Amagansett	New York	36
Anaho Island	Nevada	248
Anahuac	Texas	21,758
Ankeny	Oregon	2,796
Antioch Dunes	California	55
Appert Lake	North Dakota	908
Aransas	Texas	98,721
Arapaho	Colorado	17,654
Arctic	Alaska	19,046,382
Ardoch	North Dakota	2,696
Arrowwood	North Dakota	15,934
Ash Meadows	Nevada	11,173

Attwater Prairie Chicken	Texas	7,984
Audubon	North Dakota	14,736
Back Bay	Virginia	4,589
Bamforth	Wyoming	1,166
Bandon Marsh	Oregon	289
Banks Lake	Georgia	3,550
Basket Slough	Oregon	2,492
Bear Butte	South Dakota	374
Bear Lake	Idaho	17,605
Bear River	Utah	65,030
Bear Valley	Oregon	1,733
Becharof	Alaska	1,200,000
Benton Lake	Montana	12,383
Big Boggy	Texas	3,564
Big Lake	Arkansas	11,036
Big Stone	Minnesota	10,794
Bitterlake	New Mexico	23,350
Blackbeard Island	Georgia	5,618
Black Coulee	Montana	1,309
Blackwater	Maryland	14,263
Block Island	Rhode Island	29
Blowing Wind Cave	Alabama	264
Blue Ridge	California	897
Bogue Chitto	Mississippi, Louisiana	18,637
Bombay Hook	Delaware	15,122
Bone Hill	North Dakota	640
Bonsecour	Alabama	3,765
Bosque del Apache	New Mexico	57,191
Bowdoin	Montana	12,577
Brazoria	Texas	10,407
Breton	Louisiana	9,047
Brown's Park	Colorado	13,375
Brumba	North Dakota	1,977
Buffalo Lake	Texas	9,761
Butte Sink	California	1,490
Cabeza Prieta	Arizona	860,000
Caloosahatchee	Florida	40
Camas	Indiana	10,578
Camp Lake	North Dakota	585
Canfield	North Dakota	313
Cape Charles	Virginia	183

	State(s)	*Acreage*
Cape Mears	Oregon	139
Cape Romain	South Carolina	34,229
Carolina Sandhills	South Carolina	45,591
Castle Rock	California	14
Catahoula	Louisiana	5,309
Cedar Island	North Carolina	12,526
Cedar Keys	Florida	721
Cedar Point	Ohio	2,445
Charles M. Russell	Montana	897,129
Chase Lake	North Dakota	4,385
Chassahowitzka	Florida	30,436
Chautauqua	Illinois	6,197
Chincoteague	Virginia, Maryland	9,931
Choctaw	Alabama	4,218
Cibola	Arizona, California	11,428
Clarence Cannon	Mississippi	3,737
Clear Lake	California	33,440
Cold Springs	Oregon	3,117
Columbia	Washington	28,952
Columbian White-Tailed Deer	Washington, Oregon	4,757
Colusa	California	4,040
Conboy Lake	Washington	5,509
Conscience Point	New York	60
Copalis	Washington	61
Cottonwood	North Dakota	1,013
Crab Orchard	Illinois	43,550
Creedman Coulee	Montana	2,728
Crescent Lake	Nebraska	45,818
Crocodile Lake	Florida	1,466
Cross Creeks	South Dakota	8,862
Cross Island	Maine	1,355
Crystal River	Florida	33
Currituck	North Carolina	512
Dakota Lake	North Dakota	2,756
D'Arbonne	Louisiana	17,420
Deer Flat	Idaho, Oregon	11,410
Delevan	California	5,634
Delta	Louisiana	48,799

Desert	Nevada	1,588,779
Des Lacs	North Dakota	19,544
De Soto	Iowa, Nebraska	7,823
Dungeness	Washington	756
Eastern Neck	Maryland	2,286
Edwin B. Forsythe	New Jersey	30,606
Egmont Key	Florida	328
Elizabeth Morton	New York	187
Ellicott Slough	California	126
Ernie	Oregon	7,994
Eufaula	Alabama, Georgia	11,160
Fallon	Nevada	17,902
Farallon	California	211
Featherstone	Virginia	164
Felsenthal	Arkansas	64,599
Fern Cave	Alabama	199
Fisherman Island	Virginia	1,025
Fish Springs	Utah	17,992
Flattery Rocks	Washington	125
Flint Hills	Kansas	18,463
Florence Lake	North Dakota	1,888
Fort Niobrana	Nebraska	18,667
Fox River	Wisconsin	641
Franklin Island	Maine	12
Grasslands	California	24,484
Gravel Island	Wisconsin	27
Gray's Lake	Idaho	16,153
Great Dismal Swamp	North Carolina, Virgina	101,873
Great Meadows	Massachusetts	2,878
Great Swamp	New Jersey	6,793
Great White Heron	Florida	7,404
Green Bay	Wisconsin	2
Grulla	New Mexico, Texas	3,236
Hagerman	Texas	11,320
Hailstone	Montana	920
Halfbreed Lake	Montana, North Dakota	3,257
Hanalei	Hawaii	917
Harbor Island	Michigan	695
Harris Neck	Georgia	2,687
Hart Mountain	Oregon	249,239
Hatchie	Tennessee	11,556

	State(s)	Acreage
Havasu	Arizona, California	45,851
Hawaiian Islands	Hawaii	254,418
Hewitt Lake	Montana	1,680
Hiddenwood	North Dakota	568
Hillside	Mississippi	15,406
Hobart Lake	North Dakota	2,076
Hobe Sound	Florida	969
Holla Bend	Arkansas	4,083
Hopper Mountain	California	1,871
Horicon	Wisconsin	20,976
Huleia	Hawaii	238
Humboldt Bay	California	559
Huron	Michigan	147
Hutchinson Lake	North Dakota	479
Hutton Lake	Wyoming	1,428
Imperial	Arizona, California	15,764
Innoko	Alaska	3,850,000
Iroquois	New York	10,818
Island Bay	Florida	20
Izembek	Alaska	320,893
James C. Campbell	Hawaii	145
J. Clark Salyer	North Dakota	58,693
J. N. "Ding" Darling	Florida	5,014
Johnson Lake	North Dakota	2,007
Kakahaia	Hawaii	45
Kanuti	Alaska	1,430,000
Karl E. Mundt	Nebraska, South Dakota	1,082
Kelly's Slough	North Dakota	1,270
Kenai	Alaska	1,970,000
Kern	California	10,618
Kesterson	California	5,900
Key West	Florida	2,019
Kirtland Warbler	Michigan	1,896
Klamath Forest	Oregon	16,377
Kodiak	Alaska	1,865,000
Kofa	Arizona	660,000
Kootenai	Idaho	2,764
Koyukuk	Alaska	3,550,000
Lacassine	Louisiana	31,776

Lacreek	South Dakota	16,260
Laguna Alascosca	Texas	45,187
Lake Alice	North Dakota	10,954
Lake Andes	South Dakota	940
Lake Elsie	North Dakota	635
Lake George	North Dakota	3,119
Lake Ilo	North Dakota	4,033
Lake Isom	South Dakota	1,846
Lake Mason	Montana	16,968
Lake Nettie	North Dakota	2,895
Lake Otis	North Dakota	320
Lake Thibadeau	Montana	3,868
Lake Woodruff	Florida	18,506
Lake Zahl	North Dakota	3,823
Lambs Lake	North Dakota	1,207
Lamesteer	Montana	800
Las Vegas	New Mexico	8,672
Lee Metcalf	Montana	2,696
Lewis and Clark	Oregon	38,000
Little Goose	North Dakota	288
Little Pend Oreille	Washington	40,175
Long Lake	North Dakota	22,310
Lords Lake	North Dakota	1,915
Lost Lake	North Dakota	960
Lostwood	North Dakota	24,810
Lower Hatchie	South Dakota	2,628
Lower Klamath	California	40,295
Lower Rio Grande Valley	Texas	8,345
Lower Suwannee	Florida	22,821
Loxahatchee	Florida	145,635
MacKay Island	North Carolina, Virginia	7,056
Malheur	Oregon	183,964
Maple River	North Dakota	712
Mark Twain	Illinois, Iowa	25,768
Martin	Maryland	4,424
Marumsco	Virginia	63
Mason Neck	Virginia	1,935
Massasoit	Massachusetts	184
Mathews Brake	Mississippi	807
Matlacha Pass	Florida	231
Mattamuskeet	North Carolina	50,180

	State(s)	Acreage
Maxwell	New Mexico	3,699
McFaddin	Texas	42,956
McKay Creek	Oregon	1,837
McLean	North Dakota	760
McNary	Washington	3,629
Medicine Lake	Montana	22,824
Merced	California	2,562
Meredosia	Illinois	1,850
Merritt Island	Michigan	363
Mille Lacs	Minnesota	.6
Mingo	Mississippi	21,676
Minidoka	Idaho	20,721
Minnesota Valley	Minnesota	4,878
Missisquoi	Vermont	5,839
Mississippi River Cave	Illinois, Iowa, Wisconsin, Minnesota	106,197
Moapa Valley	Nevada	33
Modoc	California	6,283
Monomoy	Massachusetts	2,702
Monte Vista	Colorado	14,189
Montezuma	New York	6,432
Moody	Texas	3,517
Moosehorn	Maine	22,745
Morgan Brake	Mississippi	1,465
Muleshoe	Texas	5,809
Muscatatuck	Indiana	7,724
Nansemond	Virginia	208
Nantucket	Massachusetts	40
National Bison Range	Montana	18,541
National Elk	Wyoming	24,247
National Key Deer	Florida	5,816
Necedah	Wisconsin	39,549
Nine Pipe	Montana	2,542
Ninigret	Rhode Island	408
Nisqually	Washington	2,824
Nomans Land Island	Massachusetts	620
North Platte	Nebraska	5,047
Nowitna	Alaska	1,560,000
Noxubee	Mississippi	46,324

Okefenokee	Florida, Georgia	395,080
Optima	Oklahoma	4,333
Oregon Islands	Oregon	575
Ottawa	Ohio	5,794
Ouray	Utah	11,483
Overflow	Arkansas	6,790
Oxbow	Massachusetts	662
Oyster Bay	New York	3,204
Pablo	Montana	2,542
Pahranagat	Nevada	5,381
Panther Swamp	Mississippi	22,797
Parker River	Massachusetts	4,650
Passage Key	Florida	36
Pathfinder	Wyoming	16,807
Patuxent	Maryland	4,682
Pea Island	North Carolina	5,915
Pearl Harbor	Hawaii	61
Pee Dee	North Carolina	8,438
Pelican Island	Florida	4,396
Petit Manan	Maine	3,310
Piedmont	Georgia	34,863
Pierce	Washington	319
Pinckney Island	South Carolina	4,053
Pine Island	Florida	404
Pinellas	Florida	392
Pixley	California	5,187
Pleasant Lake	North Dakota	898
Plum Tree Island	Virginia	3,276
Pocasse	South Dakota	2,540
Pond Island	Maine	10
Presquile	Virginia	1,329
Pretty Rock	North Dakota	800
Prime Hook	Delaware	9,701
Protection Land	Washington	4
Pungo	North Carolina	12,380
Quillayute Needles	Washington	300
Quivira	Kansas	21,820
Rabb Lake	North Dakota	261
Rachel Carson	Maine	2,736
Red Rock Lakes	Montana	32,468
Reelfoot	Kentucky	10,428

	State(s)	Acreage
Rice Lake	Minnesota	16,516
Ridgefield	Washington	3,017
Rock Lake	North Dakota	5,507
Rose Lake	North Dakota	836
Ruby Lake	Nevada	37,632
Sabine	Louisiana	139,437
Sachuest Point	Rhode Island	228
Sacramento	California	10,783
Saddle Mountain	Washington	30,810
St. Johns	Florida	6,254
St. Marks	Florida	64,600
St. Vincent	Florida	12,490
Salt Meadow	Connecticut	183
Salton Sea	California	37,378
Salt Plains	Oklahoma	31,996
San Andres	New Mexico	57,215
San Bernard	Texas	24,454
San Bernardino	Arizona	2,309
Sand Lake	South Dakota	19,804
San Francisco Bay	California	17,218
San Juan Island	Washington	451
San Luis	California	7,430
San Pablo Bay	California	11,634
Santa Ana	Texas	2,088
Santee	South Carolina	43,636
Savannah	South Carolina, Georgia	26,584
School Section Lake	North Dakota	680
Seal Beach	California	911
Seal Island	Maine	65
Seatuck	New York	183
Seedskadee	Wyoming	14,842
Selawik	Alaska	2,150,000
Seney	Michigan	95,455
Sequoyah	Oklahoma	20,800
Sevilleta	New Mexico	228,134
Sheldon	Nevada, Oregon	571,048
Shell Keys	Louisiana	8
Shell Lake	North Dakota	1,835
Sherburne	Minnesota	29,583

Sheyenne Lake	North Dakota	797
Shiawassee	Michigan	8,984
Sibley Lake	North Dakota	1,077
Silver Lake	North Dakota	3,348
Slade	North Dakota	3,000
Snyder Lake	North Dakota	1,500
Springwater	North Dakota	640
Squaw Creek	Missouri	5,919
Stewart Lake	North Dakota	2,230
Stillwater	Nevada	24,203
Stoney Slough	North Dakota	880
Storm Lake	North Dakota	686
Stump Lake	North Dakota	27
Sullys Hill	North Carolina	1,674
Sunburst Lake	North Dakota	328
Supawna Meadows	New Jersey	1,718
Susquehanna	Maryland	4
Sutter	California	2,591
Swan Lake	Missouri	10,669
Swanquarter	North Carolina	15,643
Swan River	Montana	1,569
Tamarac	Minnesota	35,191
Target Rock	New York	80
Tennessee	Tennessee	51,358
Tetlin	Alaska	700,000
Tewaukon	North Dakota	9,273
Texas Point	Texas	8,952
Thacher Island	Massachusetts	22
Three Arch Rocks	Oregon	15
Tijuana Slough	California	472
Tinicum	Oregon	898
Tishomingo	Oklahoma	16,464
Togiak	Alaska	4,105,000
Tomahawk	North Dakota	440
Toppenish	Washington	1,763
Trempealeau	Wisconsin	5,617
Trustom Pond	Rhode Island	579
Tule Lake	California	39,396
Turnbull	Washington	15,565
Tybee	Georgia	100
Ul Bend	Montana	55,489

	State(s)	Acreage
Umatilla	Oregon, Washington	22,885
Union Slough	Iowa	2,200
Upper Klamath	Oregon	12,457
Upper Mississippi	Illinois, Iowa, Wisconsin, Minnesota	88,900
Upper Ouachita	Louisiana	20,905
Upper Souris	North Dakota	32,092
Valentine	Nebraska	67,097
Wallops Island	Virginia	3,373
Wapack	New Hampshire	1,674
Wapanocca	Arkansas	5,484
War Horse	Montana	3,192
Washita	Oklahoma	8,084
Wassaw	Georgia	10,070
Watercress Darter	Alabama	7
Waubay	South Dakota	2,585
Wertheim	New York	2,395
West Sister Island	Ohio	77
Wheeler	Alabama	34,119
White Lake	North Dakota	1,040
White River	Arkansas	112,399
Wichita Mountains	Oklahoma	59,019
Wild Rice Lake	North Dakota	779
Willapa	Washington	14,297
William L. Finley	Oregon	5,325
Willow Lake	North Dakota	2,621
Wintering River	North Dakota	239
Wolf Island	California	5,126
Wood Lake	North Dakota	280
Wyandotte	Michigan	304
Yazoo	Mississippi	12,471
Yukon Delta	Alaska	19,624,458
Yukon Flats	Alaska	8,630,000

NOTE: Not included here are individual units of the Alaska Maritime National Wildlife Refuge System. These units, ranging from tiny offshore islets to full-sized islands like Attu in the Aleutians, comprise an additional 4.5 million acres.

THE NATIONAL WILDERNESS PRESERVATION SYSTEM

The acreage figures given are totals. The first year designated for each wilderness is the year it was established; any subsequent year designated indicates when an addition was made.

Wilderness	Agency	Acreage	Year Designated
ALABAMA			
Cheaha	USFS	6,780	1983
Sipsey	USFS	12,646	1975
		State Total 19,426	
ALASKA			
Admiralty Island National Monument	USFS	937,396	1980
Aleutian Islands	FWS	1,300,000	1980
Andreafsky	FWS	1,300,000	1980
Arctic	FWS	8,000,000	1980
Becharof	FWS	400,000	1980
Bering Sea	FWS	81,340	1970
Bogoslof	FWS	175	1970
Chamisso	FWS	455	1975
Coronation Island	USFS	19,232	1980
Denali	NPS	1,900,000	1980
Endicott River	USFS	98,729	1980
Forrester Island	FWS	2,832	1970
Gates of the Arctic	NPS	7,052,000	1980
Glacier Bay	NPS	2,770,000	1980
Hazy Islands	FWS	32	1970
Innoko	FWS	1,240,000	1980
Izembek	FWS	300,000	1980
Katmai	NPS	3,473,000	1980
Kenai	FWS	1,350,000	1980
Kobuk Valley	NPS	190,000	1980
Koyukuk	FWS	400,000	1980
Lake Clark	NPS	2,470,000	1980
Maurelle Islands	USFS	4,937	1980
Misty Fjords National Monument	USFS	2,142,243	1980
Noatak	NPS	5,800,000	1980

Wilderness	Agency	Acreage	Year Designated
ALASKA (*cont'd*)			
Nunivak	FWS	600,000	1980
Petersburg Creek– Duncan Salt Creek	USFS	46,777	1980
Russell Fjord	USFS	348,701	1980
St. Lazaria	FWS	65	1970
Selawik	FWS	240,000	1980
Semidi	FWS	250,000	1980
Simeonof	FWS	25,855	1976
South Baranof	USFS	319,568	1980
South Prince of Wales	USFS	90,996	1980
Stikine-LeConte	USFS	448,841	1980
Tebenkof	USFS	66,839	1980
Togiak	FWS	2,270,000	1980
Tracy-Arm-Ford- Terror	USFS	653,179	1980
Tuxedni	FWS	5,566	1970
Unimak	FWS	910,000	1980
Warren Island	USFS	11,181	1980
West Chichagof– Yakobi	USFS	264,747	1980
Wrangell–St. Elias	NPS	8,700,000	1980
	State Total	56,484,686	
ARIZONA			
Apache Creek	USFS	5,420	1984
Aravaipa Canyon	BLM	6,670	1984
Bear Wallow	USFS	11,080	1984
Beaver Dam Mountains	BLM	17,003	1984
Castle Creek	USFS	26,030	1984
Cedar Bench	USFS	14,950	1984
Chiricahua	USFS	87,700	1964 1984
	NPS	10,290	1976 1984

Cottonwood Point	BLM	6,500	1984
Escudilla	USFS	5,200	1984
Fossil Springs	USFS	11,550	1984
Four Peaks	USFS	53,500	1984
Galiuro	USFS	76,317	1964
			1984
Grand Wash Cliffs	BLM	36,300	1984
Granite Mountain	USFS	9,800	1984
Hellsgate	USFS	36,780	1984
Juniper Mesa	USFS	7,600	1984
Kachina Peaks	USFS	18,200	1984
Kanab Creek	USFS	68,250	1984
	BLM	8,850	1984
Kendrich Mountain	USFS	6,510	1984
Mazatzal	USFS	251,912	1964
			1984
Miller Peak	USFS	20,190	1984
Mount Baldy	USFS	7,079	1970
Mount Logan	BLM	14,600	1984
Mount Trumbull	BLM	7,900	1984
Mount Wrightson	USFS	25,260	1984
Munds Mountain	USFS	18,150	1984
Organ Pipe Cactus	NPS	312,600	1978
Paiute	BLM	84,700	1984
Pajarita	USFS	7,420	1984
Paria Canyon–			
Vermillion Cliff	BLM	90,046	1984
Petrified Forest	NPS	50,260	1970
Pine Mountain	USFS	20,061	1972
Pusch Ridge	USFS	56,933	1978
Red-Rock–Secret			
Mountain	USFS	43,950	1984
Rincon Mountain	USFS	38,590	1984
Saddle Mountain	USFS	40,600	1984
Saguaro	NPS	71,400	1976
Salome	USFS	18,950	1984
Salt River Canyon	USFS	32,800	1984
Santa Teresa	USFS	26,780	1984
Sierra Ancha	USFS	20,850	1964
Strawberry Crater	USFS	10,140	1984
Superstition	USFS	159,757	1964
			1984

Wilderness	Agency	Acreage	Year Designated
ARIZONA (cont'd)			
Sycamore Canyon	USFS	47,757	1972
		8,180	1984
West Clear Creek	USFS	13,600	1984
Wet Beaver	USFS	6,700	1984
Woodchute	USFS	5,600	1984
	State Total	2,037,265	
ARKANSAS			
Big Lake	FWS	2,144	1976
Black Fork Mountain	USFS	7,568	1984
Buffalo National River	NPS	10,529	1978
Caney Creek	USFS	14,344	1975
Dry Creek	USFS	6,310	1984
East Fork	USFS	10,777	1984
Flatside	USFS	10,105	1984
Hurricane Creek	USFS	15,177	1984
Leatherwood	USFS	16,956	1984
Poteau Mountain	USFS	10,884	1984
Richland Creek	USFS	11,822	1984
Upper Buffalo	USFS	11,746	1975
			1984
	State Total	128,362	
CALIFORNIA			
Ansel Adams	USFS	228,669	1964
			1984
	NPS	665	1984
Aqua Tibia	USFS	15,933	1975
Bucks Lake	USFS	21,000	1984
Caribou	USFS	20,625	1964
			1984
Carson-Iceberg	USFS	160,000	1984
Castle Craigs	USFS	7,300	1984
Chanchelvilla	USFS	8,200	1984

Cucamonga	USFS	12,981	1964
			1984
Desolation	USFS	63,475	1969
Dick Smith	USFS	65,130	1984
Dinkey Lakes	USFS	30,000	1984
Domeland	USFS	94,686	1964
			1984
Emigrant	USFS	112,191	1975
			1984
Farallon	FWS	141	1974
Golden Trout	USFS	303,287	1978
Granite Chief	USFS	25,000	1984
Hauser	USFS	8,000	1984
Hoover	USFS	48,601	1964
Ishi	USFS	41,600	1984
	BLM	240	1984
Jennie Lakes	USFS	10,500	1984
John Muir	USFS	580,675	1964
			1984
Joshua Tree	NPS	429,690	1976
Kaiser	USFS	22,700	1976
Lassen Volcanic	NPS	78,982	1972
Lava Beds	NPS	28,460	1972
Machesna Mountain	USFS	19,880	1984
	BLM	120	
Marble Mountain	USFS	241,744	1964
			1984
Mokelumne	USFS	104,461	1964
			1984
Monarch	USFS	45,000	1984
Mount Shasta	USFS	37,000	1984
North Fork	USFS	8,100	1984
Pine Creek	USFS	13,100	1984
Pinnacles	NPS	12,952	1976
Point Reyes	NPS	25,370	1976
			1985
			1985
Red Buttes	USFS	16,150	1984
Russian	USFS	12,000	1984
San Gabriel	USFS	36,118	1968
San Gorgonio	USFS	56,722	1964
			1984

Wilderness	Agency	Acreage	Year Designated
CALIFORNIA (cont'd)			
San Jacinto	USFS	32,040	1964
			1984
San Mateo Canyon	USFS	39,540	1984
San Rafael	USFS	150,610	1968
			1984
Santa Lucia	USFS	18,679	1978
	BLM	1,733	1978
Santa Rosa	USFS	20,160	1984
Sequoia–Kings Canyon	NPS	736,980	1984
Sheep Mountain	USFS	43,600	1984
Siskiyou	USFS	153,000	1984
Snow Mountain	USFS	37,000	1984
South Sierra	USFS	63,000	1984
South Warner	USFS	70,385	1964
			1984
Thousand Lakes	USFS	16,335	1964
Trinity Alps	USFS	495,377	1984
	BLM	4,623	1984
Ventana	USFS	164,144	1969
			1978
			1984
Yolla Bolly–Middle Eel	USFS	145,404	1964
			1984
	BLM	8,500	1984
Yosemite	NPS	677,600	1984
	State Total	5,925,278	
COLORADO			
Big Blue	USFS	98,320	1980
Black Canyon of the Gunnison	NPS	11,180	1976
Cache La Padre	USFS	9,238	1980
Collegiate Peaks	USFS	166,654	1980
Comanche Peak	USFS	66,791	1980
Eagles Nest	USFS	133,325	1976
Flat Tops	USFS	235,035	1975

Great Sand Dunes	NPS	33,450	1976
Holy Cross	USFS	122,037	1980
Hunter–Fryingpan	USFS	74,250	1978
Indian Peaks	USFS	70,374	1978
	NPS	2,922	1980
La Garita	USFS	103,986	1964
			1980
Lizard Head	USFS	41,189	1980
Lost Creek	USFS	105,090	1980
Maroon Bells–Snow			
Mass	USFS	181,138	1980
Mesa Verde	NPS	8,100	1976
Mount Evans	USFS	74,401	1980
Mount Massive	USFS	27,980	1980
	FWS	2,560	1980
Mount Sneffels	USFS	16,505	1980
Mount Zirkel	USFS	139,818	1964
			1980
Neota	USFS	9,924	1980
Never Summer	USFS	13,702	1980
Platte River	USFS	770	1984
Raggeds	USFS	59,519	1980
Rawah	USFS	73,020	1964
			1980
South San Juan	USFS	127,690	1980
Weminuche	USFS	459,804	1975
			1980
West Elk	USFS	176,092	1964
			1980
	State Total	2,644,864	

FLORIDA

Alexander Springs	USFS	7,700	1984
Big Gum Swamp	USFS	13,600	1984
Billies Bay	USFS	3,120	1984
Bradwell Bay	USFS	24,602	1975
			1984
Cedar Keys	FWS	379	1972
Chassahowitzka	FWS	23,580	1976
J.N. "Ding" Darling	FWS	2,619	1976
Everglades	NPS	1,296,500	1978

351

Wilderness	Agency	Acreage	Year Designated
FLORIDA (cont'd)			
Florida Keys	FWS	6,245	1975
			1982
Island Bay	FWS	20	1970
Juniper Prairie	USFS	13,260	1984
Lake Woodruff	FWS	1,066	1976
Little Lake George	USFS	2,500	1984
Mud Swamp/New River	USFS	7,800	1984
Passage Key	FWS	36	1970
Pelican Island	FWS	6	1970
St. Marks	FWS	17,350	1975
	State Total	1,420,420	
GEORGIA			
Big Frog	USFS	83	1984
Blackbeard Island	FWS	3,000	1975
Cohutta	USFS	32,307	1974
Cumberland Island	NPS	8,840	1982
Ellicott Rock	USFS	2,181	1975
			1984
Okefenokee	FWS	353,981	1974
Southern Nanahala	USFS	12,439	1984
Wolf Island	FWS	5,126	1975
	State Total	417,957	
HAWAII			
Haleakala	NPS	19,270	1976
Hawaii Volcanoes	NPS	123,100	1978
	State Total	142,370	
IDAHO			
Craters of the Moon	NPS	43,243	1970
Frank Church– River of No Return	USFS	2,232,311	1964
	BLM	720	1980

Gospel Hump	USFS		205,900	1978
Hells Canyon	USFS		83,800	1975
Sawtooth	USFS		217,088	1972
Selway-Bitterroot	USFS		1,089,017	1964
				1980
		State Total	3,872,079	

ILLINOIS

Crab Orchard	FWS		4,050	1976

INDIANA

Charles C. Dean	USFS		12,935	1982

KENTUCKY

Beaver Creek	USFS		4,756	1975

LOUISIANA

Breton	FWS		5,000	1975
Kisatchie	USFS		8,700	1980
Lacassine	FWS		3,346	1976
		State Total	17,046	

MAINE

Moosehorn	FWS		7,386	1970
				1975

MASSACHUSETTS

Monomoy	FWS		2,420	1970

MICHIGAN

Huron Islands	FWS		147	1970
Isle Royal	NPS		131,880	1976
Michigan Islands	FWS		12	1970
Seney	FWS		25,150	1970
		State Total	157,189	

Wilderness	Agency	Acreage	Year Designated
MINNESOTA			
Agassiz	FWS	4,000	1976
Boundary Waters		798,309	1964
Canoe Area	USFS		1978
Tamarac	FWS	2,180	1976
	State Total	804,489	
MISSISSIPPI			
Black Creek	USFS	4,560	1984
Gulf Islands	NPS	1,800	1978
Leaf	USFS	940	1984
	State Total	7,300	
MISSOURI			
Bell Mountain	USFS	8,817	1980
Devil's Backbone	USFS	6,595	1980
Hercules-Glades	USFS	12,314	1976
Irish	USFS	16,500	1984
Mingo	FWS	7,730	1976
Paddy Creek	USFS	6,728	1983
Piney Creek	USFS	8,087	1980
Rockpile Mountain	USFS	4,089	1980
	State Total	70,860	
MONTANA			
Absaroka-Beartooth	USFS	920,310	1978
			1983
Anaconda-Pintler	USFS	157,874	1964
Bob Marshall	USFS	1,009,356	1964
			1978
Cabinet Mountains	USFS	94,272	1964
Gates of the Mountains	USFS	28,562	1964
Great Bear	USFS	286,700	1978
Lee Metcalf	USFS	248,944	1983
	BLM	6,000	1983
Medicine Lake	FWS	11,366	1976

Mission Mountains	USFS		73,877	1975
Rattlesnake	USFS		29,824	1980
Red Rock Lakes	FWS		32,350	1976
Scapegoat	USFS		239,296	1972
Selway-Bitterroot	USFS		248,893	1964
Ul Bend	FWS		20,819	1976
				1983
Welcome Creek	USFS		28,135	1978
		State Total	3,436,578	

NEBRASKA

Fort Niobrara	FWS		4,635	1976

NEVADA

Jarbidge	USFS		64,667	1964

NEW HAMPSHIRE

Great Gulf	USFS		5,552	1964
Pemigewasset	USFS		45,000	1984
Presidential Range– Dry River	USFS		27,380	1975 1984
Sandwich Range	USFS		25,000	1984
		State Total	102,932	

NEW JERSEY

Brigantine	FWS		6,681	1975
Great Swamp	FWS		3,660	1968
		State Total	10,341	

NEW MEXICO

Aldo Leopold	USFS		201,966	1980
Apache Kid	USFS		44,650	1980
Bandelier	NPS		23,267	1976
Bisti	BLM		3,968	1984
Blue Range	USFS		30,000	1980
Bosque del Apache	FWS		30,287	1975
Capitan Mountains	USFS		34,513	1980
Carlsbad Mountains	NPS		33,125	1978

Wilderness	Agency	Acreage	Year Designated
NEW MEXICO (cont'd)			
Chama River Canyon	USFS	50,260	1978
Cruces Basin	USFS	18,000	1980
De-na-zin	BLM	23,872	1984
Dome	USFS	5,200	1980
Gila	USFS	557,819	1964
			1980
Latir Peak	USFS	20,000	1980
Manzano Mountain	USFS	36,650	1978
Pecos	USFS	223,333	1964
			1980
Salt Creek	FWS	9,621	1970
Sandia Mountain	USFS	37,028	1978
			1980
			1984
San Pedro Parks	USFS	41,132	1964
Wheeler Peak	USFS	19,661	1964
			1980
White Mountain	USFS	48,366	1964
			1980
Withington	USFS	18,869	1980
	State Total	1,511,587	
NEW YORK			
Fire Island	NPS	1,363	1980
NORTH CAROLINA			
Birkhead Mountains	USFS	4,790	1984
Catfish Lake South	USFS	7,600	1984
Ellicott Rock	USFS	4,022	1975
			1984
Joyce Kilmer	USFS	13,181	1975
			1984
Linville Gorge	USFS	10,975	1964
			1984
Middle Prong	USFS	7,900	1984
Pond Pine	USFS	1,860	1984

Pocosin	USFS		11,000	1984
Sheep Ridge	USFS		9,540	1984
Shining Rock	USFS		18,450	1964
				1984
Southern Nantahala	USFS		10,900	1984
Swanquarter	FWS		8,785	1976
		State Total	109,003	

NORTH DAKOTA

Chase Lake	FWS		4,155	1975
Lostwood	FWS		5,577	1975
Theodore Roosevelt	NPS		29,920	1978
		State Total	39,652	

OHIO

West Sister Island	FWS		77	1975

OKLAHOMA

Wichita Mountains	FWS		8,570	1970

OREGON

Badger Creek	USFS	24,000	1984	
Black Canyon	USFS	13,400	1984	
Boulder Creek	USFS	19,100	1984	
Bridge Creek	USFS	5,400	1984	
Bull of the Woods	USFS	34,900	1984	
Columbia	USFS	39,000	1984	
Cummins Creek	USFS	9,300	1984	
Diamond Peak	USFS	52,337	1964	
			1984	
Drift Creek	USFS	5,800	1984	
Eagle Cap	USFS	358,461	1964	
			1972	
			1984	
Gearhart Mountain	USFS	22,809	1964	
			1984	
Grassy Knob	USFS	17,200	1984	
Hells Canyon	USFS	130,095	1975	1984
	BLM	1,038	1984	
Kalmiopsis	USFS	179,700	1964	
			1978	

Wilderness	Agency	Acreage	Year Designated
OREGON (cont'd)			
Menagerie	USFS	4,725	1984
Middle Santiam	USFS	7,500	1984
Mill Creek	USFS	17,400	1984
Monument Rock	USFS	19,800	1984
Mountain Lake	USFS	23,071	1964
Mount Hood	USFS	46,520	1964
			1978
Mount Jefferson	USFS	107,008	1968
			1984
Mount Thielsen	USFS	55,100	1984
Mount Washington	USFS	52,516	1964
			1984
North Fork John Day	USFS	121,400	1984
North Fork Umatilla	USFS	20,200	1984
Oregon Islands	BLM	5	1978
	FWS	480	1970
			1978
Red Buttes	USFS	3,750	1984
Rock Creek	USFS	7,400	1984
Rogue-Umpqua Divide	USFS	33,200	1984
Salmon Huckleberry	USFS	44,560	1984
Skylake	USFS	116,300	1984
Strawberry Mountain	USFS	68,303	1964
			1984
Table Rock	BLM	5,500	1984
Three Arch Rocks	FWS	15	1970
Three Sisters	USFS	285,202	1964
			1978
			1984
Waldo Lake	USFS	39,200	1984
Wenaha-Tucannon	USFS	66,375	1978
Wild Rogue	USFS	25,658	1978
	BLM	10,160	1978
State Total		2,093,888	

PENNSYLVANIA

Allegheny Islands	USFS		368	1984
Hickory Creek	USFS		9,337	1984
		State Total	9,705	

SOUTH CAROLINA

Cape Romain	FWS		29,000	1975
Ellicott Rock	USFS		2,809	1974
Hell Hole Bay	USFS		1,980	1980
Little Wambaw Swamp	USFS		5,000	1980
Wambaw Creek	USFS		1,640	1980
Wambaw Swamp	USFS		5,100	1980
		State Total	45,529	

SOUTH DAKOTA

Badlands	NPS		64,250	1976
Black Elk	USFS		9,824	1980
		State Total	74,074	

TENNESSEE

Bald River Gorge	USFS		3,887	1984
Big Frog	USFS		7,942	1984 1986
Citico Creek	USFS		16,000	1984
Cohutta	USFS		1,795	1975
Gee Creek	USFS		2,493	1975
Joyce Kilmer– Slickrock	USFS		3,832	1974
		State Total	35,979	

TEXAS

Big Slough	USFS		3,000	1984
Guadalupe Mountains	NPS		46,850	1978
Indian Mounds	USFS		9,946	1984
Little Lake Creek	USFS		4,000	1984
Turkey Hill	USFS		5,400	1984

Wilderness	Agency	Acreage	Year Designated
TEXAS (cont'd)			
Upland Island	USFS	12,000	1984
		State Total 81,196	
UTAH			
Ashdown Gorge	USFS	7,000	1984
Beaver Dam Mountains	BLM	2,597	1984
Box-Death Hollow	USFS	26,000	1984
Dark Canyon	USFS	45,000	1984
Deseret Peak	USFS	25,500	1984
High Uintas	USFS	460,000	1984
Lone Peak	USFS	30,088	1978
Mount Naomi	USFS	44,350	1984
Mount Nebo	USFS	28,000	1984
Mount Olympus	USFS	16,000	1984
Mount Timpanogos	USFS	10,750	1984
Paria Canyon– Vermillion Cliffs	BLM	19,954	1984
Pine Valley Mountain	USFS	50,000	1984
Twin Peaks	USFS	13,100	1984
Wellsville Mountain	USFS	23,850	1984
		State Total 802,189	
VERMONT			
Big Branch	USFS	6,720	1984
Breadloaf	USFS	21,480	1984
Bristol Cliffs	USFS	3,738	1975 1976
George D. Aiken	USFS	5,060	1984
Lye Brook	USFS	14,621	1975 1984
Peru Peak	USFS	6,920	1984
		State Total 58,539	

VIRGINIA

Beartown	USFS		6,375	1984
James River Face	USFS		8,903	1975
				1984
Kimberling Creek	USFS		5,802	1984
Lewis Fork	USFS		5,730	1984
Little Dry Run	USFS		3,400	1984
Little Wilson Creek	USFS		3,855	1984
Mountain Lake	USFS		8,253	1984
Peters Mountain	USFS		3,326	1984
Ramsey's Draft	USFS		6,725	1984
Saint Mary's	USFS		10,090	1984
Shenandoah	NPS		79,579	1976
Thunder Ridge	USFS		2,450	1984
		State Total	144,488	

WASHINGTON

Alpine Lakes	USFS	305,407	1976	
Boulder River	USFS	49,000	1984	
Buckhorn	USFS	44,474	1984	1986
Clearwater	USFS	14,300	1984	
Colonel Bob	USFS	12,120	1984	
Glacier Peak	USFS	576,648	1964	
			1968	
			1984	
Glacier View	USFS	3,050	1984	
Goat Rocks	USFS	105,023	1964	
			1984	
Henry M. Jackson	USFS	102,671	1984	
Indian Heaven	USFS	20,650	1984	
Juniper Dunes	BLM	7,140	1984	
Lake Chelan– Sawtooth	USFS	150,704	1984	
Mount Adams	USFS	46,776	1964	
			1984	
Mount Baker	USFS	117,580	1984	1986
Mount Skokomish	USFS	15,686	1984	
Noisy-Diobsud	USFS	14,300	1984	
Norse Peak	USFS	50,902	1984	
Pasayten	USFS	529,850	1968	
			1984	

361

Wilderness	Agency	Acreage	Year Designated
WASHINGTON (cont'd)			
Salmo-Priest	USFS	41,335	1984
San Juan Islands	FWS	353	1976
Tatoosh	USFS	15,720	1984
The Brothers	USFS	16,682	1984 1986
Trapper Creek	USFS	6,050	1984
Washington Islands	FWS	485	1970
Wenaha-Tucannon	USFS	111,048	1978
William O. Douglas	USFS	166,603	1984
Wonder Mountain	USFS	2,320	1984
	State Total	2,528,561	
WEST VIRGINIA			
Cranberry	USFS	35,864	1983
Dolly Sods	USFS	10,215	1975
Laurel Fork North	USFS	6,055	1983
Laurel Fork South	USFS	5,997	1983
Otter Creek	USFS	20,000	1974
	State Total	78,131	
WISCONSIN			
Blackjack Springs	USFS	5,886	1978
Headwater	USFS	19,950	1984
Porcupine Lake	USFS	4,195	1984
Rainbow Lake	USFS	6,583	1975
Whisker Lake	USFS	7,345	1978
Wisconsin Islands	FWS	29	1970
	State Total	43,988	
WYOMING			
Absaroka-Beartooth	USFS	23,750	1984
Bridger	USFS	428,169	1964
			1984
Cloud Peak	USFS	195,500	1984
Encampment River	USFS	10,400	1984
Fitzpatrick	USFS	198,838	1976
			1984

Gros Ventre	USFS	287,000	1984
Huston Park	USFS	31,300	1984
Jedediah Smith	USFS	116,535	1984
North Absaroka	USFS	350,538	1964
Platte River	USFS	22,230	1984
Popo Agie	USFS	101,991	1984
Savage Run	USFS	14,940	1978
Teton	USFS	585,468	1964
			1984
Washakie	USFS	703,981	1964
			1972
			1984
Winegar Hole	USFS	14,000	1984
	State Total	3,084,640	

THE WILD AND SCENIC RIVERS SYSTEM

	State(s)	Miles
Alagnak	Alaska	67
Alatna	Alaska	83
Allagash Wilderness Waterway	Maine	95
American (Lower)	California	23
American (North Fork)	California	38.3
Andreafsky	Alaska	262
Aniakchak	Alaska	63
Au Sable	Michigan	23
Beaver Creek	Alaska	127
Birch Creek	Alaska	126
Charley	Alaska	208
Chattooga	North Carolina, South Carolina, Georgia	56.9
Chilikadrotna	Alaska	11
Delaware Middle	New York, Pennsylvania, New Jersey	35
Delaware Upper	New York, Pennsylvania	75.4
Delta	Alaska	62
Eel	California	364

	State(s)	Miles
Eleven Point	Missouri	44.4
Feather	California	77.6
Flathead	Montana	219
Fortymile	Alaska	392
Gulkana	Alaska	181
Illinois	Oregon	50.4
Ivishak	Alaska	80
John	Alaska	52
Klamath	California	286
Kobuk	Alaska	110
Koyukuk (North Fork)	Alaska	102
Little Beaver	Ohio	33
Little Miami	Ohio	66
Little Miami	Ohio	28
Middle Fork Clearwater	Idaho	185
Middle Fork Salmon	Idaho	104
Missouri	Montana	149
Missouri	Nebraska, South Dakota	59
Mulchatna	Alaska	24
New	North Carolina	26.5
Noatak	Alaska	330
Nowitna	Alaska	225
Obed	Tennessee	45.2
Owyhee	Oregon	112
Pere Marquette	Michigan	66.4
Rapid	Idaho	26.8
Rio Grande	New Mexico	52.75
Rio Grande	Texas	191.2
Rogue	Oregon	84.5
St. Croix	Minnesota, Wisconsin	200
St. Croix (Lower)	Minnesota, Wisconsin	27
St. Croix (Lower)	Minnesota, Wisconsin	25
St. Joe	Idaho	67.3
Salmon	Alaska	70
Salmon	Idaho	125
Selawik	Alaska	160
Sheenjek	Alaska	160
Skagit	Washington	157.5
Smith	California	340
Snake	Idaho, Oregon	66.9

Tinayguk	Alaska	44
Tlikakila	Alaska	51
Trinity	California	203
Tuolumne	California	83
Unalakleet	Alaska	80
Verde	Arizona	40.5
Wind	Alaska	140
Wolf	Wisconsin	25

THE NATIONAL TRAILS SYSTEM

SCENIC TRAILS

	State(s)	*Miles*
Appalachian	Georgia, North Carolina, Virginia, Maryland, Pennsylvania, New Jersey, New York, Connecticut, Massachusetts, Vermont, New Hampshire, Maine	2,000
Continental Divide	Montana, Wyoming, Colorado, New Mexico	3,100
Florida	Florida	1,300
Ice Age	Wisconsin	1,000
Natchez Trace	Mississippi, Tennessee	694
North Country	North Dakota, Minnesota, Wisconsin, Michigan, Ohio, Pennsylvania	3,200
Pacific Crest	Washington, Oregon, California	2,350
Potomac Heritage	Virginia, Maryland, West Virginia	704

HISTORIC TRAILS

Iditarod	Alaska	2,037
Lewis and Clark	Washington, Montana, North Dakota, South Dakota, Nebraska, Iowa, Missouri	3,700
Mormon Pioneer	Utah, Wyoming, Nebraska, Iowa	1,300
Oregon	Oregon, Idaho, Wyoming, Nebraska, Kansas, Missouri	2,000
Overmountain		
Victory	South Carolina	272

APPENDIX

MAJOR PUBLIC LAND LEGISLATION

	Date Passed	*Application*
Preemption Act	1841	Sale and disposal of public lands.
Homestead Act	1862	Unrestricted settlement on public lands to all settlers, requiring only the residence, improvement, and cultivation of a tract of 160 acres.
General Mining Law	1872	Opened all public lands to private prospecting and development.
Desert Land Act	1877	Authorized the purchase of 640 acres of public land at $1.25 an acre, providing that the settler irrigated the tract within three years.
General Revision Act	1891	Repealed the Preemption Act, reduced the acreage limitation under the Desert Land Act from 640 to 320 acres, and put limits on the auction sale of land. Section 24 of the act, the "Forest Reserve Act," authorized the President of the United States to withdraw from settlement or exploitation any forest area of the public domain that, in the opinion of the Secretary of the Interior, required watershed protection and timber preservation.
Forest "Organic Act"	1897	Declared that forest reserves were established to "improve and protect the forest within the boundaries for the purpose of securing favorable conditions of water flow, and to furnish a continuous supply of

timber for the use and necessities of citizens of the United
States." Placed reserves under
the administration of the General Land Office of the Department of the Interior.

Newlands (Reclamation) Act	1902	Authorized the financing and construction of federal irriga-tion projects on public lands in the West, with restrictions on the private use of public water; amended in 1982 to relieve those restrictions.
Reorganization Act	1905	Transferred forest reserves to the Department of Agriculture and created the U.S. Forest Service.
Weeks Act	1911	Appropriated $9 million for the purchase of private land in order to establish national for-ests in the eastern United States.
National Park "Organic Act"	1916	Established the National Park Service under the Department of the Interior; established guidelines for the management of the national park system.
Mineral Leasing Act	1920	Authorized the federal govern-ment to lease public lands for the private extraction of oil, gas, coal, phosphates, sodium, and other minerals.
Taylor Grazing Act	1934	Closed to indiscriminate set-tlement and use all remaining unreserved and unappropriated public-domain land in nine Western states and the Terri-tory of Alaska; placed 142 million acres into grazing dis-

	Date Passed	*Application*
		tricts and created the Grazing Service to administer them.
Reorganization Act	1946	Created the Bureau of Land Management within the Department of the Interior, merging the Grazing Service with the General Land Office.
Outdoor Recreation Resources Review Commission Act	1958	Established commission to study present and future recreation needs on all federal land systems.
Multiple Use and Sustained Yield Act	1960	Redefined the purposes of the national forests to include recreation, soil, range, timber, watershed, wildlife, fishing, hunting, and mining on a "most judicious use" basis.
Public Land Law Review Commission Act	1961	Created a body to investigate all existing statutes and regulations governing the retention, management, and disposal of public lands and to determine present and future demands on the public domain.
Classification and Multiple Use Act	1964	Directed the Bureau of Land Management to classify public lands, determining which were suitable for disposal and which were suitable for retention and management by the government.
Wilderness Act	1964	Established the National Wilderness Preservation System to be composed of portions of national parks, forests, and wildlife refuges designated by

		Congress as "Wilderness Areas."
Land and Water Conservation Fund Act	1964	Provided funds for and authorized federal assistance to the states in planning, acquisition, and development of needed land and water areas and facilities; and provided funds for the federal acquisition and development of lands for national parks, wildlife refuges, wild and scenic rivers, and other federal conservation programs.
National Wild and Scenic Rivers Act	1968	Provided for the establishment of a system of river segments to be preserved as free-flowing streams accessible for public use and enjoyment.
National Trails System Act	1968	Authorized National Scenic Trails for public enjoyment and appreciation of open-air outdoor areas of the nation; later amended to include Historic Trails.
National Environmental Policy Act	1969	Required public involvement and development of environmental impact statements in the formulation and adoption of all federal land management plans.
Forest and Rangeland Renewable Resources Planning Act	1974	Established planning process for comprehensive long-range and continuous inventory of all forest and rangeland resources under federal, state, local, and private ownership.
Eastern Wilderness Act	1974	Added sixteen designated areas in the East to the Na-

	Date Passed	*Application*
		tional Wilderness Preservation System.
National Forest Management Act	1976	Mandated the development of fifty-year unit-by-unit manage-ment plans for all U.S. Forest Service lands—planning to in-clude economic, wildlife, wil-derness, and recreation uses.
Federal Land Policy and Management Act	1976	Established public land policy guidelines for the administra-tion, protection, and develop-ment of all national resource lands of the Bureau of Land Management.
Omnibus Parks Act	1978	Established a number of new park units, including Golden Gate, Santa Monica, and Gateway national recreation areas in California and New York, and formulated guide-lines for the creation of addi-tional parks, wilderness areas, trails, and wild and scenic rivers.
Alaska National Interest Lands Conservation Act	1980	Provided for the designation and conservation of certain public lands in the state of Alaska, including the designa-tion of units of the national park system, National Wildlife Refuges, national forests, Na-tional Wild and Scenic Rivers, and National Wilderness Pres-ervation System.

APPENDIX B

Wilderness Designations, Wild and Scenic River Designations, and Park Additions Made Since 1985

WILDERNESS DESIGNATIONS

Wilderness	Agency	Acreage	Year
ALABAMA			
Sipsey	USFS	13,260	1988
ALASKA			
Chuck River	USFS	74,278	1990
Karta River	USFS	39,889	1990
Kuiu	USFS	60,581	1990
Pleasant/Lemusrier/Inian Islands	USFS	23,096	1990
South Etolin	USFS	83,371	1990
Young Lake	USFS	18,298	1990
ARIZONA			
Aravaipa Canyon	BLM	13,030	1990
Arrastra Mountain	BLM	129,800	1990
Aubrey Peak	BLM	15,400	1990
Baboquivari Peak	BLM	2,040	1990
Big Horn Mountains	BLM	21,000	1990
Cabeza Prieta	USFS	803,418	1990
Coyote Mountains	BLM	5,100	1990
Dos Cabezas Mountains	BLM	11,700	1990
Eagletail Mountains	BLM	100,600	1990
East Cactus Plain	BLM	14,630	1990
Fishhooks	BLM	10,500	1990
Havasu	USFS	14,606	1990
Gibraltar Mountain	BLM	18,790	1990

Harcuvar Mountains	BLM	25,050	1990
Harquahala Mountains	BLM	22,880	1990
Hassayampa River Canyon	BLM	12,300	1990
Hells Canyon	BLM	10,600	1990
Hummingbird Springs	BLM	31,200	1990
Imperial	USFS	9,220	1990
Kofa	USFS	516,200	1990
Mount Nutt	BLM	27,660	1990
Mount Tipton	BLM	32,760	1990
Mount Wilson	BLM	23,900	1990
Muggins Mountains	BLM	7,640	1990
Needle's Eye	BLM	8,760	1990
New Water Mountains	BLM	24,600	1990
North Maricopa Mountains	BLM	63,200	1990
North Santa Teresa	BLM	5,800	1990
Peloncillo Mountains	BLM	19,440	1990
Rawhide Mountains	BLM	38,470	1990
Redfield Canyon	BLM	9,930	1990
Sierra Estrella	BLM	14,400	1990
Signal Mountain	BLM	13,350	1990
South Maricopa Mountains	BLM	60,100	1990
Swansea	BLM	16,400	1990
Table Top	BLM	34,400	1990
Tres Alamos	BLM	8,300	1990
Trigo Mountains	BLM	30,300	1990
Upper Burro Creek	BLM	27,440	1990
Wabayuma Creek	BLM	40,000	1990
Warm Springs	BLM	112,400	1990
White Canyon	BLM	5,790	1990
Woolsey Peak	BLM	64,000	1990

CALIFORNIA

Chumash	USFS	38,150	1992
Garcia	USFS	14,100	1992
Matilija	USFS	29,600	1992
San Rafael	USFS	46,400	1992
Sespe	USFS	219,700	1992
Silver Peak	USFS	14,500	1992
Ventana	USFS	38,000	1992

COLORADO

Buffalo Peaks	USFS	23,570	1993
Buffalo Peaks	USFS	19,840	1993
Byers Peak	USFS	8,095	1993
Fossil Ridge	USFS	32,838	1993
Greenhorn Mountain	USFS	22,040	1993
Hunter-Fryingpan	USFS	8,330	1993
La Garita	USFS	25,640	1993
Lost Creek	USFS	14,700	1993
Mount Zirkel	USFS	20,750	1993
Never Summer	USFS	6,990	1993
Powderhorn	USFS	13,599	1993
Powderhorn	BLM	48,115	1993
Ptarmigan Peak	USFS	13,175	1993
Raggeds-Oh-Be-Joyful	USFS	5,009	1993
Sangre de Cristo	USFS	226,420	1993
Sarvis Creek	USFS	47,140	1993
South San Juan-South San Juan Wilderness Expansion	USFS	31,100	1993
Uncompahgre	USFS	815	1993
Uncompahgre	BLM	3,390	1993
Vasquez Peak	USFS	12,300	1993
Weminuche-West Needles	USFS	28,740	1993

GEORGIA

Blood Mountain	USFS	7,800	1991
Brasstown	USFS	11,178	1986
Cohutta	USFS	2,900	1986
Mark Trail	USFS	16,400	1991
Raven Cliffs	USFS	8,562	1986
Rich Mountain	USFS	9,476	1986
Tray Mountain	USFS	9,702	1986

ILLINOIS

Bald Knob	USFS	5,863	1990
Bay Creek	USFS	2,866	1990
Burden Falls	USFS	3,671	1990
Clear Springs	USFS	4,730	1990
Garden of the Gods	USFS	3,268	1990

Lusk Creek	USFS	4,466	1990
Panther Den	USFS	685	1990

KENTUCKY

Clifty	USFS	11,662	1985

MAINE

Caribou-Speckled Mountain	USFS	12,000	1990

MICHIGAN

Big Island Lake	USFS	5,856	1987
Delerium	USFS	11,870	1987
Horseshoe Bay	USFS	3,790	1987
Mackinac	USFS	12,230	1987
McCormick	USFS	16,850	1987
Nordhouse Dunes	USFS	3,450	1987
Rock River Canyon	USFS	4,640	1987
Round Island	USFS	378	1987
Sturgeon River Gorge	USFS	14,500	1987
Sylvania	USFS	18,327	1987

NEBRASKA

Soldier Creek	USFS	7,794	1986

NEVADA

Alta Toquima	USFS	38,000	1989
Arc Dome	USFS	115,000	1989
Arc Dome	BLM	20	1989
Boundary Peak	USFS	10,000	1989
Currant Mountain	USFS	36,000	1989
Currant Mountain	BLM	3	1989
East Humboldts	USFS	36,900	1989
Grant Range	USFS	50,000	1989
Jarbridge	USFS	48,500	1989
Mount Charleston	USFS	43,000	1989
Mount Moriah	USFS	70,000	1989
Mount Moriah	BLM	6,435	1989

Mount Rose	USFS	28,000	1989
Quin Canyon	USFS	27,000	1989
Ruby Mountains	USFS	90,000	1989
Santa Rosa-Paradise Peak	USFS	31,000	1989
Table Mountain	USFS	98,000	1989

NEW MEXICO

Cebolla	BLM	62,800	1987
West Malpais	BLM	39,700	1987

OKLAHOMA

Black Fork Mountain	USFS	4,629	1988
Upper Kiamichi River	USFS	9,802	1988

SOUTH CAROLINA

Congaree Swamp	NPS	15,010	1988

TENNESSEE

Big Frog	USFS	2,221	1986
Big Laurel Branch	USFS	6,251	1986
Little Frog Mountain	USFS	4,684	1986
Pond Mountain	USFS	6,626	1986
Sampson Mountain	USFS	7,991	1986
Unaka Mountain	USFS	4,700	1986

TEXAS

Indian Mounds	USFS	971	1986
Turkey Hill	USFS	73	1986
Upland Island	USFS	1,330	1986

VIRGINIA

Rich Hole	USFS	6,450	1988
Rough Mountain	USFS	9,300	1988
Shawyers Run	USFS	101	1988
Shawyers Run	USFS	3,366	1988

WASHINGTON

Mount Rainier	NPS	228,488	1988
Olympic	NPS	876,669	1988
Stephen Mather	NPS	634,614	1988

WEST VIRGINIA

| Mountain Lake | USFS | 2,721 | 1988 |

WILD AND SCENIC RIVER DESIGNATIONS

River	*State(s)*	*Mileage*
Allegheny	Pennsylvania	85
Bear Creek	Michigan	6.5
Big Marsh Creek	Oregon	15
Big Piney	Arkansas	45.2
Big Sur	California	19.5
Black	Michigan	14
Black Creek	Mississippi	14
Black Creek	Mississippi	21
Bluestone	West Virginia	17
Buffalo River	Arkansas	15.8
Cache La Poudre	Colorado	76
Carp	Michigan	27.8
Cassatot River	Arkansas	30.8
Chetco	Oregon	44.5
Clackamas	Oregon	47
Clarks Fork of the Yellowstone	Wyoming	20.5
Cossatot River	Arkansas	30.8
Crescent Creek	Oregon	10
Crooked	Oregon	15
Deschutes	Oregon	173.4
Donner Und Blitzen	Oregon	72.7
Eagle Creek	Oregon	27
East Fork of the Jemez	New Mexico	11
Elk	Oregon	19
Grand Ronde	Oregon	43.8
Great Egg Harbor River	New Jersey	129
Horsepasture	North Carolina	4.2
Hurricane Creek	Arkansas	15.5

Imnaha	Oregon	77
Indian	Michigan	51
John Day	Oregon	147.5
Joseph Creek	Oregon	8.6
Kern	California	151
Kings	California	81
Klickitat	Washington	10
Little Deschutes	Oregon	12
Little Missouri	Arkansas	15.7
Lostine	Oregon	16
Loxahatchie	Florida	7.5
McKenzie	Oregon	12.7
Malheur	Oregon	13.7
Manistee	Michigan	26
Maurice	New Jersey	35.4
Metolius	Oregon	28.6
Merced	California	122
Middle Fork of the Vermillion	Illinois	17.1
Minam	Oregon	39
Missouri	Missouri, Nebraska, South Dakota	39
Mulberry	Arkansas	56
Niobrara	Nebraska	103
North Fork Crooked	Oregon	32.3
North Fork John Day	Oregon	54.1
North Fork Malheur	Oregon	25.5
North Fork of Middle Fork, Willamette	Oregon	42.3
North Fork Owyhee	Oregon	9.6
North Fork Smith	Oregon	13
North Fork Sprague	Oregon	15
North Powder	Oregon	6
North Sylamore Creek	Arkansas	14.5
North Umpqua	Oregon	33.8
Ontonagon	Michigan	157.4
Paint	Michigan	51
Pecos	New Mexico	20.5
Pine	Michigan	25
Presque Isle	Michigan	57
Powder	Oregon	11.7
Quartzville Creek	Oregon	12
Red River	Kentucky	19.4

Rio Chama	New Mexico	24.6
Richland Creek	Arkansas	16.5
Roaring	Oregon	13.7
Saline Bayou	Louisiana	19
Salmon	Oregon	33.5
Sandy	Oregon	24.9
Sespe Creek	California	31.5
Sipsey Fork of the West Fork	Alabama	61.4
Siquoc River	California	33
South Fork John Day	Oregon	47
Squaw Creek	Oregon	15.4
Sturgeon	Michigan	43.9
Sturgeon	Michigan	25
Sycan	Oregon	59
Tahquamenon, East Branch	Michigan	13.2
Upper Rogue	Oregon	40.3
Wenaha	Oregon	21.5
Westfield River	Massachusetts	42.3
West Little Owyhee	Oregon	57.6
White	Oregon	46.5
Whitefish	Michigan	33.6
White Salmon	Washington	9
Wildcat Creek	New Hampshire	14.5
Yellow Dog	Michigan	4

NATIONAL PARK ADDITIONS

Park	State	Acreage
Dry Tortugas	Florida	64,700
Great Basin	Nevada	77,199
Samoa	American Samoa	9,000

SELECTED BIBLIOGRAPHY

The list of secondary sources below is by no means exhaustive. It is meant only to highlight the publications that were most valuable to me in the preparation of this book. I have concentrated on listing books, since the government documents, magazines, newspapers, and unpublished agency reports I consulted for this book are too numerous to mention. Nevertheless, I think the entries indicate the breadth of material available on the subject of public lands, and cover all aspects of their historical, political, social, economic, ecological, and, yes, even spiritual significance. They are a good place to start for anyone wishing to study the matter further.   —D.Z.

GENERAL REFERENCES

Arrandale, Thomas. *The Battle for Natural Resources*. Washington, D.C.: Congressional Quarterly, 1983.

Coggins, George Cameron, and Charles F. Wilkinson. *Federal Public Land and Resource Law*. University Casebook Law Series. Mineola, N.Y.: Foundation Press, 1981.

Cronon, William. *Changes in the Land*. New York: Hill & Wang, 1983.

Dana, Samuel Trask. *Forest and Range Policy*. New York: McGraw-Hill, 1956.

Fox, Stephen. *John Muir and His Legacy: The American Conservation Movement*. Boston: Little, Brown, 1981.

Gates, Paul W. *The History of Public Land Law Development*. Washington, D.C.: Public Land Law Review Commission, 1968.

Hays, Samuel P. *Conservation and the Gospel of Efficiency: The Progressive Conservation Movement, 1890–1920*. Cambridge: Harvard University Press, 1959.

Nash, Roderick. *Wilderness and the American Mind*. New Haven: Yale University Press, 1982.

Robbins, Roy. *Our Landed Heritage: The Public Domain 1776–1970*. Lincoln: University of Nebraska Press, 1976.

Wilderness (magazine). Special issues: Spring, Summer, Fall, Winter 1983; Spring, Summer, Fall 1984.

Wyant, William K. *Westward in Eden*. Berkeley: University of California Press, 1982.

1. THE PLEASURING GROUNDS

Abbey, Edward. *Desert Solitaire*. New York: Ballantine Books, 1968.

Darling, F. Frazer, and Noel D. Eichhorn. *Man and Nature in the National Parks*. Washington, D.C.: The Conservation Foundation, 1971.

Everhart, William C. *The National Park Service*. Boulder: Westview Press, 1985.

Foresta, Ronald A. *America's National Parks and Their Keepers*. Washington, D.C.: Resources for the Future, 1984.

Hampton, H. Duane. *How the U.S. Cavalry Saved Our National Parks*. Bloomington: Indiana University Press, 1971.

Ise, John. *Our National Park Policy, a Critical History*. Baltimore: Johns Hopkins University Press, 1961.

Lee, Ronald F. *The Family Tree of the National Park System*. Philadelphia: Eastern National Parks and Monuments Association, 1972.

Runte, Alfred. *The National Parks: An American Experience*. Lincoln: University of Nebraska Press, 1979.

Sax, Joseph L. *Mountains Without Handrails: Reflections on the National Parks*. Ann Arbor: University of Michigan Press, 1981.

Shankland, Robert. *Steve Mather of the National Parks*. New York: Alfred A. Knopf, 1951.

Tilden, Freeman. *The National Parks*. New York: Alfred A. Knopf, 1983.

2. A HEART OF WOOD

Catton, Bruce. *Waiting for the Morning Train*. New York: Doubleday, 1972.

Clawson, Marion. *Forests for Whom and for What?* Baltimore: Resources for the Future, 1975.

DeVoto, Bernard. *The Easy Chair*. Boston: Houghton Mifflin, 1955.

Frome, Michael. *Whose Woods These Are: The Story of the National Forests*. Garden City, N.Y.: Doubleday, 1962.

Ise, John. *The United States Forest Policy*. New Haven: Yale University Press, 1920.

Lillard, Richard G. *The Great Forest*. New York: Da Capo, 1947.

Maclean, Norman. *A River Runs Through It and Other Stories*. Chicago: University of Chicago Press, 1976.

Marsh, George Perkins. *Man and Nature*. Cambridge: Harvard University Press, 1965.

Pinchot, Gifford, *Breaking New Ground*. New York: Harcourt Brace and Co., 1946.

Platt, Rutherford. *The Great American Forest*. Englewood Cliffs, N.J.: Prentice-Hall, 1971.

Robinson, Glen O. *The Forest Service: A Study in Public Land Management*. Baltimore: Resources for the Future, 1977.

Shands, William E., and Robert G. Healy. *The Lands Nobody Wanted*. Washington, D.C.: The Conservation Foundation, 1977.

Steen, Harold K. *The U.S. Forest Service: A History*. Seattle: University of Washington Press, 1976.

Stegner, Wallace. *The Uneasy Chair: A Biography of Bernard DeVoto*. Garden City, N.Y.: Doubleday, 1974.

Tichi, Cecelia. *New World, New Earth*. New Haven: Yale University Press, 1979.

3. THE LEFTOVER LEGACY

Clawson, Marion. *The Land System of the United States: An Introduction to the History and Practice of Land Use and Land Tenure*. Lincoln: University of Nebraska Press, 1972.

———. *Uncle Sam's Acres*. New York: Dodd, Mead, 1951.

Foss, Philip. *Politics and Grass: The Administration of Grazing on the Public Domain*. New York: Greenwood Press, 1960.

Peffer, E. Louise. *The Closing of the Public Domain: Disposal and Reservation Policies 1900–1950*. Stanford, Calif.: Stanford University Press, 1951.

Stegner, Wallace. *Angle of Repose*. New York: Doubleday, 1971.

———. *Beyond the Hundredth Meridian: John Wesley Powell and the Second Opening of the West*. Lincoln: University of Nebraska Press, 1982.

Voigt, William, Jr. *Public Grazing Lands: Use and Misuse by Industry and Government*. New Brunswick, N.J.: Rutgers University Press, 1976.

Watkins, T. H., and Charles S. Watson, Jr. *The Lands No One Knows*. San Francisco: Sierra Club Books, 1975.

Webb, Walter Prescott. *The Great Plains*. Lincoln: University of Nebraska Press, 1981.

Zaslowsky, Dyan. "Does the West Have a Death Wish?" *American Heritage*, Spring/Summer 1982.

4. ISLANDS OF LIFE

Allen, Durwood L. *Our Wildlife Legacy*. New York: Funk & Wagnalls, 1954.

Bean, Michael J. *The Evolution of National Wildlife Law*. Revised and expanded edition. New York: Praeger, 1983.

Brooks, Paul. *Speaking for Nature: How Literary Naturalists from Henry Thoreau to Rachel Carson Have Shaped America*. Boston: Houghton Mifflin, 1980.

Defenders of Wildlife. *A Report on the National Wildlife Refuge System*. Washington, D.C.: Defenders of Wildlife, 1977.

Doherty, Jim. "An Audubon Report: America's Incomparable, Troubled National Wildlife Refuges System." *Audubon*, July 1983.

Giles, Robert H., Jr. *Wildlife Management*. San Francisco: W. H. Freeman, 1978.

Graham, Edward H. *The Land and Wildlife*. New York: Oxford University Press, 1947.

Laycock, George. *The Sign of the Flying Goose: A Guide to the National Wildlife Refuges*. Garden City, N.Y.: Doubleday/Natural History Press, 1965.

Leopold, Aldo. *Game Management*. New York: Scribner's, 1933.

McCullough, David. *Mornings on Horseback*. New York: Simon & Schuster, 1981.

Reed, Nathaniel P., and Dennis Drabell. *The U.S. Fish and Wildlife Service*. Boulder: Westview Press, 1984.

Reiger, John F. *American Sportsmen and the Origins of Conservation*. Lincoln: University of Nebraska Press, 1975.

Riley, Laura and William. *Guide to the National Wildlife Refuges*. Garden City, N.Y.: Doubleday, 1979.

U.S. Department of the Interior. Fish and Wildlife Service. *The Final Environmental Statement on the Operation of the National Wildlife Refuge System*. Washington, D.C., 1979.

382

5. THE FREEDOM OF THE WILDERNESS

Dubos, René. *The Wooing of Earth*. New York: Scribner's, 1980.

Frome, Michael. *Battle for the Wilderness*. New York: Praeger, 1974.

Hendee, John C., George H. Stankey, and Robert C. Lucas. *Wilderness Management*. Publication of the U.S. Department of Agriculture. Washington, D.C., 1978.

Leopold, Aldo. *A Sand County Almanac*. New York: Ballantine Books, 1978.

Marshall, Robert. "The Problems of Wilderness." *Scientific Monthly*, Spring 1930.

McCloskey, Maxine E., and James P. Gilligan, eds. *Wilderness and the Quality of Life*. San Francisco: Sierra Club Books, 1969.

Thoreau, Henry David. *Walden: Or, Life in the Woods*. New York: Signet, 1960.

Turner, Frederick. *Beyond Geography: The Western Spirit Against the Wilderness*. New York: Viking, 1981.

———. *Rediscovering America: John Muir in His Time and Ours*. New York: Viking, 1985.

Turner, Frederick Jackson. "The Significance of the Frontier in American History." In *Problems in American Civilization*, edited by George Rogers Taylor. Boston: D. C. Heath and Co., 1956.

Watkins, T. H. *John Muir's America*. Portland, Ore.: Graphic Arts Center Publishing Company, 1976.

6. INLAND PASSAGES

Appalachian Mountain Club. *The A.M.C. White Mountain Guide*. Boston: Appalachian Mountain Club, 1979.

DeVoto, Bernard. *Across the Wide Missouri*. Boston: Houghton Mifflin, 1947.

———. *Mark Twain's America*. New York: Chautauqua Institution, 1933.

———, ed. *The Journals of Lewis and Clark*. Boston: Houghton Mifflin, 1953.

Ford, Daniel. *The Country Northward*. Somersworth: New Hampshire Publishing Company, 1976.

Fradkin, Philip L. *A River No More: The Colorado River and the West*. New York: Alfred A. Knopf, 1981.

Huser, Verne. "Wild and Scenic Rivers: Alive But Not Well." *American Forests*, November 1982.

Kauffmann, John, M. *Flow East*. New York: McGraw-Hill, 1973.

McPhee, John. *Encounters with the Archdruid*. New York: Farrar, Straus and Giroux, 1982.

Nichols, John. *The Milagro Beanfield War*. New York: Ballantine Books, 1974.

Palmer, Tim. *Stanislaus: The Struggle for a River*. Berkeley: University of California Press, 1982.

Robbins, Michael. *Along the Continental Divide*. Washington, D.C.: National Geographic Society, 1981.

Twain, Mark. *Life on the Mississippi*. New York: Penguin Books, 1984.

Waterman, Laura and Guy. *Backwoods Ethics: Environmental Concerns for Hikers and Campers*. Boston: Stone Wall Press, 1979.

7. THE STATE OF NATURE

Cahn, Robert. *The Fight to Save Wild Alaska*. New York: National Audubon Society, 1982.

Chevigny, Hector. *Russian America: The Great Alaskan Venture 1741–1867*. New York: Ballantine Books, 1973.

Gruening, Ernest. *The State of Alaska*. New York: Random House, 1968.

Hanrahan, John, and Peter Gruenstein. *Lost Frontier: The Marketing of Alaska*. New York: W. W. Norton, 1977.

London, Jack. *The Call of the Wild*. New York: Grosset & Dunlap, 1931.

Marshall, Robert. *Alaska Wilderness*. Berkeley: University of California Press, 1970.

———. *Arctic Village*. New York: Random House, 1933.

McGinniss, Joe. *Going to Extremes*. New York: Alfred A. Knopf, 1980.

McPhee, John. *Coming into the Country*. New York: Farrar, Straus and Giroux, 1977.

Murie, Margaret E. *Two in the Far North*. Anchorage: Alaska Northwest Publishing Company, 1957.

Nelson, Richard K., Kathleen Mautner, and G. Ray Bane. *Tracks in the Wild: A Portrayal of Koyukon and Nunamiut Subsistence*. Fairbanks: University of Alaska, 1982.

Norton, Boyd. *Alaska: Wilderness Frontier*. New York: Reader's Digest Press, 1977.

Rakestraw, Lawrence W. *A History of the United States Forest Service in Alaska*. Anchorage: Alaska Historical Commission, 1981.

Williss, G. Frank. *Do It Right the First Time: The National Park Service and the Alaska National Interest Lands Conservation Act of 1980*. Publication of the U.S. Department of the Interior. Washington, D.C., 1986.

ADDITIONAL READINGS

As Dyan Zaslowsky noted at the time, there were a wealth of publications available already when she and the staff of The Wilderness Society produced the first edition of *These American Lands*. That abundance swelled to astonishing proportions in the years that followed, as the environmental consciousness of the publishing world, like that of the general public, was intensified by the increasingly sharp lines of conflict that developed between the conservation community and the Reagan and Bush administrations over issues involving the American public lands. What follows, then, is, like the earlier bibliography, more selective than comprehensive. For this edition, I also have included those special issues and individual articles published by *Wilderness* magazine that bear most directly on the problems (and recommended solutions) discussed in this book. —T.H.W.

GENERAL REFERENCES

Allen, Thomas B. *Guardians of the Wild: The Story of the National Wildlife Federation, 1936-1986.* Bloomington: University of Indiana Press, 1987.

Brant, Irving. *Adventures in Conservation with Franklin D. Roosevelt.* Flagstaff, Arizona: Northland Publishing, 1989.

Brower, David. *For Earth's Sake: The Life and Times of David Brower.* Layton, Utah: Gibbs Smith, 1990.

_____. *Work in Progress.* Layton, Utah: Gibbs Smith, 1991.

Cohen, Michael. *The History of the Sierra Club.* San Francisco: Sierra Club Books, 1988.

Conaway, James. *The Kingdom in the Country.* Boston: Houghton Mifflin, 1987.

Fox, Stephen. "We Want No Straddlers." (History of The Wilderness Society.) *Wilderness*, Winter 1984.

Graham, Frank J. *The Audubon Ark: A History of the National Audubon Society.* Austin: University of Texas Press, 1990.

Hays, Samuel P., and Barbard D. Hays. *Beauty, Health, and Permanence: Environmental Politics in the United States, 1955-1985.* New York: Cambridge University Press, 1987.

Hoyle, Russ, ed. *Gale Environmental Almanac*. Detroit: Gale Research, Inc., 1993.

Nash, Roderick Frazier. *American Environmentalism: Readings in Conservation History*. New York: McGraw Hill, 1990.

_____. *The Rights of Nature: A History of Environmental Ethics*. Madison: University of Wisconsin Press, 1989.

Robbins, Jim. *Last Refuge: The Environmental Showdown in Yellowstone and the American West*. New York: William Morrow, 1993.

Shabecoff, Philip. *A Fierce Green Fire: The American Environmental Movement*. New York: Hill & Wang, 1993.

Stegner, Wallace. *The American West as Living Space*. Ann Arbor: University of Michigan Press, 1987.

Turner, Tom, and Carr Clifton. *Wild By Law: The Sierra Club Legal Defense Fund and the Places It Has Saved*. San Francisco: Sierra Club Books, 1990.

Udall, Stewart L. *The Quiet Crisis and the Next Generation*. Layton, Utah: Gibbs Smith, 1988.

Wallach, Bret. *At Odds with Progress: Americans and Conservation*. Tucson: University of Arizona Press, 1991.

Watkins, T. H. *Righteous Pilgrim: The Life and Times of Harold L. Ickes, 1874-1952*. New York: Henry Holt: 1990.

Wilkinson, Charles F. *Crossing the Next Meridian: Land, Water, and the Future of the West*. Washington, D. C.: Island Press, 1992.

Worster, Donald. *Under Western Skies: Nature and History in the American West*. New York: Oxford University Press, 1992.

1. THE PLEASURING GROUNDS

Boucher, Norman. "Thinking Like Gods." (Recovery efforts in Everglades National Park.) *Wilderness*, Winter 1991.

Douglas, Marjorie Stoneman. *Voice of the River: An Autobiography*. Englewood, Florida: Pineapple Press, 1987.

Hartzog, George B. *Battling for the National Parks*. Mt. Kisco, New York: Moyer Bell, 1988.

Lien, Carsten. *Olympic Battleground: The Power Politics of Timber Preservation*. San Francisco: Sierra Club Books, 1991.

Reinhardt, Richard. "Careless Love." (Yosemite National Park.) Wilderness, Summer 1989.

Runte, Alfred. *Yosemite: The Embattled Wilderness*. Lincoln: University of Nebraska Press, 1990.

Sellars, Richard West. "Science or Scenery?" (Priorities in National Park management.) *Wilderness*, Summer 1989.

2. A HEART OF WOOD

Daniel, John. "The Long Dance of the Trees." (Old growth forests of the Pacific Northwest.) *Wilderness*, Spring 1988.

Kelly, David, and Gary Braasch. *Secrets of the Old Growth Forest*. Layton, Utah: Gibbs Smith, 1988.

Manning, Richard. *Last Stand: Logging, Journalism, and the Case for Humility*. Layton, Utah: Gibbs Smith, 1991.

Norse, Elliott. *Ancient Forests of the Pacific Northwest*. Washington, D. C.: Island Press, 1990.

Seideman, David. *Showdown at Opal Creek: The Battle for America's Last Wilderness*. New York: Carroll and Graf, 1993.

Turner, Frederick. "In the Highlands." (Threatened forest ecosystems in the Southern Appalachian Highlands.) *Wilderness*, Fall 1990.

Wuerthner, George. "Dimming the Range of Light." (Threatened Sierra Nevada forest ecosystems.) *Wilderness*, Winter 1993.

3. THE LEFTOVER LEGACY

Leshy, John. *The Mining Law: A Study in Perpetual Motion*. Washington, D. C.: Resources for the Future, 1986.

Ferguson, Denzel, and Nancy Ferguson. *Sacred Cows at the Public Trough*. Bend, Oregon: Maverick Publications, 1983.

Russell, Sharmon Apt. *Kill the Cowboy: A Battle of Mythology for the West*. New York: Addison-Wesley, 1993.

Wilderness. Special issue: "Dips, Spurs, and Angles." (General Mining Law of 1872.) Summer 1992.

Wilderness. Special issue: "The Unperceived Wilderness: Treasures of the BLM." Summer 1986.

Wuerthner, George. "How the West Was Eaten." *Wilderness*. Spring 1991.

4. ISLANDS OF LIFE

Barker, Rocky. *Saving all the Parts: Reconciling Economics and the Endangered Species Act.* Washington, D. C.: Island Press, 1993.

DiSilvestro, Roger G. *The Endangered Kingdom: The Struggle to Save America's Wildlife.* New York: Wiley & Sons, 1989.

Dunlop, Thomas R. *Saving America's Wildlife.* Princeton, N. J.: Princeton University Press, 1988.

Ehrlich, Paul. *The Machinery of Nature.* New York: Simon & Schuster, 1986.

Kellert, Stephen R., and Edward O. Wilson, eds. *The Biophilia Hypothesis.* Washington, D. C.: Island Press, 1993.

Little, Charles. "The Old Wild Life." (Reintroduction of Wolves.) *Wilderness.* Summer 1991.

Matthieson, Peter. *Wildlife in America.* New York: Viking, 1987.

Norton, Bryan G. *The Preservation of Species.* Princeton, N. J.: Princeton University Press, 1986.

Riley, Laura, and William Riley. *Guide to the National Wildlife Refuges.* New York: Macmillan, 1992.

Wilderness. Special issue: "Biodiversity and the Public Lands." Spring 1987.

Wilson, Edward O. *The Diversity of Life.* Cambridge, Mass.: Harvard University Press, 1992.

5. THE FREEDOM OF THE WILDERNESS

Brown, David E. "A Gift to the Young." (Arizona BLM wilderness proposals.) *Wilderness,* Spring 1988.

Callicott, J. Baird, ed. *Companion to a Sand County Almanac.* Madison: University of Wisconsin Press, 1987.

Glover, James A. *A Wilderness Original: The Life of Bob Marshall.* Seattle: The Mountaineers, 1986.

Graf, William L. *Wilderness Preservation and the Sagebrush Rebellions.* Savage, Maryland: Rowan and Littlefield, 1990.

Lavender, David. "The Mudgetts Equation." (New Mexico BLM wilderness proposals.) *Wilderness,* Winter 1988.

Little, Charles E. "The Challenge of Greater Yellowstone: An Ecosystem Report." *Wilderness,* Winter 1987.

Martin, Russell. *A Story that Stands Like a Dam: Glen Canyon and the Struggle for the Soul of the West.* New York: Henry Holt, 1989.

Meine, Curt. *Aldo Leopold: His Life and Work.* Madison: University of Wisconsin Press, 1988.

Mitchell, John G. "To the Edge of Forever." (Utah BLM wilderness proposals.) *Wilderness*, Fall 1988.

Reinhardt, Richard. "Desert Storm." (Oregon BLM wilderness proposals.) Wilderness, Fall 1992.

Reisner, Marc. "A Decision for the Desert." (California Desert Protection Act.) *Wilderness*, Winter 1986.

Utah Wilderness Coalition. *Wilderness at the Edge: A Citizen's Proposal to Protect Utah's Canyons and Deserts.* Salt Lake City: Utah Wilderness Coalition, 1990.

Vickery, Jim Dale. *Wilderness Visionaries.* Harrisburg, Penna.: Stackpole Books, 1987.

Watkins, T. H. *Time's Island: The California Desert.* Layton, Utah: Gibbs Smith, 1989.

———. "Untrammeled by Man." (History of the Wilderness Act.) Audubon, November 1989.

Wilderness. Special issue: "Wilderness America: A Vision for the Future of the Nation's Wildlands." Spring 1989.

Zaslowsky, Dyan. "The Unfinished Wilderness." (Wilderness proposals for Montana and Idaho.) *Wilderness*, Summer 1987.

6. INLAND PASSAGES

Doppelt, Bob, et al. *Entering the Watershed: A New Approach to Save America's River Ecosystems.* Washington, D. C.: Island Press, 1993.

Echeverria, John D., et al. *Rivers at Risk: The Concerned Citizen's Guide to Hydropower.* Washington, D. C.: Island Press, 1989.

Jackson, Donald Dale. "The Long Way 'Round." (The history of the National Trails System.) *Wilderness*, Summer 1987.

Pern, Stephen. *The Great Divide: A Walk Through America Along the Continental Divide.* New York: Viking, 1988.

Palmer, Tim. *Endangered Rivers and the Conservation Movement.* Berkeley: University of California Press, 1986.

_____. *The Wild and Scenic Rivers of America*. Washington, D. C.: Island Press, 1993.

Reisner, Marc. *Cadillac Desert: The American West and Its Disappearing Water*. New York: Viking, 1986.

Ryan, Karen-Lee, ed. *Trails for the Twenty-First Century: Planning, Design, and Management Manual for Multi-Use Trails*. Washington, D. C.: Island Press, 1993.

Worster, Donald. *Rivers of Empire: Water, Aridity, and the Growth of the American West*. New York: Pantheon Books, 1985.

7. THE STATE OF NATURE

Daniel, John. "A Chance to Do It Right." (Alaska's national parks.) *Wilderness*, Summer 1993.

Davidson, Art. *In the Wake of the Exxon Valdez: The Devastating Impact of the Alaska Oil Spill*. San Francisco: Sierra Club Books, 1990.

Hedin, Robert, and Gary Holthaus, eds. *Alaska: Reflections on Land and Spirit*. Tucson: University of Arizona Press, 1989.

Jackson, Donald Dale. "The Floor of Creation." (Arctic National Wildlife Refuge.) *Wilderness*, Fall 1986.

Miller, Debbie S. *Midnight Wilderness: Journeys in Alaska's Arctic National Wildlife Refuge*. San Francisco: Sierra Club Books, 1990.

Strohmeyer, John. *Extreme Conditions: Big Oil and the Transformation of Alaska*. New York: Simon and Schuster: 1993.

Watkins, T. H. *Vanishing Arctic: Alaska's National Wildlife Refuge*. New York: Aperture Books, 1988.

Wilderness. Special issue: "The Perils of Expedience." (Alaska after passage of ANILCA.) Winter 1990.

INDEX

Abbey, Edward, 42
Acid rain, 48
Air pollution, 48
Alaska, 279–322; climate of, 280; colonization of, 282; discovery of, 281; Forest Service in, 288–89; gold rush, 284–85; National Interest Lands of, *see* National Interest Lands of Alaska; oil and gas resources, 291–92, 295, 297–99, 302, 309–13; pipe-line, 30, 298, 299; rivers of, 316–17; road building in, 318; statehood, 294–95; U.S. acquisition of, 283; wildlife of, 280–81, 285–86, 293, 308–309, 311, 313, 314–15
Alaska Coalition, 301, 304, 305, 309, 310, 313
Alaska Coalition for American Energy Security, 311
Alaska Homestead Act, 289
Alaska Maritime National Wildlife Refuge, 178, 319
Alaska National Interest Lands Conservation Act (ANILCA) (Alaska Lands Act), 40, 192, 218, 269, 280, 301–307, 309, 313, 314, 318
Alaska Native Claims Settlement Act (ANCSA), 298, 299–300, 301, 303
Alaskan Federation of Natives, 297
Albright, Horace, 24, 29–30, 31, 37
American Bison Society, 166
American Forestry Association, 65
American Ornithologists Union, 160, 165
American Rivers, 269, 270
American Rivers Conservation Council, 248
America's National Parks and Their Keepers (Foresta), 13, 24
Ancient Forest Alliance, 95–96
Anderson, Harold, 204
Andrus, Cecil, 220, 249, 301, 303–304
Antiquities Act, 32, 296, 303
Appalachian Mountain Club, 255, 257
Appalachian Trail, 204, 232–33, 256–68, 261, 272, 274

"Appalachian Trail: A Project in Regional Planning, An," 256
Appalachian Trail Conference (ATC), 257, 258, 260, 263, 276
Arctic National Wildlife Refuge, 294–95, 302, 304, 308, 309–13, 320
Arizona Desert Wilderness Act, 219–20
Army Corps of Engineers, U.S., 48, 50, 51, 184, 238, 240, 252
Aspinall, Wayne, 297
Atlantic Monthly, The, 5
Atlantic Richfield Company, 179, 298, 311
Atomic Energy Commission, 295–96
Audubon Society, 163, 165, 248
Avery, Milton, 258

Babbitt, Bruce, 44, 50, 140–41, 145, 182
Back Bay National Wildlife Refuge, 179
Baker, James, 134
Ballard, Edward B., 258
Ballinger, Richard, 75, 289, 290
Barrett, Frank, 32, 81
Beach, Ben, 181, 182
Bean, Michael J., 158, 160
Ben-Gurion, David, 7
Benton MacKaye Trail, 261–62, 273, 274–75
Bering, Vitus, 281
Berry, Russell, 317, 321
Beyond the Hundredth Meridian (Stegner), 2, 110
Big Cypress National Preserve, 49, 50
Biological Survey, U.S., 80, 160–61, 188
Bitterroot National Forest, 87, 88
Borah, William E., 110
Boucher, Norman, 49
Boxer, Barbara, 221
Bradford, William, 60
Breaking New Ground (Pinchot), 70
Bridger, Jim, 16
Broome, Harvey, 204
Brower, David, 243–44
Bryce, James, 27

ABOUT THE AUTHORS

Dyan Zaslowsky is a free-lance writer and *New York Times* correspondent who lives in Evergreen, Colorado, with her husband and two children. She is the author of numerous articles on the environment and other subjects for such magazines as *American Heritage, Atlantic Monthly, Audobon,* and *Wilderness,* and she is currently at work on a biography of Rosalie Edge, a conservation pioneer.

T. H. Watkins is editor of *Wilderness* and a former senior editor of *American Heritage.* He is the author of numerous books, among them *Righteous Pilgrim,* a prize-winning biography of FDR's Interior Secretary, Harold L. Ickes, and *The Great Depression: America in the 1930s.* His *Stone Time: An essay in words and photographs on the unprotected wildlands of Southern Utah* will be published in the fall.